DATE DUE

			PRINTED IN U.S.A.

SOMETHING ABOUT THE AUTHOR®

Something about
the Author *was named
an "Outstanding
Reference Source"
the highest honor given
by the American
Library Association
Reference and Adult
Services Division.*

ISSN 0276-816X

R

SOMETHING ABOUT THE AUTHOR®

**Facts and Pictures about Authors
and Illustrators of Books for Young People**

EDITED BY
DIANE TELGEN

VOLUME 73

 **Gale Research Inc.** • *DETROIT* • *WASHINGTON, D.C.* • *LONDON*

STAFF

Editor: Diane Telgen

Associate Editor: Elizabeth A. Des Chenes

Senior Editor: James G. Lesniak

Sketchwriters: Shelly Andrews, Marilyn K. Basel, Sonia Benson, Laura Standley Berger, Joanna Brod, Bruce Ching, Kevin S. Hile, Anne Janette Johnson, Jane M. Kelly, Jeanne M. Lesinski, Mark F. Mikula, Tom Pendergast, Cornelia A. Pernik, Nancy Rampson, Susan M. Reicha, Terrie M. Rooney, Pamela L. Shelton, Deborah A. Stanley, Elizabeth Wenning, and Thomas Wiloch

Research Manager: Victoria B. Cariappa
Research Supervisor: Mary Rose Bonk
Editorial Associates: Reginald A. Carlton, Clare Collins, Andrew Guy Malonis, and Norma Sawaya
Editorial Assistants: Patricia Bowen, Rachel A. Dixon, Eva Marie Felts, Shirley Gates, Sharon McGilvray, and Devra M. Sladics

Picture Permissions Supervisor: Margaret A. Chamberlain
Permissions Associates: Pamela A. Hayes and Keith Reed
Permissions Assistants: Arlene Johnson and Barbara Wallace

Production Director: Mary Beth Trimper
External Production Assistant: Mary Kelley
Art Director: Cynthia Baldwin
Desktop Publishers/Typesetters: Sherrell Hobbs, Nick Jakubiak, C. J. Jonik, and Yolanda Y. Latham

This book is printed on acid-free paper that meets the minimum requirements of American National Standard for Information Sciences—Permanence Paper for Printed Library Materials, ANSI Z39.48-1984.

Library of Congress Catalog Card Number 72-27107

ISBN 0-8103-2283-8 ISSN 0276-816X

Printed in the United States of America

Published simultaneously in the United Kingdom by Gale Research International Limited
(An affiliated company of Gale Research Inc.)

The trademark **ITP** is used under license.
10 9 8 7 6 5 4 3 2 1

Contents

Introduction

Something about the Author (*SATA*) is an ongoing reference series that deals with the lives and works of authors and illustrators of children's books. *SATA* includes not only well-known authors and illustrators whose books are widely read, but also those less prominent people whose works are just coming to be recognized. This series is often the only readily available information source on emerging writers or artists. You'll find *SATA* informative and entertaining whether you are a student, a librarian, an English teacher, a parent, or simply an adult who enjoys children's literature for its own sake.

What's Inside SATA

SATA provides detailed information about authors and illustrators who span the full time range of children's literature, from early figures like John Newbery and L. Frank Baum to contemporary figures like Judy Blume and Richard Peck. Authors in the series represent primarily English-speaking countries, particularly the United States, Canada, and the United Kingdom. Also included, however, are authors from around the world whose works are available in English translation. The writings represented in *SATA* include those created intentionally for children and young adults as well as those written for a general audience and known to interest younger readers. These writings cover the entire spectrum of children's literature, including picture books, humor, folk and fairy tales, animal stories, mystery and adventure, science fiction and fantasy, historical fiction, poetry and nonsense verse, drama, biography, and nonfiction.

Obituaries are also included in *SATA* and are intended not only as death notices but as concise views of people's lives and work. Additionally, each edition features newly revised and updated entries for a selection of *SATA* listees who remain of interest to today's readers and who have been active enough to require extensive revision of their earlier biographies.

Two Convenient Indexes

In response to suggestions from librarians, *SATA* indexes no longer appear in each volume, but are included in alternate (odd-numbered) volumes of the series, beginning with Volume 57.

SATA continues to include two indexes that cumulate with each alternate volume: the Illustrations Index, arranged by the name of the illustrator, gives the number of the volume and page where the illustrator's work appears in the current volume as well as all preceding volumes in the series; the Author Index gives the number of the volume in which a person's Biographical Sketch or Obituary appears in the current volume as well as all preceding volumes in the series.

These indexes also include references to authors and illustrators who appear in Gale's *Yesterday's Authors of Books for Children, Children's Literature Review,* and the *Something about the Author Autobiography Series.*

Easy-to-Use Entry Format

Whether you're already familiar with the *SATA* series or just getting acquainted, you will want to be aware of the kind of information that an entry provides. In every *SATA* entry the editors attempt to give as complete a picture of the person's life and work as possible. A typical entry in *SATA* includes the following clearly labeled information sections:

- *PERSONAL:* date and place of birth and death, parents' names and occupations, name of spouse, date of marriage, and names of children, educational institutions attended, degrees received, religious and political affiliations, hobbies and other interests.

- *ADDRESSES:* complete home, office, and agent's address.

- *CAREER:* name of employer, position, and dates for each career post; military service.

- *MEMBER:* memberships and offices held in professional and civic organizations.

- *AWARDS, HONORS:* literary and professional awards received.

- *WRITINGS:* title-by-title chronological bibliography of books written and/or illustrated, listed by genre when known; lists of other notable publications, such as plays, screenplays, and periodical contributions.

- *ADAPTATIONS:* a list of films, television programs, plays, and other media which have been adapted from the author's work.

- *WORK IN PROGRESS:* description of projects in progress.

- *SIDELIGHTS:* a biographical portrait of the author's development, either directly from the person—and often written specifically for the *SATA* entry—or gathered from diaries, letters, interviews, or other published sources.

- *FOR MORE INFORMATION SEE:* references for further reading.

- *EXTENSIVE ILLUSTRATIONS:* photographs, movie stills, manuscript samples, book covers, and other interesting visual materials supplement the text.

How a SATA Entry Is Compiled

A *SATA* entry progresses through a series of steps. If the biographee is living, the *SATA* editors try to secure information directly from him or her through a questionnaire. From the information that the biographee supplies, the editors prepare an entry, filling in any essential missing details with research and/or telephone interviews. When necessary, the author or illustrator is sent a copy of the entry to check for accuracy and completeness.

If the biographee is deceased or cannot be reached by questionnaire, the *SATA* editors examine a wide variety of published sources to gather information for an entry. Biographical and bibliographic sources are consulted, as are book reviews, feature articles, published interviews, and material sometimes obtained from the biographee's family, publishers, agent, or other associates. Entries compiled entirely from secondary sources are marked with an asterisk (*).

We Welcome Your Suggestions

We invite you to examine the entire *SATA* series, starting with this volume. Please write and tell us if we can make *SATA* even more helpful to you. Send comments and suggestions to: The Editor, *Something about the Author,* Gale Research Inc., 835 Penobscot Bldg., Detroit, Michigan 48226.

Acknowledgments

Grateful acknowledgment is made to the following publishers, authors, and artists whose works appear in this volume.

JOAN AIKEN. Jacket of *Give Yourself a Fright,* by Joan Aiken. Delacorte Press, 1989. Copyright © 1987 by Joan Aiken Enterprises, Ltd. Jacket illustration copyright © 1989 by Beau Daniels. Used by permission of Delacorte Press, a division of Bantam Doubleday Dell Publishing Group, Inc./ Jacket of *Past Eight O'Clock,* by Joan Aiken. Text copyright © 1986 by Joan Aiken Enterprises Ltd. Jacket illustration copyright © 1986 by Jan Pienkowski. Reprinted by permission of Viking Penguin, a division of Penguin USA Inc. In Canada by Jonathan Cape Ltd./ Jacket of *The Last Slice of Rainbow,* by Joan Aiken. Text copyright © 1985 by Joan Aiken Enterprises Ltd. Jacket art copyright © 1988 by Alix Berenzy. Reprinted by permission of HarperCollins Publishers./ Photograph © Jerry Bauer.

RUTH AINSWORTH. Jacket of *The Phantom Cyclist, and Other Ghost Stories,* by Ruth Ainsworth. Copyright © 1971 by Ruth Ainsworth. Cover illustration copyright © 1974 by Follett Publishing Company, a division of Follett Corporation./ Photograph by Turners.

BETTY LOU BAKER. Jacket of *Walk the World's Rim,* by Betty Lou Baker. Copyright © 1965 by Betty Baker Venturo. Jacket by The Etheredges. Reprinted by permission of HarperCollins Publishers./ Cover of *The Pig War,* by Betty Lou Baker. Text copyright © 1969 by Betty Baker. Pictures copyright © 1969 by Robert Lopshire. Reprinted by permission of HarperCollins Publishers./ Jacket of *The Shaman's Last Raid,* by Betty Lou Baker. Copyright © 1963 by Betty Baker Venturo. Pictures by Leonard Shortall. Reprinted by permission of HarperCollins Publishers.

DUNCAN BALL. Jacket of *Jeremy's Tail,* by Duncan Ball. Text copyright © 1990 by Duncan Ball. Jacket illustration copyright © 1990 by Donna Rawlins. Reprinted by permission of Orchard Books, New York./ Illustration from *Emily Eyefinger,* by Duncan Ball. Simon & Schuster, 1992. Illustrated by George Ulrich. Reprinted by permission of the publisher./ Photograph courtesy of Duncan Ball.

PATRICIA BEATTY. Cover of *Be Ever Hopeful, Hannalee,* by Patricia Beatty. Troll Associates, 1991. Copyright © 1988 by Patricia Beatty. Reprinted by permission of Troll Associates./ Cover of *Charley Skedaddle,* by Patricia Beatty. Troll Associates, 1988. Cover illustration copyright © 1987 by Jon Weiman. Reprinted by permission of Morrow Junior Books, a division of William Morrow & Company, Inc./ Jacket of *Jayhawker,* by Patricia Beatty. Jacket illustration copyright © 1991 by Stephen Marchesi. Reprinted by permission of Morrow Junior Books, a division of William Morrow & Company, Inc.

DONNA BERGMAN. Cover of *City Fox,* by Donna Bergman. Jacket illustration copyright © 1992 by Peter E. Hanson. Reprinted with the permission of Atheneum Publishers, an imprint of Macmillan Publishing Company./ Photograph courtesy of Donna Bergman.

N. M. BODECKER. Illustrations by N. M. Bodecker from his *Snowman Sniffles and Other Verse.* Margaret K. McElderry Books, 1985. Copyright © 1983 by N. M. Bodecker. Reprinted by permission of Margaret K. McElderry Books, an imprint of Macmillan Publishing Company./ Cover of *Quimble Wood,* by N. M. Bodecker. Margaret K. McElderry Books, 1981. Illustrations copyright © 1981 by Branka Starr. Reprinted by permission of Margaret K. McElderry Books, an imprint of Macmillan Publishing Company./ Illustrations by N. M. Bodecker from his *Hurry, Hurry Mary Dear! And Other Nonsense Poems.* Margaret K. McElderry Books, 1976. Copyright © 1976 by N. M. Bodecker. Reprinted by permission of Margaret K. McElderry Books, an imprint of Macmillan Publishing Company.

NANNETTE BROPHY. Photograph courtesy of Nannette Brophy.

CRAIG MCFARLAND BROWN. Illustration from *My Barn,* by Craig McFarland Brown. Copyright © 1991 by Craig McFarland Brown. Reprinted by permission of Greenwillow Books, a division of William Morrow & Company, Inc./ Photograph courtesy of Craig McFarland Brown.

DOROTHY BUTLER. Jacket of *Higgledy Piggledy Hobbledy Hoy,* by Dorothy Butler. Jacket art copyright © 1991 by Lyn Kriegler. Reprinted by permission of Greenwillow Books, a division of William Morrow and Company, Inc.

GUS CAZZOLA. Cover of *The Bells of Santa Lucia,* by Gus Cazzola and Pierr Morgan. Copyright © 1991 by Gus Cazzola. Illustrations copyright © 1991 by Pierr Morgan. Reprinted by permission of Philomel Books.

SOOK NYUL CHOI. Jacket of *Year of Impossible Goodbyes,* by Sook Nyul Choi. Houghton Mifflin Company, 1991. Copyright © 1991 by Sook Nyul Choi. Jacket art by Marie Garafano. Reprinted by permission of Houghton Mifflin Company./ Photograph courtesy of Sook Nyul Choi.

ANNA COATES. Cover of *Dog Magic,* by Anna Coates. Bantam Skylark, 1991. Copyright © 1991 by Anna Kate Scotti. Cover art copyright © 1991 by Bill Schmidt. Reprinted by permission of Bantam Books, a division of Bantam Doubleday Dell Publishing Group, Inc./ Photograph courtesy of Anna Coates.

CHRISTIN COUTURE. Photograph by David Gottleib.

BARBARA A. LEWIS. Photograph from *Kids with Courage,* by Barbara A. Lewis. Reprinted by permission of *Tacoma Morning News Tribune.*/ Cover of *The Kid's Guide to Social Action,* by Barbara A. Lewis. Copyright © 1991 by Barbara A. Lewis. Reprinted by permission of Free Spirit Publishing Inc.

GARY A. LIPPINCOTT. Photograph courtesy of Gary A. Lippincott.

MORAG LOH. Cover of *Tucking Mommy In,* by Morag Loh. Text copyright © 1987 by Morag Loh. Illustrations copyright © 1987 by Donna Rawlins. Reprinted by permission of Orchard Books, New York./ Photograph courtesy of Morag Loh.

MARETHA MAARTENS. Jacket of *Paper Bird: A Novel of South Africa,* by Maretha Maartens. Copyright © 1989 by Maretha Maartens. Jacket art copyright © 1991 by Paul Morin. Reprinted by permission of Houghton Mifflin Company./ Photograph courtesy of Maretha Maartens.

RUTH MANNING-SANDERS. Illustration from *A Book of Ghosts and Goblins,* by Ruth Manning-Sanders. Copyright © 1968 by Ruth Manning-Sanders./ Photograph courtesy of Ruth Manning-Sanders.

JAMES MARSH. Photograph and illustration courtesy of James Marsh.

GREGORY MATLOFF. Cover of *The Urban Astronomer,* by Gregory Matloff. Reprinted by permission of John Wiley & Sons, Inc.

MERCER MAYER. Illustration from *Little Monster's Counting Book,* by Mercer Mayer. Copyright © 1978 by Mercer Mayer. Reprinted by permission of Mercer Mayer./ Illustration from *A Boy, a Dog, a Frog, and a Friend,* by Mercer and Marianna Mayer. Copyright © 1971 by Mercer and Marianna Mayer. Reprinted by permission of Dial Books for Young Readers./ Jacket of *Appelard and Liverwurst,* by Mercer Mayer. Jacket illustration copyright © 1978 by Steven Kellogg. Reprinted by permission of Morrow Junior Books, a division of William Morrow & Company, Inc./ Illustration by Mercer Mayer from his *There's A Nightmare in My Closet.* Copyright © 1968 by Mercer Mayer. Reprinted by permission of Dial Books for Young Readers./ Jacket of *The Sleeping Beauty,* retold and illustrated by Mercer Mayer. Copyright © 1984 by Mercer Mayer. Jacket copyright © 1984 by Macmillan Publishing Company, a division of Macmillan, Inc. Reprinted by permission of Macmillan Publishing Company./ Photograph courtesy of Mercer Mayer.

YONA ZELDIS MCDONOUGH. Photograph by Paul A. McDonough, courtesy of Yona Zeldis McDonough.

FREDRICK MCKISSACK. Cover of *Frederick Douglass: The Black Lion,* by Patricia and Fredrick McKissack. Copyright © 1987 by Regensteiner Publishing Enterprises, Inc. Cover illustration by Len W. Meents. Reprinted by permission of Childrens Press./ Photograph courtesy of Fred McKissack.

PATRICIA MCKISSACK. Jacket of *The Long Hard Journey: The Story of the Pullman Porter,* by Patricia and Fredrick McKissack. Jacket photos (left to right) courtesy of A. Philip Randolph Institute, World Arts Foundation, Inc., and A. Philip Randolph Institute. Jacket design by Michael Chesworth. Reprinted by permission of Walker and Company./ Illustration from *Mirandy and Brother Wind,* by Patricia C. McKissack. Text copyright © 1988 by Patricia C. McKissack. Illustrations copyright © 1988 by Jerry Pinkney. Reprinted by permission of Alfred A. Knopf, Inc./ Cover of *Mary McLeod Bethune,* by Patricia C. McKissack. Copyright © 1985 by Regensteiner Publishing Enterprises, Inc. Cover illustration by Len W. Meents. Reprinted by permission of Childrens Press.

SHERRY MEIDELL. Photograph courtesy of Sherry Meidell.

EVE MERRIAM. Cover of *Where Is Everybody?,* by Eve Merriam. Text copyright © 1989 by Eve Merriam. Illustrations by Diane de Groat. Reprinted by permission of Simon & Schuster Books for Young Readers, New York./ Illustration from *Good Night to Annie,* by Eve Merriam. Four Winds Press, 1980. Text copyright © 1980 by Eve Merriam. Illustrations copyright © 1980 by John Wallner. Reprinted by permission of John Wallner./ Jacket of *Blackberry Ink: Poems,* by Eve Merriam. Jacket illustration copyright © 1985 by Hans Wilhelm, Inc. Reprinted by permission of Morrow Junior Books, a division of William Morrow & Company, Inc./ Photograph by Layle Silbert.

BEN MIKAELSEN. Jacket of *Rescue Josh McGuire,* by Ben Mikaelsen. Text copyright © 1991 by Ben Mikaelsen. Jacket illustration copyright © 1991 by Stephen Marchesi. Reprinted by permission of Hyperion Books for Children./ Photograph by Kenneth D. Albertsen.

JEWEL MILLER. Photograph courtesy of Jewel Miller.

MARYANN MILLER. Cover of *Coping with Cults,* by Maryann Miller. The Rosen Publishing Group, Inc., 1990. Copyright © 1990 by Maryann Miller. Reprinted by permission of The Rosen Publishing Group, Inc./ Photograph courtesy of Maryann Miller.

URSULA MORAY WILLIAMS. Cover of *Johnnie Golightly and His Crocodile,* by Ursula Moray Williams. Text copyright © 1970 by Ursula John. Illustrations copyright © 1970 by Faith Jaques./ Illustration from *The Toymaker's Daughter,* by Ursula Moray Williams. Meredith, 1968. Text copyright © 1968 by Ursula Moray Williams. Illustrations copyright © 1968 by Shirley Hughes. Reprinted by permission of Shirley Hughes.

JEFF MOSS. Illustration from *The Sesame Street Songbook,* by Jeffrey Moss. Macmillan Publishing Company, 1992. Copyright © 1992 Children's Television Workshop. Illustration by David Prebenna. Reprinted by permission of the Children's Television Workshop./ Illustration from *The Butterfly Jar: Poems,* by Jeff Moss. Bantam Books, 1989. Text copyright © 1989 by Jeff Moss. Illustrations copyright © 1989 by Chris Demarest. Reprinted by permission of Chris Demarest./ Jacket of *The Butterfly Jar: Poems,* by Jeff Moss.

Bantam Books, 1989. Text copyright © 1989 by Jeff Moss. Illustrations copyright © 1989 by Chris Demarest. Used by permission of Bantam Books, a division of Bantam Doubleday Dell Publishing Group, Inc./ Jacket of *The Other Side of the Door: Poems,* by Jeff Moss. Jacket illustration © 1991 by Chris Demarest. Reprinted by permission of Chris Demarest./ Photograph © 1989 by Blaivas.

PETER N. NELSON. Cover of *Deadly Games,* by Peter N. Nelson. Copyright © 1992 by Pocket Books. Cover photographs by Michel Legrou/MPG. Reprinted by permission of Pocket Books, a division of Simon & Schuster, Inc./ Photograph courtesy of Peter N. Nelson.

JOE NICKELL. Photograph courtesy of Joe Nickell.

NICHOLAS NUGENT. Photograph courtesy of Nicholas Nugent.

PEGGY PARISH. Cover of *Haunted House,* by Peggy Parish. Copyright © 1971 by Macmillan Publishing Co., Inc. Illustrations by Paul Frame. Reprinted by permission of Macmillan Publishing Company, a Division of Macmillan, Inc./ Cover of *Play Ball, Amelia Bedelia,* by Peggy Parish. Text copyright © 1972 by Margaret Parish. Pictures copyright © 1972 by Wallace Tripp. Reprinted by permission of HarperCollins Publishers./ Illustration from *The Cats' Burglar,* by Peggy Parish. Illustrations copyright © 1983 by Lynn Sweat. Reprinted by permission of Greenwillow Books, division of William Morrow & Company, Inc.

PATRICK QUINN. Cover of *Matthew Pinkowski's Special Summer,* by Patrick Quinn. Kendall Green Publications, Gallaudet University Press, 1991. Copyright © 1991 by Patrick J. Quinn. Cover illustration by Laura Stutzmann. Reprinted by permission of Kendall Green Publications, an imprint of Gallaudet University Press./ Photograph courtesy of Patrick Quinn.

CATHERINE REEF. Cover of *Gettysburg,* by Catherine Reef. Dillon, 1992. Reprinted by permission of James Blank./ Cover of *Jaques Cousteau: Champion of the Sea,* by Catherine Reef. Illustrations copyright © 1992 by Twenty-first Century Books. Cover illustration by Larry Raymond. Reprinted by permission of Henry Holt and Company, Inc./ Photograph courtesy of Catherine Reef.

ANITA RIGGIO. Illustration by Anita Riggio from *Coal Mine Peaches,* by Michelle Dionetti. Text copyright © 1991 by Michelle Dionetti. Illustrations copyright © 1991 by Anita Riggio. Reprinted by permission of Orchard Books, New York./ Photograph by Paul Cryan.

POLLY M. ROBERTUS. Photograph courtesy of Polly M. Robertus.

IAN SERRAILLIER. Cover of *The Gorgon's Head: The Story of Perseus,* by Ian Serraillier. Copyright © 1961 by Ian Serraillier. Reprinted by permission of Scholastic, Inc./ Cover of *Escape from Warsaw,* by Ian Serraillier. Reprinted by permission of Scholastic, Inc./ Photograph courtesy of Ian Serraillier.

BRENDA SILSBE. Photograph courtesy of Brenda Silsbe.

SEYMOUR SIMON. Jacket of *Deserts,* by Seymour Simon. Morrow Junior Books, 1990. Copyright © 1990 by Seymour Simon. Jacket photograph courtesy of Chuck Place. Reprinted by permission of Morrow Junior Books, a division of William Morrow & Company, Inc./ Jacket of *Oceans,* by Seymour Simon. Copyright © 1990 by Seymour Simon. Jacket photograph courtesy of Chuck Place. Reprinted by permission of Morrow Junior Books, a division of William Morrow & Company, Inc./ Illustration from *Neptune,* by Seymour Simon. Copyright © 1991 by Seymour Simon. Photograph courtesy of Jet Propulsion Laboratory/NASA. Reprinted by permission of Morrow Junior Books, a division of William Morrow & Company, Inc./ Jacket of *Earthquakes,* by Seymour Simon. Copyright © 1991 by Seymour Simon. Jacket photograph courtesy of The Image Bank/Garry Gay. Reprinted by permission of Morrow Junior Books, a division of William Morrow & Company, Inc./ Photograph by William Gottlieb.

MARC SIMONT. Illustration by Marc Simont from *The Philharmonic Gets Dressed,* by Karla Kuskin. Text copyright © 1982 by Karla Kuskin. Illustrations copyright © 1982 by Marc Simont. Reprinted by permission of HarperCollins Publishers./ Illustration by Marc Simont from *The Three Day Enchantment,* by Mollie Hunter. Text copyright © 1985 by Maureen Mollie Hunter McIlwraith. Illustrations copyright © 1985 by Marc Simont. Reprinted by permission of HarperCollins Publishers./ Illustration by Marc Simont from *The Happy Day,* by Ruth Krauss. Copyright © 1949 by Ruth Krauss. Pictures copyright © 1949 by Marc Simont. Reprinted by permission of HarperCollins Publishers./ Photograph by Larry Kaufman, courtesy of Marc Simont.

IRENE SMALLS-HECTOR. Cover of *Jonathan and His Mommy,* by Irene Smalls-Hector. Text copyright © 1991 Irene Smalls-Hector. Illustrations copyright © 1992 by Michael Hays. Reprinted by permission of Little, Brown and Company./ Photograph courtesy of Irene Smalls-Hector.

JOSEPH A. SMITH. Photograph courtesy of Joseph A. Smith.

DONALD J. SOBOL. Cover of *The Amazing Power of Ashur Fine,* by Donald J. Sobol. Troll Associates, 1987. Copyright © 1986 by Donald J. Sobol. Reprinted by permission of Troll Associates./ Cover of *Encyclopedia Brown's Record Book of Weird And Wonderful Facts,* by Donald J. Sobol. Copyright © 1979 by Donald J. Sobol. Illustrations copyright © 1979 by Sal Murdocca. Used by permission of Dell Books, a division of Bantam Doubleday Dell Publishing Group, Inc./ Cover of *The Wright Brothers at Kitty Hawk,* by Donald J. Sobol. Copyright © 1961 by Donald J. Sobol. Reprinted by permission of Scholastic, Inc./ Cover of *Encyclopedia Brown Keeps the Peace,* by Donald J. Sobol. Copyright © 1969 by Donald J. Sobol. Bantam Skylark, 1978. Reprinted by permission of Bantam Books, a division of Bantam Doubleday Dell Publishing Group, Inc./ Photograph courtesy of Donald J. Sobol.

LAURA A. SONNENMARK. Photograph courtesy of Laura A. Sonnenmark.

something about the author

AIKEN, Joan (Delano) 1924-

PERSONAL: Born September 4, 1924, in Rye, Sussex, England; daughter of Conrad Potter (a poet) and Jessie (McDonald) Aiken; married Ronald George Brown (a journalist), July 7, 1945 (deceased, 1955); married Julius Goldstein (a painter and teacher), September 2, 1976; children: (first marriage) John Sebastian, Elizabeth Delano. *Education:* Attended schools in Oxford, England. *Politics:* Liberal. *Religion:* Agnostic.

ADDRESSES: Home—The Hermitage, East St., Petworth, West Sussex GU28 0AB, England; New York, NY. *Agent*—A. M. Heath, 40-42 William IV St., London WC2N 4DD, England; Brandt & Brandt, 1501 Broadway, New York, NY 10036.

CAREER: British Broadcasting Corp., BBC Registry Department, Goring-on-Thames, Berkshire, England, clerk, 1941-43; United Nations Information Office, London, England, secretary and librarian, 1943-49; worked at St. Thomas' Hospital, London, 1943; *Argosy* (magazine), London, features editor, 1955-60; J. Walter Thompson Advertising Agency, London, advertising copywriter, 1961; full-time writer, 1961—. Writer in residence, Lynchburg College, 1988.

MEMBER: Authors Society, Writers Guild, Mystery Writers Circle.

AWARDS, HONORS: Lewis Carroll Shelf Award, 1965, for *The Wolves of Willoughby Chase;* Guardian Award for Children's Fiction, and Carnegie Award runner-up, both 1969, both for *The Whispering Mountain;* Edgar

JOAN AIKEN

Allan Poe Award, best juvenile mystery, Mystery Writers of America, 1972, for *Night Fall; Midnight Is a Place* was selected one of the *New York Times* Outstanding

Books, 1974; *The Skin Spinners* was included in the American Institute of Graphic Arts Book Show, 1975.

WRITINGS:

FOR CHILDREN

All You've Ever Wanted and Other Stories, illustrated by Pat Marriott, J. Cape, 1953.

More Than You Bargained For and Other Stories, illustrated by Marriott, J. Cape, 1955, Abelard, 1957.

The Kingdom and the Cave, illustrated by Dick Hart, Abelard, 1960, new edition, illustrated by Victor Ambrus, Doubleday, 1974.

The Wolves of Willoughby Chase, Doubleday, 1962.

Black Hearts in Battersea (sequel to *The Wolves of Willoughby Chase*), illustrated by Robin Jacques, Doubleday, 1964, British edition, illustrated by Marriott, J. Cape, 1964.

Night Birds on Nantucket, illustrated by Jacques, Doubleday, 1966, British edition published as *Nightbirds on Nantucket,* illustrated by Marriott, J. Cape, 1966.

Armitage, Armitage, Fly Away Home, illustrated by Betty Fraser, Doubleday, 1968.

The Whispering Mountain, illustrated by Frank Bozzo, J. Cape, 1968, Doubleday, 1969.

A Necklace of Raindrops and Other Stories, illustrated by Jan Pienkowski, J. Cape, 1968, Doubleday, 1969.

A Small Pinch of Weather and Other Stories, illustrated by Marriott, J. Cape, 1969.

Night Fall, Macmillan (England), 1969, Holt, 1970.

Smoke from Cromwell's Time and Other Stories, Doubleday, 1970.

Winterthing: A Child's Play, (first produced in London, England, at the Young Vic Theatre, 1970, and in the United States in Albany, NY, 1977, music by John Sebastian Brown), illustrated by Arvis Stewart, Holt, 1972, published in England with *The Mooncusser's Daughter,* J. Cape, 1973.

The Cuckoo Tree, illustrated by Susan Obrant, Doubleday, 1971, British edition, illustrated by Marriott, J. Cape, 1971.

The Kingdom under the Sea and Other Stories, illustrated by Pienkowski, J. Cape, 1971.

All and More (stories; originally published as *All You've Ever Wanted* and *More Than You Bargained For*), J. Cape, 1971.

A Harp of Fishbones and Other Stories, illustrated by Marriott, J. Cape, 1972.

The Escaped Black Mamba, (produced on BBC-TV), illustrated by Quentin Blake, BBC Books, 1973, published as *Arabel and the Escaped Mamba,* Knight, 1984.

The Mooncusser's Daughter (play; first produced in London at the Unicorn Theatre, 1973, music by Brown), Viking, 1973, published in England with *Winterthing,* J. Cape, 1973.

The Bread Bin (produced on BBC-TV), illustrated by Blake, BBC Books, 1974.

All but a Few, Penguin, 1974.

Midnight Is a Place, illustrated by Marriott, Viking, 1974.

Tales of Arabel's Raven (produced on BBC-TV), illustrated by Blake, J. Cape, 1974, published as *Arabel's Raven,* Doubleday, 1974.

Not What You Expected: A Collection of Short Stories, Doubleday, 1974.

The Skin Spinners: Poems, illustrated by Ken Rinciari, Viking, 1976.

A Bundle of Nerves: Stories of Horror, Suspense, and Fantasy, Gollancz, 1976.

Mortimer's Tie (produced on BBC-TV, 1976), illustrated by Blake, BBC Books, 1976.

(Translator from the French) Sophie de Segur, *The Angel Inn,* illustrated by Marriott, J. Cape, 1976, Stemmer House, 1978.

Go Saddle the Sea, illustrated by Marriott, Doubleday, 1977.

The Far Forests: Tales of Romance, Fantasy, and Suspense, Viking, 1977.

The Faithless Lollybird and Other Stories, illustrated by Marriott, J. Cape, 1977, United States edition, illustrated by Eros Keith, Doubleday, 1978.

Street (play; first produced at the Unicorn Theatre, 1977, music by Brown), illustrated by Stewart, Viking, 1978.

Tale of a One-Way Street and Other Stories, illustrated by Pienkowski, J. Cape, 1978, Doubleday, 1980.

Mice and Mendelson, illustrated by Babette Cole, published with music by Brown, J. Cape, 1978.

Mortimer and the Sword Excalibur, (produced on BBC-TV), illustrated by Blake, BBC Books, 1979.

The Spiral Stair, illustrated by Blake, BBC Books, 1979.

A Touch of Chill, Gollancz, 1979, Delacorte, 1980.

Arabel and Mortimer (includes *Mortimer's Tie, The Spiral Stair,* and *Mortimer and the Sword Excalibur*), illustrated by Blake, J. Cape/BBC Books, 1980, Doubleday, 1981.

The Shadow Guests, Delacorte, 1980.

The Stolen Lake, illustrated by Marriott, Delacorte, 1981.

Mortimer's Portrait on Glass (produced on BBC-TV), illustrated by Blake, BBC Books, 1982.

The Mystery of Mr. Jones's Disappearing Taxi (produced on BBC-TV), illustrated by Blake, BBC Books, 1982.

A Whisper in the Night (horror stories), Gollancz, 1982, Delacorte, 1984.

Moon Hill (play), first produced at the Unicorn Theatre, 1982.

Bridle the Wind (sequel to *Go Saddle the Sea*), illustrated by Marriott, Delacorte, 1983.

The Kitchen Warriors, illustrated by Jo Worth, BBC Books/Knight Books, 1983.

Mortimer's Cross (includes *The Mystery of Mr. Jones's Disappearing Taxi* and *Mortimer's Portrait on Glass*), illustrated by Blake, J. Cape/BBC Books, 1983, Harper, 1984.

Fog Hounds, Wind Cat, Sea Mice (stories), Macmillan, 1984.

Up the Chimney Down and Other Stories, illustrated by Marriott, J. Cape, 1984, Harper, 1985.

Mortimer Says Nothing (stories), illustrated by Blake, J. Cape, 1985, Harper, 1986.

The Last Slice of Rainbow, illustrated by Margaret
    Walty, J. Cape, 1985, illustrated by Alix Berenzy,
    Harper, 1988.
Past Eight O'Clock (stories), illustrated by Pienkowski,
    Cape, 1986, Viking, 1987.
Dido and Pa, J. Cape, 1986, Delacorte, 1987.
The Moon's Revenge, illustrated by Lee Alan, Knopf,
    1987.
The Teeth of the Gale, Harper, 1988.
The Erl King's Daughter, Heinemann, 1988.
Give Yourself a Fright, Delacorte, 1989.
Return to Harken House, Delacorte, 1990.
A Fit of Shivers: Tales for Late at Night, Gollancz, 1990,
    Delacorte, 1992.
Mortimer and Arabel, BBC Books, 1992.
A Foot in the Grave, illustrated by Pienkowski, Viking,
    1992.
Is, Cape, 1992, Delacorte, 1993.
Creepy Company, Gollancz, 1993.
The Midnight Moropus, Simon & Schuster, 1993.

Also author of a television play, *The Dark Streets of
Kimballs Green.*

FOR ADULTS

The Silence of Herondale, Doubleday, 1964.
The Fortune Hunters, Doubleday, 1965.
Beware of the Bouquet, Doubleday, 1966, published in
    England as *Trouble with Product X,* Gollancz, 1966.
Dark Interval, Doubleday, 1967, published in England
    as *Hate Begins at Home,* Gollancz, 1967.
The Ribs of Death, Gollancz, 1967, published as *The
    Crystal Crow,* Doubleday, 1968.
*The Windscreen Weepers and Other Tales of Horror and
    Suspense,* Gollancz, 1969, published as *Green Flash
    and Other Tales of Horror, Suspense, and Fantasy,*
    Holt, 1971.
The Embroidered Sunset, Doubleday, 1970.
The Butterfly Picnic, Gollancz, 1970, published as *A
    Cluster of Separate Sparks,* Doubleday, 1972.
Died on a Rainy Sunday, Holt, 1972.
Voices in an Empty House, Doubleday, 1975.
Castle Barebane, Viking, 1976.
The Five-Minute Marriage, Gollancz, 1977, Doubleday,
    1978.
Last Movement, Doubleday, 1977.
The Smile of the Stranger, Doubleday, 1978.
The Lightning Tree, Gollancz, 1980, published as *The
    Weeping Ash,* Doubleday, 1980.
The Young Lady from Paris, Gollancz, 1982, published
    as *The Girl from Paris,* Doubleday, 1982.
The Way to Write for Children, St. Martin's, 1982.
Foul Matter, Doubleday, 1983.
Mansfield Revisited, Gollancz, 1984, Doubleday, 1985.
Deception, Gollancz, 1987, published in the United
    States as *If I Were You,* Doubleday, 1987.
Blackground, Doubleday, 1989.
Jane Fairfax, Gollancz, 1990, St. Martin's 1991.
The Haunting of Lamb House, Cape, 1991, St. Martin's,
    1993.
Morningquest, Gollancz, 1992, St. Martin's, 1993.

Contributor to anthology *Sixteen: Short Stories by
Outstanding Writers for Young Adults,* edited by Donald
R. Gallo, Dell, 1984. Also contributor of short stories to
*Abinger Chronicle, Argosy, Everywoman, John Bull,
Vogue, Good Housekeeping, Housewife, Vanity Fair,
New Statesman, Woman's Own, Woman's Journal,* and
of reviews to *History Today* and *Washington Post.*

ADAPTATIONS: Midnight Is a Place was adapted as a
thirteen-part serial and broadcast on Southern Televi-
sion in England, 1977; *Armitage, Armitage, Fly Away
Home* was adapted for broadcast on BBC-TV, 1978; *The
Wolves of Willoughby Chase* was adapted for film by
Atlantic/Zenith, 1988; *Apple of Discord* and *The Rose of
Puddle Fratrum* were adapted from Aiken's short stories
and broadcast on BBC-TV. *The Wolves of Willoughby
Chase* and *A Necklace of Raindrops and Other Stories*
were released on audiocassette by Caedmon, 1978.

SIDELIGHTS: British author Joan Aiken has been
publishing her fiction for children since 1953, and she
has written for adults since the mid-1960s. She is
perhaps best known for the series of children's novels
she began with *The Wolves of Willoughby Chase,* books
set in the fictional reigns of James III and Richard IV

In this collection of "bedtime" stories, Aiken weaves
tales about sleeping, dreaming, and waking. (Cover
illustration by Jan Pienkowski.)

during the nineteenth century in England. Lauded by critics for her lively imagination, intricate plots, and humorous characters, Aiken has often been compared to Charles Dickens. She has also written horror and suspense stories for younger readers, and won the Edgar Allan Poe Award for best juvenile mystery for her novel *Night Fall.* Aiken's work for adults ranges from horror to historical fiction; one noteworthy example is *Mansfield Revisited,* her sequel to Jane Austen's *Mansfield Park.*

Aiken was born September 4, 1924, in Rye, Sussex, England. Her father was the American-born poet Conrad Aiken; he and Aiken's Canadian mother moved to England feeling that schooling there would be better for Aiken's older siblings. Ironically, while her elder brother and sister attended English boarding schools, Aiken was taught at home by her mother, and, as she recalled in an essay for *Something about the Author Autobiography Series* (*SAAS*), obtained a better education than she would have in the small village school.

By the time Aiken was four years old, her parents divorced. Her mother then married another writer, Martin Armstrong. Perhaps because of the influence of both of her father figures, Aiken knew that she wanted to become a writer herself from an early age. From the

Aiken invites her readers into imaginative worlds of mischievous ghosts in this collection of stories. (Cover illustration by Beau Daniels.)

time she was five years old, she continuously kept notebooks of poems and stories. She reminisced in her *SAAS* essay: "I knew I was going to be a writer, like Conrad, like Martin, whose books were to be seen around the house. I knew that writers didn't make much money." In addition, Aiken read a great deal; some of her favorite books included Rudyard Kipling's "Jungle" books, Walter de la Mare's *Peacock Pie,* E. Nesbit's stories, and Hodgson Burnett's *A Little Princess.*

When Aiken was twelve she was finally sent to boarding school at Wychwood near Oxford, England. She recounted her first impressions for *SAAS:* "Severe the agony certainly was. The contrast between our small, orderly, quiet house filled with ancient, beautiful objects and civilised practices—and this noisy, bare, crowded, ugly barrack, and its bleak, trampled garden, both filled with girls in uniform, came as an inconceivable shock." But, as Aiken explained further, "after a couple of terms I began to realise what it had to offer . . . . School stirred up a strong competitive spirit . . . in no time I was devoting all my energy to getting the highest marks in class, getting parts in school plays, getting poems into the school magazine, being elected Form Representative, and so on."

But before Aiken left Wychwood, the school was forced to combine with the Oxford High School due to the hardships of World War II. She told *SAAS:* "The sudden amalgamation with a larger school completely threw me; I developed a swollen gland in my neck which would not respond to treatment, spent a term in bed, had two operations, and my schoolwork went to pieces." She also "refus[ed] to attend classes at the larger school." Because of these misfortunes, when the time came for Aiken to take the entrance exams for Oxford University, she failed. Instead, she took a clerical job with the British Broadcasting Corporation (BBC), although she admitted to *SAAS:* "What I really wanted was to marry a rich man who would support me in the country while I wrote books."

Somewhat bored at the BBC, Aiken moved on to work at the United Nations information office in London. There she met Ronald Brown, whom she married in 1945. But in the meantime Aiken had continued with her writing. Two of her children's stories had been purchased by the BBC, a few of her poems were accepted by the magazine *Abinger Chronicle,* and she completed a children's novel. The latter she entered in a contest, but did not win. While starting to raise her two children, John and Elizabeth, she began getting more of her short stories accepted by magazines, and, in 1953, published her first book of short stories for children, *All You've Ever Wanted and Other Stories.* Aiken followed this in 1955 with *More Than You Bargained For and Other Stories.*

At about the same time, however, Aiken's husband died of cancer, and she was left with his debts. As the sole means of support for her two children, she took a job as a story editor with *Argosy* magazine and continued to supplement her income with short story sales. But after

Bonnie and Sylvia are imprisoned by an evil governess in the film of *The Wolves of Willoughby Chase*, the first novel in Aiken's alternate history of nineteenth-century Britain.

getting rid of an agent who felt she would only succeed writing short fiction as opposed to novels, Aiken revised her earlier children's novel and published it in 1960 as *The Kingdom and the Cave.* Two years after the publication of her first novel, Aiken followed the effort with *The Wolves of Willoughby Chase,* regarded by many critics to be her most substantial novel for young readers.

The Wolves of Willoughby Chase centers on a conflict between the fictional legitimate Stuart king, James III, and plotters from the community of Hanover who want to put the pretender Bonnie Prince Georgie on the throne. Against this backdrop, the main characters in the story, schoolmates Bonnie and Sylvia, must contend with wolves and evil governesses and tolerate injustices while living in an orphanage. For her work, Aiken gained popularity with both readers and several critics—many of whom hailed her use of alternative history. She then continued the story line with *Black Hearts in Battersea,* which several reviewers praised for

its colorful use of language and humorous tone. In the second book of the series Aiken introduces the dynamic orphan girl Dido Twite, who becomes the heroine in further stories spawned by *The Wolves of Willoughby Chase.*

Over the course of more than twenty years Aiken employed the same alternative history in books such as *Night Birds on Nantucket, The Cuckoo Tree,* and *The Stolen Lake.* In *Dido and Pa,* a 1986 addition to the series, the main character is kidnapped by her own father and is taken to London where she is called into service by the Hanoverians, who hope to overthrow King Richard IV by preparing an imposter to take the monarch's place. Several reviewers complimented Aiken for her rich cast of characters and her thoughtful re-creation of nineteenth-century London in the story. Reflecting upon *Dido and Pa,* Susan Dooley of the *Washington Post Book World* noted, "If *Dido and Pa* is your introduction to Joan Aiken, you will be delighted by the wit and imagination with which she creates her

Enchantments, fairies, spirits, and other mysterious creatures inhabit this collection of fantastic fiction. (Cover illustration by Alix Berenzy.)

own special world." And Edward Blishen of the *Times Literary Supplement* remarked, "In the end, what this warm book in this warm series offers, apart from the pleasure of making a mess of history, is the joy of a sort of heroic gossip." Elaborating further on Aiken's talent, he wrote that "her skill lies in a buoyancy of invention that keeps the reader in a state of constant happiness."

In the mid-1960s, Aiken realized her longtime ambition of writing for adults as well. Some of her adult novels, such as *The Smile of the Stranger, The Weeping Ash,* and *The Girl from Paris,* are set in historical times at her English home, the Hermitage in Petworth, West Sussex. Of her acclaimed *Mansfield Revisited,* written as a sequel to early nineteenth-century author Jane Austen's *Mansfield Park,* she claimed in an interview for *Authors and Artists for Young Adults* that "it was different from writing any of the others. I did it very carefully with a copy of [lexicographer Samuel] Johnson's dictionary to make sure I wasn't using words that weren't in use during that time. I re-read Jane Austen at least once a year, so her style is very much in my ear. I read all the biographies of her that I could lay my hands on." Aiken likes, as a general rule, to alternate writing her children's and adult books.

Other well-known children's books by Aiken include those in her series about Mortimer the raven and his human friend Arabel, and those about half-English, half-Spanish Felix Brooke—*Go Saddle the Sea, Bridle the Wind,* and *The Teeth of the Gale.* The last three works,

which are regarded by Aiken as among her favorites, are set in early-nineteenth-century Europe. In *Go Saddle the Sea,* the main character Felix is mistreated by his Spanish grandfather and leaves his home to embark on a series of adventures en route to meet his other forebears in England. When he encounters his English relatives, he discovers that they are just as disagreeable as those he left behind in Spain.

Bridle the Wind tracks Felix after he decides to return to his Spanish grandfather's home. During his journey he is shipwrecked on the coast of France and, after losing his memory, finds himself working in a monastery which is ruled by a sinister abbot. Felix escapes from the community in the company of Juan, who has been kidnapped from the Basque regions of nineteenth-century Spain. Felix and Juan develop a solid friendship as they travel back to their homeland, and Felix eventually discovers that his companion is a girl. Although some critics felt that supernatural elements detracted from *Bridle the Wind,* several reviewers praised Aiken's strong characters and the rapid pace of the narrative.

Felix and Juan, renamed Juana, reunite several years later in *The Teeth of the Gale.* Juana, who is preparing to enter the sisterhood in a French convent, calls upon Felix to help in the rescue of a group of children from an old castle atop a two-hundred foot crag. During the mission, Felix's rescuing party must overcome numerous obstacles including blizzards, attacks by bears, and incidents of poisoning. In the *Times Literary Supplement* Patricia Craig remarked that *The Teeth of the Gale* "is recounted in Aiken's usual boisterous, full-blooded and dashing manner. Once an Aiken plot gets going, there is no let-up at all in animation or intrigue."

Aiken has also written plays for children, including *Winterthing* and *The Mooncusser's Daughter;* poetry collections, such as *The Skin Spinners;* and several short story anthologies. *The Last Slice of Rainbow,* published in 1985, contains nine tales, many of which rely on fantastic situations. Included in the collection are stories about a girl with telepathic powers, a princess who is cursed with hair that continually chastises her, and a tree that sends love letters to a young woman. Andrew Wawn of the *Times Literary Supplement* wrote that "the trail of such ideas in the tales and the shrewdness of their linguistic expression will engage, and delight tellers and listeners alike."

In 1976 Aiken married American painter and teacher Julius Goldstein. Since then she has divided her time between her home in West Sussex and her husband's native Manhattan, New York. She continues to write, and she and her older sister Jane, who is also a writer, critique each other's work before they submit it for publication.

WORKS CITED:

Aiken, Joan, essay in *Something about the Author Autobiography Series,* Volume 1, Gale, 1986, pp. 17-37.

Aiken, Joan, interview in *Authors and Artists for Young Adults,* Gale, 1989.
Blishen, Edward, review of *Dido and Pa, Times Literary Supplement,* November 28, 1986, p. 1343.
Craig, Patricia, "The Elements of Adventure," *Times Literary Supplement,* May 6, 1988, p. 513.
Dooley, Susan, review of *Dido and Pa, Washington Post Book World,* November 9, 1986, p. 18.
Wawn, Andrew, review of *The Last Slice of Rainbow, Times Literary Supplement,* November 29, 1985, p. 1360.

FOR MORE INFORMATION SEE:

BOOKS

Cadogan, Mary, and Patricia Craig, *You're A Brick, Angela! A New Look at Girls' Fiction From 1839-1975,* Gollancz, 1976.
Children's Literature Review, Volume 19, Gale, 1990.
Contemporary Literary Criticism, Volume 35, Gale, 1985.
Egoff, Sheila A., *Thursday's Child: Trends and Patterns in Contemporary Children's Literature,* American Library Association, 1981.
Townsend, John Rowe, *A Sense of Story: Essays on Contemporary Writers for Children,* Lippincott, 1971.

PERIODICALS

Children's Literature in Education, spring, 1988.
Times Literary Supplement, July 12, 1991, p. 20.
Washington Post Book World, October 9, 1988, p. 11.

* * *

AINSWORTH, Ruth (Gallard) 1908-

PERSONAL: Full name Ruth Gallard Ainsworth Gilbert; born October 16, 1908, in Manchester, England; daughter of Percy Clough (a Methodist minister) and Gertrude (Fisk) Ainsworth; married Frank Lathe Gilbert (a managing director of chemical works), March 29, 1935; children: Oliver Lathe, Christopher Gallard, Richard Frank. *Education:* Attended Froebel Training Centre, Leicester, England. *Politics:* Labour.

ADDRESSES: Home—Field End, Corbridge, Northumberland NE45 5JP, England.

CAREER: Writer.

WRITINGS:

CHILDREN'S BOOKS

Tales about Tony, illustrated by Cora E. M. Paterson, Epworth, 1936.
Mr. Popcorn's Friends, Epworth, 1938.
The Gingerbread House, Epworth, 1938.
The Ragamuffins, Epworth, 1939.
Richard's First Term: A School Story, Epworth, 1940.
All Different (poems), illustrated by Linda Bramley, Heinemann, 1947.
Five and a Dog, Epworth, 1949.

"Listen with Mother" Tales (selected from *Listen with Mother* radio program, British Broadcasting Corp. [BBC]), illustrated by Astrid Walford, Heinemann, 1951.
Rufty Tufty the Golliwog, illustrated by Dorothy Craigie, Heinemann, 1952.
The Ruth Ainsworth Readers (contains *The Cottage by the Sea; Little Wife Goody; The Robber; The Wild Boy; A Comfort for Owl; Sugar and Spice; Fun, Fires and Friends; Black Bill; A Pill for Owl; Tortoise in Trouble; The Pirate Ship;* and *Hob the Dwarf*), Heinemann, 1953-55.
Rufty Tufty at the Seaside, illustrated by Craigie, Heinemann, 1954.
Charles Stories, and Others from "Listen with Mother" (selected from *Listen with Mother* program), illustrated by Sheila Hawkins, Heinemann, 1954.
More about Charles, and Other Stories from "Listen with Mother" (selected from *Listen with Mother* program), illustrated by Hawkins, Heinemann, 1954.
Three Little Mushrooms: Four Puppet Plays (contains *Here We Go round the Buttercups, Lob's Silver Spoon, Hide-and-Seek,* and *Hay-Making*), Heinemann, 1955.
More Little Mushrooms: Four Puppet Plays (contains *Three Clever Mushrooms, Tick-Tock, Christmas Eve,* and *The White Stranger*), Heinemann, 1955.
The Snow Bear, illustrated by Rosemary Trew, Heinemann, 1956.
Rufty Tufty Goes Camping, illustrated by Craigie, Heinemann, 1956.
Rufty Tufty Runs Away, illustrated by Craigie, Heinemann, 1957.

RUTH AINSWORTH

Five "Listen with Mother" Tales about Charles (selected from *Listen with Mother* program), illustrated by Matvyn Wright, Adprint, 1957.

Nine Drummers Drumming (stories), illustrated by John Mackay, Heinemann, 1958.

Rufty Tufty Flies High, illustrated by D. G. Valentine, Heinemann, 1959.

Cherry Stones: A Book of Fairy Stories, illustrated by Pat Humphreys, Heinemann, 1960.

Rufty Tufty's Island, illustrated by Valentine, Heinemann, 1960.

Lucky Dip: A Selection of Stories and Verses, illustrated by Geraldine Spence, Penguin, 1961.

Rufty Tufty and Hattie, illustrated by Valentine, Heinemann, 1962.

Far-Away Children, illustrated by Felice Trentin, Heinemann, 1963, Roy, 1968.

The Ten Tales of Shellover, illustrated by Antony Maitland, Deutsch, 1963, Roy, 1968.

The Wolf Who Was Sorry, illustrated by Doritie Kettlewell, Heinemann, 1964, Roy, 1968.

(Editor) James H. Fassett, *Beacon Readers,* Ginn, 1964-65.

Rufty Tufty Makes a House, illustrated by Valentine, Heinemann, 1965.

Jack Frost, illustrated by Jane Paton, Heinemann, 1966.

Daisy the Cow, illustrated by Sarah Garland, Hamish Hamilton, 1966.

Horse on Wheels, illustrated by Janet Duchesne, Hamish Hamilton, 1966.

The Look about You Books, illustrated by Jennie Corbett, Heinemann, Book 1: *In Woods and Fields,* 1967, Book 2: *Down the Lane,* 1967, Book 3: *Beside the Sea,* 1967, Book 4: *By Pond and Stream,* 1969, Book 5: *In Your Garden,* 1969, Book 6: *In the Park,* 1969.

(Reteller) *My Monarch Book of Little Red Riding Hood,* Bancroft & Co., 1967, published as *Little Red Riding Hood,* Purnell, 1977.

(Reteller) *My Monarch Book of Goldilocks and the Three Bears,* Bancroft & Co., 1967, published as *Goldilocks and the Three Bears,* Purnell, 1980.

(Reteller) *My Monarch Book of Cinderella,* Bancroft & Co., 1967, published as *Cinderella,* Purnell, 1980.

Roly the Railway Mouse, illustrated by Leslie Atkinson, Heinemann, 1967, published as *Roly the Railroad Mouse,* F. Watts, 1969.

More Tales of Shellover, illustrated by Maitland, Roy, 1968.

The Aeroplane Who Wanted to See the Sea, Bancroft & Co., 1968.

Boris the Teddy Bear, Bancroft & Co., 1968.

Dougal the Donkey, Bancroft & Co., 1968.

Mungo the Monkey, Bancroft & Co., 1968.

The Old-Fashioned Car, Bancroft & Co., 1968.

The Rabbit and His Shadow, Bancroft & Co., 1968.

The Noah's Ark, illustrated by Elsie Wrigley, Lutterworth, 1969.

The Bicycle Wheel, illustrated by Shirley Hughes, Hamish Hamilton, 1969.

Look, Do and Listen (anthology), illustrated by Bernadette Watts, F. Watts, 1969.

(Reteller) *My Monarch Book of Puss in Boots,* Purnell, 1969, published as *Puss in Boots,* 1977.

(Reteller) *My Monarch Book of Jack and the Beanstalk,* Purnell, 1969, published as *Jack and the Beanstalk,* 1977.

(Reteller) *My Monarch Book of Snow White and the Seven Dwarfs,* Purnell, 1969, published as *Snow White,* 1977.

(Reteller) *My Monarch Book of Beauty and the Beast,* Purnell, 1969, published as *Beauty and the Beast,* 1977.

(Editor) *Book of Colours and Sounds,* Purnell, 1969.

The Ruth Ainsworth Book (stories), illustrated by Hughes, F. Watts, 1970.

The Phantom Cyclist, and Other Stories, illustrated by Maitland, Deutsch, 1971, published in United States as *The Phantom Cyclist, and Other Ghost Stories,* Follett, 1974.

Fairy Gold: Favourite Fairy Tales Retold for the Very Young, illustrated by Barbara Hope Steinberg, Heinemann, 1972.

Another Lucky Dip, illustrated by Hughes, Penguin, 1973.

Three's Company, illustrated by Prudence Seward, Lutterworth, 1974.

Ruth Ainsworth's Bedtime Book, Purnell, 1974.

The Phantom Fisherboy: Tales of Mystery and Magic, illustrated by Hughes, Deutsch, 1974.

Three Bags Full, illustrated by Sally Long, Heinemann, 1975.

The Bear Who Liked Hugging People, and Other Stories, illustrated by Maitland, Heinemann, 1976, Crane Russak, 1978.

(Reteller) *The Sleeping Beauty,* Purnell, 1977.

Up the Airy Mountain: Stories of Magic, illustrated by Eileen Browne, Heinemann, 1977.

The Phantom Roundabout, and Other Ghostly Tales, illustrated by Hughes, Deutsch, 1977, published in United States as *The Phantom Carousel, and Other Ghostly Tales,* Follett, 1978.

Mr. Jumble's Toyshop, illustrated by Paul Wrigley, Lutterworth, 1978.

The Talking Rock, illustrated by Joanna Stubbs, Deutsch, 1979.

(Reteller) *Hansel and Gretel,* Purnell, 1980.

(Reteller) *The Three Little Pigs,* Purnell, 1980.

(Reteller) *The Pied Piper of Hamelin,* Purnell, 1980.

(Reteller) *Rumplestiltskin,* Purnell, 1980.

The Mysterious Baba and Her Magic Caravan: Two Stories, illustrated by Joan Hickson, Deutsch, 1980.

Mermaids' Tales, illustrated by Dandi Palmer, Lutterworth, 1980.

The Pirate Ship and Other Stories, illustrated by Hughes, Heinemann, 1980.

The Little Yellow Taxi and His Friends, illustrated by Gary Inwood, Lutterworth, 1982.

EDUCATIONAL BOOKS WITH RONALD RIDOUT

Look Ahead Readers (eight books, with supplementary readers), illustrated by John Mackay, Heinemann, 1956-58.

Books for Me to Read, Red Series: *Jill and Peter, The House of Hay, Come and Play, A Name of My Own,*

The Duck That Ran Away, and *Tim's Hoop,* illustrated by Ingeborg Meyer-Rey, Blue Series: *At the Zoo, What Are They?, Colours, Silly Billy, A Pram and a Bicycle,* and *Pony, Pony,* illustrated by Gwyneth Mamlock, Green Series: *Susan's House, What Can You Hear?, Tim's Kite, Flippy the Frog, Huff the Hedgehog,* and *A House for a Mouse,* illustrated by William Robertshaw, Bancroft & Co., 1965.

Dandy the Donkey, Bancroft & Co., 1971.

The Wild Wood, illustrated by Leslie Orriss, Bancroft & Co., 1971.

OTHER

The Evening Listens (adult poems), Heinemann, 1953.

Also author of plays and stories for television; contributor of stories to BBC programs, including *Listen with Mother* and *English for Schools.*

SIDELIGHTS: British children's author Ruth Ainsworth spent her own childhood by the sea in Suffolk, which accounts for the appearance of lonely beaches, mermaids, and sand dunes in many of her writings. "I am told that I began making up poems when I was three, and wrote an exercise book of fairy tales when I was eight," she recalls. "Throughout my childhood I enjoyed writing, whether diaries, school essays or stories." The numerous warm and gentle stories which fill Ainsworth's works are written primarily for younger readers, falling somewhere between picture books and books for more advanced readers. "It is like coming home, to open a book by Ruth Ainsworth," asserts a *Junior Bookshelf* contributor. "Here is security, an affectionate welcome, and a warm happy tale without surprises or excessive excitement but with plenty of gentle fun."

Ainsworth continued writing throughout her childhood and into her teens, and by the age of fifteen she was published in a national daily. She moved with her family to Leicester two years later, the large library there adding a new dimension to her life. Soon after, her poetry was published in a number of magazines and journals, including *Spectator* and *Country Life,* and when she won a Gold Medal for original work, the publication of more poems ensued as part of the prize. Her first break came when Heinemann published *All Different,* a book of her children's poetry. At the same time, Ainsworth began writing regularly for *Listen with Mother,* a BBC radio program, and Heinemann also published these stories in 1951 as *"Listen with Mother" Tales.* From then on, the books followed steadily.

Many of these books consist of an assortment of short stories compiled in one volume. *The Ruth Ainsworth Book,* published in 1970, collects a number of Ainsworth's previously published short stories and adds a variety of new selections. The book contains a range of stories, from simple tales for the very young, to longer and more substantial narratives for older children. Everything from realism to fantasy is covered; and a *Bulletin of the Center for Children's Books* contributor maintains that "the collection on the whole has variety

Ainsworth provides portraits of gentle, friendly spirits in this collection of ghost stories. (Cover illustration by Mike Eagle.)

and is sturdy enough to be useful for reading aloud, particularly in home collections." In such works as *The Phantom Fisherboy: Tales of Mystery and Magic* and *The Phantom Cyclist, and Other Stories,* Ainsworth delves into the unknown and presents a number of modern ghosts. These spooky spirits appear to various young children, but like Ainsworth's other characters, they are gentle, kind, and even friendly. The stories in *The Phantom Cyclist* are "told in a simple and effective style," describes a *Times Literary Supplement* reviewer. And Catherine Storr concludes in *New Statesman:* "Ainsworth will earn the gratitude of the children who always ask for ghost stories, and of parents who dread the waking and shrieking the following night, with her book of unalarming, but definitely inexplicable eerie tales."

In longer works, such as *The Talking Rock* and *The Mysterious Baba and Her Magic Caravan: Two Stories,* Ainsworth continues to mix elements of fantasy and reality. *The Talking Rock* revolves around six-year-old Jakes and his adventures on a beach in England. Quarantined with the measles, he must remain in England for a short time when his family moves to Nigeria. While staying by the sea with friends of the family, Jakes makes a boy in the sand who magically comes to life. Sand Boy, a young mermaid, and Jakes spend a few wonderful days on the beach until they, along with all the other sea creatures, are threatened by the sea monster Glumper. Jakes must climb to the top of Talking Rock to find out how to fight Glumper, and by the time he rejoins his family all is well. "This is a pleasant fantasy, not epic, but nicely written," remarks *School Library Journal* contributor Janice Giles. With *The Talking Rock,* asserts a *Junior Bookshelf* reviewer, Ainsworth presents "her most ambitious, and in many ways her most successful, story."

The two stories that make up *The Mysterious Baba and Her Magic Caravan* are set in the Left-Over Land, the place toys retire to when they are not sold. A doll family is among the inhabitants of this land, and they encounter a series of mysteries when they take in Baba, a homeless Russian doll. The other dolls are baffled by the size of some of her clothes and by the amount of food she eats until they find out that she is a Russian nested doll, with six other little Babas inside her. The family accepts Baba and her children, and the second story in the book picks up where the first left off, relating the adventures of the Baba children and their friends. *Baba and Her Magic Caravan* "is an amusing and ingenious story with a satisfying ending," relates Frances Ball in the *British Book News Children's Supplement.* "Warmth and generosity distinguish all the characters, who retain their doll-like qualities along with their human traits," concludes *School Library Journal* contributor Susan Cain.

Ainsworth sees writing as a pleasure, and claims to "write from a top layer of happiness.... If I live long enough to write stories for my great-grandchildren," she continues, "I suppose my characters will behave much as they have always done, building sandcastles, making houses, and meaning well, though this sometimes turns out badly. They experience the anguish of separation and disappointment, but there is usually a comforting, solid figure near at hand, an eternal Mrs. Golliwog."

Children find magic in the everyday life of play and family. My sources spring from just that. Only children and birds 'Know the sweetness of cherries, / The goodness of bread.'"

WORKS CITED:

Ainsworth, Ruth, essay in *Something about the Author,* Volume 7, Gale, 1975, pp. 1-4.

Ball, Frances, review of *The Mysterious Baba and Her Magic Caravan: Two Stories, British Book News Children's Supplement,* autumn, 1980, p. 15.

Cain, Susan, review of *The Mysterious Baba and Her Magic Caravan: Two Stories, School Library Journal,* September, 1980, p. 55.

Giles, Janice, review of *The Talking Rock, School Library Journal,* January, 1980, p. 64.

Review of *The Mysterious Baba and Her Magic Caravan: Two Stories, Junior Bookshelf,* October, 1980, p. 236.

Review of *The Phantom Cyclist, and Other Stories, Times Literary Supplement,* October 22, 1971, p. 1321.

Review of *The Ruth Ainsworth Book, Bulletin of the Center for Children's Books,* March, 1971, p. 101.

Storr, Catherine, "Fantasy, Fakes and Fact," *New Statesman,* November 12, 1971, p. 663.

Review of *The Talking Rock, Junior Bookshelf,* December, 1979, pp. 321-322.

FOR MORE INFORMATION SEE:

PERIODICALS

Bulletin of the Center for Children's Books, December, 1979.

Junior Bookshelf, April, 1977.

Library Journal, September 15, 1974.

Newsweek, November 9, 1979.

Saturday Review, May 27, 1978.

School Library Journal, April, 1971; October, 1978; December, 1980.

Times Literary Supplement, December 2, 1977; November 21, 1980.

B

BAKER, Betty Lou 1928-1987

PERSONAL: Born June 20, 1928, in Bloomsburg, PA; died November 6, 1987, in Tucson, AZ; daughter of Robert Weidler and Mary (Wentling) Baker; married Robert George Venturo, 1947 (divorced, 1965); children: Christopher Patrick. *Education:* Attended school in Orange, NJ. *Hobbies and other interests:* Western history, wildlife, and, "of course, Indians."

CAREER: Writer. Worked as a dental assistant and owner of a gift shop. Lecturer to groups and instructor of writing for children.

MEMBER: Arizona Press Women.

AWARDS, HONORS: Western Heritage Award, 1963, for *Killer-of-Death,* and 1970, for *And One Was a Wooden Indian;* Spur Award, Western Writers of America, 1966, for *Walk the World's Rim;* Western Writers Award (fiction), 1968, for *The Dunderhead War;* Children's Book Showcase Award, 1977, for *Dupper.*

WRITINGS:

The Sun's Promise, Abelard, 1962.
Little Runner of the Longhouse, Harper, 1962.
The Shaman's Last Raid, Harper, 1963, revised edition published as *The Medicine Man's Last Stand,* Scholastic, 1965.
Killer-of-Death, Harper, 1963.
The Treasure of the Padres, Harper, 1964.
Walk the World's Rim, Harper, 1965.
The Blood of the Brave, Harper, 1966.
The Dunderhead War, Harper, 1967.
Great Ghost Stories of the Old West, Four Winds, 1968.
Do Not Annoy the Indians, Macmillan, 1968.
The Pig War, Harper, 1969.
Arizona, Coward, 1969.
And One Was a Wooden Indian, Macmillan, 1970.
A Stranger and Afraid, Macmillan, 1972.
The Big Push, Coward, 1972.
At the Center of the World: Based on Papago and Pima Myths, Macmillan, 1973.

BETTY LOU BAKER

The Spirit Is Willing, Macmillan, 1974.
Three Fools and a Horse (Apache folktale), Macmillan, 1975.
Dupper, Greenwillow, 1976.
Settlers and Strangers: Native Americans in the Desert Southwest and History as They Saw It, Macmillan, 1977.
Save Sirrushany!, Macmillan, 1978.
No Help at All (Mayan legend), Greenwillow, 1978.
Partners, Greenwillow, 1978.

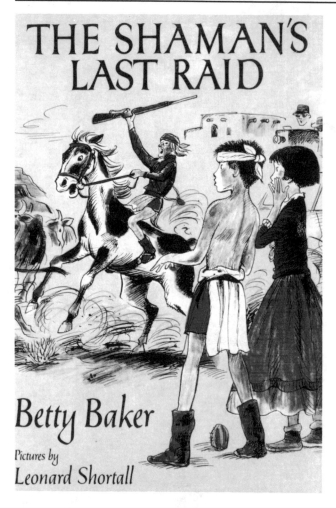

Baker's interest in the interactions between Native Americans and other cultures provides the background for this story of two contemporary Indian children. (Cover illustration by Leonard Shortall.)

Latki and the Lightning Lizard (Indian folktale), Macmillan, 1979.
All-By-Herself, Greenwillow, 1980.
Rat Is Dead, Harper, 1980.
The Great Desert Race, Macmillan, 1980.
Santa Rat, Greenwillow, 1980.
And Me, Coyote! (Indian folktales), Harper, 1981.
Worthington Botts and the Steam Machine, Macmillan, 1981.
Danby and George, Greenwillow, 1981.
Rat Is Dead and Ant Is Sad (Pueblo folktale), Harper, 1981.
Seven Spells to Farewell, Macmillan, 1982.
The Turkey Girl, Macmillan, 1983.
My Sister Says, Macmillan, 1984.
The Night Spider Case, Macmillan, 1984.

Baker's papers are housed at the University of California Library, Los Angeles; and in the Kerlan Collection, University of Minnesota, Minneapolis.

SIDELIGHTS: Betty Lou Baker specialized in writing historical fiction about the southwestern United States. Many of her books were retellings of American Indian

legends and myths; other works featured themes tied to historical events, such as the Mexican War of 1846. Baker was inspired to write, in part, by the "boring sketchiness and occasional inaccuracies" of her son's history books. In an essay for the *Third Book of Junior Authors,* Baker further explained what inspired her work: "Though I usually begin with an intriguing historical situation, people soon involve me and history is relegated to the background .... Primarily, I write the sort of book I liked to read, about interesting people involved in lots of action and none of the boring stuff I skip when I read."

In Baker's 1965 work, *Walk the World's Rim,* Chakoh, a sixteenth-century Avavare Indian boy, leaves his starving village to join Cabeza de Vaca's historic expedition from Cuba to Texas. On the way, he learns of other Indian tribes, as well as other religions. Enjoying the selfish spirit of the Spaniards with whom he travels, Chakoh learns to despise Esteban, the black slave who accompanies them. But when Esteban is killed searching for gold in Cibola, Chakoh mourns the loss of his friendship, and comes to value Esteban's courage. *New York Times Book Review* contributor Thomas Fall

A sixteenth-century native joins the exploration of Texas by the Spaniard Cabeza de Vaca and learns about friendship and honor in Baker's historical novel. (Cover illustration by the Etheredges.)

found *Walk the World's Rim*'s characters weak, but noted the book's "richness of incident." A *Bulletin of the Center for Children's Books* reviewer lauded the novel's "economy of construction."

In 1971, Baker published *And One Was a Wooden Indian,* another work centering on a young Native American's first interactions with people of other cultures. Hatilshay and Turtlehead, two mid-nineteenth-century Apache boys, are traveling in the desert. After Turtlehead is injured, the two encounter a group of white soldiers who treat the wound and show the boys a carved wooden Indian figure that resembles Turtlehead. The nephew of a shaman, Turtlehead becomes convinced that the statue is intended to turn him into wood, and that he must destroy it. Although Hatilshay questions his friend's belief, he agrees to help him steal the carving. The two boys follow the white men's trail, encountering people of different races and religions—Mexicans, Papago, Yuma, and Catholics—and discover new ways of looking at the world. Reviewers praised the novel's humor and authenticity. Although she found the plot confusing, *New York Times Book Review* contributor Miriam Gurko called *And One Was a Wooden Indian* an "engaging story." A reviewer for *Horn Book* lauded the manner in which Baker "sympathetically and convincingly" renders Hatilshay's point of view.

Baker's 1983 book, *The Turkey Girl,* is rooted in folklore, which a *Kirkus Reviews* critic identified as the source of its "reader-snagging strength." Tally, a poor girl, lives alone, caring for the mayor's turkeys in exchange for food. Secretly she dreams of a real home and a family. The turkeys, grateful for Tally's devoted care, try to fulfill her wish by magically providing a beautiful gown that hides her identity. When Tally attends the town party, the prince takes an interest in her. But when she later kills a wolf the prince is stalking, he is angered. One of the prince's hunters, however, is impressed by the girl's spirit, and he and his wife decide to adopt Tally and her turkeys. Reviewers generally enjoyed the characters and storyline, although they found flaws in Baker's writing style. A *School Library Journal* critic commented that Baker's tone "rings true."

Other of Baker's works have been praised for both their historical context and their colorful characterizations. "A nicely crafted fantasy," noted Zena Sutherland, writing in the *Chicago Tribune Book World* of *Seven Spells to Farewell.* And a *Bulletin of the Center for Children's Books* reviewer extolled *The Spirit is Willing* by saying: "The writing style is vivacious, the characters come alive, the details of the period and locale are vivid, and the author has created a family and community that are believable and enjoyable."

Baker was a disciplined writer who produced five thousand words a day; she also lectured and travelled extensively. During her travels, Baker continually looked for new book ideas. "Writing is the only job I've ever had that doesn't bore me," she once commented. "Every book is different, not just different in background and characters, but different problems to be

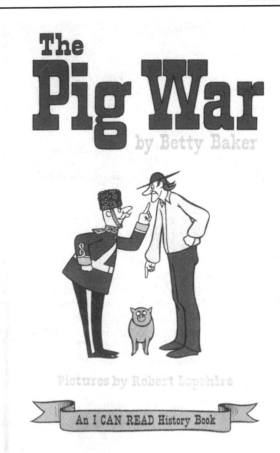

Baker searches for the interesting people and events in history, as in this tale of Revolutionary America. (Cover illustration by Robert Lopshire.)

solved. Somehow what you learn on one book never applies to the next. And the subject matter can always change to suit my interests."

WORKS CITED:

Review of *And One Was a Wooden Indian, Horn Book,* April, 1971.

Baker, Betty, essay in *Third Book of Junior Authors,* edited by Doris de Montreville and Donna Hill, Wilson, 1972, pp. 24-25.

Fall, Thomas, review of *Walk the World's Rim, New York Times Book Review,* July 11, 1965, p. 34.

Gurko, Miriam, review of *And One Was a Wooden Indian, New York Times Book Review,* February 14, 1971, p. 20.

Palmer, Nancy, review of *The Turkey Girl, School Library Journal,* May, 1983.

Review of *The Spirit is Willing, Bulletin of the Center for Children's Books,* July-August, 1974.

Sutherland, Zena, review of *Seven Spells to Farewell, Chicago Tribune Book World,* June 6, 1982.

Review of *The Turkey Girl, Kirkus Reviews,* March 1, 1983.

Review of *Walk the World's Rim, Bulletin of the Center for Children's Books,* June, 1965, p. 141.

FOR MORE INFORMATION SEE:

BOOKS

Twentieth Century Children's Writers, edited by D. L. Kirkpatrick, St. Martin's, 1978, pp. 53-54.

PERIODICALS

Booklist, June 15, 1983, p. 1343.
Bulletin of the Center for Children's Books, February, 1971, p. 87; March, 1978; May, 1982.
Horn Book, April, 1965, p. 174; October, 1978.

*   *   *

BALL, Duncan 1941-

PERSONAL: Born February 9, 1941, in Boston, MA; son of Donald (a civil engineer) and Theodora (a social worker; maiden name, Yates) Ball; married second wife, Jill Quin (a violist), March 26, 1988; children: Eliot, Ian. *Education:* Received B.A. from Boston University. *Politics:* "Left of center." *Religion:* None.

ADDRESSES: Home—Sydney, Australia. *Agent*—Joanna Cole, 532 West 114th St., New York, NY 10025.

CAREER: Chemist, part-time painter and writer, and editor, *School Magazine,* until 1982; free-lance writer, 1982—.

AWARDS, HONORS: West Australian Young Readers' Awards, best book in the primary section, 1987, for *Selby's Secret,* 1990, for *Selby Speaks,* and 1991, for *Selby Screams;* West Australian Young Readers' Award,

best Australian book in the primary section, 1989, for *The Ghost and the Gory Story.*

WRITINGS:

"GHOST" SERIES; NOVELS FOR CHILDREN

The Ghost and the Goggle Box, Angus & Robertson, 1984.
The Ghost and the Gory Story, Angus & Robertson, 1987.
The Ghost and the Shutterbug, Angus & Robertson, 1989.

"SELBY" SERIES; COMBINED STORIES AND NOVELS FOR CHILDREN

Selby's Secret, Angus & Robertson, 1985.
Selby Speaks, Angus & Robertson, 1988.
Selby Screams, Angus & Robertson, 1989.

"EMILY EYEFINGER" SERIES; ILLUSTRATED BY GEORGE ULRICH; FOR CHILDREN

Emily Eyefinger, Simon & Schuster, 1992.
Emily Eyefinger, Secret Agent, Simon & Schuster, 1993.

OTHER; FOR CHILDREN, EXCEPT WHERE NOTED

The Great Australian Snake Exchange (adult novel), Hutchinson (Australia), 1978.
My Dog's a Scaredy-Cat (picture book), illustrated by Craig Smith, Walter McVitty Books, 1987.
Comedies for Kids (plays), Angus & Robertson, 1988.
Jeremy's Tail (picture book), illustrated by Donna Rawlins, Ashton Scholastic, 1990.
(With son, Ian Ball) *The Spy Code Handbook* (activity book), Collins/Angus & Robertson, 1990.
Piggott Place (novel), Collins/Angus & Roberston, 1992.

SIDELIGHTS: Duncan Ball told *SATA:* "As a child, I was not a good reader. Let's be frank—I could barely read at all. My family moved a lot so my education was continually interrupted and I didn't develop the necessary skills. I didn't develop 'the reading habit' until I was in high school. But, from an early age, I always loved stories in all forms—being read to, listening to the radio, going to movies, and making up stories of my own. Ultimately that, coupled with a terror of a very conscientious—but tough—high school English teacher, gave me the motivation to read and, eventually, an interesting occupation.

"Though we usually lived in Boston, my parents, sister, and brother spent four years in Anchorage, Alaska, returning when I was ten or eleven. Then, when I was in my mid-teens, we spent three years in Spain. I loved being there, but my English didn't develop much during this time. I desperately wanted to be a bullfighter at this time. Fortunately no one encouraged this early career choice. Also in Madrid (thanks to the Prado) I became interested in paintings. I made some attempts at painting that were crude but gave me a lot of satisfaction.

"Part way through high school we moved back to Boston, and I discovered books—books by Fyodor Dostoyevsky and Franz Kafka and Ernest Hemingway and John Steinbeck. At this point I wanted to be a

DUNCAN BALL

Young Jeremy travels the world and encounters danger—blindfolded—while trying to the pin the tail on the donkey. (Cover illustration by Donna Rawlins.)

painter, but I heard that no one can really make a living in the arts so I studied first civil engineering and then mathematics at university, graduating from Boston University with a B.A. in mathematics and a minor in chemistry. In the midst of my studies I went to Paris and met some real artists, mainly painters and writers. (Some of them were even making a living at it.) After a year, out of money, I returned once again to the United States and the real world.

"For some years I worked as a chemist while writing and painting in my spare time and raising a family. Then, footloose once again, I moved to Sydney, Australia, in 1974—my principal residence since then.

"My first novel was an adult thriller, *The Great Australian Snake Exchange,* published in Australia and New Zealand in 1978. I gave up a job in chemical research and went to work as the editor of a literary magazine for children. It was in that job that I came to love children's books and began writing them. My own first children's books were written while I was still at the *School Magazine.* In 1982 I quit secure, well-paying, salaried work in favor of the uncertainties of free-lance writing. And I've never looked back. (Well, only once or twice a day.)

"The question most authors fear the most—and get all the time—is 'Where do your ideas come from?' In my case there are nearly as many answers as books. As with most authors, some just 'pop into my head.' One ended up on a paper napkin and then languished in my 'ideas'

file till a good friend and illustrator, Donna Rawlins, found it and decided that she would illustrate it.

"In *Jeremy's Tail,* a boy is playing pin-the-tail-on-the-donkey and he misses the donkey, goes out the door and around the world blindfolded, and then returns to the same house again. In the end he pins the tail on the donkey without knowing he's ever been away—only to be accused of peeking. Protesting his innocence, he starts off again and again heads out the door. My intention was to give the reader a bit of vicarious pleasure in seeing Jeremy in strange and dangerous situations without realizing it. But the success of the book must also be due to Donna's excellent illustrations and its educational points: a glimpse of exotic peoples and places and its demonstrating, once again, that the world is round.

"Another concept came in a very different way: A couple of years ago I was keeping an ear cocked for an idea for an early (or 'transitional') reader. When I visited schools, there was a gap in my repertoire. I had some picture books and some middle readers but nothing in between. One evening, my wife was talking about some of her early school experiences. She mentioned a second grade teacher who had once asked the class where they would like to have another eye if they had been born with a third one. After a number of

There are advantages and problems in having a third eye, as the young title character discovers in *Emily Eyefinger.* (Illustration by George Ulrich.)

answers from the class, the teacher then said, 'Think of what you could do if you had an eye on the end of your finger.' With that, my character Emily Eyefinger was born (with an eye on the end of her finger). The book, *Emily Eyefinger,* is a series of humorous episodes showing all the pros (and a few cons) of being born with an eye on the end of your finger. Happily, Olga Litowinsky at Simon & Schuster in New York saw the fun in Emily and commissioned a series of books based on the same character, beautifully illustrated by George Ulrich.

"I have now written a range of books from picture books to adult novels with the bulk of them falling in the middle readers' category. They all have humor, even when serious issues are touched upon. My intention (undoubtedly because I was a poor reader) is to write books that are as accessible as possible, to make the language flow and the stories tight—in effect, to write books that I would have liked to read as a kid."

*   *   *

BARROW, Lloyd H. 1942-

PERSONAL: Born November 2, 1942, in Fort Madison, IA; son of Robert Benton (a farmer) and Pearl (a farmer; maiden name, Perkins) Barrow; married B. Rosemary (a counseling director), June 5, 1965; children: Lon, Valerie. *Education:* Iowa State University, B.S., 1964; University of Northern Iowa, M.A., 1969; University of Iowa, Ph.D., 1973. *Hobbies and other interests:* Reading, playing bridge, watching sports, gardening.

ADDRESSES: Home—3011 Alsup, Columbia, MO 65203. *Office*—Southwestern Bell Science Education Center, University of Missouri, 108 Townsend, Columbia, MO 65211.

CAREER: Marion Schools, Marion, IA, teacher, 1965-74; Iowa City Schools, Iowa City, IA, science coordinator, 1974-77; Lenoir-Rhyne College, Hickory, NC, professor, 1977-79; University of Maine, Orono, professor, 1979-85; University of Missouri, Columbia, professor, 1985—; writer.

MEMBER: National Science Teachers Association (member of board of directors, 1983-85 and 1990-92), National Association for Research in Science Teaching, School Science and Math Association (member of board of directors, 1988-91).

AWARDS, HONORS: Iowa Teacher of the Year, Jaycees, 1974.

WRITINGS:

Adventures with Rocks and Minerals, Enslow Publications, 1991.

WORK IN PROGRESS: A second volume of *Adventures with Rocks and Minerals.*

SIDELIGHTS: Lloyd H. Barrow told *SATA:* "My motivation for writing this book was due to my interest in hands-on, minds-on geology activities to help students understand about the Earth, and my former students encouraging me to share my ideas with others."

*   *   *

BARTHOLOMEW, Jean
See BEATTY, Patricia (Robbins)

*   *   *

BEATTY, Patricia (Robbins) 1922-1991
(Jean Bartholomew)

PERSONAL: Born August 26, 1922, in Portland, OR; died July 9, 1991, in Riverside, CA; daughter of Walter M. and Jessie (Miller) Robbins; married John Louis Beatty (a professor of history and humanities), September 14, 1950 (died, 1975); married Carl G. Uhr (a professor of economics), July 31, 1977; children: (first marriage) Ann Alexandra. *Education:* Reed College, B.A., 1944; graduate study at University of Idaho, 1947-50, and University of Washington, Seattle, 1951. *Politics:* Democrat. *Religion:* Protestant. *Hobbies and other interests:* Gardening, English history, the American West, learning languages, extra-sensory perception studies, archaeology, and philosophical studies.

CAREER: High school teacher of English and history, Coeur d'Alene, ID, 1947-50; Dupont Company, Wilmington, DE, technical library worker, 1952-53; business and science librarian, Riverside, CA, 1953-56; Universi-

PATRICIA BEATTY

---

ty of California, Los Angeles, Extension Division, teacher of fiction writing for children, 1967-69. Established the John and Patricia Beatty Award California Library Association, 1988.

AWARDS, HONORS: Commonwealth Club of California Medal for best juvenile by California author, 1965, for *Campion Towers; A Donkey for the King* was named to the *Horn Book* honor list, 1966; Southern California Council on Children's and Young People's Literature Medal notable book, 1967, for *The Royal Dirk;* Golden Kite Award honor book, Society of Children's Book Writers, 1973, for *Red Rock over the River;* received California Council medal in 1974 for "distinguished body of work," and in 1976 for "comprehensive contribution of lasting value to the field of children's literature"; *By Crumbs, It's Mine!* was named a Junior Literary Guild selection in 1976, as was *I Want My Sunday, Stranger!* in 1977 and *Lacy Makes a Match* in 1979; Western Writers of America honor book, 1978, for *Wait for Me, Watch For Me, Eula Bee;* Jane Addams Children's Book Award honor book, 1982, for *Lupita Manana;* Southern California Council on Children's and Young People's Literature Medal for distinguished work of fiction, 1983, for *Jonathan Down Under;* Western Writers of America Awards, 1984, 1987; Scott O'Dell Award for Historical Fiction, 1987, for *Charley Skedaddle.*

WRITINGS:

FICTION FOR YOUNG ADULTS

Indian Canoemaker, illustrated by Barbara Beaudreau, Caxton, 1960.
Bonanza Girl, illustrated by Liz Dauber, Morrow, 1962.
(With husband, John Louis Beatty) *At the Seven Stars,* illustrated by Douglas Gorsline, Macmillan, 1963.
The Nickel-plated Beauty, illustrated by Dauber, Morrow, 1964.
(With J. L. Beatty) *Campion Towers,* Macmillan, 1965.
Squaw Dog, illustrated by Franz Altschuler, Morrow, 1965.
(With J. L. Beatty) *The Royal Dirk,* illustrated by Altschuler, Morrow, 1966.
The Queen's Own Grove, illustrated by Dauber, Morrow, 1966.
(With J. L. Beatty) *A Donkey for the King,* illustrated by Ann Siberell, Macmillan, 1966.
The Lady from Black Hawk, illustrated by Robert Frankenberg, McGraw, 1967.
(With J. L. Beatty) *The Queen's Wizard,* Macmillan, 1967.
(With J. L. Beatty) *Witch Dog,* illustrated by Altschuler, Macmillan, 1968.
Me, California Perkins, illustrated by Dauber, Morrow, 1968.
Blue Stars Watching, Morrow, 1969.
(With J. L. Beatty) *Pirate Royal,* Macmillan, 1969.
Hail Columbia, illustrated by Dauber, Morrow, 1970.
The Sea Pair, illustrated by Altschuler, Morrow, 1971.
A Long Way to Whiskey Creek, Morrow, 1971.
(With J. L. Beatty) *King's Knight's Pawn,* Morrow, 1971.

Beatty's own lonely childhood is reflected in her historical novels of children struggling to survive against long odds; in this work, a young Southern girl tries to rebuild her life after the end of the Civil War.

O the Red Rose Tree, illustrated by Dauber, Morrow, 1972.
(With J. L. Beatty) *Holdfast,* Morrow, 1972.
The Bad Bell of San Salvador, Morrow, 1973.
Red Rock over the River, Morrow, 1973.
How Many Miles to Sundown, Morrow, 1974.
(With J. L. Beatty) *Master Rosalind,* Morrow, 1974.
Rufus, Red Rufus, illustrated by Ted Lewin, Morrow, 1975.
(With J. L. Beatty) *Who Comes to King's Mountain?,* Morrow, 1975.
By Crumbs, It's Mine!, Morrow, 1976.
Something to Shout About, Morrow, 1976.
Billy Bedamned, Long Gone By, Morrow, 1977.
I Want My Sunday, Stranger!, Morrow, 1977.
Just Some Weeds from the Wilderness, Morrow, 1978.
Wait for Me, Watch for Me, Eula Bee, Morrow, 1978.
Lacy Makes a Match, Morrow, 1979.
The Staffordshire Terror, Morrow, 1979.
That's One Ornery Orphan, Morrow, 1980.
Lupita Manana, Morrow, 1981.
Eight Mules from Monterey, Morrow, 1982.
Jonathan Down-Under, Morrow, 1982.
Melinda Takes a Hand, Morrow, 1983.
Turn Homeward, Hannalee, Morrow, 1984.

The Coach That Never Came, Morrow, 1985.
Behave Yourself, Bethany Brant, Morrow, 1986.
Charley Skedaddle, Morrow, 1987.
Be Ever Hopeful, Hannalee, Morrow, 1988.
Sarah and Me and the Lady from the Sea, Morrow, 1989.
Eben Tyne, Powdermonkey, Morrow, 1990.
Jayhawker, Morrow, 1991.
Who Comes with Cannons?, Morrow, 1992.

OTHER

Station Four (novella), Science Research Associates, 1969.
(Under pseudonym Jean Bartholomew) *The English-man's Mistress* (adult gothic novel), Dell, 1974.

Also author of materials on English history for Science Research Associates.

SIDELIGHTS: A prolific and award-winning writer of historical fiction for children, Patricia Beatty enticed her readers into the past. The author recreated the eras of her fictional characters with the accuracy and attention to detail of a first-rate historian. Her heroines and heroes take part in exciting yet believable conflicts, often drawn with humor and touching on themes of heroism and morality, that make her books popular with children of many ages and interests.

Beatty was the older of two children born to Walter and Jessie Robbins. As her father was a U.S. Coast Guard commander, she grew up on the northwest coast of the United States, residing at a number of Coast Guard stations which were often located on Indian reservations. Living among the various Indian tribes gave Beatty the opportunity to learn about Native American customs and history and to develop an appreciation for the outdoors. Her interest and empathy would last a lifetime.

Like her parents, Beatty became an avid reader. At age ten she developed an infection that at that time, before antibiotics, required five months of hospitalization. She whiled away the bedridden hours reading. "I think this childhood illness had a great deal to do with my later becoming a writer," Beatty wrote in an essay for *Something about the Author Autobiography Series* (*SAAS*). "I read somewhere that many authors who write especially for young people are individuals who have had suffering in their own childhoods ... or known intense loneliness. I believe such suffering while young makes for a deeper, more sensitive person, who can feel the pain and problems of others and put himself or herself into the other person's difficult place. Putting yourself into another person's place, putting on his skin, zipping it up, and trying to think and act as he or she would is what an author does in every book he or she writes."

In 1935 the Robbins family moved to Portland, Oregon, where Beatty discovered the public library, attended junior high and high school, and became enthralled with horses. She spent many Saturdays at a riding academy

learning to ride with both English and Western saddles—skills that were to later play a part in her novels. By the time she was fifteen years old, Beatty had decided to become a high school teacher, and she entered Reed College during World War II. For a while she thought she might make a career in marine biology, but she settled on a degree in history and literature when the biology professor left Reed College. She was involved in sports, particularly fencing, which was also to become useful in her writing career. During her college years Patricia met John Beatty, whom she married in 1950 after he completed his military service.

Beatty taught English and history for several years in Idaho. While there she also learned about fishing and surviving in subzero weather. Then she worked as a librarian at various locations dictated by her husband's career as a history professor. In 1953 the couple settled in Riverside, California.

While working in the business and industry section of the Riverside Public Library, Beatty found time on her hands and decided to write her first book, *Indian Canoemaker,* about the Quillayute Indians before the coming of the white man. To her surprise it sold right away—and on the same day that her first book contract arrived, Beatty's daughter Ann Alexandra was born. Her

A Kansas farmboy determines to carry on his abolitionist father's work in this spy novel of the Civil War. (Cover illustration by Stephen Marchesi.)

second book, *Bonanza Girl,* written while Ann slept, was set in the 1880s in the mining region of northern Idaho. When it was published by Morrow in 1962 it met with instant critical success, but it unleashed a storm of protest among Beatty's friends, who thought that she must be neglecting her family and home. "Their attitude, which was compounded out of envy and combined with a real feeling I was doing something wicked to my family, struck me deeply," Beatty wrote in *SAAS.* "It turned me into a feminist, a person devoted to the interest and welfare of other women, when it could have made me hate all women as catty individuals." Thus many of Beatty's books feature courageous girls who act on their own.

Around 1960 the Beatty family went to London to live for a year. While there Patricia and her husband John were inspired to coauthor a spy novel for teenagers, *At the Seven Stars,* which focused on three famous figures from the eighteenth century. This novel led to a type of system: the Beattys published two books per year, one of English historical fiction written jointly, and another on American historical themes written solely by Patricia Beatty. This "system" lasted until John Beatty's premature death in 1975. For a few years Beatty did not write at all, but after her marriage to economics professor Carl Uhr in 1977 she regained her momentum.

Generally Beatty alternated novels written in the third person with first-person narratives. Many of what critics have called her "lighter" novels feature liberated heroines dealing with the challenges of frontier life in the West: for example, *Lacy Makes a Match* depicts a young girl's efforts at matchmaking in late 1800s California; *That's One Ornery Orphan* recounts the adventures of a plucky orphan in 1889 Texas; and *Eight Mules from Monterey* follows the daughter of a widowed librarian into the California mountains to set up library outposts in 1916. Many of Beatty's more serious novels are set during the American Civil War, such as *I Want My Sunday, Stranger,* in which a young California Mormon boy wanders battlefields of the Civil War with a photographer, and the award-winning *Charley Skedaddle,* in which a twelve-year-old boy enlists as a drummer boy, later deserts his regiment, and flees to the Blue Ridge Mountains, where he learns about the true nature of courage.

All of Beatty's novels required extensive research into the language, dress, and customs of the times they depict. While some may question the need for such accuracy in children's books, Beatty prided herself in making history come alive for her readers. "I want to share my excited sense of the past with children and I try by every means at my command, including some very laborious research, to make them aware of how life was lived at some particular period," Beatty once commented in *SATA.* "I have tried to convey a sense of the past to young readers and at the same time not overwhelm them with detail. I love to insinuate bits of historical information and educate at the same time I entertain. I think this is one of the best ways of all to teach history."

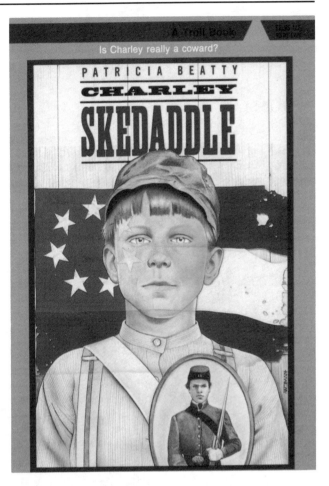

Beatty won the Scott O'Dell Award for Historical Fiction for this tale of a young boy who deserts the Union Army and must learn to believe in himself.

Beatty gained a reputation as a leading writer of historical novels for children. Some of her books have been translated into Spanish, Danish, German, and Norwegian. Herself the recipient of numerous awards, in 1988 Beatty established the John and Patricia Beatty Award through the California Library Association to encourage the writing of children's books about the culture and heritage of California. Upon her death in July 1991, Beatty left a large body of critically acclaimed work that will long continue to draw young readers into the excitement of the past.

WORKS CITED:

Beatty, Patricia, essay in *Something about the Author Autobiography Series,* Volume 4, Gale, 1987, pp. 35-52.
Something about the Author, Volume 30, Gale, 1983, pp. 48-53.

FOR MORE INFORMATION SEE:

PERIODICALS

Children's Book World, November 5, 1967.
Christian Science Monitor, February 23, 1969.
National Observer, November 4, 1968.
Saturday Review, April 17, 1971.

Writer, March, 1989.
Young Readers' Review, November, 1966; October, 1967; October, 1968.*

*   *   *

BERGMAN, Donna 1934-

PERSONAL: Born March 29, 1934, in Seattle, WA; daughter of Donald T. ("worked for a contractor and once said, 'I wish I was a writer'") and Emma Lou (an assistant treasurer in a brokerage firm; maiden name, Laffort) Webster; married Robert D. Bergman (an insurance underwriter), June 6, 1955; children: Randall. *Education:* University of Washington, B.A., earned teaching certificate, 1955; pursued postgraduate study. *Politics:* Independent. *Religion:* Presbyterian.

ADDRESSES: Home—4037 56th Street S.W., Seattle, WA 98116. *Agent*—Renee Cho, McIntosh & Otis, Inc., 310 Madison Avenue, New York, NY 10017.

CAREER: Seattle Public Schools, Seattle, WA, teacher of art and language arts, grades 7-9, 1955-1987; free-lance writer, 1987—. Served as handwriting and communication consultant for local businesses, including an insurance company, bank, and credit union.

MEMBER: National Writers Club (director of chapter services, Seattle chapter), Society of Children's Book Writers (vice-president, Seattle chapter, and regional

DONNA BERGMAN

advisor), Pacific Northwest Writers Conference (vice-president).

AWARDS, HONORS: First place award for a children's picture book, Pacific Northwest Writers Conference, 1989, for *City Fox*; fifth place short story award in national writing contest, National Writers Club, 1990, for "Under the Pines."

WRITINGS:

(Contributor) Ann Saling, editor, *Sasquatch Sightings* (contains "A Handsome Giant"), Edmonds Art Commission Books, 1987.
City Fox, illustrated by Peter E. Hanson, Atheneum, 1992.
Timmy Green's Blue Lake, illustrated by Ib Ohlsson, Morrow, 1992.

Contributor of short stories to periodicals, including *Just a Moment, Sunshine,* and *The Columbia.*

WORK IN PROGRESS: "A number of picture books are in the works, as well as a longer piece about a young boy who loves farming but is forced to move to the city."

SIDELIGHTS: Donna Bergman turned her attention to writing books for children after engaging in a teaching career that spanned thirty years. She was an art and language arts instructor for the school system in Seattle, Washington, the city where she herself was raised. Bergman told *SATA:* "My interest in writing blossomed into a passion during the years I helped ninth grade students in my classes with an assignment that involved writing and illustrating a children's book." Although she left the classroom in 1987 to devote her full time to her writing, Bergman still remains interested in young people. She is especially attuned to the problems faced by eight-to-twelve-year-old students in areas of language and communication due to the increasingly diverse ethnic mix among them.

Bergman has also expressed concern for the area in which she lives. "I was born in Seattle and still live here in a house that sits high on a hill. The house looks out across Puget Sound to the islands and to the Olympic Mountains beyond. My den—where I write—is upstairs and, from my window, I watch seagulls and crows swoop and soar. The view, which also includes magnificent fir trees and an ancient pine, often serves as a setting in my stories. I like to think of the natural environment as one of the characters in my stories, and I feel every bit as protective of it as a mother does of her child." It was the concern Bergman felt over a fox she discovered living on the hillside below her house that prompted her to write *City Fox.*

"In addition to our Northwest environment, the years I spent as an artist and art teacher also influenced my writing," Bergman explained to *SATA.* "The idea for *Timmy Green's Blue Lake,* my second book, came from seeing old things in new ways, which artists often do: found art, collages, abstractions." Although trained as an artist, Bergman has come to love writing to the point

The wildlife that can exist on the edge of the big city became the focus of Bergman's first book. (Cover illustration by Peter E. Hanson.)

that she is content to leave the work of illustrating her picture books to someone else. "My experience, so far, has been that the artists have enriched the stories with their drawings," she noted. "Now *I* play around with words and themes, as before, I fooled around with lines and colors and shapes."

Bergman is active in a host of activities that bring her into contact with other local writers. "As most writers do, I love to read the work of other authors, finding it both a way to stimulate my ideas and an inspiration for working on my craft—I try to read the work of only the best writers. I also attend writers' conferences and workshops. I belong to a writer's critique group. And I've come to see *rewriting* as part of the writing process. Writers, I've discovered, never stop learning."

*   *   *

BERTOLET, Paul
See McLAUGHLIN, Frank

*   *   *

BODECKER, N(iels) M(ogens) 1922-1988

PERSONAL: Born January 13, 1922, in Copenhagen, Denmark; immigrated to the United States, 1952; died of cancer of the colon, February 1, 1988, in Hancock, NH; married Mary Ann Weld, 1952 (marriage dissolved, 1959); children: three sons. *Education:* Attended Technical Society's Schools (Copenhagen), School of Architecture, 1939-41, School of Applied Arts, 1941-44, and Copenhagen School of Commerce, 1942-44.

ADDRESSES: Home—Hancock, NH 03449.

CAREER: Free-lance writer and illustrator. *Military service:* Royal Danish Artillery, 1945-47.

AWARDS, HONORS: Spring Book Festival honor awards, 1954, for *Half Magic,* and 1959, for *Magic or Not?;* Ohioana Book Award, Ohioana Library Association, 1957, for *Knight's Castle,* and 1963, for *Seven-Day Magic;* Society of Illustrators citation, 1965, for *David Copperfield; Miss Jaster's Garden* was named among the year's ten best illustrated books, *New York Times,* 1972; American Library Association notable book citation, best books of the year citation, School Library Association, best children's books of the year citation, National Book League of the United Kingdom, all 1973, Christopher Award, 1974, and Biennial of Illustration selection, American Institute of Graphic Artists, 1976, all for *It's Raining Said John Twaining: Danish Nursery Rhymes; The Mushroom Center Disaster* was named a Children's Book Showcase title, 1975; Christopher Award, 1977, for *Hurry, Hurry, Mary Dear! and Other Nonsense Poems; A Little at a Time* was named a Children's Book Showcase title, 1977.

WRITINGS:

POETRY

Digtervandring (title means "Poets Ramble"), Forum, 1943.
Graa Fugle (title means "Grey Birds"), Prior, 1946.

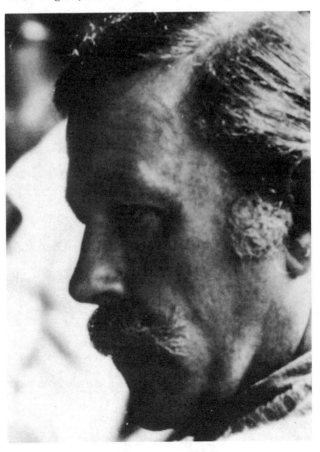

N. M. BODECKER

HOUSE FLIES

What makes
common house flies
trying
is
that they keep
multiflieing.

Bodecker's whimsical drawings often accentuate the humor of his verse. (Illustration from *Hurry, Hurry, Mary Dear.*)

JUVENILES

The Mushroom Center Disaster, illustrated by Erik Blegvad, Atheneum, 1974.
Quimble Wood, illustrated by Branka Starr, Atheneum, 1981.
Carrot Holes and Frisbee Trees, illustrated by Nina Winters, Atheneum, 1983.
Water Pennies and Other Poems, illustrated by Blegvad, Macmillan, 1991.

SELF-ILLUSTRATED JUVENILES ·

Miss Jaster's Garden, Golden Press, 1972.
(Translator and editor) *It's Raining Said John Twaining: Danish Nursery Rhymes,* Atheneum, 1973.
Let's Marry Said the Cherry, and Other Nonsense Poems, Atheneum, 1974.
Hurry, Hurry, Mary Dear! And Other Nonsense Poems, Atheneum, 1976.
A Person from Britain Whose Head Was the Shape of a Mitten, and Other Limericks, Atheneum, 1980.
The Lost String Quartet, Atheneum, 1981.

Pigeon Cubes and Other Verse, Atheneum, 1982.
Snowman Sniffles and Other Verse, Atheneum, 1983.

ILLUSTRATOR

Sigfred Pedersen, *Spillebog for Hus, Hjem og Kro* (title means "Book of Games for House, Home and Inn"), Erichsen (Copenhagen), 1948.
Patric Dennis, *Oh! What a Wonderful Wedding,* Crowell, 1953.
Roger Eddy, *The Bulls and the Bees,* Crowell, 1956.
Russell Lynes, *Cadwallader: A Diversion,* Harper, 1959.
Mark Caine, *The S-Man,* Houghton, 1960.
Agnes DeMille, *The Book of the Dance,* Golden Press, 1963.
Charles Dickens, *David Copperfield,* Macmillan, 1966.

ILLUSTRATOR OF JUVENILES

Edward Eager, *Half Magic,* Harcourt, 1954.
Evan Commager, *Cousins,* Harper, 1956.
Eager, *Knight's Castle,* Harcourt, 1956.
Anne Barrett, *Songberd's Grove,* Bobbs-Merrill, 1956.
Eager, *Magic by the Lake,* Harcourt, 1957, revised edition, 1985.
Commager, *Beaux,* Harper, 1958.
Eager, *The Time Garden,* Harcourt, 1958.
Eager, *Magic or Not?,* Harcourt, 1959.
Eager, *The Well-Wishers,* Harcourt, 1960.
Adelaide Holl, *Sylvester, the Mouse with the Musical Ear,* Golden Press, 1961.
Eager, *Seven-Day Magic,* Harcourt, 1962.
Miriam Schlein, *The Snake in the Carpool,* Abelard, 1963.
Doris Adelberg, *Lizzie's Twins,* Dial, 1964.
Josephine Gibson, *Is There a Mouse in the House?,* Macmillan, 1965.
Mary Francis Shura, *Shoe Full of Shamrock,* Atheneum, 1965.
Robert Kraus, *Good Night, Little One,* Springfellow Books, 1972.
Kraus, *Good Night, Richard Rabbit,* Springfellow Books, 1972.
Kraus, *Good Night, Little A.B.C.,* Springfellow Books, 1972.
Michael Jennings, *Mattie Fritts and the Flying Mushroom,* Windmill Books, 1973.
Kraus, *The Night-Lite Calendar 1974,* Windmill Books, 1973.
Kraus, *The Night-Lite Calendar 1975,* Windmill Books, 1974.
Kraus, *The Night-Lite Storybook,* Windmill Books, 1975.
David A. Adler, *A Little at a Time,* Random House, 1976.

OTHER

Poetry represented in the anthology *Ung Dansk Lyrik* (title means "Young Danish Poetry"), edited by Niels Kaas Johansen, Hirschsprung (Copenhagen), 1949.
Contributor of illustrations to books, including *Helen Gould Was My Mother-in-Law,* by Celeste Andrews Seton and Clark Andrews, Crowell, 1953; *Confessions of a Dilettante,* by Russell Lynes, Harper, 1966; *Fun and Laughter: A Treasure House of Humor,* Reader's Digest,

1967; *English Drama in Transition,* edited by Henry F. Salerno, Pegasus, 1968; *The English Short Story in Transition,* edited by Helmut E. Gerber, Pegasus, 1968; and *English Poetry in Transition,* edited by John M. Munro, Pegasus, 1968. Also contributor of illustrations to magazines, including *Holiday, McCall's, Saturday Evening Post, Esquire,* and *Ladies' Home Journal.* Bodecker's books have been published in Canada, England, France, Sweden, Denmark, Italy, Germany, Holland, and Spain.

SIDELIGHTS: N. M. Bodecker was an author and illustrator of children's books whose first love was poetry. After publishing two books of verse in Danish, he began illustrating, predominately children's books, and eventually began to write and illustrate his own books for young readers. He was perhaps best known as translator, editor, and illustrator of *It's Raining Said John Twaining: Danish Nursery Rhymes,* a collection that was named one of 1973's notable books by the School Library Association, the American Library Association, and the National Book League of the United Kingdom. Bodecker enjoyed writing books for children, and once remarked, "I have retained strong emotional ties to the childhood condition and need to share my imaginings with a sympathetic audience." By the time of his death, Bodecker had illustrated or contributed

illustrations to over forty books and received many awards both for his writing and illustrations.

Bodecker was born in Copenhagen, Denmark, on January 13, 1922. He received an extensive education in Copenhagen that included several years each at the School of Architecture, the School of Applied Arts, and the Copenhagen School of Commerce, and then two years with the Royal Danish Artillery. His first book of poetry, *Digtervandring,* was published while he was still in school in 1943. After the military, he did some work as an illustrator in Denmark before coming to the United States at the age of thirty, where he married Mary Ann Weld. They eventually had three sons, but the marriage ended a few years afterwards. Bodecker then lived for a while in New York City and Westport, Connecticut, finally settling in Hancock, New Hampshire. He worked for twenty years as an illustrator while he was learning to write poetry in English, ultimately beginning to write and illustrate his own books for children. "Writing for children took me by surprise," he commented in *Twentieth-Century Children's Writers.* "I hadn't planned it, it just happened."

Bodecker's sons became the inspiration for one of his own attempts at a children's book—*It's Raining Said John Twaining: Danish Nursery Rhymes.* A collection of

SPRING GALE

The world is spinning madly,
I can feel the way it scoots,
shaking loose a million, billion
dandelion parachutes.
The birds cling to the maple trees
with little squeaks and hoots;
the maples cling to rocks and earth
for dear life with their roots

—but Dad and I are safe
in our great, big rubber boots.

Bodecker's strong recollections of his own childhood inform poems such as this piece from *Snowman Sniffles and Other Verse*. (Illustration by the author.)

Danish nursery rhymes he had translated for his sons, edited, and then illustrated, the volume was well-received by critics. Full of nonsense verse, "the poems have a tongue-twisting rhythm and logical illogic which cry to be read aloud," as Margaret F. Maxwell explained in *Twentieth-Century Children's Writers*. The collection includes such tales as the one about guinea pigs who go to see the King, and a woman who takes her mice with her on trips across ice. A reviewer in the *New York Times Book Review* praised Bodecker's work, claiming the rhymes were "nimbly translated." Jean Mercier in *Publishers Weekly* commented that the illustrations were perfectly suited to the tales and called the collection "fresh and funny."

Bodecker's talent for whimsy was shown in books like *The Lost String Quartet,* in which the members of the Daffodil String Quartet, on their way to a concert, end up giving a performance of the "Spring Quartet in E Minor" using string beans, an alpenhorn, a tirelin (once a violin), and a viola constrictor. After a wrong turn

---

BICKERING

The folks in Little Bickering
they argue quite a lot.
Is tutoring in bickering
required for a tot?
Are figs the best for figuring?
Is pepper ice cream hot?
Are wicks the best for wickering
a wicker chair or cot?
They find this endless dickering
and nonsense and nit-pickering
uncommonly invigor'ing,
I find it downright sickering!
You do agree!
Why not?

The author's talent for clever rhymes and rhythms are evident in this poem about an argumentative little town. (Illustration by the author from *Hurry, Hurry, Mary Dear.*)

takes them into one disaster after another, including the almost total destruction of their instruments (a boa swallows one of the instruments, so they rent the boa and play a viola constrictor, for example), the quartet finally arrive for their performance and find an enthusiastic audience. Both written and illustrated by Bodecker, the book received mixed reviews. The text was often criticized as uneven, or as Holly Sanhuber in the *School Library Journal* claimed, "choppy." A reviewer in the *Bulletin for the Center of Children's Books* declared that the "abrupt end" was disappointing and distracting. Critics generally praised the drawings, however, with Mercier calling them "magnetically wild." And the *Bulletin for the Center of Children's Books* reviewer commented that the illustrations closely reflect the "lunatic quality of the text."

Bodecker illustrated many of his other works, including *Pigeon Cubes and Other Verse.* A look at the comic realities of life, the collection wryly discusses such topics as a tulip blooming in a garbage dump, piles of loose photos that multiply before they can be put into an album, and the fate of the early worm at the mercy of the early bird. Mercier commented that Bodecker expresses feelings "in sharp but not cruel satire and just as often in sensitive contemplation." Ethel R. Twichell in *Horn Book* noted the "sly humor and ... skillful manipulation of rhyme," and remarked that Bodecker's drawings add a "touch of whimsical humor." "Text and illustration are inseparable," concluded Peter Neumeyer in the *School Library Journal.*

In *Carrot Holes and Frisbee Trees,* Bodecker turns from poetry and rhyme to straight story-telling, presenting the tale of William and Pippin Plumtree. A happily married couple, the Plumtrees grow the best and largest vegetables in the neighborhood within their garden, and are very content—until their carrots grow to the size of a third grade child. Problems mount as the Plumtrees try to utilize the surplus, first canning, then eventually starting a post hole business (capitalizing on the size of the holes left when the growing carrots are removed from the ground). But each solution has its own problems, such as frisbee-sized carrot seeds. In the end, the lumber industry has a promising use for the gigantic carrots. Marge Loch-Wouters, writing in the *School Library Journal,* called *Carrot Holes and Frisbee Trees* "an unusual tale that sparkles with humor and absurd situations." Mercier praised Bodecker's "bone-dry" presentation, which "increases the fun in the fantasy." Mary B. Burns, writing in *Horn Book,* asserted that the line drawings by Nina Winters complement the "original and engaging" text, and concluded: "A fresh, funny story, ideal for reading aloud."

Bodecker's last and posthumously published work, *Water Pennies and Other Poems,* is a collection of short poems about the small wonders of nature to be found around a pond. From butterflies and moths to grasshoppers and slugs, Bodecker uses his imagination as he reveals the tiny creatures for young readers. The delicate line drawings were done by Erik Blegvad, a fellow Dane who had previously illustrated *The Mushroom Center*

Disaster, and complemented the world Bodecker created with his words. Ann Stell, writing in the *School Library Journal,* commented on the "whimsical reinvention" of the pond creatures, but noted that the collection often lacked the clever wording for which Bodecker was known. Nancy Vasilakis in *Horn Book,* on the other hand, lauded the "strong, insistent rhythms," and called the book a "beautiful little volume" that conveyed the "buzz and busyness" of the world of the pond. A reviewer in the *New York Times Book Review* had a similar view, and declared that *Water Pennies* was "full of small delights." Today, Bodecker's name remains most often associated with his nonsense verse for children.

WORKS CITED:

Burns, Mary B., review of *Carrot Holes and Frisbee Trees, Horn Book,* February, 1984, p. 49.

Review of *It's Raining Said John Twaining: Danish Nursery Rhymes, New York Times Book Review,* November 13, 1977, p. 40.

Loch-Wouters, Marge, review of *Carrot Holes and Frisbee Trees, School Library Journal,* January, 1984, p. 72.

Review of *The Lost String Quartet, Bulletin of the Center for Children's Books,* September, 1981, p. 6.

Maxwell, Margaret F., essay on N. M. Bodecker, *Twentieth-Century Children's Writers,* edited by Tracy Chevalier, 3rd edition, St. James Press, 1989, pp. 110-11.

Mercier, Jean F., review of *Carrot Holes and Frisbee Trees, Publishers Weekly,* September 9, 1983, p. 64.

Mercier, Jean F., review of *It's Raining Said John Twaining: Danish Nursery Rhymes, Publishers Weekly,* December 3, 1973, p. 40.

Mercier, Jean F., review of *The Lost String Quartet, Publishers Weekly,* May 29, 1981, p. 43.

Mercier, Jean F., review of *Pigeon Cubes and Other Verse, Publishers Weekly,* September 10, 1982, p. 75.

Neumeyer, Peter, review of *Pigeon Cubes and Other Verse, School Library Journal,* November, 1982, p. 77.

Sanhuber, Holly, review of *The Lost String Quartet, School Library Journal,* August, 1981, p. 63.

Stell, Ann, review of *Water Pennies and Other Poems, School Library Journal,* January, 1992, pp. 101-02.

Twichell, Ethel R., review of *Pigeon Cubes and Other Verse, Horn Book,* February, 1983, pp. 56-57.

Vasilakis, Nancy, review of *Water Pennies and Other Poems, Horn Book,* January/February, 1992, p. 85.

Review of *Water Pennies and Other Poems, New York Times Book Review,* February 2, 1992, p. 30.

FOR MORE INFORMATION SEE:

PERIODICALS

Bulletin for the Center of Children's Books, February, 1973, p. 86; October, 1974, p. 24; March, 1975, p. 106.

Horn Book, April, 1977, p. 181; October, 1980, pp. 532-33; June, 1983, p. 318.

The adventures of four little people who tumble from a car into the forest form the basis of this story. (Cover illustration by Branka Starr.)

New York Times Book Review, June 21, 1981, p. 37.

Publishers Weekly, November 18, 1974, p. 53; November 22, 1976, p. 52; April 23, 1979, p. 80; March 4, 1983, p. 100; August 10, 1984, p. 83.

School Library Journal, November, 1978, p. 30; September, 1980, p. 66; May, 1983, pp. 56, 58.

OBITUARIES:

PERIODICALS

New York Times, February 3, 1988.
Publishers Weekly, February 26, 1988.
School Library Journal, March, 1988.*

                    —Sketch by Terrie M. Rooney

*   *   *

BROPHY, Nannette 1963-

PERSONAL: Last name rhymes with "trophy"; born July 27, 1963, in Pottsville, PA; daughter of Martin (a retired surveyor) and Dolores (a retired teacher's aide; maiden name, Kocur) Brophy; married Mark T. Major (a genealogist/historian), December 27, 1986; children: Lawrence. *Education:* Pennsylvania State University,

NANNETTE BROPHY

associate degree, 1983; Joe Kubert School of Cartoon and Graphic Art, Inc., diploma, 1986; Institute of Children's Literature, diploma, 1991. *Politics:* Nonpartisan. *Religion:* Christian.

ADDRESSES: Home—708 W. Norwegian St., Pottsville, PA 17901.

CAREER: Author, illustrator, cartoonist, caricaturist. Schuylkill County Council for the Arts, member of advisory council, 1991—.

WRITINGS:

(Self-illustrated) *The Color of My Fur,* Winston-Derek, 1992.

WORK IN PROGRESS: A picture book about materialism entitled *Larry's Loot.*

SIDELIGHTS: In a letter to *SATA,* Nannette Brophy quoted early twentieth-century artist and teacher Robert Henri: "'Find out what you really like if you can. Find out what is really important to you. Then sing your song. You will have something to sing about and your whole heart will be in the singing.' This quote expresses perfectly how I feel about what I do.

"Presently I am an author and an illustrator, but I consider myself an artist first," Brophy continued. "This may be a slight exaggeration, but I believe that the very day my little left hand picked up its first crayon is the day I decided to become an artist. What a magnificent thing it is to create worlds, both real and imaginary, by simply putting marks on a piece of paper! A few years later, I discovered that the same is true of writing. A single sentence, a single word even, can conjure up tons of visual images. And when words and pictures come together, magic is made.

"As is true of most, if not all, human beings, I have opinions inside of me that scream to be released. Lucky me, I have a way to reach the masses. Through storybooks, I can encourage children to become people of honor and goodness. I would like to give them thoughtful stories and vibrant pictures that demean social injustice and promote peace between people. This was my motivation for creating *The Color of My Fur.* It is a book about the silliness of prejudice. The opening pages throw you smack dab in the middle of feuding purple and orange bunnies—fighting only because their fur colors are different.

"Animals tell the story instead of people to avoid making it blatantly obvious what the book is about. I felt that bunnies, the talking cloud, and other make-believe devices softened the harshness for the young reader without sacrificing the lesson to be learned. Bright hues are used in the full color illustrations to enhance the dullness of the gray washes. Isn't the message obvious? The world would be truly boring if we were all the same.

"Though *The Color of My Fur* is my only published work, I am hopeful that there will be more to follow. I would like to continue to address social issues through children's books, perhaps making it my niche, or trademark if you will—to entertain and educate at the same time.

"To make a difference, to sing my song, this is why I write and draw."

* * *

BROWN, Craig McFarland 1947-

PERSONAL: Born September 4, 1947, in Fairfield, IA; son of Carl (in sales) and Jane (a teacher; maiden name, McFarland) Brown; divorced; children: Heather Jean, Cory McFarland. *Education:* Layton School of Art, B.F.A., 1969; attended University of Wisconsin-Milwaukee, 1971-73, and Uri Shulevitz Workshop on writing and illustrating children's books, 1985. *Politics:* Independent.

ADDRESSES: Home and office—1615 South Tejon #3, Colorado Springs, CO 80906.

CAREER: American Greetings Corporation, Cleveland, OH, artist, 1969-71; *Astronomy* magazine, Milwaukee, WI, art director, 1973-75; Koss Corporation, Milwaukee, packaging designer, 1975-77; W. C. Brown Publishing Co., Dubuque, IA, art director, 1977-81; Current, Inc., Colorado Springs, CO, artist 1, 1981-87; author and illustrator, 1987—. Teacher at Taos Institute of Arts; member of a Hospice bereavement team. *Exhibitions:* Children's Book of Art, Boston, 1989; Society of Illustrators, New York City, Our Own Show, 1990 and 1991, and Annual Show, 1990; 25th Exhibition of Original Pictures of International Children's Books, Japan, 1990.

MEMBER: Toastmasters.

AWARDS, HONORS: Design award for best juvenile book, Rocky Mountain Book Publishers Association, 1990; Children's Books of the Year citation, Child Study Children's Book Committee at Bank Street College, 1991, for *The Ornery Morning.*

WRITINGS:

SELF-ILLUSTRATED

The Patchwork Farmer, Greenwillow, 1988.
My Barn, Greenwillow, 1991.
City Sounds, Greenwillow, 1992.
The Bandshell, Greenwillow, 1993.
In the Spring, Greenwillow, 1993.

CRAIG McFARLAND BROWN

ILLUSTRATOR

Amy Lawson, *The Talking Bird and the Storypouch,* Harper, 1988.
Toni Knapp, *The Gossamer Tree,* Rockrimmon Press, 1988.
Peter and Connie Roop, *Snips the Tinker,* edited by Patricia and Fredrick McKissack, Milliken, 1989.
Knapp, *The Six Bridges of Humphrey the Whale,* Rockrimmon Press, 1989.
Craig Kee Strete, *Big Thunder Magic,* Greenwillow, 1990.
Lael Littke, *Storm Monster,* Silver Burdett, 1990.
Tom Raabe, *Biblioholism,* Fulcrum Publishing, 1990.
Patricia Brennan Demuth, *The Ornery Morning,* Dutton, 1991.

WORK IN PROGRESS: Research on scarecrows, dolls, and myths.

SIDELIGHTS: Raised in a rural farming community, Craig McFarland Brown had many opportunities to develop his drawing talent. He described his younger years to *SATA* as a time full of freedom and carefree days. He recalled rising early and riding his bike out into the country where he could draw and paint the countryside, including its barns, animals, fields, and flowers. Fishing was another favored morning activity that allowed him time to draw. The afternoons were devoted to baseball or swimming, until it was time to head home for dinner. In the evenings, Brown remembers the hours he spent downtown reading books and magazines at the Soda Fountain. He commented that it was "quite a full day" for a young boy.

Brown explained that he became interested in drawing while in the third grade, creating caricatures of classmates and teachers. This early interest in art was encouraged throughout his primary and secondary education. At Layton School of Art, Brown developed an interest in children's books that he claimed "later turned into a love affair." After sixteen years of working in advertising, he left to become a full-time free-lance illustrator. His drawing is done with a technique called "stippling." Brown explained: "It is created by placing dots next to each other—the closer the dots the darker the value, the further apart the dots the lighter the value. When the stippling is done, then pastels are added for the color." He noted that his "interest in stippling was generated while at Layton School of Art and during visits to the Chicago Art Institute, where each visit would start and end at the paintings of George Seurat." He includes Grant Wood, Maurice Sendak, and Uri Schulevitz as other artists that have affected his style and peaked his interest.

Brown's childhood memories also influence his work, and were at the heart of the first two books he wrote and illustrated. Brown commented that *The Patchwork Farmer* was based on his "feelings for farmers," the respect he has for "how hard they work—their perseverance and willingness to come back day after day." He noted that he admires farmers and has always noticed "the patchwork look of the fields" whenever he was

I like the sound

OINK OOOOINK OINNNK OINK OINK...

the sound a pig makes.

Brown's childhood in a farming community provided him with the background for his self-illustrated book about a barn and its inhabitants. (Illustration by the author from his *My Barn.*)

traveling through the countryside. His second book explores the barnyard. Brown wrote: *"My Barn* was written to give children the authentic sound animals make and a look at a barn's architecture." He also wanted them to "have fun repeating the sounds that each animal makes." A rooster, for example, goes "Er Er Er Er Er Errrrrrr Errrrr" instead of "Cock-A-Doodle-Do." Brown divides his time between writing, illustrating, and as he explained, "working with students at schools and workshops, helping to promote their own creativity and self worth," where he presents himself as part of a trio that includes his two dogs, Max and Moe.

* * *

BUTLER, Dorothy 1925-

PERSONAL: Born in 1925 in Auckland, New Zealand; daughter of William and Emily (Brown) Norgrove; married Roy Edward Butler (an engineer); children: Catherine Butler Darroch, Christine Butler Sidwell, Patricia Butler Yeoman, Vivien Butler Mulgrew, Anthony, Simon, Susan, Josephine. *Education:* University of Auckland, B.A., 1946, diploma in education, 1975; Auckland Teachers College, teacher's certificate, 1947. *Religion:* Unitarian-Universalist.

ADDRESSES: Home—132 Sunnybrae Rd., Takapuna, Auckland 10, New Zealand. *Office*—Dorothy Butler Children's Bookshop Ltd., Fountain Court, Three Lamps, Ponsonby, Auckland, New Zealand.

CAREER: High school English teacher; worked as play center supervisor, university lecturer in children's literature, and teacher of night classes for Auckland Technical Institute, 1946-65; Dorothy Butler Children's Bookshop Ltd., Auckland, New Zealand, owner and managing director, 1965—. Owner of Dorothy Butler Reading Centre, 1978-84; children's editor for Reed Methuen, 1984. May Hill Arbuthnot Honor Lecturer in the United States, 1982; Anne Carroll Moore Spring Lecturer, Lincoln Center, 1982; guest lecturer, Northern Territories Library Service (Australia) and Australian Book Council, 1984, and Japan Foundation, 1985. Member of National Council of Booksellers, 1974-80.

MEMBER: International PEN, New Zealand Children's Literature Association, New Zealand Reading Association.

AWARDS, HONORS: Eleanor Farjeon Award, 1979; *Cushla and Her Books* was cited as an "outstanding book on a disabled person" by the American Library Association's Committee for the Year of the Disabled Person, 1981.

WRITINGS:

(With Marie Clay) *Reading Begins at Home: Preparing Children for Reading Before They Go to School,* Heinemann (New Zealand), 1979, (with Bobbye S. Goldstein) Heinemann (United States), 1980, revised edition, 1987.
The Dorothy Butler Pre-Reading Kit, Heinemann, 1980.
Babies Need Books, Atheneum, 1980, revised edition, Penguin, 1988.
Babies Need Books, (television adaptation), Television New Zealand, 1983.
Five to Eight (nonfiction), illustrated by Shirley Hughes, Bodley Head, 1986.

FOR CHILDREN

Cushla and Her Books, Hodder & Stoughton, 1979, Horn Book, 1980.
(Editor) *The Magpies Said: Stories and Poems from New Zealand,* illustrated by Lyn Kriegler, Puffin, 1980.
(Editor) *For Me, Me, Me: Poems for the Very Young,* Hodder & Stoughton, 1983.
I Will Build You a House: Poems, illustrated by Megan Gressor, Hodder & Stoughton, 1984.
Come Back, Ginger: A Tale of Old New Zealand (picture book), illustrated by Kriegler, Reed Methuen, 1987.
A Bundle of Birds (picture book), illustrated by Kriegler, Reed Methuen, 1987.
My Brown Bear Barney, illustrated by Elizabeth Fuller, Greenwillow, 1989.
Lulu (poetry), Hodder & Stoughton, 1990.
A Happy Tale, illustrated by John Hurford, Crocodile, 1990.

Another Happy Tale, illustrated by Hurford, Crocodile, 1991.
Higgledy Piggledy Hobbledy Hoy, illustrated by Kriegler, Greenwillow, 1991.
My Brown Bear Barney in Trouble, illustrated by Fuller, Greenwillow, 1993.

Contributor to magazines in England, the United States, and New Zealand.

SIDELIGHTS: Children's author Dorothy Butler once said, "With my own family, I became convinced that children need books from birth if reading is to 'take.' I am actively opposed to television. The 'videobook' concept is dedicated to producing narrative text and static images for children for whom television is the only thing available."

Aidan Chambers commented in *Horn Book,* "Dorothy Butler loves people and is passionately convinced of the importance of literature. And she wants more than anything to bring the two together; especially she wants to bring children and books together."

Butler's conviction is in part due to the true story of Cushla Yeoman, one of her granddaughters. Born with severe handicaps and requiring round-the-clock care, Cushla's early years proved more difficult than many families could have handled, but her parents and family worked together to help her. *Cushla and Her Books*'s "account of Cushla's growth, by slow degrees, into a vital, aware child, who by the age of six could scramble about and talk and who, most astonishingly of all, had taught herself to read is one I wish every parent and particularly every professional involved with children would study," Chambers declared. Originally written as a thesis for her diploma in education from Auckland University, Cushla's story earned Butler a citation from the American Library Association's Committee for the Year of the Disabled Person in 1981.

WORKS CITED:

Chambers, Aidan, "Letter from England: Dorothy Butler," *Horn Book,* August, 1980, pp. 450-452.

FOR MORE INFORMATION SEE:

PERIODICALS

Horn Book, September, 1989, p. 609.
Los Angeles Times Book Review, September 15, 1985, p. 2.

Dorothy Butler's strong belief that children should learn to love books at an early age has led to a second career as an author. (Cover illustration by Lyn Kriegler.)

Observer, September 16, 1990, p. 55.
School Librarian, November, 1990, p. 141.
School Library Journal, January, 1990, p. 78.

Times Educational Supplement, June 24, 1988, p. 28; May 12, 1989, p. B8.
Times Literary Supplement, July 18, 1980; November 21, 1980; February 20, 1987, p. 197.*

C

CARWELL, L'Ann
  See McKISSACK, Patricia C.

*   *   *

CASTLE, Paul
  See HOWARD, Vernon (Linwood)

*   *   *

CAZZOLA, Gus 1934-

PERSONAL: Born August 19, 1934, in Jersey City, NJ; son of August S. (a civil servant) and Edith (Golinski) Cazzola; married Angela Maria DeStephano (a teacher), June, 1957; children: Camille Cazzola Miller, Nadine, Michael. *Education:* Seton Hall University, B.A. (English), 1960; Trenton State College, B.A. (education), 1970; Monmouth College, M.A., 1973.

ADDRESSES: Home—114 Maple Ave., Island Heights, NJ, 08732.

CAREER: Hudson Dispatch, Union City, NJ, reporter, 1953-57; mail carrier and clerk, 1957-65; Hooper Avenue School, Toms River, NJ, teacher, 1965-86; Beachwood Elementary School, Toms River, reading and writing teacher, 1986-92; writer. Writing judge for New Jersey Council of the Arts, 1979. Worked variously as a reading and writing teaching specialist, cartoonist, and college and television lecturer. Playground and recreation director for Dover Township, in Toms River, 1965-74. *Military service:* U.S. Army, paratrooper and public relations representative, 1954-56.

MEMBER: Society of Children's Book Writers, New Jersey Education Association.

AWARDS, HONORS: Best novel award, New Jersey Education Association, 1976, for unpublished novel, *The Day They Burned Toms River;* Helen Keating Ott Award, Church and Library Association, 1980, and award from New Jersey Writers Conference, 1981 and 1982, for *A Chisel for Ezekiel;* literacy award from International Reading Association, 1988.

WRITINGS:

A Chisel for Ezekiel, Concordia, 1979.
To Touch the Deer, Westminster, 1982.
The Bells of Santa Lucia, Philomel Books, 1991.
Dismas My Brother, Shining Star Press, 1992.

A fire brings a young girl out of her grief in Gus Cazzola's picturebook.

Also author of *The Day They Burned Toms River* and *The Evil Eye of Michael S. Crisp,* Simon & Schuster. Work represented in anthologies, including *The World Beyond,* Xerox Publishing, 1976. Contributor to periodicals, including *Young World, True Experiences, Reporter, Organic Gardening,* and *Christian Living.* Author of educational writing kits for Xerox Personalized Reading Service, *Reader's Digest* Educational Service, Point 32, and Xerox Pal Paperback Service. Contributor to the American College Test (ACT).

WORK IN PROGRESS: The Reunion, a horror novel; *The Long Run Home,* a juvenile novel.

SIDELIGHTS: In addition to teaching reading and writing to children for more than twenty-five years, Gus Cazzola has authored several books exploring various themes, including survival and social responsibility. In 1982 Cazzola published *To Touch the Deer,* which revolves around a teenage boy caught in a fantasy world where his mother has died and he has run away from his stepfather. The boy ventures into the New Jersey Pine Barrens where he must learn to survive. He receives help from a deer who guides and protects him, and when the game boy touches the buck, he returns to the real world. Cazzola's next book, *The Bells of Santa Lucia,* is a picture book featuring a young girl from an Italian village who is infatuated with the sounds of bells. When her grandmother, who would ring a bell to summon the girl, passes away, the girl becomes disenchanted with all chimes. She is deaf to the tolls of the bells in the village, until fire rages through an animal's stall, and it becomes essential for her to ring the largest bell in the village in order to warn the community. Diane Roback, writing in her review for *Publisher's Weekly,* described *The Bells of Santa Lucia* as a "sweet and compassionate story" that is "substantial and deftly told."

WORKS CITED:

PERIODICALS

Roback, Diane, review of *The Bells of Santa Lucia, Publisher's Weekly,* November 8, 1991, p. 63.

FOR MORE INFORMATION SEE:

PERIODICALS

School Library Journal, November, 1981, p. 88; January, 1992, p. 89.

* * *

CHOI, Sook Nyul

PERSONAL: Born in Pyongyang, Korea; came to the United States; children: two daughters. *Education:* Received B.A. from Manhattanville College.

ADDRESSES: Home—Cambridge, MA.

CAREER: Writer; teacher of creative writing to high school students. Boston Public Library, selected author for creative writing workshop, 1992. Former teacher of elementary school students in New York City.

MEMBER: Authors Guild, Authors League of America, Society of Children's Book Writers, National Writers Union, Women's National Book Association.

AWARDS, HONORS: Bulletin Blue Ribbon citation, *Bulletin of the Center for Children's Books,* and Judy Lopez Book Award, both 1991, Young Adults Library Services Association best book for young adults citation, New York Public Library best book for the teen age citation, and American Library Association notable book citation, all for *Year of Impossible Goodbyes;* Cambridge YWCA Women of Achievement Award, 1992.

WRITINGS:

Year of Impossible Goodbyes (novel for young adults), Houghton, 1991.
Echoes of the White Giraffe (sequel to *Year of Impossible Goodbyes*), Houghton, in press.
Halmoni and the Picnic (picture book), illustrated by Karen Milone-Dugan, Houghton, in press.

WORK IN PROGRESS: A picture book.

SIDELIGHTS: Set in 1945 Korea, Sook Nyul Choi's *Year of Impossible Goodbyes* focuses on ten-year-old Sookan, a resident of Pyongyang who struggles to preserve her identity while her homeland is under Japanese colonial rule. The Japanese force Korean men to serve in labor camps, require Koreans to attend

SOOK NYUL CHOI

Set in the turbulent war years of Choi's native Korea, *Year of Impossible Goodbyes* presents the struggle of a young girl's family to survive the Japanese military occupation and escape to freedom in the south. (Cover illustration by Marie Garafano.)

Japanese schools and places of worship, and outlaw their language. While living in this restrictive environment, Sookan studies the Korean language at night behind the darkened windows of her home. Her mother, meanwhile, supervises a sock factory and serves as a champion to her female work force. During the summer of 1945, the Japanese are defeated and Russian troops occupy the northern part of the territory while Americans control the south. The Russians prove to be no more respectful of the Koreans than the Japanese. When they begin using psychological warfare on Koreans, Sookan's mother decides to lead an escape to the American zone with her young children rather than wait for her husband, who is in Manchuria, and her sons, who are held in the Japanese labor camps, to return home. Michael Shapiro of the *New York Times Book Review* deemed *Year of Impossible Goodbyes* a "powerful and moving autobiographical novel" and added that while Choi intended the work for a young audience, it "should also be read by adults—both for its poignancy and for its capacity to illuminate."

Choi told *SATA:* "I have always loved books. As a young girl growing up in Korea, I loved collecting books. I

loved the feel and the smell of books; I liked the sound of pages turning; and I liked arranging them on my bookshelf. Sitting under the trellis of grapevines in our backyard, I would sit and read for hours as I snacked on the bitter green grapes. Through books, I could travel to the far corners of the world and meet people from distant lands and cultures. Through books, I could even travel through time.

"As a grammar school student in Korea, I began writing short stories and poetry. I loved to write, for through writing, I could express my thoughts, ideas, and feelings, and could even express my dreams and visions of the fantastic.

"Thirty years later, after emigrating to the United States and after teaching in American schools for almost twenty years, I began writing once again, but this time in English. I now have two countries, my native country of Korea, and my adopted country, the United States. Through my writing, I want to bring to life the history and culture of Korea, to share with all my American friends. I hope that through my books, Americans can gain insight into this very different and interesting culture."

WORKS CITED:

Shapiro, Michael, review of *Year of Impossible Goodbyes, New York Times Book Review,* November 10, 1991, p. 42.

*   *   *

COATES, Anna 1958-
(Anne Joseph, Anna Scotti)

PERSONAL: Born December 7, 1958, in Philadelphia, PA; daughter of Joseph F. (a futurist) and Vary (a

ANNA COATES

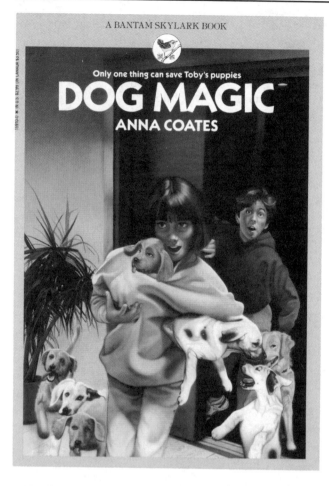

A BANTAM SKYLARK BOOK

Only one thing can save Toby's puppies

DOG MAGIC
ANNA COATES

The family dog speaks to enlist Matt and Kate's help in finding his missing puppies in Anna Coates's first novel for children. (Cover illustration by Bill Schmidt.)

political scientist; maiden name, Taylor) Coates; married Frederick Scotti, Jr. (a record promoter), 1986. *Education:* Antioch College, B.A., 1979.

ADDRESSES: Agent—Curtis Brown, 10 Astor Place, New York, NY 10002.

CAREER: Writer, 1984—. Free-lance script analyst.

WRITINGS:

Dog Magic (suspense), Bantam, 1991.

UNDER PSEUDONYM ANNE JOSEPH

Sweet Dreams, My Darling (suspense), Pinnacle, 1990.
Grandfather (horror), Zebra Books, 1991.

OTHER

Contributor to periodicals, including *Los Angeles Times Magazine, Buzz,* and *Writer.*

WORK IN PROGRESS: A children's novel.

SIDELIGHTS: Two children are amazed when their pet dog talks to them in Anna Coates's *Dog Magic,* but they quickly learn that the dog's puppies are in danger and set out to rescue them from a product-testing laboratory.

"Adults may find [the premise] hard to accept . . . . But, this is, after all, a fantasy, and one that kids are likely to enjoy," Kay Weisman commented in *Booklist.* Anne Connor, writing in *School Library Journal,* similarly believes *Dog Magic* "should appeal to animal lovers with a conscience."

Coates told *SATA:* "I write for children as 'Anna Coates' and for adults as 'Anna Scotti.' My nonfiction has appeared in the *Los Angeles Times Magazine, Buzz, Writer,* and other magazines. I also free-lance as a script analyst for various entertainment firms. I enjoy hearing from young readers and do my best to answer every letter."

WORKS CITED:

Connor, Anne, review of *Dog Magic, School Library Journal,* January, 1992, p. 108.
Weisman, Kay, review of *Dog Magic, Booklist,* January 1, 1992.

* * *

COUTURE, Christin 1951-

PERSONAL: Born August 21, 1951, in Springfield, MA; daughter of Raymond and Therese (Le Blanc) Couture. *Education:* University of Massachusetts, B.F.A. (magna cum laude), 1974; attended Brooklyn Museum School, 1974-75.

ADDRESSES: Home—103 East Second St., New York, NY 10009. *Office*—Farrar, Straus, Giroux, Inc., 19 Union Square W., New York, NY 10013.

CAREER: Professional painter and free-lance graphic artist, 1975—. *Exhibitions:* Work has appeared in solo exhibitions, including Monique Knowlton Gallery, New York City, 1979, 1980, and 1982; Galeria Arvil, Mexico City, Mexico (traveling), 1983, 1988; Centro Cultural Vanguardia, Saltillo, Coahuila, Mexico, 1984; Fauve Gallery, Amherst, MA, 1987; and Forbes Gallery, Northampton, MA, 1992. Work has also appeared in group shows, including University of Massachusetts, Herter Gallery, 1974, Fine Arts Gallery, 1984; Monique Knowlton Gallery, 1978, 1983, and 1985; Chicago International Art Exposition, 1981, 1982, and 1983; University of Oklahoma, Museum of Art, 1982; Sioux City Arts Center (traveling), 1984; Secreteria de la Contraloria, Mexico City, 1988; Staemfli Gallery, New York City, 1990; and Mount Holyoke College Art Museum, 1992. Works are in private collections in the United States and Latin America.

MEMBER: National Women's Caucus for Art, Authors Guild, Inwood-Heights Parks Alliance.

AWARDS, HONORS: Brooklyn Museum School fellowship, 1974; MacDowell Colony, 1980; Yaddo Residency, 1987; and Foundation Karolyi fellowship, 1989.

CHRISTIN COUTURE

WRITINGS:

SELF-ILLUSTRATED

The House on the Hill, Farrar, Straus, 1991.
A Walk in the Woods, Farrar, Straus, 1992.

WORK IN PROGRESS: A new series of paintings, and several book ideas.

SIDELIGHTS: Christin Couture told *SATA:* "Making picture books, for me, is a natural extension of painting. My ideas come from a deep personal source causing me to get very excited and totally obsessed with the project at hand. This leads to new adventures and further exploration of the material. In my case, the text is secondary to the visual image which must be strong enough to stand alone on each page—like a series of narrative paintings. The text gently pulls the reader along, serving as an amusing understatement or a stand-in when multiple action is taking place."

Couture's paintings in *The House on the Hill* were inspired by a trip to Mexico in which she had the opportunity to search through, as she phrased it, an "extraordinary house." It was filled with priceless antiques, treasures, and unusually decorated rooms. Once back in the United States, she looked for the

unique around her—in her own home (the "House on the Hill"), her friends' homes, and wherever else it captured her artistic imagination and caused the "excitement of discovery." Couture's paintings were done in predella format, a style she once described as "a long horizontal cut-away view of an interior or landscape." Dating from the early Italian Renaissance, this type of painting was originally reserved for religious use—adorning altars with depictions of the lives of saints.

Couture continued with the same painting technique in *A Walk in the Woods.* Here, she focused on the change of seasons, specifically the transformations of a "northeastern forest from late spring to late summer," as she once explained. Drawing inspiration from her early experiences hiking along the Holyoke Range in Massachusetts with her family, Couture recreated her vision for all to share. Interested in more than just images as she sketched the individual trees, she noted patterns and styles of leaves. She researched the tree names and learned to identify them through their bark types and unique leaf shapes. *A Walk in the Woods* also encompasses her impressions of rivers, such as the Oxbow of the Connecticut River, a water tower, lakes, a cave in Shutesbury, Massachusetts, and even a cow pasture at the Pocantico Hills. Couture wrote, "Although I've had a lot of exposure to nature, I paid little attention to the different types of plants until I began work on *A Walk in the Woods.*"

*   *   *

CRISMAN, Ruth 1914-

PERSONAL: Born June 16, 1914, in Oak Park, IL; daughter of John Henry (a bookkeeper) and Ruth Ethel (a beautician; maiden name, Stiles) Thorup; married Chester Tresenriter, 1935 (divorced, 1940); married James Lester Crisman, July 7, 1941 (died, 1991); children: (second marriage) Carol Ann, James Alan. *Education:* Attended University of Southern California; California State University, Los Angeles, B.A., 1966, M.A., 1971. *Politics:* Republican. *Religion:* Episcopalian.

ADDRESSES: Home—Glendale, CA. *Office*—P.O. Box 4411, Glendale, CA 91202. *Agent*—Kendra Marcus, Bookstop Literary Agency, 67 Meadow View Rd., Orinda, CA 94563.

CAREER: Worked as a dental assistant, 1931-41; Los Angeles Board of Education, clerk typist and library assistant, 1956-64; elementary school teacher in various fields, including child care, reading, and special education for the physically handicapped, 1965-1979; writer. Substitute teacher, 1980-84.

MEMBER: Society of Children's Book Writers, PEN Women, Professional Writers League, California Writers Club, St. Martha's Guild, Monday Writers, California Federation of Chaparral Poets, Pi Lambda Theta.

RUTH CRISMAN

WRITINGS:

FOR CHILDREN

The Mississippi, Franklin Watts, 1984.
Hot off the Press, Lerner, 1991.
Thomas Jefferson: Man with a Vision (biography), Scholastic, 1992.
Racing the Iditarod Trail, Dillon, 1993.

Contributor of articles to periodicals, including *Los Angeles Times, Los Angeles Herald Examiner, Your Health, The Waterways Journal, Career World, Changes,* and *Instructor Magazine.*

SIDELIGHTS: Ruth Crisman told *SATA:* "My love of books and children led to careers as teacher, author, and free-lance writer. I have travelled extensively in the United States, Canada, New Zealand, and Mexico, with special interest in our nation's rivers."

*   *   *

CROMPTON, Anne Eliot 1930-

PERSONAL: Born April 6, 1930, in Springfield, MA; daughter of Samuel Atkins (a professor of drama) and Ethel (a writer; maiden name, Cook) Eliot; married Willard Crompton (a woodworker), November 24, 1951; children: Carrie Elliott, Joseph, Nancy, Catherine

Utera, Samuel. *Education:* Attended Kenwood Academy, 1943-48, and Newton College of the Sacred Heart, 1948-49. *Hobbies and other interests:* Ecology, piano, gardening, painting, family.

ADDRESSES: Home—Chesterfield, MA.

CAREER: Free-lance writer. Chesterfield Arts Council, chair, 1991-92.

MEMBER: Society of Children's Book Writers.

WRITINGS:

The Sorcerer, Little, Brown, 1971.
Deer Country, Little, Brown, 1973.
The Winter Wife, Little, Brown, 1975.
The Rain-Cloud Pony, Holiday House, 1977.
A Woman's Place, Little, Brown, 1978.
The Lifting Stone, Holiday House, 1978.
Queen of Swords, Methuen, 1980.
The Ice Trail, Methuen, 1980.
The Untamed, Pinnacle, 1981.
Warrior Wives, Pinnacle, 1982.
Johnny's Trail, Swedenborg Foundation, 1986.
The Snow Pony, Henry Holt, 1991.

Contributor of reviews to *New York Times, Orion Nature Quarterly,* and *Parent's Choice.*

ANNE ELIOT CROMPTON

A pair of ice skates raises puzzling memories in the mind of a colonial boy raised by an Indian tribe. (Cover illustration by Elise Primavera.)

WORK IN PROGRESS: The Rainbow Pony, a novel for middle readers.

SIDELIGHTS: Anne Eliot Crompton told *SATA:* "When I was small and looking ahead at my life, I made three wishes. I wished for my own family. I wished to live in the country. And I wished to write fiction.

"Someone once said, 'Life is a tale told by the lips of God.' When my mother talked about people, she helped you feel that. She was a born writer and the author of many books for children and adults. Even in conversation, she made common truth sound like a fairy tale. 'Mr. X saw an angel and changed his life.' 'Aunt M met her husband-to-be during a power failure on the subway.' 'Mr. L bought the wrong business and went bankrupt, which saved his marriage.'

"I grew up loving fiction, respecting its magic, and wanting to tell stories. Every day I saw stories, but I could never tell them because I could hardly talk—I had a speech impediment. So early on I decided to write books, like my mother. She bought me a typewriter for my fifteenth birthday and showed me how to prepare a manuscript, and I was in business. At age eighteen I sold a short story to *Seventeen* magazine, and walked on air. The joy of communicating—and not to one listener, but many readers—was almost too much to bear.

"However, my first two wishes had to come first before writing. I had to achieve the family—a good husband and five children—and the country. And these goals needed all my time and energy until I was thirty-seven. That year my youngest child started school, and suddenly I had free time. Right away I hauled out the old typewriter and went back into the magic business of storytelling. My first sale was to a religious magazine. Crazily I danced around the house shouting 'Thirty dollars! THIRTY DOLLARS!' Someone thought my short story was worth that much!

"My niece asked cautiously, 'Don't you mean thirty *thousand* dollars?'

"'No, I mean thirty! Thirty! Thirty! And hundreds of people will read it!' My niece shook her head, amazed.

"So far all my stories have been about nature and the human spirit. I have written picture books, middle-grade books, young-adult novels, adult novels, and short stories. My three wishes have been granted. And now I wish only to write more, richer, deeper fiction, that will touch and interest more readers."

FOR MORE INFORMATION SEE:

PERIODICALS

Horn Book, August, 1975; April, 1979.
New York Times Book Review, December 10, 1978.
Los Angeles Times Book Review, August 29, 1982.

D

DADEY, Debbie 1959-

PERSONAL: Full name is Debra Gibson Dadey; last name is pronounced "Day-dee"; born May 18, 1959, in Morganfield, KY; daughter of Voline (a model maker) and Rebecca (a teacher; maiden name, Bailey) Gibson; married Eric Dadey (a chemist), June 11, 1981; children: Nathan Leigh. *Education:* Western Kentucky University, B.S., M.S.L.S. *Politics:* Democrat. *Religion:* Catholic.

ADDRESSES: Home—2513 Wilma Lane, Plano, TX 75074. *Agent*—Pesha Rubinstein, 37 Overlook Ter., #10, New York, NY 10033.

CAREER: St. Romuald Elementary School, Hardinsburg, KY, teacher, 1981-83; St. Leo Elementary School, Versailles, KY, teacher, 1983-84; Sayre School, Lexington, KY, began as teacher, became librarian, 1986-1990; Tates Creek Elementary School, Lexington, librarian, 1990-92. Free-lance writer, Argus Communications, 1989; instructor, University of Kentucky, 1990-92; writing consultant, Scott County Schools, 1991-92.

MEMBER: International Reading Association (Bluegrass Chapter vice-president), Society of Children's Book Writers, National Education Association, Kentucky Education Association, Fayette County Education Association.

WRITINGS:

WITH MARCIA THORNTON JONES

Vampires Don't Wear Polka Dots, Scholastic, 1990.
Werewolves Don't Go to Summer Camp, Scholastic, 1991.
Santa Claus Doesn't Mop Floors, Scholastic, 1991.
Leprechauns Don't Play Basketball, Scholastic, 1992.
Ghosts Don't Eat Potato Chips, Scholastic, 1992.
Aliens Don't Wear Braces, Scholastic, 1993.
Frankenstein Doesn't Plant Petunias, Scholastic, 1993.
Genies Don't Chew Bubblegum, Scholastic, 1993.
Pirates Don't Wear Pink Sunglasses, Scholastic, 1993.

DEBBIE DADEY

Contributing editor to *Kidstuff* magazine. Contributor to *Kicks* magazine.

WORK IN PROGRESS: Indian Sister.

SIDELIGHTS: "I have always been a daydreamer, sometimes to my teachers' chagrin," Debbie Dadey told *SATA.* "I think anyone who can dream can write. All it takes is the desire and the dream." Dadey began achieving her dream four years ago with the help of Marcia Thornton Jones, when Dadey was working as a librarian at an elementary school where Jones taught. "It was one of those days when the kids didn't seem to be paying attention to anything we had to say," Dadey recalled for *SATA.* "We decided if we grew horns, sprouted fangs, had steam rolling out of our ears, and were 15 feet tall the kids in our school would really pay attention to us. That's the reason we wrote *Vampires Don't Wear Polka Dots.* It's a story about a tough group of third graders who get an even tougher teacher ... she might even be a monster or vampire!"

Memories of summer camp inspired the pair's next book, *Werewolves Don't Go to Summer Camp.* "We had been to short little camps as kids," Dadey told *SATA,* but the book expanded on their rather ordinary experiences to focus on a week-long camp where the counselor is rumored to be a real werewolf. Despite the fun of writing books with werewolves and vampires as characters, Dadey and Jones told *SATA* that their favorite book is *Santa Claus Doesn't Mop Floors* because of its insight into the character of Eddie, whom they describe as a "stinker." The book shows how Eddie discovers "that miracles really can happen," Dadey said.

One of Dadey's and Jones's recent efforts is *Leprechauns Don't Play Basketball,* a story which pits a vampire and a leprechaun against one another right in the middle of an elementary school. "It was interesting because of the research we did into leprechauns and vampires," the authors told *SATA.* "If we write about a certain creature, we always read as much as we can about it. We come up with some interesting tid-bits and try to include them in our stories." While writing *Ghosts Don't Eat Potato Chips,* the pair "read so many ghost books we had to check under our beds before we went to sleep at night!" Dadey and Jones continue to research supernatural creatures for future novels; upcoming books will feature witches and pirates.

*   *   *

DAHL, Roald 1916-1990

PERSONAL: Given name is pronounced "Roo-aal"; born September 13, 1916, in Llandaff, South Wales; died November 23, 1990, in Oxford, England; son of Harald (a shipbroker, painter, and horticulturist) and Sofie (Hesselberg) Dahl; married Patricia Neal (an actress), July 2, 1953 (divorced, 1983); married Felicity Ann Crosland, 1983; children: (first marriage) Olivia (deceased), Tessa, Theo, Ophelia, Lucy. *Education:* Graduate of British public schools, 1932.

ADDRESSES: Agent—Watkins Loomis Agency, 150 East 35th St., New York, NY 10016.

CAREER: Shell Oil Co., London, England, member of eastern staff, 1933-37, member of staff in Dar-es-Salaam, Tanzania, 1937-39; writer. Host of a series of half-hour television dramas, *Way Out,* during early 1960s.

Military service: Royal Air Force, fighter pilot, 1939-45; became wing commander.

AWARDS, HONORS: Edgar Awards, Mystery Writers of America, 1954, 1959, and 1980; New England Round Table of Children's Librarians award, 1972, and Surrey School award, 1973, both for *Charlie and the Chocolate Factory;* Surrey School award, 1975, and Nene award, 1978, both for *Charlie and the Great Glass Elevator;* Surrey School award, 1978, and California Young Reader Medal, 1979, both for *Danny: The Champion of the World;* Federation of Children's Book Groups award, 1982, for *The BFG;* Massachusetts Children's award, 1982, for *James and the Giant Peach;* New York Times Outstanding Books award, 1983, Whitbread Award, 1983, and West Australian award, 1986, all for *The Witches;* World Fantasy Convention Lifetime Achievement Award, and Federation of Children's Book Groups award, both 1983; Kurt Maschler award runner-up, 1985, for *The Giraffe and the Pelly and Me; Boston Globe/Horn Book* nonfiction honor citation, 1985, for *Boy: Tales of Childhood;* International Board on Books for Young People awards for Norwegian and German translations of *The BFG,* both 1986; Smarties Award, 1990, for *Esio Trot.*

ROALD DAHL

WRITINGS:

FOR CHILDREN

The Gremlins, illustrations by Walt Disney Productions, Random House, 1943.

James and the Giant Peach: A Children's Story, illustrations by Nancy Ekholm Burkert, Knopf, 1961, published with illustrations by Michel Simeon, Allen & Unwin, 1967.

Charlie and the Chocolate Factory, illustrations by Joseph Schindelman, Knopf, 1964, revised edition, 1973, published with illustrations by Faith Jaques, Allen & Unwin, 1967.

The Magic Finger, illustrations by William Pene du Bois, Harper, 1966, illustrations by Pat Marriott, Puffin Books, 1974.

Fantastic Mr. Fox, illustrations by Donald Chaffin, Knopf, 1970.

Charlie and the Great Glass Elevator: The Further Adventures of Charlie Bucket and Willy Wonka, Chocolate-Maker Extraordinary, illustrations by Schindelman, Knopf, 1972, published with illustrations by Jaques, Allen & Unwin, 1973.

Danny: The Champion of the World, illustrations by Jill Bennett, Knopf, 1975.

The Enormous Crocodile, illustrations by Quentin Blake, Knopf, 1978.

The Complete Adventures of Charlie and Mr. Willy Wonka (contains *Charlie and the Chocolate Factory* and *Charlie and the Great Glass Elevator*), illustrations by Jaques, Allen & Unwin, 1978.

The Twits, illustrations by Blake, J. Cape, 1980, Knopf, 1981.

George's Marvelous Medicine, illustrations by Blake, J. Cape, 1981, Knopf, 1982.

Roald Dahl's Revolting Rhymes, illustrations by Blake, J. Cape, 1982, Knopf, 1983.

The BFG, illustrations by Blake, Farrar, Straus, 1982.

Dirty Beasts (verse), illustrations by Rosemary Fawcett, Farrar, Straus, 1983.

The Witches, illustrations by Blake, Farrar, Straus, 1983.

Boy: Tales of Childhood (autobiography), Farrar, Straus, 1984.

The Giraffe and Pelly and Me, illustrations by Blake, Farrar, Straus, 1985.

Matilda, illustrations by Blake, Viking Kestrel, 1988.

Roald Dahl: Charlie and the Chocolate Factory, Charlie and the Great Glass Elevator, The BFG (boxed set), Viking, 1989.

Rhyme Stew (comic verse), illustrations by Blake, J. Cape, 1989, Viking, 1990.

Esio Trot, illustrations by Blake, Viking, 1990.

The Dahl Diary, 1992, illustrations by Blake, Puffin Books, 1991.

The Vicar of Nibbleswicke, illustrations by Blake, Viking, 1992.

SHORT FICTION

Over to You: Ten Stories of Flyers and Flying, Reynal, 1946.

Someone Like You, Knopf, 1953.

Kiss, Kiss, Knopf, 1959.

Charlie, his parents and grandparents, and Mr. Wonka travel the universe in Wonka's fantastic contraption in Dahl's sequel to *Charlie and the Chocolate Factory.* (Cover illustration by Joseph Schindelman.)

Selected Stories of Roald Dahl, Modern Library, 1968.

Twenty-nine Kisses from Roald Dahl (contains *Someone Like You* and *Kiss, Kiss*), M. Joseph, 1969.

Switch Bitch, Knopf, 1974.

The Wonderful World of Henry Sugar and Six More, Knopf, 1977 (published in England as *The Wonderful Story of Henry Sugar and Six More,* Cape, 1977).

The Best of Roald Dahl (selections from *Over to You, Someone Like You, Kiss Kiss,* and *Switch Bitch*), introduction by James Cameron, Vintage, 1978.

Roald Dahl's Tales of the Unexpected, Vintage, 1979.

Taste and Other Tales, Longman, 1979.

A Roald Dahl Selection: Nine Short Stories, edited and introduced by Roy Blatchford, photographs by Catherine Shakespeare Lane, Longman, 1980.

More Tales of the Unexpected, Penguin, 1980 (published in England as *More Roald Dahl's Tales of the Unexpected,* Joseph, 1980, and as *Further Tales of the Unexpected,* Chivers, 1981).

(Editor) *Roald Dahl's Book of Ghost Stories,* Farrar, Straus, 1983.

Two Fables (contains "Princess and the Poacher" and "Princess Mammalia"), illustrations by Graham Dean, Viking, 1986.

The Roald Dahl Omnibus, Hippocrene Books, 1987.
A Second Roald Dahl Selection: Eight Short Stories, edited by Helene Fawcett, Longman, 1987.
Ah, Sweet Mystery of Life, illustrations by John Lawrence, J. Cape, 1988, Knopf, 1989.

Contributor of short fiction to *Penguin Modern Stories 12,* 1972.

SCREENPLAYS

"Lamb to the Slaughter" (teleplay), *Alfred Hitchcock Presents,* Columbia Broadcasting System (CBS-TV), 1958.
(With Jack Bloom) *You Only Live Twice,* United Artists, 1967.
(With Ken Hughes) *Chitty Chitty Bang Bang,* United Artists, 1968.
The Night-Digger (based on *Nest in a Falling Tree,* by Joy Crowley), Metro-Goldwyn-Mayer, 1970.
Willie Wonka and the Chocolate Factory (motion picture; adaptation of *Charlie and the Chocolate Factory*), Paramount, 1971.

Also author of screenplays *Oh Death, Where Is Thy Sting-a-Ling-a-Ling?,* United Artists, *The Lightning Bug,* 1971, and *The Road Builder.*

OTHER

Sometime Never: A Fable for Supermen (adult novel), Scribner, 1948.
The Honeys (play), produced in New York City, 1955.
My Uncle Oswald (adult novel), M. Joseph, 1979, Knopf, 1980.
Going Solo (autobiography), Farrar, Straus, 1986.

Contributor to anthologies and to periodicals, including *Harper's, New Yorker, Playboy, Collier's, Town and Country, Atlantic, Esquire,* and *Saturday Evening Post.*

ADAPTATIONS: Dahl's short story "Beware of the Dog" was made into the film *36 Hours* by Metro-Goldwyn-Mayer, 1964; an excerpt from the film *Willie Wonka and the Chocolate Factory* was distributed as the film *Delicious Inventions* and the filmstrips *Willie Wonka and the Chocolate Factory—Storytime* and *Willie Wonka and the Chocolate Factory—Learning Kit,* all by Films, Inc., 1976; *The Witches* was filmed by Lorimar in 1990. *Tales of the Unexpected* was broadcast by WNEW-TV, 1979. Richard George wrote the play adaptations *Roald Dahl's Charlie and the Chocolate Factory: A Play,* Knopf, 1976, and *Roald Dahl's James and the Giant Peach: A Play,* Penguin, 1982. Dahl has recorded *Charlie and the Chocolate Factory,* Caedmon, 1975, *James and the Giant Peach,* Caedmon, 1977, *Fantastic Mr. Fox,* Caedmon, 1978, and *Roald Dahl Reads His "The Enormous Crocodile" and "The Magic Finger,"* Caedmon, 1980, as well as an interview, *Bedtime Stories to Children's Books,* Center for Cassette Studies, 1973; *The Great Switcheroo,* read by Patricia Neal, was recorded by Caedmon, 1977.

SIDELIGHTS: Roald Dahl, best known as the author of children's books such as *Charlie and the Chocolate*

Factory and *James and the Giant Peach,* was also noted for his short stories for adults, and his enchanting autobiographical descriptions of growing up in England and flying in World War II. His children's fiction is known for its sudden turns into the fantastic, its wheeling, fast-moving prose, and its decidedly harsh treatment of any adults foolish enough to cause trouble for the young heroes and heroines. Similarly, his adult fiction often relies on a sudden twist that throws light on what has been happening in the story, a trait most evident in *Tales of the Unexpected,* which was made into a television series.

Dahl was born on September 13, 1916, the son of an adventurous shipbroker. He was an energetic and mischievous child and from an early age proved adept at finding trouble. His very earliest memory was of pedalling to school at breakneck speed on his tricycle, his two sisters struggling to keep up as he whizzed around curves on two wheels. In *Boy: Tales of Childhood,* Dahl recounted many of these happy memories from his childhood, remembering most fondly the trips that the entire family took to Norway, which he always consid-

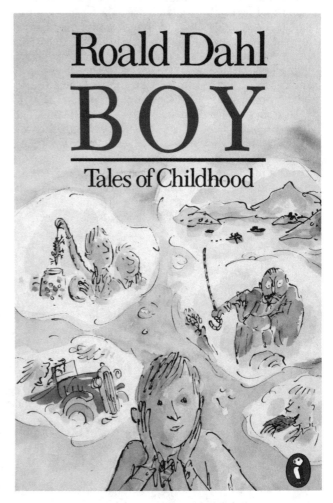

Dahl's tales of mischievous children who encounter nasty adults had a basis in his own childhood; he relates interesting episodes from his youth in this autobiography for children. (Cover illustration by Quentin Blake.)

ered home. Each summer the family would tramp aboard a steamer for the two-day trip to Oslo, where they were treated to a Norwegian feast with his grandparents, and the next day board a smaller ship for a trip north to what they called "Magic Island." On the island the family whiled away the long summer days swimming and boating.

Though Dahl's father died when the author was four, his mother abided by her husband's wish to have the children attend English schools, which he considered the best in the world. At Llandaff Cathedral School the young Dahl began his career of mischievous adventures and met up with the first of many oppressive, even cruel, adults. One exploit in particular foretold both the author's career in school and the major themes of his adult work. Each day on the way to and from school the seven-year-old Dahl and his friends passed a sweetshop. Unable to resist the lure of "Bootlace Liquorice" and "Gobstoppers"—familiar candy to *Charlie and the Chocolate Factory* fans—the children would pile into the store and buy as much candy as they could with their limited allowances. Day after day the grubby, grouchy storekeeper, Mrs. Pratchett, scolded the children as she dug her dirty hands into the jars of candy; one day the kids had had enough of her abuse, and Dahl hatched the perfect plan to get back at her. The very next day, when she reached into the jar of Gobstoppers she clamped her hand around a very stiff, dead mouse and flung the jar to the ground, scattering Gobstoppers and glass all over the store floor. Mrs. Pratchett knew who to blame, and when the boys went to school the next day she was waiting, along with a very angry Headmaster Coombes. Not only did Coombes give each of the boys a severe beating, but Mrs. Pratchett was there to witness it. "She was bounding up and down with excitement," Dahl remembered in *Boy,* "'Lay it into 'im!' she was shrieking. 'Let 'im 'ave it! Teach 'im a lesson!'"

Dahl's mother complained about the beating the boys were given, but was told if she didn't like it she could find another school. She did, sending Roald to St. Peters Boarding School the next year, and later to Repton, a renowned private school. Of his time at St. Peters, Dahl said in *The Wonderful World of Henry Sugar and Six More:* "Those were days of horrors, of fierce discipline, of not talking in the dormitories, no running in the corridors, no untidiness of any sort, no this or that or the other, just rules, rules and still more rules that had to be obeyed. And the fear of the dreaded cane hung over us like the fear of death all the time."

Dahl received undistinguished marks while attending Repton, and showed little sign of his future prowess as a writer. His end-of-term report from Easter term, 1931, which he saved, declared him "a persistent muddler. Vocabulary negligible, sentences mal-constructed. He reminds me of a camel." Nevertheless, his mother offered him the option of attending Oxford or Cambridge when he finished school. His reply, recorded in *Boy,* was, "No, thank you. I want to go straight from school to work for a company that will send me to wonderful faraway places life Africa or China." He got his wish, for he was soon hired by the Shell Oil Company, and later shipped off to Tanganyika (now Tanzania), where he enjoyed "the roasting heat and the crocodiles and the snakes and the log safaris up-country, selling Shell oil to the men who ran the diamond mines and the sisal plantations.... Above all, I learned how to look after myself in a way that no young person can ever do by staying in civilization."

In 1939, Dahl's adventures took on a more dangerous cast as he joined the Royal Air Force training squadron in Nairobi, Kenya. World War II was just beginning, and Dahl would soon make his mark as a fighter pilot combatting the Germans all around the Mediterranean

Charlie and other lucky children tour a marvelous—and dangerous—candy plant in *Willy Wonka and the Chocolate Factory,* for which Dahl wrote the screenplay.

Sea. While strafing a convoy of trucks near Alexandria, Egypt, his plane was hit by machine-gun fire. The plane crashed to the ground and Dahl crawled from the wreckage as the gas tanks exploded. The crash left his skull fractured, his nose crumpled, and his eyes temporarily stuck shut. After six months of recovery he returned to his squadron in Greece and shot down four enemy planes, but frequent blackouts as a result of his earlier injuries eventually rendered him unable to fly.

Dahl was soon transferred to Washington, D.C., to serve as an assistant air attache. One day C. S. Forester interviewed Dahl over lunch for an article he was writing for the *Saturday Evening Post,* but was too engrossed in eating to take notes himself. The notes that Dahl took for him turned out to be a story, which Forester sent to the magazine under Dahl's name. The magazine paid Dahl one thousand dollars for the story, which was titled "Piece of Cake" and later published in *Over to You: Ten Stories of Fliers and Flying.* Soon his stories appeared in *Collier's, Harper's, Ladies' Home Journal, Tomorrow,* and *Town and Country.* Dahl indicated in a *New York Times Book Review* profile by Willa Petschek that "as I went on, the stories became less and less realistic and more fantastic. But becoming a writer was pure fluke. Without being asked to, I doubt if I'd ever have thought of it."

In 1943, Dahl wrote his first children's story, and coined a term, with *The Gremlins.* Gremlins were tiny saboteurs who lived on fighter planes and bombers and were responsible for all crashes. Mrs. Roosevelt, the president's wife, read the book to her children and liked it so much that she invited Dahl to dinner, and he and the president soon became friends. Through the 1940s and into the 1950s Dahl continued as a short story writer for adults, establishing his reputation as a writer of macabre tales with an unexpected twist. J. D. O'Hara, writing in *New Republic,* labelled him "our Supreme Master of Wickedness," and his stories earned him three Edgar Allan Poe Awards from the Mystery Writers of America.

In 1953 he married Hollywood actress Patricia Neal, star of such movies as *The Fountainhead* and, later, *Hud,* for which she won an Academy Award. Dahl recalled in Barry Farrell's biography *Pat and Roald* that "she wasn't at all movie-starish; no great closets filled with clothes or anything like that. She had a drive to be a great actress, but it was never as strong as it is with some of these nuts. You could turn it aside." Although the marriage did not survive, it produced five children. As soon as the children were old enough, he began making up stories for them each night before they went to bed. These stories became the basis for his career as a children's writer, which began in earnest with the publication of *James and the Giant Peach* in 1961. Dahl insisted that having to invent stories night after night was perfect practice for his trade, telling the *New York Times Book Review:* "Children are a great discipline because they are highly critical. And they lose interest so quickly. You have to keep things ticking along. And if you think a child is getting bored, you must think up something that jolts it back. Something that tickles. You

Threatened by giants whose favorite breakfast is fried children, young Sophie enlists the help of the BFG to stop them. (Cover illustration by Blake.)

have to know what children like." Sales of Dahl's books certainly attest to his skill: *Charlie and the Chocolate Factory* and *Charlie and the Great Glass Elevator* have sold over one million hardcover copies in America, and *James and the Giant Peach* more than 350,000.

James and the Giant Peach recounts the fantastic tale of a young boy who travels thousands of miles in a house-sized peach with as bizarre an assemblage of companions as can be found in a children's book. After the giant peach crushes his aunts, James crawls into the peach through a worm hole, making friends with a centipede, a silkworm, a spider, a ladybug, and a flock of seagulls that lifts the peach into the air and carries it across the ocean to Central Park. Gerald Haigh, writing in *Times Educational Supplement,* said that Dahl had the ability to "home unerringly in on the very nub of childish delight, with brazen and glorious disregard for what is likely to furrow the adult brow."

One way that Dahl delighted his readers was to exact often vicious revenge on cruel adults who harmed children. In *Matilda,* the Amazonian headmistress Miss Turnbull, who deals with unruly children by grabbing them by the hair and tossing them out windows, is

The Grand High Witch begins her nefarious plot to turn all of England's children into mice in the movie version of Dahl's
The Witches.

finally banished by the brilliant, triumphant Matilda. *The Witches,* released as a movie in 1990, finds the heroic young character, who has been turned into a mouse, thwarting the hideous and diabolical witches who are planning to kill all the children of England. But even innocent adults receive rough treatment: parents are killed in car crashes in *The Witches,* and eaten by a rhinoceros in *James and the Giant Peach;* aunts are flattened by a giant peach in *James and the Giant Peach;* and pleasant fathers are murdered in *Matilda.* Many critics have objected to Dahl's rough treatment of adults. Eleanor Cameron, for example, in *Children's Literature in Education,* found that "Dahl caters to the streak of sadism in children which they don't even realize is there because they are not fully self-aware and are not experienced enough to understand what sadism is." And in *Now Upon a Time: A Contemporary View of Children's Literature,* Myra Pollack Sadker and David Miller Sadker criticized *Charlie and the Chocolate Factory* for its "ageism": "The message with which we close the book is that the needs and desires and opinions of old people are totally irrelevant and inconsequential."

However, Dahl explained in the *New York Times Book Review* that the children who wrote to him "invariably pick out the most gruesome events as the favorite parts

of the books . . . . They don't relate it to life. They enjoy the fantasy. And my nastiness is never gratuitous. It's retribution. Beastly people must be punished." Alasdair Campbell, writing in *School Librarian,* similarly argued that "normal children are bound to take some interest in the darker side of human nature, and books for them should be judged not by picking out separate elements but rather on the basis of their overall balance and effect." He found books such as *James and the Giant Peach, Charlie and the Chocolate Factory,* and *The Magic Finger* "ultimately satisfying, with the principles of justice clearly vindicated."

In Mark I. West's *Trust Your Children: Voices Against Censorship in Children's Literature,* Dahl contended that adults may be disturbed by his books "because they are not quite as aware as I am that children are different from adults. Children are much more vulgar than grownups. They have a coarser sense of humor. They are basically more cruel." Dahl often commented that the key to his success with children was that he conspired with them against adults. Vicki Weissman, in her review of *Matilda* in the *New York Times Book Review,* agreed that Dahl's books are aimed to please children rather than adults in a number of ways. She thought that "the truths of death and torture are as distant as when the magician saws the lady in half," and delighted that "anarchic and patently impossible plots romp along with no regard at all for the even faintly likely." Just as children are more vulgar than adults, so too do they have more tolerance for undeveloped characters, loose linking of events, ludicrous word play, and mind-boggling plot twists. Eric Hadley, in his sketch of Dahl in *Twentieth Century Children's Writers,* suggested that the "sense of sharing, of joining with Dahl in a game or plot, is crucial: you admire him and his cleverness, *not* his characters." The result, according to Hadley, is that the audience has the "pleasure of feeling that they are in on a tremendous joke."

"The writer for children must be a jokey sort of a fellow...," Dahl once told *Writer.* "He must like simple tricks and jokes and riddles and other childish things. He must be unconventional and inventive. He must have a really first-class plot." As a writer, Dahl encountered difficulty in developing plots. He filled an old school exercise book with ideas that he had jotted down in pencil, crayon, or whatever was handy, and insisted in *The Wonderful Story of Henry Sugar and Six More* that every story he had ever written, for adults or for children, "started out as a three- or four-line note in this little, much-worn, red-covered volume." And each children's book was written in a tiny brick hut in an orchard outside his home in Buckinghamshire, England. The little hut was rarely cleaned, and the walls were lined with "ill-fitting sheets of polystyrene, yellow with

A young girl puts the "magic finger" on the Gregg family—who then shrink, grow bird wings in place of their arms, and must live in a tree while trying to get their own shapes back. (Cover illustration by William Pene du Bois.)

age and tobacco smoke, and spiders ... [making] pretty webs in the upper corners," Dahl once recalled for *SATA.* "The room itself is of no consequence. It is out of focus, a place for dreaming and floating and whistling in the wind, as soft and silent and murky as a womb."

Looking back on his years as a writer in *Boy,* Dahl contended that "the life of a writer is absolute hell compared with the life of a businessman. The writer has to force himself to go to work.... Two hours of writing fiction leaves this particular writer absolutely drained. For those two hours he has been miles away, he has been somewhere else, in a different place with totally different people, and the effort of swimming back into normal surroundings is very great. It is almost a shock. The writer walks out of his workroom in a daze. He wants a drink. He needs it. It happens to be a fact that nearly every writer of fiction in the world drinks more whisky than is good for him. He does it to give himself faith, hope, and courage. A person is a fool to become a writer. His only compensation is absolute freedom. He has no master except his own soul, and that, I am sure, is why he does it."

WORKS CITED:

Cameron, Eleanor, "A Question of Taste," *Children's Literature in Education,* summer, 1976, pp. 59-63.
Campbell, Alisdair, "Children's Writers: Roald Dahl," *School Librarian,* June, 1981, pp. 108-114.
Dahl, Roald, *The Wonderful Story of Henry Sugar and Six More,* Knopf, 1977.
Dahl, Roald, *Boy: Tales of Childhood,* Farrar, Straus, 1984.
Farrell, Barry, *Pat and Roald,* Random House, 1969.
Hadley, Eric, "Roald Dahl," *Twentieth-Century Children's Writers,* 3rd edition, St. James Press, 1989, pp. 255-256.
Haigh, Gerald, "For Non Squiffletrotters Only," *Times Educational Supplement,* November 19, 1982, p. 35.
O'Hara, J. D., *New Republic,* October 19, 1974, p. 23.
Petschek, Willa, "Roald Dahl at Home," *New York Times Book Review,* December 25, 1977, p. 6, 15.
Sadker, Myra Pollack, and David Miller Sadker, *Now Upon a Time: A Contemporary View of Children's Literature,* Harper, 1977.
Weissman, Vicki, review of *Matilda, New York Times Book Review,* January 15, 1989, p. 31.
West, Mark I., interview with Dahl in *Trust Your Children: Voices against Censorship in Children's Literature,* Neal-Schuman, 1988, pp. 71-76.
Writer, August, 1976, pp. 18-19.

FOR MORE INFORMATION SEE:

BOOKS

Children's Literature Review, Gale, Volume 1, 1976, Volume 7, 1984.
Contemporary Literary Criticism, Gale, Volume 1, 1973, Volume 6, 1976, Volume 18, 1981.
Dahl, Roald, *Going Solo,* Farrar, Straus, 1986.

McCann, Donnarae, and Gloria Woodard, editors, *The Black American in Books for Children: Readings in Racism,* Scarecrow, 1972.

Powling, Chris, *Roald Dahl,* Hamish Hamilton, 1983.

Wintle, Justin, and Emma Fisher, *The Pied Pipers: Interviews with the Influential Creators of Children's Literature,* Paddington Press, 1975.

PERIODICALS

Atlantic, December, 1964.

Chicago Sunday Tribune, February 15, 1960; November 12, 1961.

Chicago Tribune, October 21, 1986.

Chicago Tribune Book World, August 10, 1980; May 17, 1981.

Children's Literature in Education, spring, 1975; summer, 1988; fall, 1988.

Christian Science Monitor, November 16, 1961.

Commonweal, November 15, 1961.

Horn Book, October, 1972; December, 1972; February, 1973; April, 1973; June, 1973.

Kenyon Review, Volume 31, number 2, 1969.

Life, August 18, 1972.

New Republic, April 19, 1980.

New Statesman, October 29, 1960; March 5, 1971; November 4, 1977.

New York, December 12, 1988.

New York Herald Tribune Book Review, November 8, 1953; February 7, 1960.

New York Review of Books, December 17, 1970; December 14, 1972.

New York Times, November 8, 1953; April 29, 1980;

New York Times Book Review, February 7, 1960; November 12, 1961; October 25, 1964; November 8, 1970; September 17, 1972; October 27, 1974; October 26, 1975; September 30, 1979; April 20, 1980; March 29, 1981; January 9, 1983; January 20, 1985; October 12, 1986.

People, November 3, 1986; May 9, 1988.

Punch, November 29, 1967; December 6, 1978.

Saturday Review, December 26, 1953; February 20, 1960; February 17, 1962; November 7, 1964; March 10, 1973.

Sewanee Review, winter, 1975.

Spectator, December, 1977.

Times (London), December 22, 1983; April 21, 1990.

Times Literary Supplement, October 28, 1960; December 14, 1967; June 15, 1973; November 15, 1974; November 23, 1979; November 21, 1980; July 24, 1981; July 23, 1982; November 30, 1984; September 12, 1986; May 6, 1988.

Washington Post, October 8, 1986.

Washington Post Book World, November 13, 1977; April 20, 1980; May 8, 1983; January 13, 1985.*

*   *   *

DAVIS, Nelle 1958-

PERSONAL: Born August 12, 1958, in Hartford, CT; daughter of Kelso Davis and Helen (Hewes) Fletcher; married Benjamin O. Rosenthal (a photographer), July 11, 1984. *Education:* Attended Franklin College, Lugano, Switzerland, 1976-77; Pratt Institute, B.F.A., 1981.

ADDRESSES: Home and office—New York, NY.

CAREER: Illustrator.

ILLUSTRATOR:

Lee Bennett Hopkins, editor, *Munching: Poems about Eating,* Little, Brown, 1985.

Alvin and Virginia Silverstein, *The Mystery of Sleep,* Little, Brown, 1987.

Betty Miles, *Save the Earth: An Action Handbook for Kids,* revised edition, Knopf, 1991.

SIDELIGHTS: Illustrator Nelle Davis was born August 12, 1958, in Hartford, Connecticut. She attended Franklin College in Lugano, Switzerland, and went on to complete her bachelor's degree in fine arts at New York City's prestigious Pratt Institute in 1981. Since embarking on a career as an illustrator, Davis has three published children's books to her credit, and has received praise from reviewers for her vibrant cartoon-like illustrations. *Horn Book* reviewer Ethel R. Twichell describes Davis's humorous approach to *Munching: Poems about Eating:* the fried eggs that "stare unwinking from their yolky faces" and the children "prepared to plunge into a huge bowl of bananas and cream." Davis's gray-wash line drawings for *The Mystery of Sleep* have also been well-received by critics for the gentle humor they bring to Alvin and Virginia Silverstein's popular text.

WORKS CITED:

Twichell, Ethel R., review of *Munching: Poems about Eating, Horn Book,* March/April, 1986, p. 214.

FOR MORE INFORMATION SEE:

PERIODICALS

Booklist, January 15, 1986, p. 759; December 15, 1987, p. 713.

Horn Book, March/April, 1988, p. 225.

*   *   *

DOUGLAS, Carole Nelson 1944-

PERSONAL: Born November 5, 1944, in Everett, WA; daughter of Arnold Peter (a fisherman) and Agnes Olga (a teacher; maiden name, Lovchik) Nelson; married Sam Douglas (an artist), November 25, 1967. *Education:* College of St. Catherine, B.A., 1966.

ADDRESSES: Home—3920 Singleleaf Lane, Fort Worth, TX 76133. *Agent*—Howard Morhaim, 175 Fifth Avenue, 14th floor, New York, NY, 10010.

CAREER: St. Paul Pioneer Press & Dispatch (now *St. Paul Pioneer Press*), St. Paul, MN, various writing and editorial positions, 1967-84; full-time novelist, 1984—. First woman show chair of annual Gridiron, 1971; member of board of directors, Twin Cities local of The Newspaper Guild, 1970-72.

CAROLE NELSON DOUGLAS

MEMBER: Mystery Writers of America, Science Fiction and Fantasy Writers of America, Romance Writers of America, Sisters in Crime.

AWARDS, HONORS: Honorary member of board of directors of St. Paul Public Library Centennial, 1981; Silver Medal, Sixth Annual West Coast Review of Books, 1982, for *Fair Wind, Fiery Star;* Science Fiction/Fantasy Award, 1984, Popular Fiction Award, Science Fiction, 1987, and Lifetime Achievement Award for Versatility, 1991, all from *Romantic Times;* Nebula Award nomination, Science Fiction Writers of America, 1986, for *Probe;* Best Novel of Romantic Suspense citation, American Mystery Awards, 1990, and *New York Times Book Review* notable book citation, 1991, for *Good Night, Mr. Holmes.*

WRITINGS:

Amberleigh, Jove, 1980.
Fair Wind, Fiery Star, Jove, 1981.
The Best Man, Ballantine, 1983.
Lady Rogue, Ballantine, 1983.
Azure Days and Quicksilver Nights, Bantam, 1985.
Probe, Tor Books, 1985.
The Exclusive, Ballantine, 1986.
Counterprobe, Tor Books, 1988.
Crystal Days and Crystal Nights, two volumes, Bantam, 1990.

Cup of Clay, Tor Books, 1991.
Catnap, Tor Books, 1992.
Seed Upon the Wind, Tor Books, 1992.

"SWORD AND CIRCLET" FANTASY NOVELS

Six of Swords, Del Rey, 1982.
Exiles of the Rynth, Del Rey, 1984.
Keepers of Edanvant, Tor Books, 1987.
Heir of Rengarth, Tor Books, 1988.
Seven of Swords, Tor Books, 1989.

"IRENE ADLER" SERIES

Good Night, Mr. Holmes, Tor Books, 1990.
Good Morning, Irene, Tor Books, 1991.
Irene at Large, Tor Books, 1992.

Also author of *In Her Prime* and *Her Own Person,* both 1982. Editorial writer for the *Fort Worth Star-Telegram,* 1985—; columnist for *Mystery Scene* magazine, 1991.

WORK IN PROGRESS: Two novels in the *Taliswoman* trilogy; novels about Irene Adler; novels in the "Midnight Louie" series. Research on "late 19th-century art, fashion, household objects, clothing, manners, food, transportation and language usage, in London, Paris, and such exotic places as Afghanistan and Tibet," and research on Las Vegas.

SIDELIGHTS: Carole Nelson Douglas told *SATA:* "An only child who often had to amuse myself, I used to think that everybody made up poems and descriptive sentences when lying on the grass and looking up at the clouds, or when riding on a bus. Now I know that I was a writer for as long as I can remember, and that writing isn't much different from thinking or daydreaming, except that you make the effort to record it.

"My own writing applies the techniques of poetry to prose. Poetry influenced my younger school years, especially Edgar Allan Poe, a master of rhythm and word choice. My fantasy novels particularly reflect my interest in playing with language as I invent lands, people, animals and every kind of phenomena, and have a historical feel as well.

"[The] Sword and Circlet fantasies document the [protagonists'] magical adventures, a means of exploring relationships and the search for self. I describe the series as a 'domestic epic,' because it examines how men and women can form lasting alliances without losing their individuality and independence. By the fifth book, Irissa and Kendric's children are teenagers confronting the same relationship quandaries as their parents. One child is magically gifted; the other not. Each has a special bond with the opposite parent. Fantasy novels offer a writer a subtle means of dealing with contemporary issues like gender role reversal, animal rights and ecology without getting on a soapbox.

"Although I wrote my fantasy novels as an adult, for adults, library magazines reviewed them as 'YA,' young adult. This pleasant surprise was also accurate: I get many charming fan letters from young readers, who absorb my fantasy worlds and themes more readily than many adult reviewers and readers.... Magic in fantasy is a metaphor for personal power and self-realization, a word that many young readers may not be able to define, but they grasp the concepts instinctively when they read it.

"I was surprised again recently when my novel about Irene Adler, the only woman to outwit Sherlock Holmes [in Arthur Conan Doyle's —"A Scandal in Bohemia"], *Good Night, Mr. Holmes,* was reviewed as both an adult and young readers' novel. Again, I hadn't aimed for a young audience; I've never written 'down' or simplified my vocabulary. This book evolved the way most of my ideas come to me: I realized that all the recent novels set in the Sherlock Holmes world were written by men. Yet I had loved the stories as a youngster. My years as a newspaper reporter taught me that when men monopolize anything it's time for women to examine it from a female point of view.... My Irene Adler is as intelligent, self-sufficient and serious about her professional and personal integrity as Sherlock Holmes, and far too independent to be anyone's mistress but her own. She also moonlights as an inquiry agent while building her performing career, so she is a professional rival of Holmes's rather than a romantic interest. Her adventures intertwine with Holmes's, but she is definitely her own woman in these novels.

"Another favorite character of mine is Midnight Louie, an 18-pound, crime-solving black tomcat who is the part-time narrator of a new mystery series that begins with *Catnap.* Like many of my creations, Louie goes way back. He was a real if somewhat larger-than-life stray cat I wrote a feature story about for my newspaper in 1973.

"I want my books to appeal to a wide variety of readers on different levels, and to contain enough levels that they bear re-reading. Although labeled as science fiction novels, *Probe* and *Counterprobe* are contemporary-set suspense/psychological adventure stories with a strong feminist subtext, the kind that husbands recommend to wives, and vice versa; teenagers to parents, and vice versa. To write books that cross common ground between the sexes and span the generation gap is rewarding, especially in this pigeon-holed publishing world."

In college, Douglas majored in theater and English literature. Upon graduating, she took "a lowly merchandising position with the local newspaper," then tried her hand at writing, eventually becoming a reporter. "I loved newspaper reporting and feature writing," the author stated, "but truly creative writers are not appreciated in a journalism-dominated atmosphere. My work was recognized everywhere but where I was employed. Women weren't made reviewers or given columns or often promoted to editor positions in newspapers then (and now).

"When a particularly good story of mine was radically cut, I took a YWCA writing class (everybody thought a

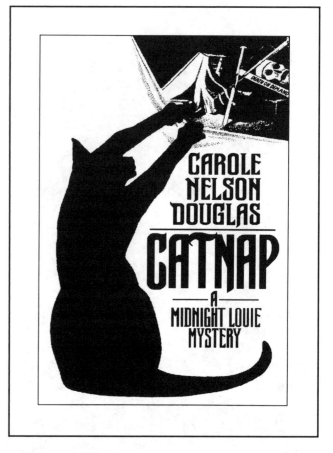

Douglas's fantasy and mystery novels appeal to young adults for their independent, intelligent protagonists—including "Midnight Louie," an eighteen-pound, crime-solving tomcat. (Cover illustration by the author.)

published journalist was crazy to take a writing course) to learn the mechanics of submitting national-level nonfiction." But when called upon to read to the class from her own work, "I dug out a novel I had begun in college and read from it," the author remembered, adding that "the enthusiastic instructor, the well-known children's author Judy Delton, shooed me out of class with the irresistible injunction to 'write that book and sell it.'"

Commenting on similarities between fiction-writing and journalism, Douglas further stated that "a professional novelist needs many of the skills learned in writing for a newspaper: you must write day in and day out, often under time constraints, and still meet your own standards of quality. You must be tenacious and you must believe in what you are doing, that the 'story' needs to be told, and that you are the only one to tell it.

"If I had known how many setbacks awaited the career novelist I might not have tried doing it. But ignorance is sometimes motivation. I've had twenty-four novels published since 1980 in a number of genres. My books are classified as fantasy or science fiction, romance, mystery, women's mainstream fiction and historical novels. But many of these elements blend in each book, and none of my novels fits any category formula. Being different is satisfying, though it is frustrating when your work needs to be put into a category for marketing reasons.

"Yet I've never gone wrong following my talents and my interests. I've survived because I took risks and followed my instincts. When I majored in theater everybody (including me) thought I'd never get a well-paying job. I found myself a well-paid newspaper reporter within a year of graduation. When I left that substantial job security, everybody feared that I'd be unable to replace that salary with book income. When I began to write novels in a variety of so-called genres under my own name, everybody said that wasn't smart marketing. There have been handicaps and setbacks, but I survived. That same Everybody discouraged my novel writing by saying I was too young, but I later discovered that there were a lot of other Everybodies out there more worth heeding: the readers one's work reaches. Their enthusiastic reactions to my writing and my books has kept me going for years. Now all those Everybodies are growing up or developing wider reading tastes, and they're finding my books in different sections of the bookstore."

* * *

DUMBLETON, Mike 1948-

PERSONAL: Born January 6, 1948, in Chipping Norton, England; son of Ernest George (an industrial planner) and Susie (Jean) Dumbleton; married Linda Jean Collard (a teacher), June 28, 1969; children: Jay, Luke, Nathan. *Education:* Nottingham University, B.Ed., 1970, teaching certificate, 1970. *Religion:* Christian. *Hobbies and other interests:* Sports.

ADDRESSES: Home—1 Foord Ave., Gawler E., South Australia 5118. *Agent*—Australian Literary Management, 2A Armstrong St., Middle Park, Victoria, Australia 3206.

CAREER: South Australian Education Department, Adelaide, English teacher, 1973-74, faculty coordinator, 1975-87, deputy principal, 1988, literacy projects coordinator, 1989—; writer.

MEMBER: South Australian Writers Centre.

AWARDS, HONORS: Dial-a-Croc was named to the American Booksellers Association/Children's Book Council "Children's Books Mean Business" list, 1992.

WRITINGS:

PICTURE BOOKS

Dial-a-Croc, illustrated by Ann James, Orchard Books, 1991.
Granny O'Brien and the Diamonds of Selmore, illustrated by David Cox, Omnibus Books, 1993.
Melissa the Kisser, illustrated by Alex Frank, Harcourt, 1993.
Mrs. Watson's Goat, illustrated by Marina McAllan, Macmillan, 1993.
Mr. Knuckles, Allen & Unwin, 1993.

EDUCATIONAL RESOURCE MATERIALS

Can Cards, Hawker Brownlow Education, 1989.
(With Jeff Guess) *Hands On Poetry—A Practical Anthology,* Twilight Publishers, 1991, Educational Supplies, 1993.
Real Writing across the Curriculum: A Practical Guide to Improving and Publishing Student Work, South Australian Education Department, 1993.

WORK IN PROGRESS: Miss Macdonald's Farm, a picture book, for Macmillan, 1994.

SIDELIGHTS: Mike Dumbleton told *SATA:* "I was born in England and qualified as a teacher before coming to Australia with my wife, Linda, in 1972. I now live in Gawler—a small country town north of Adelaide, South Australia—and teach at a local high school.

"As a youngster I enjoyed reading and consumed endless books which belonged to popular English series at the time. They included many Enid Blyton titles and all the Biggles books, along with the books from two contrasting schoolboy series, one called William and the other called Jennings. I vividly remember being a regular customer at a well-stocked secondhand bookshop in my hometown of Cheltenham, where you could buy and sell books at prices which seemed very reasonable compared with the cost of new books. At one time I

MIKE DUMBLETON

wanted to collect all the titles for one of my favorite series. I never managed to do this because I always had to trade in books which I had read, for new titles.

"I also clearly remember reading in bed after I was supposed to have gone to sleep. I was fortunate enough to have a street lamp outside my window, and it cast enough light for me to be able to read. When my parents came to check if I'd stopped reading and turn my bedroom light off, I put the book down on the bed and pretended to be asleep.

"I've always been interested in writing but never seemed to have the time. One of the reasons is that for a long time I've been involved in sport and thoroughly enjoyed every minute of it. The other reason is that when my wife and I started our family we soon discovered that bringing up children often takes twenty-five hours a day!

"Part of my interest in writing probably stems from the fact that my grandfather, George Dumbleton, is a local village poet in Oxfordshire, England. At the age of ninety-one he no longer writes, but having been blessed with an amazing memory, he can readily recite his poems on request.

"I started writing when I decided I wasn't getting any better at basketball, and my three children were old enough to allow me some uninterrupted time. I began devising educational texts for teachers at the same time that I started writing picture book manuscripts, and it was a proposal for an educational text which was first accepted and published in Australia. *Dial-a-Croc* was accepted soon afterwards.

"The initial idea for *Dial-a-Croc* came from a play on words whereby you can reverse the syllables in the word crocodile to make the name Dial-a-Croc. The early sequences in which Vanessa heads off into the Outback are based on a real Vanessa who is mentioned in the dedication, along with my sons. She is a friend of the family and was my eldest son's girlfriend at the time. She is a self-assured, purposeful young lady, and visited us wearing fashionable safari shorts when I was planning the book. It gave me just the image I needed for the Vanessa in the story with her 'jungle jeans' and 'hunting jacket,' to which I added her 'bull whip, camping knife' and other suitable accessories before letting her venture into the 'Outback, beyond the Back of Beyond.'

"My family take an interest in my writing and help with the development of manuscripts before I send them to a publisher. My wife is a teacher with qualifications in librarianship and a keen interest in children's literature, and my sons are all willing 'in house' editors and reviewers.

"They have all become very good at providing honest and detailed feedback without making me feel bad about it. Each one of them will read and comment on my manuscripts separately so that I get fresh opinions on the work and am able to compare their responses. If they all keep coming up with the same concerns, it is

obviously something which I need to respond to. If they come up with individual points, I can balance those against my own judgments. This could be a recipe for domestic tension or divorce, but I have become better at accepting their comments without taking it personally; they are good at commenting and pointing out things in a direct but constructive way. For instance, my wife will mention some positive things about a manuscript before she says, 'but there are a couple of things which I think need looking at.' I used to think that a couple meant two, but my wife can use it to cover anything between two and twenty-two things she wants to comment on!

"I think that being a writer has developed my understanding of the difficulties confronting my students. For me, one of the benefits of being a published writer and a teacher is that when I admit my need for redrafting, using a dictionary, and working in collaboration with partners, proof-readers, and editors, the gap between student writers and published writers is narrowed. The educational text which I am currently working on is concerned with this issue and describes practical ways in which there can be a closer correlation between the writing experiences of students and those of established authors.

"I work in a fairly disjointed way, in the gaps and spaces which I can find during the week. I keep my writing

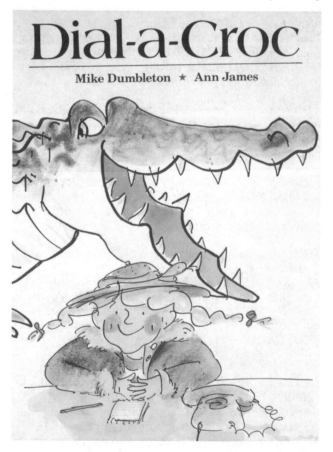

A play on words inspired this story of a young girl who traps a crocodile and starts a business with him. (Cover illustration by Ann James.)

folder close at hand just in case I find some time. With three sons who have always been involved in a range of different sports—including tennis, basketball, soccer, and surfing—I spend a lot of time driving them around, but can work in the car before and after games.

"Working within the confines of thirty-two pages can be very challenging, and although it can be frustrating at times, I enjoy the problem-solving aspect of making the text work within the page restrictions. Before I submit a manuscript to a publisher, I always set it out in the form of a book, with numbered pages, to get a better feel for the story and the illustration possibilities. It can take quite a long time to produce a picture book, and for a writer, patience can be a great virtue. It helps to be working on other projects.

"Being completely hopeless at drawing, I fully appreciate the work that is done by the illustrator, and I was delighted when my publisher arranged for Ann James to illustrate *Dial-a-Croc*. For me, one of the rewards of writing is meeting and working with the other people involved in the development and production of the book. I enjoy the contact with editors, illustrators, and designers from whom I continually learn a great deal."

E

EPLER, Doris M. 1928-

PERSONAL: Born February 5, 1928; daughter of Joseph V. (a metal worker) and Elsie (a homemaker; maiden name, Seiters) Weber; married M. Robert Epler, 1974 (died, 1980); children: Joseph M. Schaeffer, Cynthia M. Moyer. *Education:* Temple University, B.S., 1972, M.S., 1974, Ed.D. (curriculum development), 1981.

DORIS M. EPLER

ADDRESSES: Home—1254 Peggy Drive, Hummelstown, PA 17036. *Office*—Epler Enterprises, Box 13, Hummelstown, PA, 17036.

CAREER: Berks Vocational Technical School, Leesport, PA, teacher of data processing, then Adult Education administrator, 1968-82; Pennsylvania Department of Education, Harrisburg, Division Director, 1982-92. Owner, Epler Enterprises, Hummelstown, PA, 1992—. Serves on the board of Satellite Educational Resources Consortium; serves as state representative, CCSO Technology Group and liaison representative, Pennsylvania Association of Educational Communications Technology.

MEMBER: Authors League of America, American Association of School Librarians (chair, public awareness), Pennsylvania School Librarians Association, Pennsylvania Association for Educational Communications Technology.

AWARDS, HONORS: Epler has received numerous awards for outstanding contributions to school library media programs and service in the field of media communications from such organizations as Pennsylvania Library Resources Association, Pennsylvania School Librarians Association, and Pennsylvania Association for Educational Communications Technology.

WRITINGS:

(Contributor) E. Blanche Woolls and David V. Loertscher, editors, *The Microcomputer Facility and the School Library Media Specialist* (includes "Electronic Mail"), Advanced Library Systems, 1986.
Online Searching Goes to School, Oryx Press, 1992.
The Berlin Wall: How It Rose and Why It Fell, Millbrook Press, 1992.

Contributor of articles to periodicals, including *CD-ROM EndUser, Emergency Librarian, Learning and Media, Library High-tech, Library Trends, Online Inc., School Library Media Activities Monthly, School Library*

Media Annual 1992, and *School Library Media Quarterly.*

WORK IN PROGRESS: Several fictional works.

SIDELIGHTS: Doris Epler told *SATA:* "I started writing as a child. I would sneak up to the attic in my parents' house, settle down on a nice soft comforter, and, as the rain fell on the tin roof, write stories and poems. Most of my work at this time was terribly sad and even morbid. I was so afraid that others would not like my stories that I never shared my work with anyone.

"During the research process for *The Berlin Wall: How It Rose and Why It Fell,* I was astounded at how much about the Berlin Wall I had either forgotten or never knew. I kept wanting to have a hero on a white horse come racing through the resource books and rip the wall down. But the process took forty years! My hope is that the children of the world will never let another wall separate them from one another.

"While my published work to date is in the area of nonfiction, I am working on several pieces of fiction. I love to write and I am most happy when the characters and I challenge one another for control of the story. It's fascinating to watch a blank computer screen begin to fill up with words, ideas, and situations that are unique.

"The best reward of writing is seeing someone else reading your book, turning the pages, and not putting it down. The dozens of characters that are dancing in my head, coaxing me to let them out, will keep me motivated to continue my efforts to write."

*   *   *

EVANS, Greg 1947-

PERSONAL: Born November 13, 1947, in Los Angeles, CA; son of Herman (an electrical inspector) and Virginia (a homemaker; maiden name, Horner) Evans; married Betty Ransom (a teacher and city councilmember), December, 1970; children: Gary, Karen. *Education:* California State University at Northridge, B.A., 1970. *Hobbies and other interests:* Movies, plays, writing music, golf.

ADDRESSES: c/o King Features Syndicate, 235 East 45th St., New York, NY 10017.

CAREER: High school art teacher in California and Australia, 1970-74; radio and television station promotion manager in Colorado Springs, CO, 1975-80; author of comic strip "Luann," 1985—.

MEMBER: National Cartoonists Society.

WRITINGS:

SELF-ILLUSTRATED

Meet Luann, Berkeley, 1986.
Why Me?, Berkeley, 1986.

GREG EVANS

Is It Friday Yet?, Berkeley, 1987.
Who Invented Brothers Anyway?, Tor, 1989.
School and Other Problems, Tor, 1989.
Homework Is Ruining My Life, Tor, 1989.
So Many Malls, So Little Money, Tor, 1990.
Pizza Isn't Everything but It Comes Close, Tor, 1991.
Dear Diary: The Following Is Top Secret, Tor, 1991.
Will We Be Tested on This?, Tor, 1992.
There's Nothing Worse than First Period P.E., Tor, 1992.
If Confusion Were a Class I'd Get an A, Tor, 1992.
School's OK If You Can Stand the Food, Tor, 1992.

WORK IN PROGRESS: More "Luann" collections, including *I'm Not Always Confused, I Just Look That Way* and *My Bedroom and Other Environmental Hazards.*

SIDELIGHTS: Cartoonist Greg Evans describes himself as quite similar to the title character of his comic strip, "Luann." Of all the cartoon's characters, "I'm probably most like Luann, because she's not exceptional in any way; she's just an average kid and I was very average all through school," Evans commented to *SATA* interviewer Deborah A. Stanley. "I was sort of a wallflower—I wasn't the football captain or class president or anything like that. I just drifted through school, and that's kind of how Luann is." A typical teenager, Luann agonizes over her appearance, spends countless hours at the mall, does battle with her goony older brother, and, to her profound humiliation, becomes a drooling geek whenever heartthrob Aaron Hill appears. School is a source of endless frustration, from too much homework in history

Evans began his comic strip about an average kid enduring the trials of adolescence in 1985.

to too much makeup-melting sweat in gym. Luckily Luann has her friends Delta and Bernice, guidance counselor Ms. Phelps, and Puddles, her dog, to help her keep things in perspective.

Evans attributes his interest in drawing to "probably my chromosomes. I'm one of those people who was born with this cartoon disease. As far back as I can remember I would doodle and draw cartoons. I was a big fan of all the Disney characters. I grew up in Burbank near the Disney studios, and always wanted to work at Disney. I used to draw pictures of Mickey Mouse and Donald Duck; in school I'd doodle when I should have been listening to the teacher." It was in his early teens that Evans began considering a career as a cartoonist. "I started submitting cartoons to magazines," he recalled. "In fact, my first submission was to *Playboy* when I was eleven because they paid a lot of money. Of course my cartoon was rejected." Evans continued to submit his work to various publications, "all through my youth, through college and on, and I never sold anything. I started trying to create ideas for comic strips and again I didn't have any success with my first half dozen tries. Then finally I had the idea for 'Luann' in 1985 and that was the right one."

Evans believes "Luann" became a success for a number of reasons. "It was probably the right idea at the right time—it filled a niche," he noted. "[At the time] there weren't many strips with female characters or strips aimed at teenagers." Another key ingredient was his own maturity level. "I firmly believe that sometimes

you are trying before you're ready," Evans remarked. "You'll hear about somebody who's written seven books and none of them did anything, then all of a sudden their eighth book is a huge smash. I think you reach a certain level of personal development where you have the insight and you're working on something that taps the right creative flow."

The character of Luann began with Evans's observations of his daughter. "I was playing around with the idea of a strip about a saucy little five-year-old, because you know how little girls are at that age—they like to put on lipstick and Mom's big high-heeled shoes and clop around the house. As I was working around those lines, I began to realize that five was so young—you don't really have any life experiences—so I kept aging the character. Finally I said, 'Oh, I'll make her a teenager because I can remember being a teenager, and I'll have something to draw upon from my school teaching experiences.'"

Longtime "Luann" readers have probably noticed some changes in the look of the strip since its debut in 1985. "Part of that was intentional and part of it just happens over the years," Evans remarked. Some changes are the result of the artist's growing skill; others come from boredom or frustration with the material. "You'll suddenly say, 'I don't like the way I'm doing this. I'm going

As parent to a teenage son and daughter, Evans has had many chances to observe the special relationship siblings share. (From *School's OK If You Can Stand the Food.*)

His own past experiences as a high school teacher give Evans insight into recreating the school life of a teenager. (From *School's OK If You Can Stand the Food.*)

to figure out a better way,'" Evans explained. "You'll find a way to make an arm look better when it's folded or how to make a hand holding a pencil look a little better. The biggest change was a couple of years ago, when I decided to do an episode where she got her ears pierced because my daughter was wanting to get pierced earrings. Luann didn't have ears in the beginning—she had this round head and this hair and no ears. Having pierced earrings requires ears, so I redesigned Luann and gave her ears and she's had ears ever since. It makes her look different, a little cuter I think."

Along with her physical features, Luann's personality has changed as well. "In the beginning Luann was a little more cartoony and simpler, a caricature of a teenager," Evans recalled. "Now she is a much more authentic teenager. In the past few years I've been tackling more serious subject matter and more issues that teens have to deal with," giving Luann an opportunity to react like a real-life teen would. Of the realistic topics introduced in the strip, "the first one was drug abuse," Evans related. "That wasn't really difficult or controversial, because everyone agrees that drugs are a bad thing. Then I decided that with Luann being thirteen, she was right at the age when she was going to have her first period. I thought real long and hard about doing a story about it. I went ahead and tried it and finally got a story I thought worked pretty well and I got mixed reactions, mostly favorable but there were those who thought it was inappropriate for the comics page.

"Then I did a story where Brad goes out on a date and takes along a condom. That was another one that was a little controversial and you might think that wasn't appropriate for the comics page, but I didn't get any negative response on that one at all." Brad's date with the girl next door, Diane, hit a snag when the condom fell out of his pocket as he paid for their movie tickets.

An enraged Diane berated him for what she assumed were lecherous intentions, but Brad's honest and sensitive explanation saved the day, and the date: "Diane, you ... you don't know how much I care about you. I wouldn't even put my arm around you without asking. And I respect you way too much to even *think* of doing more than that .... To you, I guess it's a sign of what I *want,* but it's really a sign of what I *don't* want." Diane decides Brad's intentions weren't so bad after all. "It was almost out of character for Brad, but I had to present that point of view, and he was the one who had to say it," Evans noted.

In future stories, a new character will be introduced as a pal for Brad, and Luann may have a close encounter with Aaron Hill. Fans of the strip know that Luann has admired Aaron Hill from afar for years, but has never quite managed to speak to him. She has, however, shared many a word with the snooty, self-absorbed Tiffany; Evans reported that their feud, which has degenerated into hair-pulling matches in the past, will escalate again. "Tiffany's a good character," Evans remarked. "It's always the nasty ones that seem to generate a lot of interest. It's the evil, mean character that everybody loves to hate. She's fun to write for."

As a nationally syndicated cartoonist, Evans is a member of an elite group: the people whose names appear on the comics page, scrawled in a corner of their work, as well as cartoon artists from other mediums. Far from working in a vacuum, the artists are acquainted with each other and get together once a year to recognize the best among them with the Reuben Awards. "It's kind of like our version of the Academy Awards," Evans revealed. "The ballots go out to cartoonists around the world and we vote to nominate in various categories such as greeting card cartooning, animation, and comic strips. Then we all get together somewhere in the

Luann's crush on good-looking Aaron Hill provides her brother with multiple opportunities to tease her. (From *Will We Be Tested on This?*)

country and have a three-day bash and have the award ceremony. That's the place where most of the cartoonists see one another, which is nice because it's a very solitary profession. It's really good to get together with your peers and talk shop and just see everyone."

His fellow artists provide a nudge to Evans's creativity, but much of his inspiration comes from his children. With a seventeen-year-old son, Gary, and a thirteen-year-old daughter, Karen, Evans has ready-made storylines acted out each day in his home. Before his children became teenagers, Evans relied on his and his wife's

experiences as teachers, and spent a lot of time observing teens at the mall and at McDonald's. Evans noted that in 1993 his children will be the same ages as Luann and Brad. "I won't have to write anything," he mused. "I'll just watch my kids and take notes."

WORKS CITED:

Evans, Greg, interview with Deborah A. Stanley, December 9, 1992.

—Sketch by Deborah A. Stanley

F

FEDER, Harriet K. 1928-

PERSONAL: Surname is pronounced "*fay*-der"; born April 18, 1928, in New York, NY; daughter of Benjamin (a cabdriver) and Anna (a homemaker; maiden name, Binder) Klein; married Herbert Feder (an engineer), August 21, 1955; children: Deborah Feder-Fogelson, David, Joshua. *Education:* Attended City College of New York (now City College of the City University of New York), 1946-49, and New York University, 1949-50; Clarion State College, B.S.Ed., 1967; State University of New York at Buffalo, M.S.S., 1973. *Politics:* "Mixed." *Religion:* Jewish.

ADDRESSES: Home—132 Wickham Dr., Williamsville, NY 14221.

CAREER: Williamsville Central Schools, Williamsville, NY, teacher of social studies, 1969-86; Canisius College, Buffalo, NY, teacher of composition, 1987-88; Institute of Children's Literature, W. Redding, CT, consultant, 1990—; writer. Hadassa, The Women's Zionist Organization of America, vice president of education.

MEMBER: Society of Children's Book Writers, Mystery Writers of America, Penn Writers, National League of American Pen Women.

WRITINGS:

It Happened in Shushan, Kar-Ben, 1988.
Not Yet, Elijah, Kar-Ben, 1989.
Judah Who Always Said, "No!", Kar-Ben, 1990.
What Can You Do with a Bagel, Kar-Ben, 1991.
Mystery in Miami Beach, Lerner, 1992.

Contributor to *Children's Writer.* Also contributing editor, *Tom Thumb's Magazine,* 1951-53.

WORK IN PROGRESS: Writing *My Sister, Suzanne,* a book about a family focusing on mental illness and *Case of the Kaifeng Scroll,* a book featuring the Arab-Israeli conflict; researching Arab-Israeli history and current affairs as well as schizophrenia.

SIDELIGHTS: Harriet K. Feder told *SATA:* "I was born at the onset of the Great Depression, but my family didn't let that depress us. I remember the hand-me-down clothing I wore and the cardboard we put in our shoes to cover the holes in the soles. My mother gave French names to the dishes of rice and beans she

Vivi Hartman's "boring" vacation with her grandmother turns into an adventure after she witnesses several suspicious events in Harriet K. Feder's mystery. (Cover illustration by David Estep.)

57

cooked, and my father made old 'Good Will' tricycles look like new. For weekend entertainment, Mom banged out popular tunes on the old upright piano while the whole *mishpachah* (extended family) stood around and sang. When they weren't around, she was all business, making us practice scales for hours. My sisters aspired to playing the minute waltz in one minute, but I was Daddy's girl. My head was filled with stories.

"My father was a New York cabdriver. Born in the city, he was steeped in its history with which he liberally dosed his passengers as they passed the landmarks he cherished. Dad, of course, didn't know everything. But not to worry. The stories he didn't know he made up, and often they were better than the originals. Dad didn't remember fairy tales perfectly either, yet I always had one or two at bedtime. Though Danish storyteller Hans Christian Andersen and authors of *Grimm's Fairy Tales,* Jacob and Wilhelm Grimm, might not recognize the middles and endings, they faithfully began with 'Once upon a time.'

"I think I always knew that I was a writer. From the time I could speak I'd had a love affair with words, writing them down when I could finally master that skill. Subjects for my stories and poems were all around me. No family member could hide from my runaway pen. This holds true even now because a favorite source of ideas is my grandchildren.

"In *It Happened in Shushan* (1988) biblical era Queen Esther asks her most frequent question of the king: 'Can't we watch TV?' 'Of course not,' he tells her, 'there is no TV in Shushan.' What a bore. She never wanted to marry him anyway. Instead 'she wanted to be a doctor.'

"In *Not Yet, Elijah* (1989) a prophet waits impatiently to sip from the special cup of wine set out for him at a Passover seder. How fondly I recall watching my own father's wine glass to see if the level went down, as my little ones watch mine now. I never knew Dad's trick was to shake the table. I hope my grandchildren do not know that I have developed that skill. I describe this in my book as 'we all watch very carefully, our eyes upon the cup. Will he take one sip of wine or whoosh the whole thing up.'

"The 'No' syndrome of my two-year-old grandchild was the catalyst for *Judah Who Always Said, 'No!'* (1990), in which Judah Maccabee develops from a child who says 'No' to everything into a man who says 'No' to enslavement.

"Sitting in his high chair, cooing and chewing on a bagel, my one-year-old grandchild inspired *What Can You Do with a Bagel?* (1991) a board book for the very young.

"Less frivolous, *Mystery in Miami Beach* (1992) is based on the experience of friends who survived the Holocaust [the systematic killing of more than six million European Jews by Nazi Germany during the Second World War]. The main character is a modern

teen-age sleuth named Vivi Hartman who uncovers the Saint Louis, a ship filled with refugees, which came to our U.S. shores and was turned back to Europe where most of the people aboard were eventually killed.

"My current project, *My Sister, Suzanne,* was sparked by a friend who works with the mentally ill. Though it deals with the anguish of a family, it's a warm and hopeful story. Concurrently, I am at work on another Vivi Hartman mystery, shedding light and hope on the Arab-Israeli conflict.

"An avid fiction reader in childhood, I found well-researched stories an enjoyable way to learn about the world. I still do. My goal is to add to the collection."

* * *

FINKELSTEIN, Norman H. 1941-

PERSONAL: Born November 10, 1941, in Chelsea, MA; son of Sydney and Mollie (Fox) Finkelstein; married Rosalind Brandt (an electrologist), July 4, 1967; children: Jeffrey, Robert, Risa. *Education:* Hebrew College, B.J.Ed., 1961, M.A., 1986; Boston University, B.S., 1963, Ed.M., 1964, C.A.G.S., 1983. *Religion:* Jewish.

ADDRESSES: Office—Brookline Public Schools, 345 Harvard St., Brookline, MA 02146. *Agent*—Renee Cho,

NORMAN H. FINKELSTEIN

McIntosh & Otis, 310 Madison Ave., New York, NY 10017.

CAREER: Brookline Public Schools, Brookline, MA, library media specialist, 1970—; Hebrew College, Brookline, MA, part-time instructor, 1982—; Camp Yavneh, Northwood, NH, teacher, educational director, summers 1982-89; Massachusetts Corporation for Educational Telecommunications (MCET), host of "Thumbs Up—Thumbs Down," a program on books and media for teachers and librarians, 1990—.

MEMBER: American Library Association, Society of Children's Book Writers, Phi Delta Kappa.

AWARDS, HONORS: National Endowment for the Humanities fellowship, 1980; Holzman Award, Hebrew College, 1985, for *Remember Not to Forget: A Memory of the Holocaust;* Brookline Foundation grant, 1987; John F. Kennedy Presidential Library Foundation grant, 1987; Council for Basic Education fellowship, 1992.

WRITINGS:

FOR CHILDREN

Remember Not to Forget: A Memory of the Holocaust, illustrated by Lois and Lars Hokenson, Watts, 1984, revised edition, Mulberry/Morrow, 1993.

FOR YOUNG ADULTS

Theodor Herzl, Watts, 1985, revised edition, Lerner Publications, 1991.
Emperor General: A Biography of Douglas MacArthur, Dillon/Macmillan, 1989.
The Other 1492: Jewish Settlement in the New World, Scribners, 1989.
Captain of Innocence: France and the Dreyfus Affair, Putnam, 1991.
Sounds in the Air: Radio's Golden Age, Scribners, 1993.

WORK IN PROGRESS: "Books on the Cuban missile crisis, Edward R. Murrow, and a study of the fascinating aviator who made the second crossing of the Atlantic in 1927."

SIDELIGHTS: Norman H. Finkelstein told *SATA:* "I grew up with a pencil in one hand, a book in the other, and a radio at arm's length. When television arrived, my eyes had an extra job too. Our family was not rich; every penny was important. Yet there was always a nickel for me to exchange at Harry's Variety store for a brand-new notebook.

"Around the age of eleven, I discovered the world of current events and politics. To this very day, I cannot pass by a radio without tuning in the news. I even have a small battery-operated shortwave radio in the bathroom permanently tuned to the BBC. By age twelve I was the only kid in my neighborhood who regularly read the *New York Times.*

"As a child, I was a constant visitor to the public library. When I thought I had outgrown the basement children's room, I badgered my mother to take me 'upstairs' to the main library. For several years before I was 'legally' eligible to mingle with the adults, I checked books out on my mother's card. I liked reading histories and biographies, only occasionally straying into fiction (and then almost always historical fiction). In between the 'off the stairs' ball games with my friends during summer vacations, I could be found sitting on the front porch either drawing or reading.

"My reading habits have not changed as I've grown older. 'Fun' reading for me is still a good book on politics, diplomacy, or current issues. When I really feel the need to escape I tend to choose a spy novel. I really question whether good spy stories are still possible now that the CIA and KGB are talking to each other. As a school librarian, I now get to read and enjoy the picture books I missed as a kid.

"I enjoy writing nonfiction for young adults. Hopefully, my books allow readers to look at historical events in new ways. My writing reflects interests nurtured since childhood. The actual idea of writing a book never seriously entered my mind until I began working in the school library department of the Brookline, Massachusetts, public schools. There, I met and heard noted writers, illustrators and editors who frequently visited

Finkelstein was an avid reader of biography and history as a child, and for his second book he told the story of one man's participation in the creation of the State of Israel.

our school system. Listening to their stories inspired me to begin writing.

"My first book, *Remember Not to Forget: A Memory of the Holocaust,* resulted from teaching a high school course on the Holocaust. As I became familiar with the literature on the subject, I realized that little was available for younger readers. The resulting book was written in six weeks and then went through a year of submission and twenty-four rejections (that's right, twenty-four!) before being published by Franklin Watts.

"*Theodor Herzl,* my second book, was easier to sell. Franklin Watts published this biography of one of my favorite historical figures, the man who laid the groundwork for the establishment of the modern State of Israel fifty years before it happened. Although he is regarded as a national hero who mirrored the leadership of George Washington and the charisma of Martin Luther King, Jr., few people today recognize his name. A turning point in his conversion from respected Viennese journalist to Zionist leader was the Dreyfus Affair in France. Herzl, with fellow journalists, witnessed the degradation of the Jewish army officer falsely accused of treason. The virulent anti-Semitism that erupted so overcame Herzl, he devoted the rest of his short life to the establishment of a Jewish homeland. My research on Dreyfus for the Herzl book led to a later book for young adults, *Captain of Innocence: France and the Dreyfus Affair.*

"A vivid moment in my 'unofficial career' as a television news watcher was the return of General Douglas MacArthur to the United States in 1951. I was ten years old then but have always remembered watching this piece of history unfold on our new television. Years later, when Dillon Press invited me to write a biography of a World War II hero, I welcomed the opportunity to write about General MacArthur. *The Emperor General: A Biography of Douglas MacArthur* involved fascinating research trips to the National Archives and the Library of Congress in Washington, D.C., and the MacArthur Memorial Archives in Norfolk, Virginia.

"I think it is important to recognize the struggles and contributions of all people who are part of American society. Knowing that the upcoming commemoration of Columbus's 500th anniversary would be a milestone, I decided to write about another event of 1492—the expulsion of the Jews from Spain. *The Other 1492: Jewish Settlement in the New World* traces the path of Jews who fled Spain and focuses on a small group of twenty-three who ultimately found a new home in Columbus's New World. It is the story of heroes whose names rarely appear in school history texts.

"I sometimes think I enjoy the research part of my work more than the actual writing. Since I owe it to my readers to be factual and balanced in my presentation, I tend to read and study my subject exhaustively before distilling what I find. As I do my own research, I try to remember the three rules I teach my students: one, there is information somewhere to answer any question; two,

Expelled from their homes in the year of Columbus's landing in the New World, the large community of Spanish Jews embarked on a journey that would lead to a new life in America.

a researcher must think like a detective in order to track down appropriate source material; and three, it never hurts to ask questions."

*   *   *

FIRESIDE, Bryna J. 1932-

PERSONAL: Given name rhymes with "Dinah"; born May 5, 1932, in Elizabeth, NJ; daughter of Isador (a dentist) and Rose (a homemaker; maiden name, Shapiro) Levenberg; married Harvey Fireside (a professor), December 12, 1959; children: Leela, Douglas, Daniel. *Education:* Rutgers University, B.A., 1954; Cornell University, M.A., 1976. *Politics:* Democrat. *Religion:* Jewish. *Hobbies and other interests:* Social action work; working with Central American refugees; cooking, walking, bird watching.

ADDRESSES: Home—202 Eastwood Ave., Ithaca, NY 14850. *Office*—B. J. Fireside, 102 The Commons, Ithaca, NY 14850.

CAREER: New York City school system, New York City, elementary school teacher, 1960-68; Ithaca College, Ithaca, NY, instructor, 1972-78; Institute of Children's Literature, Danbury, CT, instructor, 1980—; State University of New York City at Cortland, supervisor of field studies, 1989-91; writer. Cofounder of The Border Fund and the Tasteful Ladies for Choice; vice president and charter member of Ithaca Reform Jewish

Temple; member, Friends of the Library (Ithaca), and Planned Parenthood.

MEMBER: Amnesty International (cofounder of Ithaca Chapter), National Writer's Union (grievance officer for upstate New York area), Society of Children's Book Writers, American Civil Liberties Union (ACLU), the Border Fund, National Women's Hall of Fame, People for the American Way, National Organization for Women (NOW), Ithaca Press Club (secretary).

AWARDS, HONORS: Human Rights Award, Tompkins County, 1992, for work with Central American refugees.

WRITINGS:

A Crow for Courage, Human Policy Press, 1978.
(With E. Lytel, R. Putter, and M. Caltado) *The Women's Encampment for a Future of Peace and Justice,* Temple University Press, 1983.
Choices: A Student Survival Guide for the 1990s, Garrett Park Press, 1989.
(With Joanne Bernstein) *Special Parents, Special Children,* Albert Whitman, 1991.
Is There a Woman in the House ... or Senate?, Albert Whitman, in press.

BRYNA J. FIRESIDE

Contributor of articles to periodicals, including *New York Times Book Review, New York Times Education Supplement, Scholastic Scope,* and *Seventeen.*

WORK IN PROGRESS: Research on "how working women won their rights—how the 1964 'sex' amendment to the Civil Rights Act sparked many lawsuits and helped pave the way for new careers for working women."

SIDELIGHTS: In 1943, when Bryna J. Fireside was eleven years old, she began working for her hometown weekly newspaper. The author told *SATA:* "Every week I delivered the news of my Girl Scout troop to the newspaper office. Every week I would stand behind the low wooden railing which separated the newspaper staff from the customers. I wished that I could sit at one of those desks and write articles for the paper. One day the editor asked me if I wanted to be the official Girl Scout reporter for the newspaper. Oh boy! Would I! It didn't take me more than thirty seconds to say yes.

"I was the only kid I knew who actually had a paying job. When my first column appeared, I discovered that I was given a byline. That meant that every week I saw my name in print. I was hooked. I was going to be a writer. But more than thirty years would go by before I would actually call myself an author. My first career was that of a teacher. That was when I discovered children's books, and began to read them both for myself and to my students. I began to wonder if I could ever write a children's book."

Fireside met and married her husband, Harvey, in 1959. The Firesides lived in New York City's Greenwich Village, where a daughter and son were born to them. They moved to Ithaca, New York, in 1968, where a third son, Daniel, was born. Fireside told *SATA:* "In Ithaca I got out into the community and volunteered to help people I admired and trusted to get elected to public office. What I was finding out was that one person could make a difference in our democracy. When I thought there was something going on in my town or in my country that I believed needed to be changed, I could help those changes along. Besides working to get people elected to public office, I joined civil rights marches, anti-nuclear demonstrations, women's marches for choice. In short, I became a social activist— a person who works and speaks out for change.

"I also began to write articles for magazines. I concentrated on writing about new ideas on how children could learn in school, and about people who were social activists. My articles began to appear in magazines and newspapers: *Jack and Jill, Ranger Rick's Nature Magazine,* the *New York Times Book Review,* and *Seventeen* magazine. But I never stopped thinking about writing a children's book.

"In 1978 it happened. My first book, *A Crow for Courage,* was published. It was about a little boy who learns how to take charge of his life even though he cannot walk. One of the reasons I wrote about a child with a handicapping condition was because my son, Doug, was going through a rough time as he learned first to accept, and then to overcome, some of the difficulties in his own life because of asthma and dyslexia. In 1991 my interest in people with handicapping conditions once again resulted in a book. With author Joanne Bernstein and her photographer husband, Michael, I wrote *Special Parents, Special Children.*

"Gradually the many strands of my life began to come together. My writing, whether for children or adults, reflected the things which were of great concern to me. In 1983, I, along with three other women, wrote a book about a women's peace camp that took root in Romulus, New York, right near a U.S. Army storage site for nuclear weapons. The book was called *The Women's Encampment for a Future of Peace and Justice.* As my children became teenagers and started to make life choices about college and careers, I began to talk to dozens of teenagers to find out how they made their decisions about their lives after high school. My book, *Choices: A Student Survival Guide for the 1990s,* was published in 1989.

"My newest book, *Is There a Woman in the House ... or Senate?,* grew out of my interest in women's issues. There were several women who had served in Congress whom I greatly admired. I knew how difficult it was for women to get elected to the Congress of the United States, and I thought that young people might want to know how they came to choose a career in politics, and what they accomplished. This book will be published in 1993.

"To me it is important to work towards making our world a better place for all of us to live. I try to do this by working for causes I believe in. In my writing, I try to show that people who believe in themselves and don't give up when things are difficult, can and do accomplish great things. I want us all to understand that one person alone can change the world ... or a little piece of it."

*   *   *

FISHER, Aileen (Lucia) 1906-

PERSONAL: Born September 9, 1906, in Iron River, MI; daughter of Nelson E. and Lucia (Milker) Fisher. *Education:* Attended University of Chicago, 1923-25; University of Missouri, B.J., 1927. *Hobbies and other interests:* Woodworking, hiking, mountain climbing.

ADDRESSES: Home and office—505 College Ave., Boulder, CO 80302.

CAREER: Women's National Journalistic Register, Chicago, IL, director, 1928-31; Labor Bureau of the Middle West, Chicago, research assistant, 1931-32; free-lance writer, 1932—.

MEMBER: Women in Communications.

AWARDS, HONORS: Silver Medal from U.S. Treasury Department, World War II; American Library Associa-

tion Notable Book of the Year, 1960, for *Going Barefoot,* 1961, for *Where Does Everyone Go?,* 1962, for *My Cousin Abe,* 1964, for *Listen, Rabbit,* 1965, for *In the Middle of the Night,* and 1966, for *Valley of the Smallest: The Life Story of a Shrew;* Western Writers of America Award for juvenile nonfiction, 1967, and Hans Christian Andersen Honor Book, 1968, both for *Valley of the Smallest: The Life Story of a Shrew;* award for children's poetry, National Council of Teachers of English, 1978. Several of Fisher's collections have been Junior Literary Guild selections.

WRITINGS:

CHILDREN'S VERSE

(Self-illustrated) *The Coffee-Pot Face,* McBride, 1933.
(Self-illustrated) *Inside a Little House,* McBride, 1938.
(Self-illustrated) *That's Why,* Thomas Nelson, 1946.
(Self-illustrated) *Up the Windy Hill: A Book of Merry Verse with Silhouettes,* Abelard, 1953.
(Self-illustrated) *Runny Days, Sunny Days: Merry Verses,* Abelard, 1958.
Going Barefoot, illustrated by Adrienne Adams, Crowell, 1960.
Where Does Everyone Go?, illustrated by Adams, Crowell, 1961.
Like Nothing at All, illustrated by Leonard Weisgard, Crowell, 1962.
I Wonder How, I Wonder Why, illustrated by Carol Barker, Abelard, 1962.
Cricket in a Thicket, illustrated by Feodor Rojankovsky, Scribner, 1963.
I Like Weather, illustrated by Janina Domanska, Crowell, 1963.
Listen, Rabbit, illustrated by Symeon Shimin, Crowell, 1964.
In the Middle of the Night, illustrated by Adams, Crowell, 1965.

AILEEN FISHER

In the Woods, in the Meadow, in the Sky, illustrated by Margot Tomes, Scribner, 1965.

Best Little House, illustrated by Arnold Spika, Crowell, 1966.

Skip around the Year, illustrated by Gioia Fiammenghi, Crowell, 1967.

My Mother and I, illustrated by Kazue Mizumura, Crowell, 1967.

We Went Looking, illustrated by Marie Angel, Crowell, 1968.

Up, up the Mountain, illustrated by Gilbert Riswold, Crowell, 1968.

In One Door and out the Other: A Book of Poems, illustrated by Lillian Hoban, Crowell, 1969.

Sing, Little Mouse, illustrated by Shimin, Crowell, 1969.

Clean as a Whistle, illustrated by Ben Shecter, Crowell, 1969.

But Ostriches . . . , illustrated by Peter Parnall, Crowell, 1970.

Feathered Ones and Furry, illustrated by Eric Carle, Crowell, 1971.

Do Bears Have Mothers, Too?, illustrated by Carle, Crowell, 1973.

My Cat Has Eyes of Sapphire Blue, illustrated by Angel, Crowell, 1975.

Once We Went on a Picnic, illustrated by Tony Chen, Crowell, 1975.

I Stood Upon a Mountain, illustrated by Blair Lent, Crowell, 1979.

Out in the Dark and Daylight, illustrated by Gail Owens, Harper, 1980.

Anybody Home?, illustrated by Susan Bonners, Crowell, 1980.

Rabbits, Rabbits, illustrated by Gail Neimann, Harper, 1983.

When It Comes to Bugs, illustrated by Chris and Bruce Degen, Crowell, 1985.

(With Jane Belk Moncure) *In Summer,* illustrated by Marie-Claude Monchaux, Children's World, 1985.

My First Hanukkah Book, illustrated by Priscilla Kiedrowski, Children's Press, 1985.

My First President's Day Book, illustrated by Lydia Halverson, Children's Press, 1987.

The House of a Mouse, illustrated by Joan Sandin, Harper, 1988.

Wishes, illustrated by Burt Dodson, DLM, 1990.

Here We Are Together, illustrated by Paul Micich, DLM, 1990.

Under the Open Sky, illustrated by Susan Edison, DLM, 1990.

Always Wondering, illustrated by Sandin, Harper, 1991.

"THE WAYS OF ANIMALS" POETRY SERIES; PUBLISHED BY BOWMAR/NOBLE

Animal Houses, illustrated by Jan Wills, 1972.

Animal Disguises, illustrated by Tim and Greg Hildebrandt, 1973.

Animal Jackets, illustrated by Muriel Wood, 1973.

Now That Days Are Colder, illustrated by Gordon Laite, 1973.

Tail Twisters, illustrated by Albert John Pucci, 1973.

Filling the Bill, illustrated by Betty Fraser, 1973.

Going Places, illustrated by Midge Quenell, 1973.

Fisher's love of animals and nature is evident in books such as this one about animal parents. (Cover illustration by Eric Carle.)

Sleepy Heads, illustrated by Phero Thomas, 1973.

You Don't Look Like Your Mother, Said the Robin to the Fawn, illustrated by Ati Forberg, 1973.

No Accounting for Tastes, illustrated by Gloria Gaulke, 1973.

"THE WAYS OF PLANTS" POETRY SERIES; PUBLISHED BY BOWMAR/NOBLE

Now That Spring Is Here, illustrated by Shimin, 1977.

And a Sunflower Grew, illustrated by Trina Schart Hyman, 1977.

Mysteries in the Garden, illustrated by Forberg, 1977.

Seeds on the Go, illustrated by Hans Zander, 1977.

Plant Magic, illustrated by Barbara Cooney, 1977.

Petals Yellow and Petals Red, illustrated by Pucci, 1977.

Swords and Daggers, illustrated by James Higa, 1977.

Prize Performance, illustrated by Tomes, 1977.

A Tree with a Thousand Uses, illustrated by James Endicott, 1977.

As the Leaves Fall Down, illustrated by Barbara Smith, 1977.

JUVENILE FICTION

Over the Hills to Nugget, illustrated by Sandra James, Aladdin, 1949.

Trapped by the Mountain Storm, illustrated by J. Fred Collins, Aladdin, 1950.

Homestead of the Free: The Kansas Story, Aladdin, 1953.

Timber!: Logging in Michigan, illustrated by Pers Crowell, Aladdin, 1955.

Off to the Gold Fields, illustrated by R. M. Powers, Thomas Nelson, 1955, published as *Secret in the Barrel,* Scholastic, 1965.

Cherokee Strip: The Race for Land, illustrated by Walt Reed, Aladdin, 1956.

A Lantern in the Window, illustrated by Harper Johnson, Thomas Nelson, 1957.

Skip, illustrated by Genevieve Vaughan-Jackson, Thomas Nelson, 1958.

Fisherman of Galilee, illustrated by John De Pol, Thomas Nelson, 1959.

Summer of Little Rain, illustrated by Gloria Stevens, Thomas Nelson, 1961.

My Cousin Abe, illustrated by Leonard Vosburgh, Thomas Nelson, 1962.

Arbor Day, illustrated by Nonny Hogrogian, Crowell, 1965.

(With Olive Rabe) *Human Rights Day,* illustrated by Lisl Weil, Crowell, 1966.

JUVENILE PLAYS

The Squanderbug's Christmas Carol, United States Treasury Department, 1943.

The Squanderbug's Mother Goose, United States Treasury Department, 1944.

A Tree to Trim: A Christmas Play, Row, Peterson, 1945.

What Happened in Toyland, Row, Peterson, 1945.

Nine Cheers for Christmas: A Christmas Pageant, Row, Peterson, 1945.

Before and After: A Play about the Community School Lunch Program, War Food Administration, 1945.

All Set for Christmas, Row, Peterson, 1946.

Here Comes Christmas!: A Varied Collection of Christmas Program Materials for Elementary Schools, Row, Peterson, 1947.

Witches, Beware: A Hallowe'en Play, Play Club, 1948.

Set the Stage for Christmas: A Collection of Pantomimes, Skits, Recitations, Readings, Plays and Pageants, Row, Peterson, 1948.

(Author of lyrics) *Christmas in Ninety-Nine Words,* with music by Rebecca Welty Dunn, Row, Peterson, 1949.

The Big Book of Christmas: A Collection of Plays, Songs, Readings, Recitations, Pantomimes, Skits, and Suggestions for Things to Make and Do for Christmas, Row, Peterson, 1951.

Health and Safety Plays and Programs, Plays, 1953.

Holiday Programs for Boys and Girls, Plays, 1953.

(With Rabe) *United Nations Plays and Programs,* Plays, 1954, 2nd edition, 1961.

(With Rabe) *Patriotic Plays and Programs,* Plays, 1956.

Christmas Plays and Programs, Plays, 1960.

Plays about Our Nation's Songs, Plays, 1962.

Bicentennial Plays and Programs, Plays, 1975.

Year-Round Programs for Young Players, Plays, 1985.

Contributor of plays to *Thirty Plays for Classroom Reading,* edited by Donald D. Durrell, Plays, 1965, and *Fifty Plays for Holidays,* edited by Sylvia E. Kamerman, Plays, 1969.

OTHER JUVENILE

Guess Again! (riddles), McBride, 1941.

All on a Mountain Day, illustrated by Gardell Christensen, Thomas Nelson, 1956.

(With Rabe) *We Dickinsons: The Life of Emily Dickinson as Seen Through the Eyes of Her Brother Austin,* Atheneum, 1965.

Valley of the Smallest: The Life Story of a Shrew, illustrated by Jean Zallinger, Crowell, 1966.

(With Rabe) *We Alcotts: The Life of Louisa May Alcott as Seen Through the Eyes of 'Marmee' ... ,* Atheneum, 1968.

Easter, illustrated by Forberg, Crowell, 1968, new edition, 1992.

Jeanne d'Arc, illustrated by Forberg, Crowell, 1970.

Contributor to periodicals, including *Story Parade, Plays, Jack and Jill,* and *Child Life.*

SIDELIGHTS: The natural world figures prominently in Aileen Fisher's books for children. Her love of plants and animals is most evident in her poetry, where she speaks of the beauty and wonder of nature; she views the outdoors "both as a naturalist and a poet," M. F. Birkett comments in *School Library Journal,* making "precise biological observations in figurative language." Fisher has also written about religious subjects and holidays, as well as two biographies of famous authors.

Growing up on a Michigan farm provided the inspiration for many of the poems in this collection. (Cover illustration by Gail Owens.)

Fisher was raised on a farm in Michigan's Upper Peninsula. The family house was big and square and set on forty acres. "We called the place High Banks," Fisher recalled in an interview with Lee Bennett Hopkins in *Language Arts,* "because it was on a high bank above the river, which was always red with water pumped from the iron mines. Still, the river was good to wade in, swim in, fish in, and skate on in winter . . . . We had all kinds of pets—cows, horses, and chickens. And we had a big garden in summer. I loved it. I have always loved the country."

After graduating from college, Fisher worked for several years in Chicago and began publishing poems in children's magazines. She wanted to find a place in the country, however. "My aim in Chicago was to save every cent I was able to so that I could escape back to the country life I loved and missed," Fisher explained to Hopkins. In 1932, she and her friend, Olive Rabe, bought a 200-acre ranch in the foothills near Boulder, Colorado, where they would live for more than thirty years. The following year, Fisher published the first of many poetry volumes, *The Coffee-Pot Face.*

Fisher and Rabe collaborated on several books together, including a biography of poet Emily Dickinson, *We Dickinsons.* "Emily Dickinson has long been our favorite poet," Fisher told *Junior Literary Guild,* "not only for her wonderful insights about nature, but for the depth of her searching thoughts about life and death, eternity and immortality. Our great devotion to this 'modern' poet of one hundred years ago led to the desire to know as much about her life as possible, and our reading and study in turn led us to want to make Emily Dickinson come alive to others."

Fisher now lives in the city of Boulder, "on a dead-end street at the foot of Flagstaff Mountain," she once stated. "Except for rabbits, I find more wildlife here at the edge of town than on the ranch; and I still enjoy many of the pleasures of country living, including what my neighbor calls a 'wild' yard. I like an organized life of peace and quiet, and so I avoid crowds, cities, noise, airports, neon lights, and confusion. My first and chief love in writing is writing children's verse." The author has over fifty volumes of poetry for children to her credit; critics praise her poems as "brief, fresh, deft, and often illuminating," as a *Bulletin for the Center of Children's Books* reviewer writes of *Out in the Dark and Daylight,* "and they are pleasant to read alone or aloud."

Speaking to Hopkins, Fisher explained: "I try to be at my desk four hours a day, from 8:00 a.m. to noon. Ideas come to me out of experience and from reading and remembering. I usually do a first draft by hand. I can't imagine writing verse on a typewriter, and for years I wrote nothing but verse so I formed the habit of thinking with a pencil or pen in hand. I usually rework my material, sometimes more, sometimes less. I *never* try out my ideas on children, except on the child I used to know—me! Fortunately I remember pretty well what I used to like to read, think about, and do. I find, even today, that if I write something I like, children are pretty

apt to like it too. I guess what it amounts to is that I never grew up."

WORKS CITED:

Birkett, M. F., review of *Out in the Dark and Daylight, School Library Journal,* September, 1980, p. 58.
Hopkins, Lee Bennett, "Profile: Aileen Fisher," *Language Arts,* October, 1978.
Junior Literary Guild, September, 1965-April, 1966, p. 36.
Review of *Out in the Dark and Daylight, Bulletin of the Center for Children's Books,* July/August, 1980, p. 211.

FOR MORE INFORMATION SEE:

BOOKS

Hopkins, Lee Bennett, *Books Are by People,* Citation Press, 1969.
Hopkins, Lee Bennett, *Pass the Poetry, Please,* Citation Press, 1972.
Twentieth-Century Children's Writers, 3rd edition, St. James Press, 1989, pp. 340-342.

PERIODICALS

Elementary English, October, 1967.

Cat Bath

After she eats,
my purry friend
washes herself
from end to end,

Washes her face,
her ears, her paws,
washes the pink
between her claws.

I watch, and think
it's better by far
to splash in a tub
with soap in a bar

And washcloth in hand
and towel on the rung
than have to do all
that work *by tongue.*

My Kitten

My kitten
has the softest fur,
as soft as silk to touch.
I smoothe her,
and she starts to purr:
"Thank you very much."

And even
when I'm doing things
or when I want to play
she smoothes herself
on me and sings:
"Thank you, anyway."

Fisher writes her poetry with an audience of one in mind—the child she used to be. (Illustration by Carle.)

New Yorker, December 14, 1968.
Young Readers' Review, November, 1968.

* * *

FISHER, Leonard Everett 1924-

PERSONAL: Born June 24, 1924, in the Bronx, NY; son of Benjamin M. and Ray M. (Shapiro) Fisher; married Margery M. Meskin (a school librarian), 1952; children: Julie Anne, Susan Abby, James Albert. *Education:* Attended Art Students League, 1941, and Brooklyn College, 1941-42; Yale University, B.F.A., 1949, M.F.A., 1950.

ADDRESSES: Home and office—7 Twin Bridge Acres Rd., Westport, CT 06880.

CAREER: Painter, illustrator, author and educator. Graduate teaching fellow, Yale Art School, 1949-50; Whitney School of Art, New Haven, CT, dean, 1951-53; faculty member, Paier College of Art, 1966-78, academic dean, 1978-82, dean emeritus, 1982—, visiting professor, 1982-87. Visiting professor, artist, or consultant at various universities and colleges, including Case Western Reserve University, Silvermine Guild School of the Arts, Hartford University School of Art, Fairfield University, and University of California. Designer of U.S. postage stamps for the U.S. Postal Service, 1972-77; design consultant, Postal Agent, Staffa and Bernera Islands, Scotland, 1979-82. Delegate to national and international conferences; member of arts councils and historical societies in Westport, CT, and Greater New Haven, CT; trustee, Westport Public Library Board of

LEONARD EVERETT FISHER

Trustees, 1982-85, vice-president, 1985-86, president, 1986-89. Lecturer and speaker at art institutes, academic seminars, education workshops and children's book programs nationwide. *Military service:* U.S. Army, Corps of Engineers, 1942-46; became technical sergeant; participated in topographic mapping of five major campaigns in European and Pacific areas.

EXHIBITIONS: Various one-man shows at museums, libraries, galleries, and universities in the United States, including Hewitt Gallery, NY; New Britain Museum (24-year retrospective), Everson Museum, University of Syracuse, NY; Kimberly Gallery, New York City; Museum of American Illustration, Society of Illustrators (50-year retrospective), New York City; Homer Babbidge Library, University of Connecticut (50-year retrospective); and special mini-exhibitions (including Smithsonian Institution, and Fairview Park Library, OH), all from 1952 to the present.

Work exhibited at various group shows at galleries, museums, and universities in the United States, including Brooklyn Museum, NY; Rockefeller Center, NY; Seligmann Galleries, NY; Eggleston Galleries, NY; Hewitt Gallery, NY; American Federation of Arts and Emily Lowe Foundation national tours; Whitney Museum, NY; National Academy (Audubon Artists), NY; New York Historical Society, NY; Society of Illustrators, NY; Yale Art Gallery, CT; and many others, all from 1939 to the present.

Work exhibited in collections of various museums, libraries, and universities, including The Library of Congress, Washington, DC; Free Library of Philadelphia, PA; Museum of American Illustration, New York, NY; Universities of Connecticut, Oregon, Minnesota, Southern Mississippi, and Appalachian State; Fairfield University, CT; The Smithsonian Institution, Washington, DC; and miscellaneous public and private collections in Iowa, Massachusetts, Michigan, Delaware, Hawaii, Maryland, New York, New Jersey, Wisconsin, California, North Carolina, and Oklahoma.

MEMBER: PEN, Society of Children's Book Writers and Illustrators, Authors Guild, Society of Illustrators, Silvermine Guild of Artists (trustee, 1970-74), New Haven Paint and Clay Club (president, 1968-70; trustee, 1968-74), Westport-Weston Arts Council (founding member; director, 1969-76; vice-president, 1972-73; president, 1973-74; board chairman, 1975-76).

AWARDS, HONORS: William Wirt Winchester traveling fellowship, Yale University, 1949; Joseph Pulitzer scholarship in art, Columbia University and the National Academy of Design, 1950; New Haven Paint and Clay Club, Carle J. Blenner Prize for painting, 1968; premio grafico, Fiera di Bologna, 5a Fiera Internazionale del Libro per l'Infanzia e la Gioventu, Italy, 1968, for *The Schoolmasters;* Mayor's Proclamation: Leonard Everett Fisher Day, Fairview Park, OH, opening National Children's Book Week, November 12, 1978; New York Library Association/School Library Media Section Award for Outstanding Contributions in the Fields of

Art and Literature, 1979; Medallion of the University of Southern Mississippi for Distinguished Contributions to Children's Literature, 1979; Christopher Medal for illustration, 1981, for *All Times, All Peoples;* National Jewish Book Award for Children's Literature, and Association of Jewish Libraries Award for Children's Literature, both 1981, both for *A Russian Farewell;* Parenting's Reading Magic Award, Time-Life, 1988, for *Monticello;* Children's Book Guild/*Washington Post* Nonfiction Award, 1989; nominee, Orbis Pictus Award for Oustanding Nonfiction for Children, National Council Teachers of English, 1989, for *The White House;* Parents' Choice Award, 1989, for *The Seven Days of Creation;* Regina Medal, Catholic Library Association, 1991, for "lifetime distinguished contributions to children's literature"; Kerlan Award, University of Minnesota, 1991, for "singular attainments in the creation of children's literature."

Fisher's books have received numerous awards or special citations from the American Institute of Graphic Arts, the *New York Times, Booklist,* the American Library Association, the National Council of Social Studies, various state library and reading organizations in Utah, Kentucky, Oklahoma, and Texas, and the National Council of Social Studies, including all books in his "Colonial Americans" and "Nineteenth-Century America" series.

WRITINGS:

SELF-ILLUSTRATED CHILDREN'S BOOKS

Pumpers, Boilers, Hooks and Ladders, Dial, 1961.
Pushers, Spads, Jennies and Jets, Dial, 1961.
A Head Full of Hats, Dial, 1962.
Two If by Sea, Random House, 1970.
Picture Book of Revolutionary War Heroes, Stockpole, 1970.
The Death of Evening Star: The Diary of a Young New England Whaler, Doubleday, 1972.
The Art Experience, F. Watts, 1973.
The Warlock of Westfall, Doubleday, 1974.
Across the Sea and Galway, Four Winds, 1975.
Sweeney's Ghost, Doubleday, 1975.
Leonard Everett Fisher's Liberty Book, Doubleday, 1976.
Letters from Italy, Four Winds, 1977.
Noonan, Doubleday, 1978, Avon, 1981.
Alphabet Art: Thirteen ABCs from Around the World, Four Winds, 1979.
A Russian Farewell, Four Winds, 1980.
Storm at the Jetty, Viking, 1980.
The Seven Days of Creation, Holiday House, 1981.
Number Art: Thirteen 1, 2, 3's from Around the World, Four Winds, 1982.
Star Signs, Holiday House, 1983.
Symbol Art: Thirteen Squares, Circles and Triangles from Around the World, Four Winds, 1984.
Boxes! Boxes!, Viking, 1984.
The Olympians: Great Gods and Goddesses of Ancient Greece, Holiday House, 1984.
The Statue of Liberty, Holiday House, 1985.
The Great Wall of China, Macmillan, 1986.

Ellis Island, Holiday House, 1986.
Symbol Art: Thirteen Squares, Circles and Triangles from Around the World, Four Winds, 1986.
Calendar Art: Thirteen Days, Weeks, Months and Years from Around the World, Four Winds, 1987.
The Tower of London, Macmillan, 1987.
The Alamo, Holiday House, 1987.
Look Around: A Book about Shapes, Viking, 1987.
Monticello, Holiday House, 1988.
Pyramid of the Sun, Pyramid of the Moon, Macmillan, 1988.
Theseus and the Minotaur, Holiday House, 1988.
The Wailing Wall, Macmillan, 1989.
The White House, Holiday House, 1989.
Prince Henry the Navigator, Macmillan, 1990.
Jason and the Golden Fleece, Holiday House, 1990.
The Oregon Trail, Holiday House, 1990.
The ABC Exhibit, Macmillan, 1991.
Sailboat Lost, Macmillan, 1991.
Cyclops, Holiday House, 1991.
Galileo, Macmillan, 1992.
Tracks Across America: The Story of the American Railroad, 1825-1900, Holiday House, 1992.
Gutenberg, Macmillan, 1993.

THE "COLONIAL AMERICANS" SERIES; SELF-ILLUSTRATED

The Glassmakers, F. Watts, 1964.
The Silversmiths, F. Watts, 1964.
The Papermakers, F. Watts, 1965.
The Printers, F. Watts, 1965.
The Wigmakers, F. Watts, 1965.
The Hatters, F. Watts, 1965.
The Weavers, F. Watts, 1966.
The Cabinet Makers, F. Watts, 1966.
The Tanners, F. Watts, 1966.
The Shoemakers, F. Watts, 1967.
The Schoolmasters, F. Watts, 1967.
The Peddlers, F. Watts, 1968.
The Doctors, F. Watts, 1968.
The Potters, F. Watts, 1969.
The Limners, F. Watts, 1969.
The Architects, F. Watts, 1970.
The Shipbuilders, F. Watts, 1971.
The Homemakers, F. Watts, 1973.
The Blacksmiths, F. Watts, 1976.

"NINETEENTH-CENTURY AMERICA" SERIES; SELF-ILLUSTRATED

The Factories, Holiday House, 1979.
The Railroads, Holiday House, 1979.
The Hospitals, Holiday House, 1980.
The Sports, Holiday House, 1980.
The Newspapers, Holiday House, 1981.
The Unions, Holiday House, 1982.
The Schools, Holiday House, 1983.

ADULT

Masterpieces of American Painting, Bison/Exeter, 1985.
Remington and Russell, W. H. Smith, 1986.

Dust rises from an Indian attack upon a train in *The Railroads,* one of Fisher's "Nineteenth Century America" series. (Illustration by the author).

ILLUSTRATOR

Geoffrey Household, *The Exploits of Xenophon,* Random House, 1955, revised edition, Shoestring Press, 1989.

Florence Walton Taylor, *Carrier Boy,* Abelard, 1956.

Manley Wade Wellman, *To Unknown Lands,* Holiday House, 1956.

Roger P. Buliard, *My Eskimos: A Priest in the Arctic,* Farrar, Straus, 1956.

Richard B. Morris, *The First Book of the American Revolution,* F. Watts, 1956, revised edition published as *The American Revolution,* Lerner Publications, 1985.

L. D. Rich, *The First Book of New England,* F. Watts, 1957.

Kenneth S. Giniger, *America, America, America,* F. Watts, 1957.

Henry Steele Commager, *The First Book of American History,* F. Watts, 1957.

James C. Bowman, *Mike Fink,* Little, Brown, 1957.

Robert Payne, *The Splendor of Persia,* Knopf, 1957.

Morris, *The First Book of the Constitution,* F. Watts, 1958, revised edition published as *The Constitution,* Lerner Publications, 1985.

Jeanette Eaton, *America's Own Mark Twain,* Morrow, 1958.

Harry B. Ellis, *The Arabs,* World, 1958.

Robert Irving, *Energy and Power,* Knopf, 1958.

Estelle Friedman, *Digging into Yesterday,* Putnam, 1958.

E. B. Meyer, *Dynamite and Peace,* Little, Brown, 1958.

E. M. Brown, *Kateri Tekakwitha,* Farrar, Straus, 1958.

C. Edell, *Here Come the Clowns,* Putnam, 1958.

L. H. Kuhn, *The World of Jo Davidson,* Farrar, Straus, 1958.

Catharine Wooley, *David's Campaign Buttons,* Morrow, 1959.

Maurice Dolbier, *Paul Bunyan,* Random House, 1959.

Edith L. Boyd, *Boy Joe Goes to Sea,* Rand McNally, 1959.

Gerald W. Johnson, *America is Born,* Morrow, 1959.

Morris, *The First Book of Indian Wars,* F. Watts, 1959, revised edition published as *The Indian Wars,* Lerner Publications, 1985.

Elizabeth Abell, editor, *Westward, Westward, Westward,* F. Watts. 1959.

Phillip H. Ault, *This is the Desert,* Dodd, 1959.

Irving, *Sound and Ultrasonics,* Knopf, 1959.

Johnson, *America Moves Forward,* Morrow, 1960.

Johnson, *America Grows Up,* Morrow, 1960.

Irving, *Electromagnetic Waves,* Knopf, 1960.

Declaration of Independence, F. Watts, 1960.

Trevor N. Dupuy, *Military History of Civil War Naval Actions,* F. Watts, 1960.

Dupuy, *Military History of Civil War Land Battles,* F. Watts, 1960.

Edward E. Hale, *The Man Without a Country,* F. Watts, 1960.

Anico Surnay, *Ride the Cold Wind,* Putnam, 1960.

Natalia M. Belting, *Indy and Mrs. Lincoln,* Holt, 1960.

Belting, *Verity Mullens and the Indian,* Holt, 1960.

Morris, *The First Book of the War of 1812,* F. Watts, 1961, revised edition published as *The War of 1812,* Lerner Publications, 1985.

Emma G. Sterne, *Vasco Nunez De Balboa,* Knopf, 1961.

James Playsted Wood, *The Queen's Most Honorable Pirate,* Harper, 1961.

Harold W. Felton, *A Horse Named Justin Morgan,* Dodd, 1962.

Charles M. Daugherty, *Great Archaeologists,* Crowell, 1962.

Margery M. Fisher, *But Not Our Daddy,* Dial, 1962.

Robert C. Suggs, *Modern Discoveries in Archaeology,* Crowell, 1962.

Paul Engle, *Golden Child,* Dutton, 1962.

Jean L. Latham, *Man of the Monitor,* Harper, 1962.

Johnson, *The Supreme Court,* Morrow, 1962.

Harold W. Felton, *Sergeant O'Keefe and His Mule, Balaam,* Dodd, 1962.

Johnson. *The Presidency,* Morrow, 1962.

Jack London, *Before Adam,* Macmillan, 1962.

Eric B. Smith and Robert Meredith, *Pilgrim Courage,* Little, Brown, 1962.

E. Hubbard, *Message of Garcia,* F. Watts, 1962.

Charles Ferguson, *Getting to Know the U.S.A.,* Coward, 1963.

A. Surany, *Golden Frog,* Putnam, 1963.

Johnson, *The Congress,* Morrow, 1963.

Margery M. Fisher, *One and One,* Dial, 1963.

Andre Maurois, *The Weigher of Souls,* Macmillan, 1963.

London, *Star Rover,* Macmillan, 1963.

Helen Hoke, editor, *Patriotism, Patriotism, Patriotism,* F. Watts, 1963.

Gettysburg Address, F. Watts, 1963.

Johnson, *Communism: An American's View,* Morrow, 1964.

Smith and Meredith, *Coming of the Pilgrims,* Little, Brown, 1964.

Richard Armour, *Our Presidents,* Norton, 1964.

Meredith and Smith, *Riding with Coronado,* Little, Brown, 1964.

Robert C. Suggs, *Alexander the Great, Scientist-King,* Macmillan, 1964.

John F. Kennedy's Inaugural Address, F. Watts, 1964.

Suggs, *Archaeology of San Francisco,* Crowell, 1965.

Martin Gardner, *Archimedes,* Macmillan, 1965.

Florence Stevenson, *The Story of Aida* (based on the opera by Giuseppe Verdi), Putnam, 1965.

Lois P. Jones, *The First Book of the White House,* F. Watts, 1965.

Ernest L. Thayer, *Casey at the Bat,* F. Watts, 1965.

John Foster, *Rebel Sea Raider,* Morrow, 1965.

Surany, *The Burning Mountain,* Holiday House, 1965.

Martha Shapp and Charles Shapp, *Let's Find Out about John Fitzgerald Kennedy,* F. Watts, 1965.

Suggs, *Archaeology of New York,* Crowell, 1966.

Clifford L. Alderman, *The Story of the Thirteen Colonies,* Random House, 1966.

Foster, *Guadalcanal General,* Morrow, 1966.

Robert Silverberg, *Forgotten by Time,* Crowell, 1966.

Johnson, *The Cabinet,* Morrow, 1966.

Washington Irving, *The Legend of Sleepy Hollow,* F. Watts, 1966.

Surany, *Kati and Kormos,* Holiday House, 1966.

Surany, *A Jungle Jumble,* Putnam, 1966.

Meredith and Smith, *Quest of Columbus,* Little, Brown, 1966.

Madeleine L'Engle, *Journey with Jonah,* Farrar, Straus, 1967.

L. Sprague and Catherine C. De Camp, *The Story of Science in America,* Scribner, 1967.

Nathaniel Hawthorne, *Great Stone Face and Two Other Stories,* F. Watts, 1967.

Johnson, *Franklin D. Roosevelt,* Morrow, 1967.

George B. Shaw, *The Devil's Disciple,* F. Watts, 1967.

Surany, *Covered Bridge,* Holiday House, 1967.

Surany, *Monsieur Jolicoeur's Umbrella,* Putnam, 1967.

Irving, *Rip Van Winkle,* F. Watts, 1967.

Morris, *The First Book of the Founding of the Republic,* F. Watts, 1968.

Surany, *Malachy's Gold,* Holiday House, 1968.

Bret Harte, *The Luck of Roaring Camp,* F. Watts, 1968.

(With Cynthia Basil) J. Foster, *Napoleon's Marshall,* Morrow, 1968.

Gerald W. Foster, *The British Empire,* Morris, 1969.

Meredith and Smith, *Exploring the Great River,* Little, Brown, 1969.

Surany, *Lora Lorita,* Putnam, 1969.

Julian May, *Why the Earth Quakes,* Holiday House, 1969.

Victor B. Scheffer, *The Year of the Whale,* Scribner, 1969.

Scheffer, *The Year of the Seal,* Scribner, 1970.

Berenice R. Morris, *American Popular Music,* F. Watts, 1970.

Scheffer, *Little Calf,* Scribner, 1970.

May, *The Land Beneath the Sea,* Holiday House, 1971.

Loren Eisely, *The Night Country,* Scribner, 1971.

Isaac B. Singer, *The Wicked City,* Farrar, Straus, 1972.

Jan Wahl, *Juan Diego and the Lady,* Putnam, 1973.

Gladys Conklin, *The Journey of the Gray Whales,* Holiday House, 1974.

James E. Gunn, *Some Dreams are Nightmares,* Scribner, 1974.

The Joy of Crafts, Blue Mountain Crafts Council, 1975.

E. Thompson, *The White Falcon,* Doubleday, 1976.

Milton Meltzer, *All Times, All Peoples: A World History of Slavery,* Harper, 1980.

Myra Cohn Livingston, *A Circle of Seasons,* Holiday House, 1982.

Richard Armour, *Our Presidents,* revised edition, Woodbridge Press, 1983.

Livingston, *Sky Songs,* Holiday House, 1984.

Livingston, *Celebrations,* Holiday House, 1985.

Livingston, *Sea Songs,* Holiday House, 1986.

Livingston, *Earth Songs,* Holiday House, 1986.

Livingston, *Space Songs,* Holiday House, 1988.

Livingston, *Up in the Air,* Holiday House, 1989.

Alice Schertle, *Little Frog's Song,* Harper, 1992.

Livingston, *If You Ever Meet a Whale,* Holiday House, 1992.

Eric A. Kimmel, editor, *The Spotted Pony: A Collection of Hanukkah Stories,* Holiday House, 1992.

ILLUSTRATOR OF TEXT BOOKS AND LEARNING MATERIALS

Our Reading Heritage (six volumes), Holt, 1956-58.

Marjorie Wescott Barrows, *Good English through Practice,* Holt, 1956.

Don Parker, editor, *The Reading Laboratories* (eight volumes), Science Research Associates, 1957-62.

M. W. Barrows and E. N. Woods, *Reading Skills,* Holt, 1958.

Dolores Betler, editor, *The Literature Sampler* (two volumes), Learning Materials, Inc., 1962, 1964.

How Things Change, Field Enterprise, 1964.

ILLUSTRATOR OF AUDIO-VISUAL FILMSTRIPS

Edgar Allan Poe, *Murders in the Rue Morgue,* Encyclopaedia Britannica, 1978.

Robert Louis Stevenson, *Dr. Jekyll and Mr. Hyde,* Encyclopaedia Britannica, 1978.

Bram Stoker, *The Judge's House,* Encyclopaedia Britannica, 1978.

A. B. Edwards, *Snow* (from *The Phantom Coach*), Encyclopaedia Britannica, 1978.

Poe, *The Tell-Tale Heart,* Encyclopaedia Britannica, 1980.

Also illustrator for *Cricket* and *Lady Bug* magazines. Many of Fisher's manuscripts, illustrations, drawings, and correspondence are housed at the Leonard Everett Fisher Archive, University of Connecticut, Storrs, the Kerlan Collection, University of Minnesota, Minneapolis, the de Grummond Collection, University of Southern Mississippi, Hattiesburg, the library of the University of Oregon, Eugene, and at the Postal History Collection, Smithsonian Institution, Washington, DC.

ADAPTATIONS: Filmstrips, all by Anico Surany and all produced by Random House: *The Golden Frog, The Burning Mountain, A Jungle Jumble, Monsieur Jolicouer's Umbrella, Ride the Cold Wind,* and *Lora Lorita.*

Fisher illuminates the lives and jobs of early settlers, such as glassblowers, in his self-illustrated "Colonial Americans" series. (Illustration from *The Glassmakers.*)

SIDELIGHTS: Leonard Everett Fisher is a prominent illustrator of both children's nonfiction and fiction books, particularly books of American and world history. He credits his father's love of art with his own decision to become an artist. The elder Fisher was a ship designer and draftsman who painted in his spare time. One of his paintings was still on the easel when two-year-old Leonard got hold of some india ink and a paint brush and added his own embellishments to his father's work. The result was an unusable mess. But instead of being punished, Fisher was given his own little studio—a converted hall closet—complete with work table, crayons, paper and pencils. "I was cozily in business," Fisher recalls in his article for *Something about the Author Autobiography Series* (*SAAS*), "ensconced in my first studio, lit from the ceiling by a naked bulb and about six steps from the kitchen."

Fisher's early efforts concentrated on scenes of wartime battle, inspired by his uncles' stories of their World War I experiences. Both uncles had fought in the trenches with the American Expeditionary Force, defending Paris from German attack. His mother, he remembers in *SAAS*, "would sit in one of the little studio chairs and read to me from *Mother Goose* or *A Child's Garden of Verses* while I drew battlefield ambulances filled with bleeding heroes."

While in school, Fisher began to win local art competitions, including several prizes sponsored by department stores. One of these was a float design for the Macy Thanksgiving Day parade. A pencil drawing was exhibited with the works of other high school students at the Brooklyn Museum. In addition to his school work, Fisher also took art classes at Moses Soyer's art studio, at the Art Students' League, and at the Heckscher Foundation. His mother also made sure he visited the art museums of New York.

After graduating from high school at the age of 16, Fisher studied art and geology at Brooklyn College for a time before entering the Army. He enlisted in 1942 and was assigned to become a mapmaker. Shipped overseas, Fisher worked at a base in Algeria drawing battle maps for the Allied campaigns in Italy, and the invasions of Normandy, southern France, and Germany. After a year, he was transferred to Hawaii to work on battle maps for the invasions of the islands of Iwo Jima and Okinawa, and for the never-executed invasion of Japan itself. His first professional writing was done at this time, with Fisher describing his unit's topographical work.

Fisher returned to college after his military service, earning two degrees from Yale University. "The Yale experience was memorable," Fisher explains in his *SAAS* article. "It prepared me for every artistic eventuality. It was up to me to discover those eventualities." Following graduation, Fisher traveled to Europe using money received from two fellowships. He visited the major art museums of London, Paris, Milan, Florence, Venice, Rome, and elsewhere in Italy. "I saw every painting I came to see and more," he remembers in *SAAS*.

Upon his return to the United States, Fisher became dean of the Whitney School of Art. He had his first New York exhibition at the Edwin C. Hewitt Gallery in 1952. Although not one painting was sold, the critical reviews were favorable and Fisher, encouraged by the response, proposed to Margery Meskin, then a systems service representative with IBM. The couple was married later that year.

Shortly after leaving the Whitney School of Art in 1953, Fisher began to illustrate books for children. His first was *The Exploits of Xenophon,* written by Geoffrey Household, which tells the story of an ancient Greek writer, historian, and military leader. Other projects soon followed, including the six-volume *Our Reading Heritage* and the *Multilevel Reading Laboratory,* an experimental concept in which 150 reading selections were printed with 150 suitable illustrations. Fisher did the illustrations for eight of the "laboratory" packages, more than 3,000 illustrations in all.

In addition to illustrating educational materials, Fisher also illustrated a number of children's picture books, working for Holiday House and Franklin Watts. These books included both fiction and nonfiction titles, including many on American history, a subject close to Fisher's heart. "American history," he explains in *SAAS,* "had a strong presence during my growing years.

An artist from an early age, Fisher has long been fascinated with the art and history of other cultures; in *Pyramid of the Sun, Pyramid of the Moon,* he portrays the sacrifice of an enemy warrior by Aztec priests.

Fisher's determination to connect today's children with the past has included many books on the immigrants who have relocated to the United States. (Illustration by the author from *Ellis Island.*)

To my parents, one an immigrant, the other the son of immigrants, the United States was heaven-sent."

Fisher has also written children's books, many of them about historical subjects. His "Nineteenth-Century America" series for Holiday House describes various aspects of American society, such as the growth of the railroads or the nation's most popular leisure-time activities, and is meant to provide a panoramic picture of the development of nineteenth century America. Fisher explains in *SAAS* that the books also "deal with my determination not to disconnect. In a culture like ours, wherein today's material gratification seems to deny any historical link, knowledge of the past is often and mistakenly brushed aside as irrelevant to our present and future values, much less the course of our nation. I try to say otherwise."

The "Colonial Americans" series from Franklin Watts consists of nineteen books describing Colonial crafts, trades, and professions. Each begins with a brief history of the craft, trade, or profession in question and then proceeds to describe the actual techniques used by Colonial craftsmen. Fisher's illustrations for the books were done in a style reminiscent of old-time engravings to give them the proper feeling. The "Colonial Americans" series, according to O. Mell Busbin in the *Dictionary of Literary Biography,* "has received wide use in classrooms throughout the United States, especially in the arts and social sciences." Over 500,000 copies of the series have been sold.

The American experience is also illuminated in Fisher's books about immigrants. *Across the Sea from Galway* tells of a group of Irish immigrants who flee famine and oppression in Ireland only to be shipwrecked off the Massachusetts coast. *Letters from Italy* is the story of several generations of an Italian-American family, be-

ginning with a grandfather who fought with Garibaldi for Italian independence to a grandson who dies in World War II fighting Mussolini. *A Russian Farewell* traces a Jewish-Ukrainian family from their trials under the Czarist government to their decision to leave for America, while *Ellis Island* profiles the famous entry point for many immigrants to the United States.

Other books were inspired by Fisher's childhood on the seashore. *The Death of Evening Star, Noonan,* and *Storm at the Jetty* are all based on his recollections of living in the family house at Sea Gate in Brooklyn. Situated on the jetty of land where the Atlantic Ocean waters met the waters of Gravesend Bay, the family house had a magnificent view of passing ships, storms at sea, and the local lighthouse. *Storm at the Jetty* is a descriptive story of how a beautiful August afternoon on the seashore gradually transforms into a violent and ugly thunderstorm at sea. *The Death of Evening Star* concerns a nineteenth century whaling ship from New England and the many tribulations of its final voyage.

Although an illustrator and author of children's books, Fisher has also created easel paintings, held exhibitions of his work, and painted murals for such public buildings as the Washington Monument. In the early 1970s he designed a number of postage stamps for the U.S. Postal Service, including a series of four stamps on American craftsmen for the Bicentennial. These stamps were first issued at Williamsburg, Virginia, on July 4, 1972. Fisher also designed the commemorative stamp *The Legend of Sleepy Hollow,* a tribute to Washington Irving's classic story.

Fisher notes a general tendency among critics to categorize him as an artist of American historical subjects, ignoring the wider range of his work, as he commented in a personal letter. "I am an artist—painter, illustrator, designer—who happens to have been immersed from time to time in colonial America, Ellis Island, the Statue of Liberty, Monticello, the White House, and the Alamo," Fisher explains. "But I do not wish my effort in this direction to detract from the energies I have devoted to my painted interpretations of poetry, Greek mythology, and world history and the artistic expressions thus generated. The three books I have published in 1991—*The ABC Exhibit, Sailboat Lost,* and *Cyclops*—are more about art and me as an artist than anything else."

Writing in *Horn Book* about the place of art in contemporary children's nonfiction, Fisher offers these observations: "We have a tendency in children's nonfiction to respond only to the desires of curriculum and educators and to ignore the other needs.... The qualities of high art are hardly ever a factor for the judgment of nonfiction. What is important about me is the quality of my thinking, what drives me to do what I am doing; not the facts of my life—but the creative impulse behind that life. I am trying to make an artistic statement logically, and a logical statement to children artistically. I think the time has come for a stronger and more artistically expansive view of nonfiction."

Fisher's recent works have included retellings of Greek myths, such as one hero's attempt to capture the magical skin of a golden sheep. (Illustration by the author from *Jason and the Golden Fleece.*)

WORKS CITED:

Busbin, O. Mell, *Dictionary of Literary Biography,* Volume 61: *American Writers for Children since 1960: Poets, Illustrators and Nonfiction Authors,* Gale, 1987, pp. 57-67.
Fisher, Leonard Everett, essay in *Something about the Author Autobiography Series,* Volume 1, Gale, 1986, pp. 89-113.
Fisher, Leonard Everett, "The Artist at Work: Creating Nonfiction," *Horn Book,* May-June, 1988, pp. 315-323.

FOR MORE INFORMATION SEE:

BOOKS

Children's Literature Review, Volume 18, Gale, 1989.
Daugherty, Charles M., *Six Artists Paint a Still Life,* North Light, 1977, pp. 10-29.
Hopkins, Lee Bennett, *More Books by More People,* Citation, 1971, pp. 159-164, 316.
Munce, Howard, editor, *Magic and Other Realism,* Hastings House, 1979, pp. 56-59.

PERIODICALS

American Artist, September, 1966, pp. 42-47, 67-70.
Catholic Library World, July-August, 1971.
Language Arts, March, 1982, pp. 224-230.
Publishers Weekly, February 26, 1982, pp. 62-63.

*   *   *

FITZHARDINGE, Joan Margaret 1912- (Joan Phipson)

PERSONAL: Born November 16, 1912, in Warrawee, New South Wales, Australia; married Colin Hardinge Fitzhardinge; children: Anna, Guy. *Education:* Frensham School, Mittagong, New South Wales, Australia.

ADDRESSES: Home—Wongalong, Mandurama, New South Wales 2792, Australia. *Agent*—A. P. Watt & Son, 20 John St., London WC1N 2DL, England.

CAREER: Author of children's books.

MEMBER: Australian Society of Authors.

AWARDS, HONORS: Children's Book Council of Australia Book of the Year Awards, 1953, for *Good Luck to the Rider,* and 1963, for *The Family Conspiracy;* Boys' Clubs of America Junior Book Award, 1963, for *The Boundary Riders;* New York Herald Tribune Children's Spring Book Festival Award, 1964, for *The Family Conspiracy;* Elizabethan Silver Medal for *Peter and Butch;* Writers Award, 1975, for *Helping Horse;* Honour Book Award, International Board on Books for Young People, 1985, for *The Watcher in the Garden.*

WRITINGS:

FICTION; UNDER PSEUDONYM JOAN PHIPSON

Good Luck to the Rider, illustrated by Margaret Horder, Angus & Robertson, 1952, Harcourt, 1968.

JOAN MARGARET FITZHARDINGE

Six and Silver, illustrated by Horder, Angus & Robertson, 1954, Harcourt, 1971.

It Happened One Summer, illustrated by Horder, Angus & Robertson, 1957.

The Boundary Riders, illustrated by Horder, Angus & Robertson, 1962, Harcourt, 1963, published with *The Family Conspiracy,* John Ferguson, 1981.

The Family Conspiracy, illustrated by Horder, Harcourt, 1962, published with *The Boundary Riders,* John Ferguson, 1981.

Threat to the Barkers, illustrated by Horder, Angus & Robertson 1963, Harcourt, 1965.

Birkin, illustrated by Horder, Harcourt, 1965.

A Lamb in the Family, illustrated by Lynette Hemmant, Hamish Hamilton, 1966.

The Crew of the "Merlin," illustrated by Janet Duchesne, Angus & Robertson, 1966, published as *Cross Currents,* Harcourt, 1967.

Peter and Butch, Longmans, 1969, Harcourt, 1970.

The Haunted Night, Harcourt, 1970.

Bass and Billy Martin, illustrated by Ron Brooks, Macmillan, 1972.

The Way Home, Atheneum, 1973.

Polly's Tiger, illustrated by Gavin Rowe, Hamish Hamilton, 1973, illustrated by Erik Blegvad, Dutton, 1974.

Helping Horse, Macmillan, 1974, published as *Horse with Eight Hands,* Atheneum, 1974.

The Cats, Macmillan, 1976, Atheneum, 1977.

Hide till Daytime, illustrated by Mary Dinsdale, Hamish Hamilton, 1977, Penguin, 1979.

Fly into Danger, Atheneum, 1978, published as *The Bird Smugglers,* Methuen, 1979.

When the City Stopped, Atheneum, 1978, published as *Keep Calm,* Macmillan, 1978.

Fly Free, Atheneum, 1979, published as *No Escape,* Macmillan, 1979.

Mr. Pringle and the Prince, illustrated by Michael Charlton, Hamish Hamilton, 1979.

A Tide Flowing, Atheneum, 1981.

The Watcher in the Garden, Atheneum, 1982.

Beryl the Rainmaker, illustrated by Laszlo Acs, Hamish Hamilton, 1984.

The Grannie Season, illustrated by Sally Holmes, Hamish Hamilton, 1985.

Dinko, Methuen, 1985.

Hit and Run, Atheneum, 1985.

Bianca, Atheneum, 1988.

The Shadow, Nelson, 1989.

OTHER; UNDER PSEUDONYM JOAN PHIPSON

Christmas in the Sun, illustrated by Horder, Angus & Robertson, 1951.

Bennelong, illustrated by Walter Stackpool, Collins, 1975.

Most of Fitzhardinge's books appear in Braille editions, and have been published in foreign editions in seven different languages.

ADAPTATIONS: The Boundary Riders, Fly into Danger, A Tide Flowing, Watcher in the Garden, Dinko, and *Hit and Run* have been recorded on audio cassette.

SIDELIGHTS: Joan Margaret Fitzhardinge, an award-winning children's novelist from Australia who writes as Joan Phipson, is widely acclaimed for her stories that accurately depict the Australian countryside and the people who live there. Ranging from her first novel, *Good Luck to the Rider,* which tells of a young girl raising a horse that no one else would love, to *The Watcher in the Garden,* in which two young misfits fall in love in a surreal garden, Fitzhardinge's stories show young people adjusting to difficult and often dangerous situations and in the process gaining confidence and learning to like themselves. Fitzhardinge earns praise from critics for her understanding and handling of the subject matter in a frank, realistic manner without resorting to unnecessary tragedy or melodrama.

Fitzhardinge traces her beginnings as a writer back to her very earliest childhood. She recalls in her autobiographical sketch for *Something about the Author Autobiography Series (SAAS)* that her father decided to move to Australia "on the strength of reading our classic novel about bushrangers, *Robbery under Arms.*" Fitzhardinge remembers having "a happy and eventful childhood, but a solitary one. And always I was an observer." It was this status as a spectator that Fitzhardinge credits most for her becoming a writer, for as a bystander she was able to soak up all the details of a situation that she could not as a participant.

Fitzhardinge certainly had many experiences to soak up. Her mother, who was homesick for England, brought her young daughter along on her many trips back and forth from England to Australia. Fitzhardinge jokes that by the time she was twenty-one she had been at sea long enough to apply for her Master's Ticket if only she could pass the examinations. During World War I she and her

Fitzhardinge, writing as Joan Phipson, combines suspense with her knowledge of the Australian bush in this novel about a teen whose joyride in a stolen car turns tragic. (Cover illustration by Gary Lang.)

mother went to live with her uncle in India, and there she was able to experience the joys of the wild firsthand, joys that were increased by her mother reading her stories by Rudyard Kipling. Fitzhardinge recalls in *SAAS* being "able to relate to *The Jungle Books* particularly because of the jackals that came nightly to scavenge our dog's bones, the leopard, always waiting during the hours of darkness to make a meal of the dog himself, and of the black panther my mother once saw lying on a rock in a clearing in the jungle."

Though Fitzhardinge always loved to read and felt that many of her best companions were books, she says in her autobiographical essay that her "real wish to write only returned after I was married and settled on a sheep and cattle property. It was not until after our daughter was born that I sat down one hot summer afternoon, pulled the typewriter towards me and, for want of something better to do, wrote a children's story." Her only guide was what she thought she would have enjoyed reading when she was nine years old. This story

was quickly published, and the publisher wrote back asking her if she would write another story for them. Fitzhardinge says, "Once a door of this kind opens before you, it takes a strong and perverse mind not to step through it." Since that time she has spent most of her life writing stories for children and young adults.

Fitzhardinge believes that she is successful as a children's writer because her childhood memories still live so strongly inside of her. "What I remembered was, not only the events, but the feelings and emotions they had caused in me, and it was this—the childish reaction to events—that, I am sure, was what stood by me," she explains in *SAAS*. These strong emotional memories, along with her vast experience with the settings in which her stories take place, allow Fitzhardinge to construct books with convincing characters and settings. A reviewer commenting on *Six and Silver* for *Junior Bookshelf* notes: "Most children enjoy recognizing their own everyday reactions in book-characters, but it takes a very perceptive author to make those reactions really recognizable, by attaching them to characters with a life of their own."

Some of Fitzhardinge's earlier books revolve around the members and close friends of a New South Wales family. In *The Family Conspiracy, Threat to the Barkers,* and *Good Luck to the Rider,* the main characters are often shunned and ignored by their peers for walking with a limp, being shy and timid, speaking with an accent, or simply for being unattractive. But as the stories progress, the characters display particular talents or abilities that win them the confidence and the admiration of others. In *The Boundary Riders,* Bobby,

One of several books concerning a New South Wales family, *The Family Conspiracy* shows the determination of the Barker children to earn enough money to pay for their sick mother's operation. (Illustration by Margaret Horder.)

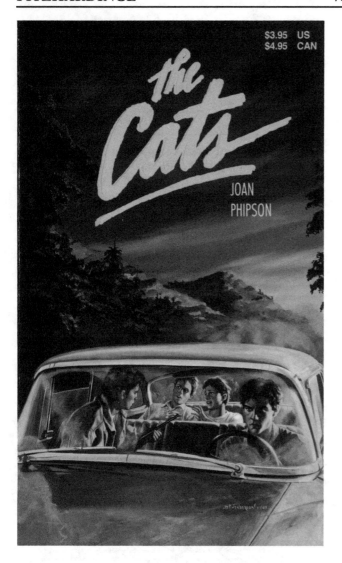

$3.95 US
$4.95 CAN

JOAN
PHIPSON

The Australian outback plays a pivotal role in this thriller about a kidnapping gone awry. (Cover illustration by Dave Henderson.)

an awkward, unattractive eleven-year-old, and his older, more confident cousin Vincent find themselves lost in the Australian bush. As the story progresses Vincent's bravado flags and only Bobby's resourcefulness and courage allow the two to find their way home. This conversion from outcast to respected member often occurs because the character is able to adapt to and function in the natural world.

In her more recent works, Fitzhardinge has depicted slightly older children in more suspenseful and often fantastic tales. *The Way Home* is the tale of three children who, after a car wreck in the Australian countryside, find themselves lost in both time and space. Two of the children are able to adapt but one of the children, who according to a *Times Literary Supplement* reviewer "was too rational and hadn't enough contact with Mother Earth," dies. In *The Watcher in the Garden,* a hilltop garden tended by the blind Mr. Lovett becomes the setting for the allegorical tale of the reconciliation of two teenagers who initially despise each other. Terry, a young criminal, and Kitty, a hot-

tempered fifteen-year-old, are both knocked unconscious and the garden's powers allow them to communicate telepathically and bridge their differences. Gale Eaton, in her review of the book for *School Library Journal,* says, "This novel is serious, exciting and nearly a masterpiece." Though the stories are set in more modern situations, it is still closeness to the earth and resourcefulness that allows the characters to gain confidence in themselves and each other.

Fitzhardinge states in *SAAS:* "I am glad I write books for children. Perhaps I should now say, 'young people,' for some of those I write are intended for teenagers. It keeps me in a world where all those who write and distribute books have the same aim: to open a world of fun, pleasure, consolation, and wisdom to those who are beginning life and who will find life so much richer for being part of this ageless inheritance."

WORKS CITED:

Eaton, Gale, review of *The Watcher in the Garden,* *School Library Journal,* November, 1982, p. 89.
Phipson, Joan, *Something about the Author Autobiographical Series,* Volume 3, Gale, 1987, pp. 205-219.
Review of *Six and Silver, Junior Bookshelf,* July, 1955, pp. 152-53.
"Testing Quests," *Times Literary Supplement,* September 28, 1973, p. 1114.

FOR MORE INFORMATION SEE:

BOOKS

Children's Literature Review, Volume 5, Gale, 1983.
McVitty, Walter, *Innocence and Experience: Essays on Contemporary Australian Children's Writers,* Nelson, 1981.
Nieuwenhuizen, Agnes, *No Kidding,* Macmillan, 1991.
Ronai, Kay, compiler, *All the Best,* Puffin, 1989.

PERIODICALS

New York Times Book Review, May 9, 1965; November 21, 1976.
Saturday Review, April 22, 1967.
Times Educational Supplement, July 29, 1983; January 9, 1987; January 16, 1987.
Times Literary Supplement, June 17, 1965; November 24, 1966; June 26, 1969; September 20, 1974; October 1, 1976; September 29, 1978; December 14, 1979; March 28, 1980; March 30, 1984; September 7, 1984.

*   *   *

FOREMAN, Michael 1938-

PERSONAL: Born March 21, 1938, in Pakefield, Suffolk, England; son of Walter Thomas (a crane operator) and Gladys (Goddard) Foreman; married Janet Charters, September 26, 1959 (divorced, 1966); married Louise Phillips, 1980; children: (first marriage) Mark; (second marriage) Ben Shahn, Jack. *Education:* Lowestoft School of Art, National Diploma in Design (painting), 1958; Royal College of Art, A.R.C.A. (with first honors), 1963.

ADDRESSES: Home—5 Church Gate, London SW6, England. *Agent*—John Locke, 15 East 76th St., New York, NY 10021.

CAREER: Graphic artist, children's author. Lecturer in graphics at St. Martin's School of Art, London, England, 1963-66, London College of Printing, 1966-68, Royal College of Art, London, 1968-70, and Central School of Art, London, 1971-72. Art director of *Ambit*, 1960—, *Playboy*, 1965, and *King*, 1966-67. *Exhibitions:* Individual show, Royal Festival Hall, London, 1985; retrospective shows in London, 1989, and Paris, France, 1991. Works exhibited in Europe, the United States, and Japan.

AWARDS, HONORS: Schweppes traveling scholarship to United States, 1961-63; Gimpel Fils Prize for young painters, 1962; Silver Eagle Award, Festival International du Livre, 1972; Francis Williams Memorial Award, Victoria and Albert Museum, 1972 and 1977, for *Monkey and the Three Wizards;* Kate Greenaway Commendation, British Library Association, 1978, for *The Brothers Grimm: Popular Folk Tales;* Carnegie Medal, British Library Association, 1980, Kate Greenaway Commendation, 1980, and Graphics Prize, International Children's Book Fair, 1982, for *City of Gold and Other Stories from the Old Testament;* Kate Greenaway Medal and Kurt Maschler/Emil Award, Book Trust of England, both 1982, for *Sleeping Beauty and Other Favourite Fairy Tales;* Kate Greenaway Medal, 1982, for *Longneck and Thunderfoot;* Federation of Children's

MICHAEL FOREMAN

Book Groups award, 1983, for *The Saga of Erik the Viking;* Kate Greenaway Commendation and *New York Times* Notable Book designation, both 1985, for *Seasons of Splendour: Tales, Myths and Legends of India;* Kate Greenaway Medal, 1990, for *War Boy: A Country Childhood.*

WRITINGS:

SELF-ILLUSTRATED

The Perfect Present, Coward, 1967.
The Two Giants, Pantheon, 1967.
The Great Sleigh Robbery, Hamish Hamilton, 1968, Pantheon, 1969.
Horatio, Hamish Hamilton, 1970, published as *The Travels of Horatio,* Pantheon, 1970.
Moose, Hamish Hamilton, 1971, Pantheon, 1972.
Dinosaurs and All That Rubbish, Hamish Hamilton, 1972, Crowell, 1973.
War and Peas, Crowell, 1974.
All the King's Horses, Hamish Hamilton, 1976, Bradbury, 1977.
Panda's Puzzle, and His Voyage of Discovery, Hamish Hamilton, 1977, Bradbury, 1978.
Panda and the Odd Lion, Hamish Hamilton, 1979.
Trick a Tracker, Philomel, 1981.
Land of Dreams, Holt, 1982.
Panda and the Bunyips, Hamish Hamilton, 1984, Schocken, 1988.
Cat and Canary, Andersen, 1984, Dial, 1985.
Panda and the Bushfire, Prentice-Hall, 1986.
Ben's Box, Hodder & Stoughton, 1986.
Ben's Baby (picture book), Andersen, 1987, Harper, 1988.
The Angel and the Wild Animal, Andersen, 1988, Atheneum, 1989.
One World, Andersen, 1990.
War Boy: A Country Childhood, Arcade, 1990.
(Editor) *Michael Foreman's Mother Goose,* foreword by Iona Opie, Harcourt, 1991.
The Boy Who Sailed with Columbus, Pavilion, 1991.
(Editor) *Michael Foreman's World of Fairy Tales,* Arcade, 1991.
Jack's Fantastic Voyage, Andersen, 1992.
Grandfather's Pencil and the Room of Dreams, Andersen, 1993.
War Game, Pavilion, 1993.

ILLUSTRATOR

Janet Charters, *The General,* Dutton, 1961.
Cledwyn Hughes, *The King Who Lived on Jelly,* Routledge & Kegan Paul, 1963.
Eric Partridge, *Comic Alphabets,* Routledge & Kegan Paul, 1964.
Derek Cooper, *The Bad Food Guide,* Routledge & Kegan Paul, 1966.
Leonore Klein, *Huit enfants et un bebe,* Abelard, 1966.
Mabel Watts, *I'm for You, You're for Me,* Abelard, 1967.
Sergei Vladimirovich Mikalkov, *Let's Fight!, and Other Russian Fables,* Pantheon, 1968.
William Ivan Martin, *Adam's Balm,* Bowmar, 1970.
C. O. Alexander, *Fisher v. Spassky,* Penguin, 1972.

Foreman began a long and fruitful partnership with actor-director Terry Jones with 1981's *Terry Jones' Fairy Tales.* (Illustration by Foreman).

William Fagg, editor, *The Living Arts of Nigeria,* Studio Vista, 1972.

Barbara Adachi, *The Living Treasures of Japan,* Wildwood House, 1973.

Janice Elliott, *Alexander in the Land of Mog,* Brockhampton Press, 1973.

Elliott, *The Birthday Unicorn,* Penguin, 1973.

Sheila Burnford, *Noah and the Second Flood,* Gollancz, 1973.

Jane H. Yolen, *Rainbow Rider,* Crowell, 1974.

Georgess McHargue, *Private Zoo,* Viking, 1975.

Barbara K. Walker, *Teeny-Tiny and the Witch-Woman,* Pantheon, 1975.

Cheng-en Wu, *Monkey and the Three Wizards,* translated by Peter Harris, Collins & World, 1976.

Alan Garner, *The Stone Book,* Collins & World, 1976.

Garner, *Tom Fobble's Day,* Collins & World, 1976.

Garner, *Granny Reardun,* Collins & World, 1977.

Hans Christian Andersen, *Hans Christian Andersen: His Classic Fairy Tales,* translated by Erik Haugaard, Gollancz, 1977.

K. Bauman, *Kitchen Stories,* Nord Sud, 1977, published as *Mickey's Kitchen Contest,* Andersen, 1978.

Garner, *The Aimer Gate,* Collins & World, 1978.

Bryna Stevens, reteller, *Borrowed Feathers and Other Fables,* Random House, 1978.

Brian Alderson, translator, *The Brothers Grimm: Popular Folk Tales,* Gollancz, 1978.

Oscar Wilde, *The Selfish Giant,* Kaye & Ward, 1978.

Seven in One Blow, Random House, 1978.

Garner, *Fairy Tales of Gold,* Volume 1: *The Golden Brothers,* Volume 2: *The Girl of the Golden Gate,* Volume 3: *The Three Golden Heads of the Well,* Volume 4: *The Princess and the Golden Mane,* Collins & World, 1979.

Bill Martin, *How to Catch a Ghost,* Holt, 1979.

Anthony Paul, *The Tiger Who Lost His Stripes,* Andersen Press, 1980.

Ernest Hemingway, *The Faithful Bull,* Emme Italia, 1980.

Aldous Huxley, *After Many a Summer,* Folio Society, 1980.

Allen Andrews, *The Pig Plantagenet,* Hutchinson, 1980.

Peter Dickenson, *City of Gold, and Other Tales from the Old Testament,* Gollancz, 1980.

Terry Jones, *Terry Jones' Fairy Tales,* Pavilion, 1981, Puffin, 1986.

John Loveday, editor, *Over the Bridge,* Penguin, 1981.

Robert McCrum, *The Magic Mouse and the Millionaire,* Hamish Hamilton, 1981.

Rudyard Kipling, *The Crab That Played with the Sea: A Just So Story,* Macmillan, 1982.

Angela Carter, selector and translator, *Sleeping Beauty and Other Favourite Fairy Tales,* Gollancz, 1982, Schocken, 1984.

Helen Piers, *Longneck and Thunderfoot,* Kestrel, 1982.

McCrum, *The Brontosaurus Birthday Cake,* Hamish Hamilton, 1982.

Jones, *The Saga of Erik the Viking,* Pavilion, 1983, Puffin, 1986.

Charles Dickens, *A Christmas Carol,* Dial, 1983.

Nanette Newman, *A Cat and Mouse Love Story,* Heinemann, 1983.

Robert Louis Stevenson, *Treasure Island,* Penguin, 1983.

Kit Wright, editor, *Poems for 9-Year-Olds and Under,* Puffin, 1984.

Helen Nicoll, editor, *Poems for 7-Year-Olds and Under,* Puffin, 1984.

Wright, editor, *Poems for 10-Year-Olds and Over,* Puffin, 1985.

Roald Dahl, *Charlie and the Chocolate Factory,* Puffin, 1985.

Madhur Jaffrey, *Seasons of Splendour: Tales, Myths and Legends of India,* Pavilion, 1985.

McCrum, *Brontosaurus Superstar,* Hamish Hamilton, 1985.

Leon Garfield, *Shakespeare Stories,* Gollancz, 1985, Houghton, 1991.

William McGonagall, *Poetic Gems,* Folio Society, 1985.

Stevenson, *A Child's Garden of Verses,* Delacorte, 1985.

Nigel Gray, *I'll Take You to Mrs Cole!* (picture book), Bergh, 1986, Kane/Miller, 1992.

Edna O'Brien, *Tales for the Telling: Irish Folk and Fairy Tales,* Pavilion, 1986, Puffin, 1988.

Eric Quayle, *The Magic Ointment, and Other Cornish Legends,* Andersen, 1986.

Jones, *Nicobobinus,* Pavilion, 1986.

Michael Moorcock, *Letters from Hollywood,* Harrap, 1986.

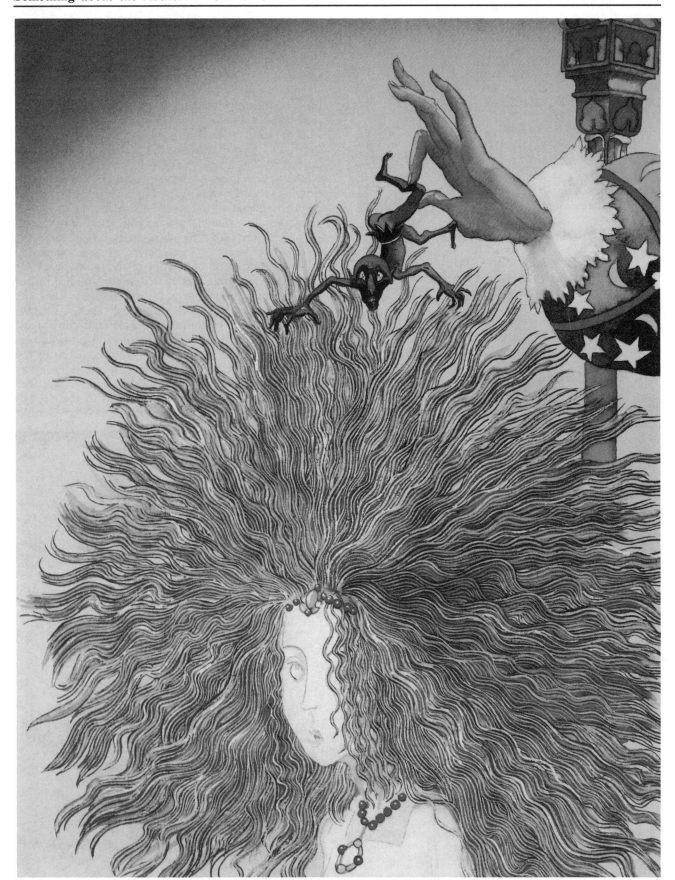

Foreman's watercolors brilliantly bring to life Jones's tale of a fantastic voyage in *The Saga of Erik the Viking*.

Charles Causley, *Early in the Morning,* Kestrel, 1986, Viking, 1987.

Kipling, *Just So Stories,* Kestrel, 1987.

Kipling, *The Jungle Book,* Kestrel, 1987.

Jan Mark, *Fun,* Gollancz, 1987, Viking, 1988.

Daphne du Maurier, *Classics of the Macabre,* Gollancz, 1987.

Clement C. Moore, *The Night before Christmas,* Viking, 1988.

Jones, *The Curse of the Vampire's Socks,* Pavilion, 1988.

J. M. Barrie, *Peter Pan and Wendy,* Pavilion, 1988.

Martin Bax, *Edmond Went Far Away,* Harcourt, 1989.

David Pelham, *Worms Wiggle,* Simon & Schuster, 1989.

Eric Quayle, editor, *The Shining Princess and Other Japanese Legends,* Arcade, 1989.

Ann Turnbull, *The Sand Horse,* Macmillan, 1989.

Johnathan Shipton, *Busy Busy Busy,* Andersen, 1990.

Kiri Te Kanawa, *Land of the Long White Cloud,* Arcade, 1990.

Alderson, translator, *The Arabian Nights,* Gollancz, 1992.

Nanette Newman, *Spider the Horrible Cat,* Pavilion, 1992.

Mary Rayner, *The Echoing Green,* Penguin Viking, 1992.

Troon Harrison, *The Long Weekend,* Andersen, 1993.

Also illustrator of *Making Music* by Gwen Clemens, 1966; *Essex Poems* by Donald Davie, 1969; *The Birthday Unicorn* by Janet Elliott, 1970; *The Pushcart War* by Jean Merrill, 1976; *The Nightingale and the Rose* by Oscar Wilde, 1981; and *The Young Man of Cury* by Charles Causley, Macmillan.

OTHER

Winter's Tales, illustrated by Freire Wright, Doubleday, 1979.

Also creator of animated films for television in England and Scandinavia.

SIDELIGHTS: Noted British artist Michael Foreman draws upon his real-life experiences in writing and illustrating his many books for children. Winner of numerous awards for his imaginative watercolor depictions of fact and fantasy, Foreman has been a prolific illustrator of the text of others, including authors Leon Garfield, Jean Merrill, Oscar Wilde, Roald Dahl, and Terry Jones. His collaboration with fellow British author Jones—of Monty Python fame—has resulted in several books, including *The Curse of the Vampire Socks, Nicobobinus,* the off-the-wall *Terry Jones' Fairy Tales,* and the award-winning *Saga of Eric the Viking.*

"I was born in a fishing village on the east coast [of England] and grew up there during the war," Foreman once wrote. "My first book, *The General,* was set there and the local people recognize the church, the ice cream hut, and other scenes in the pictures. By the time *The General* was published [in 1961], I was living in London and my second book, *The Perfect Present,* contained many London scenes. Since then I have been to many parts of the world and the sketches I bring back become the backgrounds for new books. *Rainbow Rider* is set in New Mexico and Arizona, for example, *Panda and the Odd Lion* in Africa and Venice."

Foreman turned to his native England as inspiration for *War Boy: A Country Childhood,* which was honored with the Kate Greenaway Medal in 1990. A memoir of Foreman's own experiences as a young boy living in England during World War II—his childhood village of Pakefield lies closer to Germany than any other town in Britain—*War Boy* was praised by reviewer Christopher Lehmann-Haupt of the *New York Times:* "Though his memories are haunted by enemy bombers and V1 and V2 rockets, the author recalls in delicate watercolors the many joys of being a shopkeeper's child under siege: the licorice comforts that left your teeth stained black, or the millions of flower seeds that were exploded out of gardens and showered around the district so that 'the following spring and summer, piles of rubble burst into bloom.'" From the bombing of Pakefield one August night in 1941, to the anti-tank blocks, gun-emplacements, and sea defenses which "stretched as far as the eye could see along the beach," from the soldiers stationed nearby who taught him their colorful language and filled his mother's corner shop with their rough humor and high spirits to boyhood friends like "Squirt"

Dragons soar in this scene from Jones's *Nicobobinus*.

People gave up carrying masks after a few months. We were taught to spit on the inside of the mica window to prevent it misting up. Gas masks were good for rude noises and fogged up anyway.

Foreman combined illustrations with actual wartime graphics to create a child's-eye view of England in World War II— and earned his second Greenaway Medal for illustration.

the fireman's son and "Wimps .... [who] was admired for eating horse dung, in the road, for a bet," *War Boy* contains a vivid sense of everyday life in war-torn England. *School Library Journal* reviewer Phyllis G. Sidorsky comments: "Foreman's recollections are sharp and graphic as he poignantly recalls the servicemen who crowded into his mother's shop, grateful for her welcoming cup of tea and a place to chat." Throughout the book, Foreman juxtaposes his moving pen-and-ink and watercolor illustrations with evacuation notices, cigarette cards, military diagrams, and other period publications. "The memory of those who passed through our village on the way to war will remain forever with the ghosts of us children in the fields and woods of long ago," he writes, ending his journey back to his childhood as homemade Hitlers are set ablaze on VJ Day, and the war is over.

Foreman obtains much of his inspiration, not only for illustrations but for the plots of his children's stories, from his travels around the world. In addition to numerous trips to the United States, he has traveled extensively throughout both Europe and the North African continent, viewed Siberia by railway on his way to Japan, and visited Australia and the Far East. "Sometimes the story is about travelling to many places, as with *Horatio* or *Trick a Tracker*. Occasionally, I get the idea for a story while travelling, but usually it takes a long time to get the right place, the right story, and the right character to meet." In *Cat and Canary,* all three ingredients are present, as artist/illustrator Foreman concocts a fanciful tale of a housebound cat who longs to take flight with a flock of pigeons and soar above the streets of New York City. Jennifer Taylor describes the book in *Twentieth-Century Children's Writers* as "a fantasy set against the glimmering skyline of New York as Cat is blown about at the end of a kite high above the streets—the opportunity for some dazzling perspectives."

Much of Foreman's time is spent creating illustrations for the work of other writers: "The subject matter varies

Foreman conveys the excitement of a little boy seeing soldiers on the march in *War Boy*.

from the Bible to Shakespeare to stories set in contemporary Britain or the future. My own books are never really about a place or country, but about an idea which is hopefully common to the dreams of everyone, one which works best, however, against a particular background." In his own version of the Mother Goose nursery rhymes—*Michael Foreman's Mother Goose,* published in 1991—Foreman assembles an elaborate series of colorfully-painted pictorial jokes. His depiction of such characters as Jack and Jill and the Grand Old Duke of York have caused Brian Alderson to comment on the work as "a wonderful exhibition of self-assured draughtmanship, with the artist totally in control of everything from dead pigs to dancing frogs," as the critic writes in the London *Times.*

"My books are not intended for any particular age group," Foreman once told *SATA,* "but the type is large and inviting for young readers who like to explore the pages after the story has been read to them. In addition I want the story to have some relevance for the adult reader. Less a question of age," he added. "More a state of mind."

WORKS CITED:

Alderson, Brian, "Reeling out the Rhymes," *Times* (London), August 29, 1991, p. 14.
Foreman, Michael, *War Boy: A Country Childhood,* Arcade, 1990.
Lehmann-Haupt, Christopher, "Presents of Words, Pictures and Imagination," *New York Times,* December 3, 1990.
Sidorsky, Phyllis G., review of *War Boy: A Country Childhood, School Library Journal,* May, 1990, p. 116.
Taylor, Jennifer, "Michael Foreman," *Twentieth-Century Children's Writers,* 3rd edition, St. James Press, 1989, pp. 355-356.

FOR MORE INFORMATION SEE:

BOOKS

Kingman, Lee, *Illustrators of Children's Books, 1967-1976,* Horn Book, 1977.

PERIODICALS

Graphis, number 197, 1977.
Isis, November, 1966.
New Statesman, November 27, 1987, p. 34.

New York Times Book Review, April 28, 1985, p. 26; November 11, 1990, p. 38.

Times Educational Supplement, November 14, 1986, p. 41; March 11, 1988, p. 24; June 3, 1988, p. 46; October 13, 1989, p. 28; September 21, 1990, p. R22.

Times Literary Supplement, November 26, 1982; September 7, 1984, p. 1006; November 30, 1984, p. 1379; June 6, 1986, p. 630; November 25, 1988, p. 1321; August 3, 1990, p. 833.

Washington Post Book World, September 11, 1988, p. 9; July 9, 1989, p. 10.

*   *   *

FOSTER, Leila Merrell 1929-

PERSONAL: Born February 27, 1929, in Richmond, VA; daughter of George Henry (a farm equipment dealer) and Leila (a homemaker; maiden name, Merrell) Foster. *Education:* Northwestern University, B.S., 1950, J.D., 1953, Ph.D., 1966; Garrett Theological Seminary, M.Div., 1964. *Religion:* United Methodist.

ADDRESSES: Home and office—1585 Ridge Ave., Evanston, IL 60201.

CAREER: Admitted to the Bar of Illinois, 1953; ordained United Methodist minister, 1964. Sidley, Austin, Burgess, & Smith (law firm), Chicago, IL, associate lawyer, 1953-61; United Methodist Church, Northern Illinois Conference, pastor, 1962-73; Garrett Theological Seminary, Evanston, IL, visiting lecturer, 1969-70; West Side V.A. Medical Center, Chicago, clinical psychologist, 1971-87; psychologist in private practice and writer in Evanston, 1971—. Docent at the Oriental Institute.

MEMBER: American Psychological Association (fellow), American Board of Medical Psychotherapists (fellow and diplomate), Association for the Advancement of Psychology (trustee, 1980-86), National Organization of Veterans Administration Psychologists (president, 1982-83), National Register of Health Service Providers in Psychology, American Bar Association, American Academy of Religion, Society of Biblical Literature, Association for Clinical Pastoral Education, Archaeological Institute of America, Biblical Archaeological Society, Society of Children's Book Writers, Illinois Psychological Association, Illinois State Bar Association, Chicago Bar Association, Children's Reading Round Table of Chicago, Zonta Club of Evanston (president, 1982-83).

WRITINGS:

FOR CHILDREN

Bhutan, Children's Press, 1989.
The Cold War, Children's Press, 1990.
Margaret Thatcher: First Woman Prime Minister of Great Britain, Children's Press, 1990.
Rachel Carson, Children's Press, 1990.
The Sumerians, F. Watts, 1990.

Admiral David Glasgow Farragut, Children's Press, 1991.
Iraq, Children's Press, 1991.
Jordan, Children's Press, 1991.
The Story of the Great Society, Children's Press, 1991.
The Story of the Persian Gulf War, Children's Press, 1991.
Lebanon, Children's Press, 1992.
Nien Cheng, Children's Press, 1992.

OTHER

(With Herman Schuchman) *Confidentiality* (videotape), American Orthopsychiatric Association, 1982.

Contributor of numerous articles on psychological, legal, and religious issues to professional journals.

WORK IN PROGRESS: Saudi Arabia, Kuwait, and *Oman,* all for Children's Press.

SIDELIGHTS: Leila Merrell Foster told *SATA:* "Because of my opportunities serving as a lawyer, minister, and psychologist and of traveling extensively, I enjoy a broad range of interests. As a child, I was encouraged to read widely. Now I have the opportunity of writing about many subjects to share with others."

LEILA MERRELL FOSTER

FOX, Geoffrey 1941-

PERSONAL: Born April 3, 1941, in Chicago, IL; son of Oswald Irvin (an Illinois Bell Telephone Company executive) and Dorothy (an actress and homemaker; maiden name, Knickerbocker) Fox; married Sylvia Herrera, 1966 (divorced, 1975); married Susana Torre (an architect), October 5, 1979; children: Alexander Fox, Joaquin Fox-Herrera. *Education:* Harvard University, B.A., 1963; Northwestern University, Ph.D., 1975. *Politics:* Radical democrat. *Religion:* "Pantheist. I accept authenticity of any god that humans invent."

ADDRESSES: Home and office—14 East 4th St., Rm. 812, New York, NY 10012. *Agent*—Colleen Mohyde, Doe Coover Agency, 58 Sagamore Ave., Medford, MA 02155.

CAREER: Author and editor. Universidad de Puerto Rico, Rio Piedras, instructor, 1966-67; University of Illinois at Chicago Circle, lecturer, 1970-75; Ohio Wesleyan University, Delaware, OH, assistant professor, 1976-77; St. John's University, Collegeville, MN, and College of St. Benedict, St. Joseph, MN, assistant professor, 1977-79. Held adjunct positions at New School for Social Research, 1980, 1992, Montclair State College, 1980-81, Empire State Labor College, 1980-85,

GEOFFREY FOX

Boricua College, 1981, Cornell University, 1982-84, New York University School of Continuing Education, 1985-89, and Roosevelt High School, Bronx, New York, 1988-89.

MEMBER: Authors Guild, Authors League of America, National Writers Union, Latin American Studies Association.

AWARDS, HONORS: Notable Book Citation, National Council of Social Studies/Children's Book Council, 1990, for *The Land and People of Argentina*; "Books for the Teen Age" citation, New York Public Library, 1991, for *The Land and People of Venezuela*.

WRITINGS:

Working-Class Emigres from Cuba, R & E Research Associates, 1979.
Gabriel Garcia Marquez's "100 Years of Solitude": A Critical Commentary, Simon & Schuster, 1987.
Welcome to My Contri (short stories), Hudson View Press, 1988.
The Land and People of Argentina, Harper, 1990.
The Land and People of Venezuela, HarperCollins, 1991.

Also associate editor, *Cuba Update*, 1981-83; executive editor, *Hispanic Monitor*, 1984-85; contributing editor, *Between the Lines*, 1988-90; editor of articles for *NACLA Report on the Americas*. Contributor to periodicals, including *Cuba Update, Development Forum, Hispanic Monitor, Nation, New Internationalist, New York Times,* and *Village Voice.*

WORK IN PROGRESS: Hispanic Nation, a book about U.S. Hispanics, to be completed in the fall of 1993.

SIDELIGHTS: Geoffrey Fox told *SATA:* "The earliest adventures I remember were in the forest and mountains of Dumont, New Jersey, where we lived for a year when I was five or six. The mountains were dirt hills built up each day by roaring and clanking bulldozers, as they scooped up loam from the holes they'd carved for the basements of new houses. Soldiers were coming home from World War II then and looking for homes, and houses were going up all over. Scraps of wood scattered about the construction sites were perfect for making toy airplanes and guns, and with these my playmates and I assaulted the enemies—invisible to all but us—lurking in the mountains. I loved the smell of that black dirt, and was always sure to bring plenty of it home on my face and hands and in my shoes and the cuffs of my jeans.

"The forest was really a tiny grove of saplings that the bulldozers had not yet reached and where a boy could wander and daydream, practice being an Indian or Robin Hood, gather berries and watch for birds, catch polliwogs that skittered across a scummy pond, and wonder about the connections among all these things. The leaves were gray-green and about the size of my hand, with a pungent odor and bitter taste, and when I broke a branch from a sapling, the yellowish white

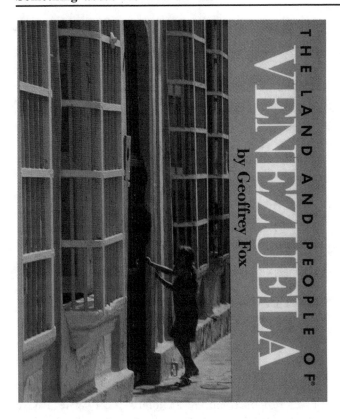

Fox's post-college travels to Caracas, where he helped improve impoverished neighborhoods, formed the basis for *The Land and People of Venezuela.* (Cover photograph by Gabriel Gazso.)

wound of the broken fibers smelled especially sharp and fresh.

"Years later I found myself on other hills, much higher than those of my boyhood, where the soil was red and smelled of iron, like a rusty nail. The plants had huge, broad green leaves, brilliant colors, and powerful aromas that I'd known before only in flower shops or perfume stores. I was in Caracas, Venezuela. Houses were going up on all these hills, too, but they were simple places made of panels of compressed cardboard, the sides of wooden crates and sheets of corrugated metal, built on terraces carved out of the hillside by the families that were going to live there. These people were not coming back from a war, but escaping high rents in the older slums of the city, and just trying to make their lives a little better. They laughed and joked and argued and flirted in a language I had never studied and seldom heard—Spanish.

"I went to Caracas in 1963, right after college, because I wanted to do something for the poorer people of the world, and because I was looking for real adventures. Even in grade school I'd become deeply troubled about injustice, such as bullies picking on little kids. Later the independence movements in Africa and Asia, the Cuban revolution, and the war in Indochina made me and other high school and college students aware of injustice worldwide. The civil rights movement at home, where ordinary, unarmed folks stood up to police clubs and

firehoses, dogs, Klansmen's shotguns, and the vicious hate of mobs, showed us it was possible for people to take action to change the world.

"In the organization ACCION en Venezuela, my job was to help the people in the shantytowns get organized to improve their lives and their neighborhoods. I learned Spanish quickly, and made many good Venezuelan friends. With pick and shovel and wheelbarrow, we worked shoulder to shoulder to build useful things like cement stairways, roads, and water and sewer lines. These were wonderful experiences, and they have shaped my writing ever since.

"In my books I try to make my readers see, feel, hear, and smell the things that I did, and especially to care about the people as much as I do. I discovered that this was almost impossible to do in my sociological articles, which had to leave out most of the description, and I began writing fiction. But in fiction, it is harder to make your readers understand how the situation your characters are in got created in the first place. I loved writing *The Land and People of Argentina* and *The Land and People of Venezuela,* because I could combine both things.

For his entries in the "Land and People of..." series, the author combines physical descriptions of the country with portraits of its inhabitants in an attempt to make readers feel they have been on actual visit. (Cover photograph by Eduardo Longoni.)

"Readers may not notice, but both these books have a 'plot,' a central theme or storyline that connects the chapters on the geography and the animals, music and literature, with those on history and economics. In my book on Argentina, the central story is the conflict between poor people seeking every opportunity to get away from the control of bosses and oppressive governments, and those trying to control and discipline them. The wide pampas, the great distances of open country between settlements, the abundance of cattle and horses after the first years of colonization, all made it easier for men and women to escape the towns and become gauchos—poor, violent, and free—whom the better-off people in the towns tried to subdue. The conflict between anarchy and authoritarianism has taken different forms but continues today, and has influenced the music, the literature, and the art.

"The story of Venezuela is of a different kind, partly because of different geography. It is about the three ethnic groups—Indians, Europeans, and Africans—who came together there because of the climate, the fertility of the valleys, and the country's location as the closest part of South America to Spain, and how, after many struggles and much bloodshed, they have become one people, their three cultural traditions combining to make something new and, as a Venezuelan might say, *sabroso* (flavorful).

"I am now working on an adult book, on the Hispanics of the United States, and writing more fiction, but I continue to be involved in young readers' projects, with introductory essays of one or possibly two new books from Henry Holt Publishers scheduled soon."

*　　*　　*

FROIS, Jeanne 1953-

PERSONAL: Born August 22, 1953, in New Orleans, LA; daughter of Cyril Joseph (a homicide detective) and Etta (O'Rourke) Frois. *Education:* Attended University of New Orleans, Delgado Community College, and Children's Institute of Literature.

ADDRESSES: Office—6660 Riverside Dr., Suite 203, Metairie, LA 70003.

CAREER: Head Start Poverty Program, Los Angeles, CA, assistant parent involvement coordinator, 1972-74; Humana Hospital, Marksville, LA, marketing and social services representative, 1987; Association of Catholic Charities, New Orleans, LA, assistant to director, 1987-89; River Bend Hospital, Metairie, LA, medical staff coordinator and assistant to administrator, 1991-92; writer.

MEMBER: Faulkner Society, American Society for the Prevention of Cruelty to Animals, Humane Society, National Association of Medical Staff Coordinators.

WRITINGS:

Louisianians All, Pelican Publishing, 1992.

Contributor to periodicals and newspapers, including *Southern Living, Old House Journal, Thema Literary Journal,* and *New Orleans Times Picayune.*

WORK IN PROGRESS: Researching and writing a novel about a young, "eccentric" girl set around the time of the fall of Vicksburg during the Civil War.

SIDELIGHTS: Jeanne Frois told *SATA:* "I was born to a family of book lovers and readers. My mother, aunts, and grandmother were generally found buried in books and newspapers at the end of the day, when their work was finished. I remember spending one dreary, rainy afternoon with my mother before the fireplace in our living room, while she read the entire text of *The Rime of the Ancient Mariner* out loud to me. How it suited that grey Sunday! Likewise, I remember spending one cold, rainy, Easter-in-March weekend on my great-grandmother's farm, slouched in a rocking chair before the fireplace in the kitchen, my thirteen-year-old mind held captive by Harper Lee's *To Kill a Mockingbird.*

"As I grew older, books became an almost natural extension of my hand. I read them on trips, took them with me to the bathtub, bed, and supper table. In the middle of teenage social functions, I'd think longingly of the good book I had left at home. And I wrote. I have always written. Through grammar school and high school, while heavily involved in art and dramatics, I also wrote stories and poems for my friends. I never once dreamed I wrote anything worth publishing, even when a published author read one of my stories and told me it was good enough to publish.... Eventually, I threw that story away. I wish I had kept it now. It was

JEANNE FROIS

only after I was well into my late twenties that I began to think my writing might be worth publishing.

"Sometimes I feel I owe the beginning of my published writing career to buses and public transportation. I once wrote an editorial to the local newspaper, complaining about the shoddy treatment the handicapped received on our local public transportation system. The day my letter was printed, the local evening news programs were filled with interviews of handicapped people who had legitimate complaints about [this problem] in New Orleans. They had come forward, and conditions improved for them greatly. The pen was mightier than the sword!"

Frois continued, citing a more personal, bus-related accident: "One morning, as I was running to catch a bus, I tripped on a curb, fell face down on a highway, and tore several ligaments in my ankle. In the ensuing immobile recovery time of three weeks, I one day hobbled into bed, drew my little dog upon my lap, and wrote a remembrance of my days spent on [my grandmother's farm]. I called it 'The Mulberry Tree,' and on a spur-of-the-moment whim, sent it to *Southern Living* magazine for consideration of publication. Six weeks later, I received a letter of acceptance and the offer to buy the story for $1,000. It was my first acceptance. I cried like a baby.

"The day I was commissioned to write my first book, *Louisianians All,* was one of the happiest of my life," Frois revealed, adding: "Especially when I was told about the nature of the project. The publisher wished to bequeath a legacy to the young people of the state of Louisiana regarding their heritage. He wanted to tell the little-heard stories about the heroes of the state, who came from all ethnic origins and religious backgrounds—French, Spanish, Greek, German, Jewish, African-American, Cajun. For a year I spent time in libraries, talked with professors and historians, and immersed myself in each person, usually long-dead, about whom I was writing. Working full time in a hospital, I wrote the book on weekends and at night. Sometimes I rose at two or three in the morning when the deadline was looming ahead. One night, dangerously close to the submission date, I wrote three chapters.

"What struck me about [the heroes included in *Louisianians All*] was the fact that they were all ordinary people who had at some point in their lives been defeated, but recovered in triumph. They were made stronger by pain, and determined to see that others would be spared the suffering they had known—either through medicine, art, writing, or charitable deeds. I discovered we live with a great deal of historical misconception, not only in Louisiana, but the entire nation.

"My experiences as a writer have taken me on a personal odyssey that has both educated and improved me in many ways. As a writer, I want to share, to do justice to a person, place, or thing—a scene, a sunset, an expression. I try to give something back by writing—a kind of thank you note for seeing something beautiful, hearing about an act of nobility, or clearing up an injustice. When I write, I hear rhythm in my mind, a kind of fantasy drum beat to which I want to adapt my idea to the music of words.

"Coming from the South, I have been made aware of a supreme irony—the South has produced some of the finest writers in the world, and yet it ranks highest in the nation for illiteracy. Teachers, parents, librarians, writers—all of us share a responsibility in rectifying this, not only in the South, but wherever unenlightenment confronts us. I hope to achieve this through writing."

G

GARLAND, Sherry 1948-
(Lynn Lawrence)

PERSONAL: Born July 24, 1948, in McAllen, TX; daughter of Joseph (a farmer and carpenter) and Desla (a homemaker) Allison; married Clyde L. Garland, July 4, 1971. *Education:* University of Texas at Arlington, B.A. (with honors), 1970, graduate studies, 1970-71. *Politics:* Independent. *Religion:* No specific branch.

ADDRESSES: Home—Houston, TX. *Office*—c/o Harcourt Brace Jovanovich, 1250 Sixth Ave., San Diego, CA 92101.

CAREER: Texas A&M University, College Station, TX, librarian in oceanography/meteorology department, 1972-75; secretarial work for various homebuilders in Houston, TX, 1976-89; lecturer and writer.

MEMBER: Society of Children's Book Writers and Illustrators, Romance Writers of America, Manuscriptor's Guild, Golden Triangle Writers' Guild, Houston Novel Writers Club.

AWARDS, HONORS: Guilded Quill Award in Juvenile Fiction, and Society of Children's Book Writers works-in-progress grant, both 1990, both for *Song of the Buffalo Boy.*

WRITINGS:

(Under pseudonym Lynn Lawrence) *The Familiar Touch* (adult), Berkley, 1982.
(Under pseudonym Lynn Lawrence) *Deep in the Heart* (adult), Berkley, 1983.
Vietnam: Rebuilding a Nation (children's nonfiction), Dillon/Macmillan, 1990.
Where the Cherry Trees Bloom (young adult novel), Verlag (Germany), 1991.
Best Horse on the Force (children's novel), Henry Holt, 1991.
Song of the Buffalo Boy (young adult novel), Harcourt, 1992.

SHERRY GARLAND

The Lotus Seed (children's picture book), illustrated by Tatsuro Kiuchi, Harcourt, 1993.
Why Ducks Sleep on One Leg (folk tale), illustrated by Jean and Mou-sien Tseng, Scholastic, 1993.
The Silent Storm (children's novel), Harcourt, 1993.
Shadow of the Dragon (young adult novel), Harcourt, in press.

WORK IN PROGRESS: Indio, a young adult novel about Southwestern Indians and Spanish conquistadors, publication by Harcourt expected in 1994; *The Summer Sands,* a picture book about the ecology of sand dunes, publication by Harcourt expected in 1994; *Dragon Tales: Selected Stories from Vietnam,* a collection of Vietnamese folk tales, illustrated by Trina Schart Hyman, publication by Harcourt expected in 1995; *My Father's Boat,* a picture book about Vietnamese-American shrimpers in the Gulf Coast; *The Friendship Doll,* a picture book about a doll sent to Japan on a friendship mission in 1927; *Three Grains of Wheat,* the story of how wheat was brought to the Americas by a slave; currently researching gang violence, the Southwest Indians who were taken as slaves to the silver mines of Mexico, and the history of Mexico.

SIDELIGHTS: Sherry Garland told *SATA:* "I was born in the Rio Grande Valley of Texas, the ninth child of a tenant farmer. I attended grades 1-8 in the small central Texas town of Weatherford, and grades 9-12 in Arlington, Texas. Living on farms and in small towns influenced me greatly. I was an outdoor child who preferred playing with animals and climbing trees to the company of other children. Many long summer days and nights were spent making up complicated stories in my head. Everything in our back yard or the nearby woods had a role to play—the roof was a palace, the porch columns were handsome guards, the swing was a chariot, the trees had names, and I danced with the rosebushes. While we lived on top of a cedar-covered mountain, I spent many hours tracking down wild birds' nests or rabbit holes.

"Although my family was extremely poor and my parents had only gone as far as junior high, they encouraged all of their nine children to excel in school and seek college educations. In high school I was in an honors English class for three years, with the same students and same teacher. I credit Mrs. Mary Galvan with inspiring me to become a writer. She made us see the beauty and power of the written word. Because of her enthusiasm, I developed an insatiable taste for the classics, from Greek plays to Shakespeare to Mark Twain and William Faulkner. I wrote poetry secretly, hiding it between mattresses or tucked away in drawers, never showing it to anyone.

"When I was seventeen, Mrs. Galvan assigned an essay called 'Why I Love Texas.' We had to make three copies—one for her, one for the city contest, and one for the state contest. To my surprise a month later I received an A++ from my teacher, an honorable mention in the state contest, and first place in the city contest. The prize money paid for my first semester's tuition at a local college. I was even on television and the essay appeared in the newspapers. All the glory made me realize that I would like to be a writer. It seemed so easy, but it was fifteen years before I sold anything else.

"I wrote poetry and short stories for the next thirteen years, but never tried to sell anything. I was married and worked full time, so writing took a back seat to making a living. One morning in 1979 I awoke from a dream so vivid that I felt as if it had really happened. The place (sixteenth-century France) and the characters' names came clearly in the dream. I wrote what had happened, embellished the story, and after one year had a 250,000-word historical novel. It hasn't sold yet, but it did signify the beginning of my writing career in earnest. From that day forth, I concentrated on becoming a writer, attending writers' conferences, joining writers' clubs, and submitting my work to publishers.

"My first two books, *The Familiar Touch* and *Deep in the Heart* were adult romances. Although one was on the best seller list and received a fair amount of success, I felt too limited while writing romances. Since I was not able to sell my historical novel, I became discouraged and decided I would never become a successful writer. I quit the romance novel business and focused on my job, and on helping Vietnamese families that I had befriended at the time.

"I could not stay away from writing for long. I had been taking kung fu and tai chi lessons for several years. One day the idea for my young adult novel, *Where the Cherry Trees Bloom,* came to me—an American girl befriends a Chinese girl who knows kung fu. I sent it out to several publishers and within one week [the publishing company] Crosswinds bought it. Unfortunately, just before the publication date, Crosswinds went out of business and my book was never published in English. It did, however, come out in German. Writing this book made me realize that I enjoyed writing for younger readers, and from that point I concentrated on young adult and children's books.

"I had been working with Vietnamese families since 1982 as a friend, advisor, and 'big sister.' I learned a lot about the Vietnamese culture—food, customs, history, festivals, weddings, etc. In 1988, I saw an ad in a writer's magazine seeking someone to write a nonfiction social studies book about Vietnam. I mailed in a proposal and was excited to learn that I had been chosen to do the project. For my book, *Vietnam: Rebuilding a Nation,* I researched Vietnamese history, conducted interviews, and provided photographs—a process that took about a year and a half. It was very hard work, but well worth it. I developed an even deeper appreciation for the Vietnamese people, and made many more friends.

"By now I knew that I wanted to write children's books, so I turned to my favorite topic—horses. One day I met a Houston mounted policeman and his horse at a city park. After hearing him explain how special these horses are and how they are trained to tolerate crowds and loud noises, and after learning that at one time teenagers did volunteer work at the stables, I knew I had the ingredients for a unique story. *Best Horse on the Force* is one of my most popular books and the one for which I receive the most fan mail.

"The Vietnam War had touched my life personally and the more I read, the more I knew that I had to tell a story about that war. I couldn't write about the war itself, since I had not been in the military. One day I saw a photograph of a beautiful Amerasian—her father had been an American GI in Vietnam. As I read about the plight of these forgotten and abandoned victims of war, I knew I had to tell their story. *Song of the Buffalo Boy* took about two years of intensive research and writing, but the hard work paid off. This young adult book has received good reviews and several awards.

"I had never considered writing picture books because they are very difficult literary forms. However, I had been working on an adult novel about the life of a Vietnamese woman. From the outline of this novel, I wrote a poem, *The Lotus Seed,* a capsule version of the woman's life—childhood, marriage, the war, coming to America, and having grandchildren who are Americans. The art director chose a new artist, Tatsuro Kiuchi, who lives in Japan, to do the beautiful, emotionally stirring illustrations.

"When an editor I met at a writer's conference in 1990 told me she was looking for Asian folk tales, I knew I had something she would like. *Why Ducks Sleep on One Leg* is light-hearted and funny, and at the same time contains a lot of Vietnamese culture. I was privileged to have the award-winning artists, Jean and Mou-sien Tseng, illustrate the book. They worked closely with the editor and me to ensure the historical and cultural accuracy of the illustrations—clothing, scenery, buildings, etc. Their bright water colors captured the flavor of the story beautifully.

"In 1983 Hurricane Alicia roared over Galveston and Houston. As I watched the trees in my backyard snap in two and saw the roads disappear under water, I was inspired to write a novel that would show the fury of a hurricane. I just *had* to name the character Alyssa, in honor of that storm. I had often visited the west end of Galveston and passed by stables where horses can be rented and ridden along the beach. Being a romantic at heart and a horse lover, I could not pass up the opportunity to write about these sturdy ponies and the hurricane. The story fell into place slowly. When I decided to make Alyssa an elective mute (she cannot speak because of the trauma of seeing her parents killed at sea), I did not realize how difficult a project I had taken on. Without speech, Alyssa could not carry on dialogue, an important vehicle in novel writing. Although very challenging, I do not regret writing *The Silent Storm,* from which I learned so much about hurricanes, shrimpers, fishermen, and the history of Galveston Island."

*   *   *

GOOD, Alice 1950-

PERSONAL: Born August 20, 1950, in Cambridge City, IN; daughter of Clarence Allen (an electrician) and Agnes Faith (associated with Appalachian Folkways; maiden name, Stallsworth) Rusk; married Steve Loner, 1974 (divorced, 1984); married Paul Edward Good (in commercial heating, ventilating, and air conditioning), 1985; children: Danielle Loner. *Education:* Attended Earlham College, 1968-69; Indiana University, B.A., 1974; Indiana University Graduate School of Library and Information Sciences, M.L.S., 1976; attended University of Colorado at Denver, 1985-87. *Politics:* Liberal. *Religion:* Pantheism.

ADDRESSES: Office—Columbine Library, 7706 West Bowles Ave., Littleton, CO 80213.

CAREER: Indiana University Library, Bloomington, reference assistant, 1975-77; Johnson County Public Library, Franklin, IN, reference librarian, 1977-79; Internal Revenue Service, Denver, CO, revenue officer, 1979-84; Denver School for Gifted and Creative Students, Denver, substitute teacher, 1987-88; Jefferson County Public Library, Lakewood, CO, reference librarian, 1988—.

AWARDS, HONORS: Indiana State Scholarship, 1968; merit scholarships from Indiana University, 1971 and 1972.

WRITINGS:

Magic Squares Puzzle Book, Price, Stern, 1991. (Self-illustrated) *Easy Holiday Cutout Patterns,* Country Thread Designs, 1991.

WORK IN PROGRESS: Concrete poetry for children; holiday door banners.

SIDELIGHTS: Alice Good told *SATA:* "My published books are the result of projects I developed when I had a long illness a few years ago. Unable to work, I wanted to produce something that would offset the major setback I experienced.

"*Magic Square Puzzles* came from my enjoyment of problem solving. Although they had been around for thousands of years, magic squares had never been used in activity books. This was a new idea that got the attention of the right publisher. *Easy Holiday Cutout Patterns* started as patterns I drew for my daughter so she could cut out decorations herself. Knowing, from my experience as a librarian, that simple holiday decoration patterns are hard to find, I thought this idea had a good chance of interesting a publisher.

"The involvement in the production of my creative ideas from beginning to end has given me enjoyment

ALICE GOOD

and satisfaction. Being published gives me a feeling of accomplishment different from that derived from my career as a librarian. I will continue to develop book ideas."

*   *   *

GROSSMAN, Patricia 1951-

PERSONAL: Born June 2, 1951, in Cleveland, OH; daughter of James (a business manager) and Carol (a journalist; maiden name, Klein) Grossman. *Education:* Pratt Institute, B.F.A., 1973; Sarah Lawrence College, M.F.A., 1976. *Politics:* Feminist progressive. *Religion:* Jewish. *Hobbies and other interests:* Drawing and painting.

ADDRESSES: Home—474 Sixth St., No. 3, Brooklyn, NY 11215. *Agent*—Marilyn Marlow (for *The Night Ones*) / Curtis Brown, 10 Astor Place, New York, NY 10003.

CAREER: Free-lance curriculum writer, 1981—. Has also held positions as a trade book editor and promotion assistant, and has worked in an art gallery. Speaks about Acquired Immune Deficiency Syndrome (AIDS) to civic and school groups.

MEMBER: Women's Action Coalition.

AWARDS, HONORS: The Night Ones was an American Booksellers Association "pick of the list" book, 1991, and received a Parent's Choice Award for illustration.

WRITINGS:

The Night Ones (for children), illustrated by Lydia Dabcovich, edited by Diane D'Andrade, Harcourt, 1991.
Inventions in a Grieving House (novel; for adults), Galileo Press, 1991.

WORK IN PROGRESS: Two picture books: *Saturday Market,* a work about a Mexican marketplace, for Lothrop, Lee & Shepard, and *Meyer the Signpainter*, a novel for adults.

SIDELIGHTS: Patricia Grossman told *SATA:* "When I write a picture book script, I am acutely aware that I am paving the way for a story in two media. This is different from writing a story to be illustrated. I have discarded many story ideas which seemed good at their inception, but ultimately were not visually suggestive enough. The picture books that interest me most are the ones where the story is advanced through the perfect interplay of words and pictures. In adult fiction, language fleshes out the subtle details of a story. In stories for very young children, words must work in concert with pictures to create a rich, fully-realized world.

"To the extent that the images are fundamental to the advancement of the story, I provide brief notes for the illustrator. Ideally for me, the illustrator embellishes in a way that is consonant with my vision for the book.

PATRICIA GROSSMAN

Lydia Dabcovich faithfully rendered my ideas for *The Night Ones,* but added many embellishments that anchored the book in its own world.

"The idea for *The Night Ones* had a simple genesis: I used to jog past a hospital whose workers often changed shifts about the time I passed by. Although I did not include a hospital in the book, I was attracted to the idea of all the workers everywhere doing a sort of *dos-a-dos* in the early-morning light.

"*Saturday Market,* forthcoming from Lothrop, Lee, and Shepard, resulted from my first trip to Mexico. There are wonderful markets every day of the week in Oaxaca, but the really big one happens on Saturday, when people from the surrounding villages make the trek on narrow, dusty roads to the vast, open-air market—a place where you can buy both a live rooster and the latest electronic gadget from Japan. My story centers on the more indigenous aspects of the market.

"I love the combination of writing for both children and adults. At their best, the two very different processes have the effect of regenerating each other."

FOR MORE INFORMATION SEE:

PERIODICALS

Booklist, March 15, 1991.
School Library Journal, August, 1991.

GUTMANN, Bessie Pease 1876-1960

PERSONAL: Born April 8, 1876, in Philadelphia, PA; died September 29, 1960, in Centerport, NY; daughter of Horace Collins (a tobacco salesman) and Margaretta Darrach (Young) Pease; married Hellmuth Gutmann (an art printer), July 14, 1906; children: Alice King, Lucille, John. *Education:* Attended Philadelphia School of Design for Women (now the Moore College of Art), 1893-94; attended the New York School of Art, 1896-98; attended Art Students League (New York), 1899-1901.

CAREER: Gutmann & Gutmann (art print firm), New York City, illustrator/artist, 1903-47.

AWARDS, HONORS: Artist of the Year award, annual reader contest, *Pictorial Review,* 1914.

WRITINGS:

SELF-ILLUSTRATED CHILDREN'S BOOKS

Our Baby's Early Days: A Chronicle of Many Happy Hours, Best & Company, 1908.
Nursery Poems and Prayers, Putnam, 1990.
Nursery Songs and Lullabies, Putnam, 1990.
I Love You, Putnam, 1991.

ILLUSTRATOR

Robert Louis Stevenson, *A Child's Garden of Verses,* Dodge, 1905.
Edmund Vance Cooke, *Chronicles of the Little Tot,* Dodge, 1905.

BESSIE PEASE GUTMANN

Agnes McClelland Dalton, *From Sioux to Susan,* The Century Company, 1905.
E. V. Cooke, *The Biography of Our Baby,* Dodge, 1906.
E. V. Cooke, *Told to the Little Tot,* Dodge, 1906.
Lewis Carroll, *Alice's Adventures in Wonderland,* Dodge, 1907.
Edith Dunham, *The Diary of a Mouse,* Dodge, 1907.
L. Carroll, *Through the Looking Glass: And What Alice Found There,* Dodge, 1909.

Gutmann's artwork has appeared in periodicals, calendars, postcards, and as separate fine art prints. Her art has also been featured on magazine covers, including *Pictorial Review, McCall's, Chicago Sunday Tribune,* and the *Washington Post.*

SIDELIGHTS: A prolific illustrator of books, magazines and commercial media, Bessie Pease Gutmann is best known for her endearing art prints featuring children and babies. In the early part of the twentieth century, Gutmann's prints were beloved not only in the United States, but also in England, Europe, Japan, Australia, and South Africa. Critics attributed her widespread popularity to the realistic depictions of the innocence and happiness of childhood. Over the course of fifty years, Gutmann published some six hundred art prints, many of which are still popular sellers today.

Bessie Collins Pease's mother noticed her daughter's interest in and talent for art while she was still a pre-schooler, wrote Victor J. W. Christie in *Bessie Pease Gutmann: Her Life and Works.* Young Pease's inclinations were encouraged by both her parents and teachers, who provided formal studies for the obviously talented child. After graduating from Mount Holly High School in New Jersey at the age of sixteen, she chose to attend the Philadelphia School of Design for Women, where she was further encouraged by the school's emphasis on both professional and fine art education.

Despite her dedication, talent and intensive, education, Pease still found herself somewhat restricted by the mores of her era. "Options open to women to earn money in the late 1800s were scarce," wrote Christie, "so Bessie Pease had to content herself with painting name cards, place cards, portrait sketches, free-lancing illustrations for local newspaper advertisers, and designs for the covers of a ladies' magazine." While Pease's work from this early period in her career was unsigned and did not enjoy any particular fame, she persevered and continued her art studies, enrolling in art classes at the Art Students League of New York in 1899.

It was at the Art Students League that Pease met and became employed by Hellmuth and Bernhard Gutmann, brothers who formed an art print firm in 1902. In 1903, Pease, who had been earning a meager living as a free-lance artist, accepted a position as a commercial artist, a career she found both financially and personally rewarding. In 1906, Pease surprised those who had predicted spinsterhood for the ambitious artist and married Hellmuth Gutmann. "It was truly a marriage of love," wrote Christie, "and it was a perfect match for both."

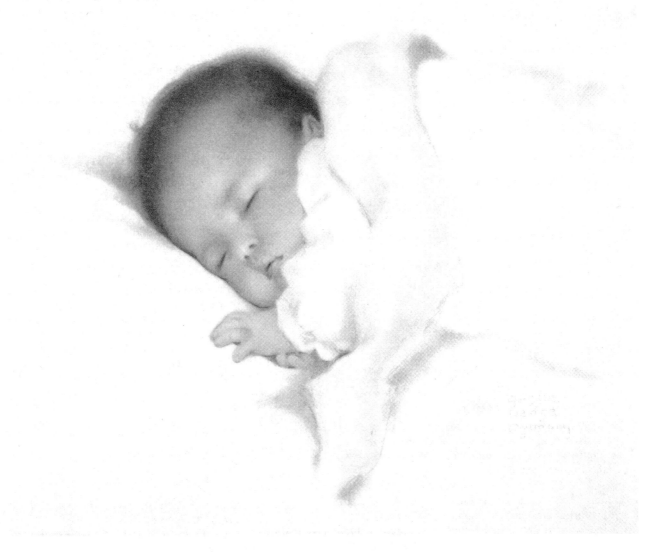

Gutmann's son and daughters provided the inspiration for her realistic portraits of children, including this famous print, "A Little Bit of Heaven."

Within three years of marriage, the Gutmann family grew by the addition of two babies, and in motherhood, Gutmann found new inspiration for her art. Gutmann's innocent yet realistic depictions of children, often modeled after her own offspring, began to attract the attention of critics and the public. "Her works became like a breath of fresh air to those who sought her work and who had grown accustomed to seeing children portrayed as solemn, formally dressed miniature adults," observed Christie.

Gutmann's unique artwork had its beginnings in the children who surrounded her on a daily basis. "Everyone has babies, you know," she once told Mary Jane Rutledge in the *Newark Sunday Call*. "My friends had them and I had three—there were always babies for models!" When Gutmann's second daughter, Lucille, was born in 1909, she became the model for what is perhaps her mother's best-known work. Gutmann made a simple sketch of her sleeping infant daughter, as she had often done in the past, and then set it aside. Seven

years later, the sketch was completed as a charcoal drawing with pale watercolor accents and reproduced as *A Little Bit of Heaven.* The simple depiction of a sleeping baby caused an unprecedented stir in the art print business. Although the Gutmann and Gutmann firm did not keep records about the exact number of prints sold, Christie reported an estimate of several million copies sold and placed in homes all over the world. Shortly thereafter, Gutmann produced a sketch of a waking baby entitled *Awakening.* Sold as a pair, these two prints achieved an even higher level of popularity than the first print had on its own. "Bessie Pease Gutmann brought a timeless quality to her babies which rendered them eternally precious and irresistible to the viewer," Christie wrote. "Few American homes were without the pair in the 1920s and 1930s and the import market was accounting for large numbers of requests.... The sales records have yet to be surpassed."

The artist's sentimental sketches of children, such as the noted "In Disgrace," have gained renewed popularity since her death in 1960.

Gutmann's second daughter, Lucille, was also the subject of another immensely popular print. *In Disgrace,* featuring the toddler Lucille and a neighbor's small collie pup, Teddy, was later paired with another print featuring the same models entitled *The Reward.* In the first one, Lucille was sketched and shaded in soft watercolors, standing in a corner, hiding her face as punishment for some childhood offense. Her faithful puppy crouches at her feet, sharing her disgrace. In the second print, the pardoned toddler shares her ice cream cone with the frolicking pup. "The heart of the public was captured when they saw the little tot, facing the wall in the corner with her best friend snuggled up against her, looking as sad as any puppy could," Christie

explained. "It wouldn't do for her to be left standing in the corner, so the public said, and the second print was prepared."

Despite Gutmann's overwhelming popularity during the 1920s and 1930s, the 1940s saw a decline in the demand for her work. At the advent of World War II early in the decade, interest in sentimental art prints featuring innocent babies faded, while wartime rations affected the availability of quality paper and sufficient labor. In 1947, Gutmann decided to stop producing art for publication when her eyesight, damaged by a childhood injury, immensely deteriorated. Hellmuth Gutmann's death in 1948 led to the sale of Gutmann & Gutmann. Although the firm never achieved the level of success it had under the direction of the Gutmann brothers, a revival of interest in Gutmann's art during the 1970s ensured the artist's reputation would live on.

While Gutmann's reputation as one of the greatest children's artists was at its height during the early part of this century, her work continues to attract admirers today. "We see the human attributes of love, freshness, warmth, sincerity, and youthful innocence in all her subjects," noted Christie. "Certainly the passage of time has not eroded her legacy." The proof of Gutmann's lasting popularity is in the continually strong sales of her art prints, the recent formation of national organizations devoted to promoting her art, and the rising value of her original prints, postcards, and other memorabilia; in recent years new books featuring her work have also appeared.

WORKS CITED:

Christie, Victor J. W., *Bessie Pease Gutmann: Her Life and Works,* Wallace-Homestead, 1990.
Rutledge, Mary Jane, article in *Newark Sunday Call,* September 30, 1934, p. 15.

FOR MORE INFORMATION SEE:

BOOKS

Christie, Victor J. W., *Bessie Pease Gutmann Published Works Catalog,* Park Avenue Publishers, 1986.
Prince, Pamela, *Sweet Dreams: The Art of Bessie Pease Gutmann,* Crown, 1985.*

—Sketch by Cornelia A. Pernik

H

HAYES, Daniel 1952-

PERSONAL: Born April 17, 1952, in Troy, NY; son of Thomas Robert (a dairy farmer) and Mary (Welch) Hayes. *Education:* State University of New York at Plattsburgh, B.S., 1973; State University of New York at Albany, M.S., 1982.

ADDRESSES: Home—RD No. 1, Route 40, Schaghticoke, NY 12154. *Agent*—Hy Cohen Literary Agency, 111 West 57th St., New York, NY 10019.

CAREER: Waterford Central Catholic High School, Waterford, NY, English teacher, 1975-84; Troy High School, Troy, NY, English teacher, 1984—; free-lance writer.

AWARDS, HONORS: Best Book for Young Adults citation, American Library Association, 1992, for *The Trouble with Lemons.*

WRITINGS:

The Trouble with Lemons, David Godine, 1991.
Eye of the Beholder, David Godine, 1992.

WORK IN PROGRESS: No Effect, a sequel to *The Trouble with Lemons* and *Eye of the Beholder.*

SIDELIGHTS: Daniel Hayes told *SATA:* "Much of my life has been spent, I think, trying out things and hoping to find what it was I could do which I not only enjoyed, but could do well. I think there exists that *thing,* or maybe more than one thing for some, that comes rather naturally for each person and at the same time makes him feel good doing it. Ideally, this *thing* becomes a career. I remember, as a freshman in high school, dreaming about and working pretty hard at becoming a star basketball player. Unfortunately, at the time I was about four feet two inches tall (my memory may have exaggerated my lack of stature some, but I do remember having to look up at almost everybody) and to be a star basketball player at that height took more ability than I was able to come by. Next, I wanted to be a rock

DANIEL HAYES

musician, and I worked pretty hard in that direction too, but to little avail. I still don't know many people who have a worse ear for music than I do.

"It wasn't until college that I decided I wanted to be a writer (to the amusement, I suspect, of some of my professors). I remember rereading books like *Huckleberry Finn* and *Great Expectations* and being so amazed by them. I'd read these books when I was younger, but at

THE
TROUBLE
WITH
LEMONS

Daniel Hayes

ALA
Best
Book

"A fast-paced
mystery
and an
excellent
coming-
of-age
story
as well."
School
Library
Journal

FAWCETT JUNIPER
70416-5 (Canada $4.99) U.S. $3.99

Tyler feels overshadowed by his famous family until he discovers a dead body while sneaking a swim in the local quarry.

the time I didn't realize how clever, how intelligent, and how funny writers like Mark Twain and Charles Dickens really were. I read plenty of books and studied writing styles so that I could become one of these people—a writer. And the difference I found with this *thing* was that I didn't have the feeling I was constantly swimming against the current. After a while I was able to sound at least a little like my favorite writers. Still, it was years before I really developed my own voice, meaning my own style of putting ideas into words. After I finished my first book, *The Trouble with Lemons,* a story told by thirteen-year-old Tyler McAllister, friends would read it and say things like, 'That's really amazing! It sounds just like you.' Perhaps what's more amazing (other than the fact that I sound like a thirteen-year-old) is that it took so long for me to learn how to sound like myself.

"I start most of my stories by getting to know my characters and then I give them things to do. The reason I do it in that order is because who the characters are— what they think about and wonder about and worry

about—is actually more important to me than what they do. I feel like all my characters (or most anyway) represent different sides of myself. A good-hearted kid like Tyler McAllister in *The Trouble with Lemons* and *Eye of the Beholder* sees things pretty much like I do at my best, but I'm not altogether a stranger to the feelings and behaviors of my less admirable characters. This is why I wouldn't be comfortable having Tyler get even with a bully like Beaver Bruckman. It would be kind of like having the victim side of myself punch out the bully side. This bully side of ourselves (most of us have a little of it, I think) is actually the more pathetic side, so it would seem almost more cruel for me to have Tyler go after Beaver than it does when Beaver goes after Tyler. Tyler has an understanding and forgiving nature (at least after the heat of the moment and he puts his fists away), so I never feel as sorry for him as I do some of my less nice characters.

"I'll probably continue using Tyler McAllister as a narrator for quite some time (I've already got quite a bit planned for him), but I'm also working on some new narrators with different points of view. I'm looking forward to all of this. It's *fun* being a writer."

*   *   *

HEITZMANN, William Ray 1948-
(Wm. Ray Heitzmann; W. R. Tolland, W. R. Vincent, pseudonyms)

PERSONAL: Born February 12, 1948, in Hoboken, NJ; son of William H. (a truck driver) and Mary (a homemaker; maiden name, Tolland) Heitzmann; married Kathleen Esnes (a school librarian), June 20, 1970 (separated); children: Richard Raymond, Mary Elizabeth. *Education:* Villanova University, B.S. (with honors), 1964; University of Chicago, M.A.T., 1966; University of Delaware, Ph.D., 1974; attended Northwestern University and California State University, San Jose (now San Jose State University). *Politics:* Independent Republican. *Religion:* Roman Catholic.

ADDRESSES: Home—Havertown, PA. *Office*—Villanova University, Liberal Arts Center, Villanova, PA 19085.

CAREER: University of Chicago, Chicago, IL, part-time social studies teacher at Laboratory Middle School, 1964-65; DuSable High School, Chicago, IL, social studies teacher, 1965-66; North Chicago High School, North Chicago, IL, social studies teacher and basketball coach, 1966-67; Highland Falls High School, Highland Falls, NY, social studies teacher and basketball coach, 1967-69; Neumann College, Aston, PA, head men's basketball coach, 1982-86; Villanova University, Villanova, PA, recruiter of minority students and basketball players, 1970-74, instructor, 1969-74, assistant professor, 1974-77, became associate professor of education and later became professor of education and human services; writer. Member of adjunct faculty in the School of Allied Health Sciences at Thomas Jefferson University; Ragdale Foundation, writer-in-residence,

1981, 1983, 1985, 1987, 1988, and 1990. Research board of advisors of American Biographical Institute, member; advisory council of International Biographical Centre, member; National Council for the Social Studies, head of committee of editors; Middle States Council for the Social Studies, member of board of directors, 1976-80, member of executive committee, 1978—; Pennsylvania Council for the Social Studies, member of executive committee, 1972—, member of board of directors, 1973—, vice president, 1977-78, president-elect, 1978-79, president, 1979-80; Pennsylvania Council Economic Education Board, board member, 1979-84. Basketball coach, Catholic Youth Organization, high schools and colleges. Conducts and directs workshops; lectures; guest on radio programs locally and nationally. President, Heitzmann's Educational Learning Product Systems (HELPS). Consultant to Airco Corporation, U.S. Naval Institute, and numerous colleges and school districts.

MEMBER: North American Society of Oceanic Historians, American Association of University Professors, U.S. Naval Institute, National Marine Education Association, Oceanic Society, International Oceanographic Society, Community College Social Science Association, Naval Historical Association, Pennsylvania Association for Curriculum Development and Supervision, Delaware Valley Reading Association, Cousteau Society, Mystic Seaport Society, Philadelphia Writers' Organization, National Association of Basketball Coaches, Llanerch Optimist Club (member of board of directors, 1983—), Kappa Delta Pi, Phi Delta Kappa, Delta Tau Kappa.

AWARDS, HONORS: Outstanding Service Award, National Council for the Social Studies, 1980; recipient of awards from Student Pennsylvania State Education Association, Weehawken School District, National

WILLIAM RAY HEITZMANN

Council for the Social Studies, and Pennsylvania Council for the Social Studies; Outstanding Alumnus Award, School of Education, University of Delaware, 1988; *MSCSS* Gold Medal, 1989, for research publications.

WRITINGS:

(Editor with Patricia Stetson) *The Psychology of Teaching and Learning,* MSS Education, 1973.

(Editor with Charles Staropoli) *Student Teaching: Classroom Management and Professionalism,* MSS Education, 1974.

Educational Games and Simulations (part of "What Research Says to the Teacher" series), National Education Association, 1974, second edition, 1983.

American Jewish Political Behavior: History and Analysis, R & E Research Associates, 1975.

Fifty Political Cartoons for Teaching United States History, J. Weston Walch, 1975.

America's Maritime Heritage and Energy Education (student workbooks), two volumes, Con-Stran Publications, 1977.

Minicourses (part of "Developments in Classroom Instruction" series), National Education Association, 1977.

The Classroom Teacher and the Student Teacher (part of "What Research Says to the Teacher" series), National Education Association, 1977.

(Contributor) Louis Thayer and Kent O. Beeler, editors, *Affective Education: Innovations for Learning,* University Associates, 1977.

Opportunities in Marine and Maritime Careers, National Textbook Co., 1979, second edition, 1988.

The Newspaper in the Classroom (part of "What Research Says to the Teacher" series), National Education Association, 1979, second edition, 1985.

Opportunities in Sports and Physical Education, National Textbook Co., 1980, second edition, 1985, and third edition, 1993, both published as *Opportunities in Sports and Athletics.*

Political Cartoons, Scholastic, 1980.

Opportunities in Sports Medicine, National Textbook Co., 1984, second edition, 1992.

Introduction to General Teaching Methods, Airco, 1984.

Guide to Introduction to General Teaching Methods, Airco, 1985.

Note Taking Tips (part of "Study Skills" series), Chubb Institute, 1989.

Test Taking Tips (part of "Study Skills" series), Chubb Institute, 1989.

Careers for Sports Nuts and Other Athletic Types, National Textbook Co., 1991.

Author has written variously under Wm. Ray Heitzmann, and under pseudonyms W. R. Tolland, and W. R. Vincent. Contributor to periodicals, including *Creative Teacher, Sea Heritage News, Beachcomber, Catholic Standard and Times,* and *Career World.* Editorial board member of *Journal of Marine Education* and *Social Studies.* Contributing editor to *Sea History* and *Long Beach Island.* Executive editor of *Social Studies;* book reviewer for *Community College Social Science Quarterly;* advertising manager of *MSCSS,* 1980-82.

SIDELIGHTS: William Ray Heitzmann told *SATA:* "The major influences upon my life (literary and personal) include: Growing up in Weehawken Township, Hudson County, New Jersey, attending St. Augustine's Elementary School in Union City, and attending high school at Power Memorial Academy in New York City; my parents whose wonderful encouragement and support continued throughout their lives; my teachers in high school and college, in particular professors and authors Mark Krug, Ph.D., at University of Chicago, James Merrill, Ph.D., and Val Armsdorf, Ph.D., at University of Delaware; residence at the Ragdale Foundation (a writers' colony) in Lake Forrest, Illinois.

"Topics for my articles, professional papers, booklets, and books have come from personal and professional interests which partially explains such an array of subjects: learning games and simulations, blimps, sea language, sports and athletics, political cartoons, humor, professional wrestling, marine and maritime studies, writing for publication, study skills, etc.

"My doctoral studies taught me painstaking research skills and the importance of absolute accuracy. My first paid publication appeared in January 1968; January 1993 marked my twenty-fifth year as writer/author."

FOR MORE INFORMATION SEE:

PERIODICALS

Asbury Park Press, July 16, 1978.
Catholic Standard and Times, December 20, 1984.
County Press, January 30, 1985.
Delaware County Daily Times, April 23, 1985.
New York Daily News, February 18, 1979.
Philadelphia Bulletin, July 21, 1978.
Suburban and Wayne Times, August 30, 1979.
Temple Telegram, November 14, 1979.
Times Herald, February 11, 1985.
Voice of Youth Advocates, June 1991, p. 123.

* * *

HEITZMANN, Wm. Ray
See HEITZMANN, William Ray

* * *

HENSTRA, Friso 1928-

PERSONAL: Born February 9, 1928, in Amsterdam, Netherlands; son of Sytze (an artist) and Anna Henstra; married Maria Sligting, March 7, 1952; children: Sylvia. *Education:* Studied at National College of Art, Amsterdam. *Hobbies and other interests:* "Nearly everything that happens."

ADDRESSES: Home—Weesperstraat 270, 1018 DN, Amsterdam, Netherlands. *Agent*—Dilys Evans, P.O. Box 400, 72 Laurel Way, Norfolk, CT 06058.

CAREER: Artist. Started as painter, switched to sculptor in 1950, and then to free-lance illustrating. Instructor at College of Art, Arnhem, 1968-86. *Exhibitions:*

Henstra's work has been shown in the Netherlands, Czechoslovakia, Germany, Belgium, England, France, the United States, and other locations, beginning in 1952. *Military service:* Dutch Army, 1948-50; served in Indonesia.

AWARDS, HONORS: Pomme d'Or (Golden Apple Prize), Bratislava Biennale d'Illustrations, 1969, for *The Practical Princess;* Citation of Merit, 1970, and Gold Medal, 1971, from Society of Illustrators; Honor Book Citations, Chicago Book Clinic Exhibition, 1971, for *Stupid Marco* and *The Round Sultan and the Straight Answer; The Silver Whistle* was named one of the fifty best books of the year by the American Institute of Graphic Arts, 1972; Children's Book Showcase awards, 1974, for *Petronella,* and 1976, for *The Little Spotted Fish;* plaque, Bratislava Biennale d'Illustrations, 1977, for *Forgetful Fred;* silver medal, Der Internationalen Buchkunst Ausstellung, Leipzig, East Germany, 1989, for *Mighty Mizzling Mouse;* Golden Brush, CPNB, Netherlands, 1992, for *Why Not?*

WRITINGS:

SELF-ILLUSTRATED

Wait and See, Addison-Wesley, 1978.
Mighty Mizzling Mouse, Lippincott, 1983.

FRISO HENSTRA

Mighty Mizzling Mouse and the Red Cabbage House, Little, Brown, 1984.

ILLUSTRATOR

H. J. Looman, *Wij en het water; de strijd der lage landen tegen de erfvijand het water in het verleden, het heden en de toekomst* (title means "We and the Water: The Struggle of the Low Countries against the Hereditary Enemy Water, in the Past, the Present, and the Future"), Elsevier, 1957.

Jay Williams, *The Practical Princess,* Parents Magazine Press, 1969.

Williams, *School for Sillies,* Parents Magazine Press, 1969.

Barbara K. Walker, *The Round Sultan and the Straight Answer,* Parents Magazine Press, 1970.

Williams, *Stupid Marco,* Parents Magazine Press, 1970.

Williams, *The Silver Whistle,* Parents Magazine Press, 1971.

Williams, *Seven at One Blow,* Parents Magazine Press, 1972.

Williams, *The Youngest Captain,* Parents Magazine Press, 1972.

Williams, *Petronella,* Parents Magazine Press, 1973.

Williams, *Forgetful Fred,* Parents Magazine Press, 1974.

Jane Yolen, *The Little Spotted Fish,* Seabury, 1975.

Williams, *The Wicked Tricks of Tyl Uilenspiegel,* Four Winds, 1978.

Herbert Montgomery, *Johnny Appleseed: A Story about John Chapman,* Winston, 1979.

Steven Kroll, *Space Cats,* Holiday House, 1979.

Lois Duncan, *The Terrible Tales of Happy Days School,* Little, Brown, 1983.

J. Patrick Lewis, *The Tsar and the Amazing Cow,* Dial, 1988.

Vit Horejs, *Pig and Bear,* Macmillan, 1989.

Lenny Hort, reteller, *The Tale of the Caliph Stork,* Dial, 1989.

Verna Aardema, *Pedro and the Padre: A Tale from Jalisco, Mexico,* Dial, 1991.

Sylvia A. Hofsepian, *Why Not?,* Macmillan, 1991.

Winifred Morris, *The Future of Yen-Tzu,* Macmillan, 1992.

Elsa Marston, *Cynthia and the Runaway Gazebo,* Morrow, 1992.

Sari Derby-Miller, *The Mouse Who Owned the Sun,* Four Winds, 1993.

Also illustrator, with others, of *Six Impossible Things before Breakfast,* written by Norma Farber, 1977. Illustrator of Dutch version of *Tomorrow's Fire,* written by Jay Williams. Contributor of illustrations to *Cricket* and other periodicals.

WORK IN PROGRESS: Illustrations for a children's book about Rembrandt.

SIDELIGHTS: Friso Henstra grew up in Amsterdam during World War II and watched as the city's beauty crumbled under the bullets and the lack of resources to repair and restore. In an essay for *Something about the Author Autobiography Series* (*SAAS*), Henstra recalled watching fighter planes from the window of his attic room. "Sometimes a plane hovers like a fish caught in the net of criss-crossed searchlights. Above the blacked-out town, dark as a wood by night, clangs the barking sound of the German anti-aircraft guns. Shell-splinters land on the tile roof with a sinister rattle, some even pierce through the tiles with a small dry sound. Elongated pieces of rough black steel with sharp jagged edges; sometimes yellow paint is visible on the smooth part. My drawings have more and more to do with the war." Henstra began drawing at age four, influenced by his father's portrait painting. He described his childhood compulsion to draw in *SAAS:* "Landscapes, men, women, clouded skies, animals: everything you can possibly imagine belongs to the painters who have painted it. I am overcome by intense jealousy and a feeling of loneliness. I will draw the world to take possession of it."

Images of the war, seen through an artist's eye, color Henstra's early memories: the grocer who allowed him to help paste strips of lime-smeared paper on the windows, the school where he and his classmates learned how to dispose of a firebomb, the sight of soldiers—"extensions of a machine"—carrying truckloads of prisoners away, the South Church he entered, hoping to sketch the interior but instead finding "a row of man-sized paper bags with stiffened bare feet sticking out."

As the war continued, Henstra and most other boys avoided school for fear of being drafted by German soldiers. His artistic talent continued to grow, however, through constant practice. When the war finally ended six years later, after occupying Henstra's life from age ten to sixteen, he sought out museums, "hungering insatiably after art. I want to see everything," and made his way to Paris with a friend where he spent two weeks drawing. Of that time he recalled, "My drawings are getting rather disoriented. If in the isolation of the war years I strove after the best possible imitation of what I saw, now on the contrary I am at the mercy of the most divergent influences. The only way I can get out from under them is to master the craft fully, once and for all." Hoping to fulfill that goal, he entered Amsterdam's National College of Art, but his studies were cut short when he was drafted to serve with the Dutch Army.

The next two years were spent preparing for and participating in the Netherlands' efforts to quell Indonesia's battle for independence from Dutch rule. As he sailed from home to his destination near Bandung, Henstra continued to practice and improve his art. "From memory I sketch what I have seen so far: Cape Saint Vincent, Malta, a gathering of sailing vessels moored by the statue of Ferdinand de Lesseps, a camel rider praying in the desert, an Arabian dhow sailing in the Red Sea. I master the technique of drawing from memory: you have to anticipate the questions that will come up later on, make comparisons with something you are already familiar with, retain numbers and proportions," he wrote in *SAAS.*

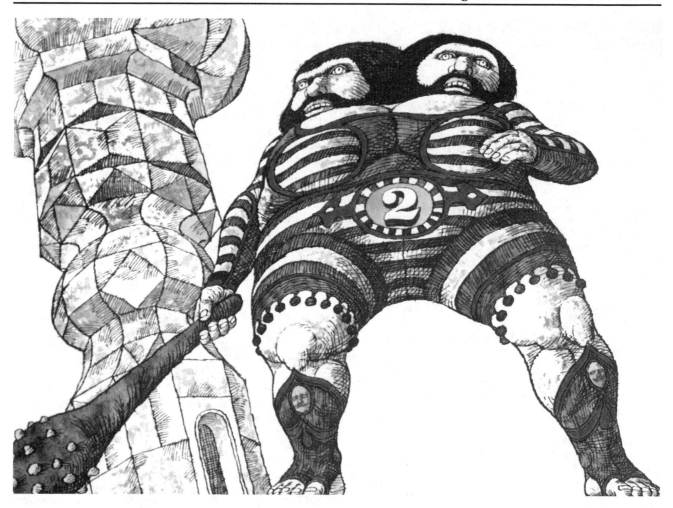

Growing up in wartime Amsterdam has colored Henstra's artwork, which is often noted for its disturbing, unconventional portraits. (Illustration by Henstra from *Stupid Marco* by Jay Williams.)

In 1952 Henstra married his wife, Rietje, "who my whole life long remains the touchstone of all my thoughts and deeds. Not a drawing leaves my drawing board without being submitted to her judgment, which I can read in her face. If she purses her lips, naturally I disagree with her—but many a drawing ends up at the bottom of a drawer as a result." Their daughter, Sylvia, was born the same year. The family lived in an attic "with the most beautiful view of Amsterdam" for seven years, as housing was extremely difficult to obtain. During that time, work was plentiful for Henstra. "Commissions for illustration come rolling in one after another, a wide variety of jobs come flocking like flies to honey," he recalled. "Curious about my own abilities, I accept nearly every offer." Among his projects were comic strips, drawings for advertisements, works for children's magazines and daily and weekly papers, and illustrations and dust jackets for books.

In 1961 Henstra returned to the Academy, this time to explore an interest in sculpture. The experience enhanced his drawing skills. "I discover that modeling clay from live models is the most effective basis for drawings. It is as if the knowledge of forms is built up through the memory of arm and hand muscles." Around the same time he accepted an invitation to teach at the

Academy of Visual Arts in Arnhem in 1968, remaining there for eighteen years.

Henstra's fortuitous teaming with author Jay Williams began around 1968 when he illustrated the Dutch version of Williams's *Tomorrow's Fire.* "The book inspires me, and I do the illustrations without much concern for conventions—I don't even use the same scale for all the illustrations," he remembered. "The nature of the subject determines how large a drawing should be—not some previously established frame that makes you feel as if you're shut up inside a cardboard box trying to catch a bird as it flies by." Williams then asked Henstra to illustrate *The Practical Princess,* for which he won the Golden Apple Prize at the Bratislava Illustration Biennial in Czechoslovakia. The prize, ten thousand kroners (about $370), was to be kept in a bank account until the winner could claim it, but since Henstra was unable to enter the Iron Curtain country, the money dwindled—the bank did not pay interest on the account, and deducted a property fine each year. When he received the award, Henstra noted, the prize money would have been enough to live on for a year.

Henstra explained in *SAAS* his affinity for Williams's books. "As a child my preference is for the fairy tales told by the Brothers Grimm—gruesome, savage tales, as are the stories drawn by Wilhelm Busch. In the Grimm stories you get strung up and left to the ravens; in Busch's you get crushed, baked, melted, and crammed in a jar. I find some of the same qualities in Jay Williams's stories: he gives a fire-breathing dragon a keg of gunpowder to eat, and to my shame I must admit that I enjoy drawing the remains of the dragon being swept up." Ironically, Henstra has been unable to find a Dutch publisher willing to publish such books. "In the Netherlands people are rather moralistic about such scenes," he commented.

In an interview with Aidan Chambers for *Horn Book,* Williams expressed regret that Henstra's illustrations have sometimes met with unfavorable reviews. "The people who dislike him usually say he's too grotesque.... If you look carefully at his pictures in my books, you'll see that his people aren't conventionally attractive. They're not pretty in any way, not cute. Friso is unrestrained with his giants and monsters. There's nothing quaint about them. They come from his own private store of images, and some adults find his images disturbing. I don't think many children do, not in the same way. They aren't threatened by them as some adults seem to be."

Henstra and Williams worked together until Williams's sudden death in 1978. Since then, Henstra has illustrated works for a number of authors, and has also written some books of his own, including *Wait and See, Mighty Mizzling Mouse,* and *Mighty Mizzling Mouse and the Red Cabbage House.* "A larky tale about a clownish hero," *Wait and See* provides "hilarity all around," a *Publishers Weekly* reviewer commented. In the story, Mighty Herman insists that someday he will get the respect he deserves. In the meantime, however, his numerous "inventions" bring him only embarrassment. In *Mighty Mizzling Mouse,* a mouse mizzles (confuses) a cat and sets off a chase that upsets tables, knocks down bystanders, breaks open a cage of lions, and leaves everyone and everything in a jumbled heap. The wordless story is a "beautifully organized, surreal, zany gallery of pictures," a *Wilson Library Bulletin* reviewer remarked. A *Bulletin of the Center for Children's Books* contributor found *Mighty Mizzling Mouse* "appealing because of the vigor and humor of the clever paintings."

Henstra's work for other authors' books has also been well-received. Many reviewers have noted that Henstra's drawings enhance the story rather than simply illustrating it. In *The Tsar and the Amazing Cow,* written by J. Patrick Lewis, "the detail of furnishings,

Henstra's long and satisfying collaboration with writer Jay Williams included *Petronella,* in which a princess must perform three dangerous tasks to rescue a prince. (Illustration by Henstra.)

costumes, and the Russian countryside and buildings along with the mannered posture of the tsar and those in his court aptly convey a sense of time and place," a *Horn Book* reviewer remarked. A *Publishers Weekly* contributor noted, "Henstra's drawings fill the wide pages with picturesque farm buildings and curious observers."

In Verna Aardema's *Pedro and the Padre: A Tale from Jalisco, Mexico,* a lazy boy is sent out to find work. He is hired by a padre, but soon his habit of lying gets him into trouble. Henstra's drawings for this book "are excellent examples of how well deserved his reputation is," Ruth Semrau wrote in *School Library Journal.* A *Publishers Weekly* reviewer noted that the drawings are effective in capturing the landscape and people of Mexico "and successfully catch the gleam in Pedro's eye." In *The Tale of the Caliph Stork,* a folk legend retold by Lenny Hort, "Henstra's ink and watercolor pictures magically convey the silly but apt transformation" of Caliph Chasid and his Grand Vizier into storks, Ruth Smith observed in *School Library Journal.* Writing in *Wilson Library Bulletin,* Donnarae MacCann and Olga Richard found that "using pen, ink, and watercolor, Henstra makes his highly personal use of line his trademark." They concluded, "It is not too much to say that would-be artists would do well to use Henstra's illustrations as a learning model."

WORKS CITED:

Chambers, Aidan, interview with Jay Williams, *Horn Book,* February, 1977, pp. 92-96.

Henstra, Friso, essay in *Something about the Author Autobiography Series,* Volume 14, Gale, 1992, pp. 125-40.

MacCann, Donnarae, and Olga Richard, review of *The Tale of the Caliph Stork, Wilson Library Bulletin,* February, 1990, p. 83.

Review of *Mighty Mizzling Mouse, Bulletin of the Center for Children's Books,* May, 1983.

Review of *Mighty Mizzling Mouse, Wilson Library Bulletin,* June, 1983, p. 865.

Review of *Pedro and the Padre, Publishers Weekly,* December 7, 1990, p. 81.

Semrau, Ruth, review of *Pedro and the Padre, School Library Journal,* May, 1991, p. 86.

Smith, Ruth, review of *The Tale of the Caliph Stork, School Library Journal,* February, 1990, p. 82.

Review of *The Tsar and the Amazing Cow, Horn Book,* May/June, 1988, p. 365.

Review of *The Tsar and the Amazing Cow, Publishers Weekly,* February 26, 1988, p. 197.

Review of *Wait and See, Publishers Weekly,* November 20, 1978.

FOR MORE INFORMATION SEE:

PERIODICALS

Booklist, March 1, 1992, p. 1283.

School Library Journal, February, 1990, p. 75; December, 1991, p. 95; March, 1992, p. 232.*

—*Sketch by Deborah A. Stanley*

HERLIHY, Dirlie Anne 1935-

PERSONAL: Born October 28, 1935, in Portsmouth, VA; daughter of George Hungerford Bailey (a machinist) and Helen MacDonald (a telephone operator; maiden name, Smith) Hickin; married James Gordon Herlihy (in sales), September 1, 1957; children: Tamara Herlihy Glass, Timothy G. Glass, J. Patrick Herlihy. *Education:* Attended Mercer University and the University of North Florida. *Politics:* "Apolitical." *Religion:* Episcopalian. *Hobbies and other interests:* Hostessing small dinner parties, witty conversation, music—especially R & B and classical—gardening, reading, golf, and travelling.

ADDRESSES: Home—Box 732, Bermuda Run, Advance, NC 27006.

CAREER: Writer. Worked variously as an advertising copywriter, secretary, department store clerk, dental assistant, and piano teacher.

AWARDS, HONORS: Ludie's Song was named one of the ten best books of 1988 by United Press International (UPI), and was recommended by *Parents'* magazine and the American Library Association, 1988.

WRITINGS:

Ludie's Song, Dial, 1988.
Don't Let the Green Grass Fool You, Dial, in press.

WORK IN PROGRESS: A book on the human connection, or "Mercy," theme.

DERLIE ANNE HERLIHY

SIDELIGHTS: Writer Dirlie Anne Herlihy was born on October 28, 1935, in Portsmouth, West Virginia, where she lived until her family moved to Macon, Georgia in 1946. Her upbringing was typical of middle-class southern families. She noted in an interview for *North Carolina Catalog of Authors,* "I continued to grow up ... among two younger siblings and the consummate 'Steel Magnolias'—my mother's three sisters—whose 'spend the days,' featuring Tony Home Permanents, chicken salad, and red Jello, provided human insights which continue to shape my life and work."

Herlihy attended Georgia's Mercer University where she majored in theatre arts. It wasn't until years later that she studied creative writing, taking selected courses at the University of North Florida. She seriously began writing when, as she describes it, "I was living in a small Ohio town and it was cold and boring and a friend gave me a typewriter."

Set in the South, amidst the racial tensions of the 1950s, *Ludie's Song,* Herlihy's first novel for young adults, describes the coming of age of a thirteen-year-old white girl through a growing friendship with a young African American woman. The book was a result of the author's

A young white girl's friendship with a black woman stirs community hatreds in Herlihy's first novel. (Cover illustration by Lonnie Knabel.)

frustration over the reaction of her family towards "different" people while she was growing up. "As a child ... [I] was unable to voice my feelings. As a teenager, these feelings were my silent rebellion, and now I write them."

WORKS CITED:

North Carolina Catalog of Authors, c. 1991.

*   *   *

HERSOM, Kathleen 1911-

PERSONAL: Born November 23, 1911, in Nottingham, England; daughter of Arthur (Her Majesty's Inspector of Schools) and Catherine Martha (Brown) Morley; married Donald Henry Hersom (a librarian), July 19, 1947; children: John, Brenda Blacklock, Mark, Helen Cowan. *Education:* Rachel McMillan Training College, teaching certificate, 1933. *Politics:* Liberal Democrat. *Religion:* Protestant.

ADDRESSES: Home—22 Market Place, Wolsingham, Durham DL3 3AB, England. *Agent*—Laura Cecil, 17 Alwyne Villas, London N1 2HG, England.

CAREER: Croydon Nursery School, Croydon, England, superintendent, 1933-36; Nelson Nursery School, Nelson, England, superintendent, 1938-41; New Brancepeth Nursery School, New Brancepeth, England, superintendent, 1942-45. Aided in voluntary war relief work with children in Holland through Save the Children Fund, 1945, and in Germany through International Voluntary Service for Peace, 1946; did voluntary work with mentally disabled children, 1971-81.

WRITINGS:

Johnny Oswaldtwistle, illustrated by Lesley Smith, Methuen, 1977.
Maybe It's a Tiger, illustrated by Niki Daly, Macmillan, 1981.
The Spitting Image, Macmillan, 1982.
Johnny Reed's Cat, and Other Northern Tales, A. & C. Black, 1987.
(With husband, Donald Hersom) *The Copycat,* Atheneum, 1989.
The Half Child, Simon & Schuster, 1989.
Listen All of You!, BBC/Longman, 1990.

Author's work has also been included in anthologies; contributor of short stories to periodicals for young readers.

WORK IN PROGRESS: Another collection of British folktales, working title *Saints, Sinners and Suchlike,* "maybe completed by 1993, or 4 or 5 or 6 ...."

SIDELIGHTS: "For as much of my life as I can remember," British author Kathleen Hersom told *SATA,* "I have enjoyed listening to and telling stories, even if my dolls were the only patient listeners." Now well into her eighties, Hersom has entertained her own four children—not to mention her seven grandchil-

The Half Child

KATHLEEN
HERSOM

A seventeenth-century girl searches for the disabled sister that no one else seems to miss in Kathleen Hersom's novel.

dren—with her engaging stories. While working in various nursery schools in her native England during her long career in education, Hersom has also shared the joy of reading both her work and the work of other children's writers to countless rapt young listeners.

"I was the youngest of three children," recalled Hersom, "and fortunate in being born into a family where reading and telling stories was a common and regular entertainment, particularly welcome in those television- and radio-less days of my early childhood. On Sunday evenings, Mother *always* read to the three of us all together. I loved those 'reads.' I remember well how I loved *Alice in Wonderland, Peter Pan, The Water Babies,* and much of Hans Christian Andersen, the Brothers Grimm, and stories taken from Sara Cone Bryant's *Stories to Tell to Children.* The very first books for all three of the children in my family were the little books of Beatrix Potter. As the boys grew out of them they were passed on to me. There is still a complete set of them (mostly very worn) in my bookcase. I have not grown out of them yet. If any of us were poorly, the invalid was always treated to a large dose of stories of their own choice, and I will always connect chicken-pox with Kipling's *Just So Stories.* My brother Jack and I shared the germs and the stories that were read to us every evening till the book was finished and we were well."

Hersom's love of books translated itself into a love of writing. Although she had one of her early stories for children published in a magazine while she was still a student and submitted several more of her works for publication over the years that followed, it wasn't until the 1970s that she seriously thought about writing books for young readers. "I attended a writer's workshop one weekend in 1972 and, during question time, I asked the tutor if he thought there was a chance of stories by complete beginners being read aloud on the 'Listen with Mother' radio programme. He said that he had no idea, and had no experience writing for young children, but if I wrote to the program's creator, Dorothy Edwards, she would probably tell me anything I wanted to know. So I did."

Edwards sent back a friendly reply to Hersom's letter and suggested that she submit three sample stories. The correspondence between the two women continued and several of Hersom's stories were eventually included in the various short-story anthologies that Edwards edited. In 1977, Hersom's work for Edwards was collected into her first "real book" and published by Methuen as *Johnny Oswaldtwistle.* In the years since, Hersom has published several more books, including *Johnny Reed's Cat, and Other Northern Tales, The Half Child,* and *The Copycat,* a book she coauthored with her husband, Donald Hersom. "As I am an extremely slow worker, I think it unlikely at my age that I will attempt any more novel-length books for children," Hersom told *SATA.* "But if any ideas crop up I will be very happy to try picture-book texts or short stories, because I *do* like writing."

* * *

HOWARD, Vernon (Linwood) 1918-1992 (Paul Castle, Don Jordan)

OBITUARY NOTICE—See index for *SATA* sketch: Born in 1918; died August 23, 1992, in Boulder City, NV. Lecturer and author. A prolific writer of children's books, plays, and self-help psychology books for adults, Howard also gave self-improvement and mysticism lectures and established the related New Life Foundation. Along with many children's books written under his own name, Howard wrote *101 Funny Things to Make and Do* under the pseudonym Paul Castle, and *Party Stunts for All* under the name Don Jordan. His self-help books include *Work Power: Talk Your Way to Life Leadership, Time Power for Personal Success, Secrets of Mental Magic: How to Use Your Full Power of Mind,* and *The Mystic Path to Cosmic Power.*

OBITUARIES AND OTHER SOURCES:

BOOKS

Authors of Books for Young People, 3rd edition, Scarecrow, 1990.

PERIODICALS

Los Angeles Times, September 6, 1992, p. A30.

J

JACKSON, Alison 1953-

PERSONAL: Born August 22, 1953, in Alhambra, CA; daughter of Samuel (a physician) and Lorayne (a musician; maiden name, Swarthout) Coombs; married Stephen Jackson (a computer analyst), September 10, 1983; children: Kyle, Quinn. *Education:* University of California, Irvine, B.A., 1975; San Jose State University, M.L.S., 1977. *Politics:* Democrat. *Religion:* Protestant. *Hobbies and other interests:* Travel, snow skiing, waterskiing.

ADDRESSES: Home—9152 Brabham Dr., Huntington Beach, CA 92646. *Office*—Fullerton Public Library, 353 West Commonwealth, Fullerton, CA 92632.

CAREER: Long Beach Public Library, Long Beach, CA, children's librarian, 1977-80; Newport Beach Public Library, Newport Beach, CA, children's librarian, 1980-87; Fullerton Public Library, Fullerton, CA, children's librarian, 1987—; writer.

MEMBER: American Library Association, Society of Children's Book Writers, California Library Association, Southern California Council on Literature for Children and Young People.

WRITINGS:

My Brother the Star, Dutton, 1990.
Crane's Rebound, Dutton, 1991.

WORK IN PROGRESS: Blowing Bubbles with the Enemy (tentative title), Dutton, in press.

SIDELIGHTS: Alison Jackson told *SATA:* "I grew up in South Pasadena, California. I was always interested in writing as a child, and I served on the staff of both my school newspaper and yearbook while attending South Pasadena High School.

"I only began writing seriously after entering college in 1971. I enrolled in the creative writing program at the University of California, Irvine, where I took a number of writing courses and learned many of the basic

ALISON JACKSON

techniques necessary in writing fiction. At that time I had written a few short stories, but I had never attempted a novel-length work. And I certainly wouldn't have dared to send anything in for publication. I didn't think I had enough talent!

"In fact, it was not until 1988 (seventeen years later) that I summoned up enough courage to submit a manuscript to a major publisher. At that time I had been working as a professional children's librarian for over ten years and was married with a tiny baby of my own at home. I decided that I had read enough good children's books in the past ten years to try writing one myself. And by that time there was no doubt in my mind that I wanted to write for children—not adults.

"The problem was ... I needed something to write about. As luck would have it, a workshop was being conducted in our library. The class was titled 'How to Get Your Child into Television Commercials,' and I thought this would be a wonderful subject to write about. Why not?, I decided. I'll write about a kid on TV.

"So I did. I invented the character of Cameron Crane, a six-year-old terror who stars in television commercials. Then I came up with the idea of an older brother, Leslie, who feels overshadowed by his brother and ignored by his parents—until he himself is given a chance to star on a county-wide basketball team. The result was *My Brother the Star,* which was published by Dutton Children's Books. I enjoyed writing about these two characters so much that I created a sequel, *Crane's Rebound,* which came out the following year.

How can a mere basketball whiz compete with the commercial kid?

Alison Jackson

In *My Brother the Star,* Leslie Crane hopes that winning a spot at county basketball camp will help draw attention away from his bratty kid brother, the star of a series of popular television commercials. (Cover illustration by Daniel Horne.)

"*Crane's Rebound* recounts Leslie's adventures at a summer sports camp. Unfortunately, competition on the basketball courts is not all Les is forced to contend with. He also has an obnoxious roommate, who happens to be a bully—and the best player on the team. In *Crane's Rebound,* I also feature a character who was introduced in my first novel. Her name is Bobby Lorimer. She is a feisty basketball-playing tomboy who develops a huge crush on Leslie while continuing to be one of his main adversaries on the court. Bobby proved to be so popular that I decided to write a third novel, just about her.

"Tentatively titled *Blowing Bubbles with the Enemy,* this third book in the series deals with Bobby's instant unpopularity when she chooses to try out for the boys' basketball team at her junior high school. Not only does this anger the boys at her school, but when Bobby is unjustly denied a spot on the team, the girls take up a crusade in her honor, nearly creating a civil war at Jefferson Junior High.

"I have always enjoyed writing books for children. I especially feel that there is a need for good, funny stories that can be enjoyed by boys in the middle (third through fifth) grades. In the future, I intend to write more books about Leslie, Cameron, and Bobby. But I would also like to branch out and create new characters with other interests.

"A number of sources have influenced my writing. One University of California, Irvine professor in particular, by the name of Oakley Hall, gave me much encouragement and advice. He taught me some of the finer points of plotting and characterization, and he continually emphasized the use of realistic detail.

"My children continue to be a source of humorous material for me. They have a logic and sense of perspective that is always fresh and entirely unique. In fact, as they grow older, I can already see a number of potential books in the works.

"I also pay close attention to the students who come into the library every day, either to do homework or just to chat with each other. I find that children will talk about almost anything, if I simply stay in the background. And I have already used quite a few of their inspirational conversations in my books.

"I think this is the real reason why I want to continue writing for children. They are so uninhibited and funny that I find them irresistible, not only as subjects in my work, but as members of my potential audience. So I feel safe in saying that as long as kids keep on reading ... I will continue writing books for them."

*   *   *

JOHNSON, Daniel Shahid 1954-

PERSONAL: Born February 5, 1954, in Danbury, CT; son of Harvey W. (a Western artist) and Ilse (maiden name, Lohman) Johnson; married Aslaug Mati Berg (a knitter), June 30, 1986. *Education:* Adams State College, B.A. *Politics:* "Non-political." *Religion:* "The religion of life."

ADDRESSES: Home and office—Box 51, Crestone, CO 81131. *Agent*—Sherry Robb Literary Properties, Los Angeles, CA.

CAREER: Poet. Worked variously as a swimming instructor, teacher, firefighter, puppetmaker, and teen workshop leader.

MEMBER: Publishers Marketing Association.

AWARDS, HONORS: Small Press Selection, Publishers Marketing Association, for *Creative Rebellion,* 1992.

WRITINGS:

Yhantishor: A Fantasy Based in Truth, Mystic Garden, 1989.
Creative Rebellion: Positive Options for Teens in the 90s, Mystic Garden, 1992.

Also author of *The Aztec Cave of Life,* 1987, and *The Kerry Lee Story,* 1992. Contributor to periodicals.

Daniel Shahid Johnson's books have been translated into German.

WORK IN PROGRESS: Two screenplays: *Under the Twisted Cross* and *The Return of Medicine Hawk.*

SIDELIGHTS: Daniel Shahid Johnson told *SATA:* "I was originally sparked in my writing career by my artistic father and my mother's creative genius in writing children's stories. My original works were tiny booklets stapled together and illustrated with colored pencils. I feel that we already know in which direction our potentials lie, even as small children. If we are supported in this direction, our lives are rich and filled with all the joys possible.

"My passion for writing was rekindled in high school where an avant-garde English teacher challenged us to put forth our best, wildest and most creative works," Johnson continued. "I once wrote her a poem written with all the letters backward. I knew she would fetch a mirror rather than trying to decipher all that writing and I purposely wrote all over the back so she couldn't hold it up to the light. It worked and she read it in her own home before a mirror. The subject of the poem was pollution and the last line stated, 'You are also responsible for this mess, how can you look at yourself in this mirror?' She later told me she was looking around the room to see if I was hiding there."

Johnson's teachers, however, were not always so encouraging. In college, he ran into a creative writing teacher who almost destroyed his career. "He was not well-traveled, nor had he kept up on the changes in our society and ways of thinking so my writings went right over his head," Johnson recalled for *SATA.* "He nearly failed me, although many in the class were enthusiastic

DANIEL SHAHID JOHNSON

about my works. Not wanting to hurt my average, I dropped the class. Now I want to tell all aspiring authors not to worry about critics and what others think of your work. Anyone can find fault and it doesn't mean you are a failure.

"For the next decade, I worked at nearly thirty jobs, in every imaginable field. This gave me a chance to meet all kinds of people, to participate in many areas of life, and to gather experience which would eventually give authenticity to my writings. For nine months, I lived absolutely alone in the Rocky Mountains, searching deep within to find the deepest expressions of myself.

"In 1986, I was involved in a freak car accident which left me with a broken back. It was obviously not time to do heavy physical labor and the experience of almost dying gave me a new zest for life. I wrote *Yhantishor: A Fantasy Based in Truth* because I had something valuable to share, and realized that it would take some time to redevelop my writing skills. It was published in 1989, received excellent reviews, and was serialized in *L.A. Resources* and *Orange County Resources* magazines for over two years. All the illustrations were done by myself, with the aid of my artist father."

In 1991, Johnson published a nonfiction work for teenagers entitled *Creative Rebellion: Positive Options for Teens in the 90s.* The book, which features forty original cartoons by Johnson, led the author to become directly involved with his young audience through workshops that began in Colorado and New Mexico and are now spreading throughout the United States. "Because I don't try to change anybody, I merely share my experiences and insights, it is easy for me to point a positive direction to anyone," Johnson told *SATA.* "We all have immense potential and sometimes we just need a little confidence to pursue our dreams. Whatever the obstacles, we can be happy and create much beauty in our world."

Johnson's first book, *Yhantishor,* was translated and released in Germany after a fan took it along to a Frankfurt book fair in 1990. His popularity in Germany was secured when another book, *The Aztec Cave of Life,* was translated and heavily promoted in bookstores. "I feel very fortunate to be associated with such diligent people," Johnson said of the individuals who helped make his books successful overseas. "Once more, I want to stress to young readers that even you, yes YOU, can succeed if you stay with it and sharpen your skills," he added.

"In early 1992, I decided to finally begin writing screenplays for movies and television," Johnson continued. "Much of the subject matter offered seemed so peripheral and violent and I was sure I could write something interesting and exciting with suggestions on how we can 'find ourselves' as individuals and live in peaceful coexistence on our planet. First, I wrote about a boy growing up in Adolph Hitler's Third Reich in *Under the Twisted Cross.* He learns by the end of the movie that it is not important just to follow orders, but to follow your heart and do only what you know is right." Johnson's second screenplay, *The Return of Medicine Hawk,* depicts an old warrior returning to his tribe, the Cheyenne Indians, in the 1920s. "It is a comedy with a message: that we are all different individuals and our differences are important to making an interesting world, yet we are all the same in that we are human beings and all must be respected as such."

Johnson's latest project is writing the life story of a prisoner in the New Mexico State Penitentiary in Santa Fe. "It is very difficult to interview someone in prison," he told *SATA.* "Prisons are horrible places where the society seeks revenge for crimes against it. I feel that everyone should visit a prison at some point, especially teens who are getting in trouble." Johnson's own experience with prisons and prisoners also taught him that "there is good in every person, even the most feared criminal."

"Whatever my longings in life have been, I have followed them," Johnson told *SATA.* "Sometimes you fail, or you are unable to make a living doing exactly what you want to do, but if you do persevere, a time comes when you have developed your genius (and we all have genius). Then life is filled with blessings of reaching to your ultimate creative peaks. Rest and enjoy life but never stop growing; there is always more up ahead."

*   *   *

JOHNSON, Neil 1954-

PERSONAL: Born September 1, 1954, in Shreveport, LA; son of Melvin F., Jr. (a physician) and Lea (in book sales; maiden name, Morton) Johnson; married Rita Hummingbird (a certified public accountant), April 30, 1988; children: Bradford, Hannah. *Education:* Washington and Lee University, B.A., 1976. *Politics:* Independent. *Religion:* Presbyterian.

ADDRESSES: Home—749 Delaware, Shreveport, LA 71106. *Office*—124 East Prospect, Shreveport, LA 71104. *Agent*—Mary Jack Wald, 111 East 14th, New York, NY 10003.

CAREER: Photo-lab technician, Shreveport, LA, 1976-80; free-lance photographer and writer, 1980—; Centenary College of Louisiana, Shreveport, photography instructor, 1982—. Marjorie Lyons Playhouse, official photographer, 1987—; Red River Rally (hot air balloon festival), founder and co-chair, 1991 and 1992.

NEIL JOHNSON

MEMBER: Media (formerly American Society of Magazine Photographers), Shreveport Chamber of Congress, Clyde Connell Art Center (formerly Stoner Art Center; member of board, 1986-88; president, 1988).

AWARDS, HONORS: Rising Young Business Leader award, 1991.

WRITINGS:

SELF-ILLUSTRATED WITH PHOTOGRAPHS

Step into China, Simon & Schuster, 1988.
Born to Run: A Racehorse Grows Up, Scholastic, 1988.
The Battle of Gettysburg, Macmillan, 1989.
All in a Day's Work, Little, Brown, 1989.
Batter Up!, Scholastic, 1990.
Fire & Silk: Flying in a Hot Air Balloon, Little, Brown, 1991.
The Battle of Lexington and Concord, Macmillan, 1992.
Jack Creek Cowboy, Dial, 1993.

PHOTOGRAPHER

Charlotte Moser, *Clyde Connell: The Art & Life of a Louisiana Woman,* University of Texas Press, 1989.
Millicent E. Selsam, *How Puppies Grow,* revised edition, Scholastic, 1990.
Selsam, *How Kittens Grow,* revised edition, Scholastic, 1992.

OTHER

Contributor of text and photos to *Louisiana Life.* Also contributor of photos to other magazines, including *Time, Audubon, National Geographic World, Art Forum, Travel and Leisure,* and *USA Today.*

WORK IN PROGRESS: A "City Book" on Shreveport/Bossier City, for Louisiana State University Press; a book on a circus, for Dial.

SIDELIGHTS: Neil Johnson told *SATA:* "Buzzing along in a two-seater ultra-light aircraft (like a big tricycle with wings), circling a hot air balloon 1000 feet over a cotton field, it hit me: This is a JOB?! I was photographing the balloon for *Fire & Silk: Flying in a Hot Air Balloon.* I would have gladly paid someone for the chance to do what I was doing. Just like the Elephant's Child, I have an insatiable curiosity for the world around me and I love to ask questions. I am a journalist, but the main medium for putting out what I learn is not the usual print journalism media—newspapers or magazines—it is books for young readers."

After a few years working at a photo-lab, learning from other photographers and refining his abilities, Johnson quit his job to become a free-lance photographer. "I realized I had *two* skills: writing *and* photography," he commented. "Why not put them together? I managed to sell these double talents to our city magazine, which hired me to do a story on an art center and then on conditions in the worst local ghetto. This latter story took me into some fairly miserable places with my camera. It surprised me to find out later that many

people who read my story and viewed the photos had no idea how bad the situation was ... until it confronted them out of the pages of the magazine. This was a very satisfying feeling." Johnson also did free-lance work for a Louisiana state magazine, including a story on thoroughbred horses and another that involved a trip to China.

"But the city and state magazine jobs did not come very often," Johnson continued. "I was forced to constantly go out searching for any kind of photography work. And many times, there simply was no work. I challenged myself to go for the national magazines. I had friends in New York City (where most national magazines are published) to stay with and a car to drive me there. My plan was to go there once a year for five years, to knock on doors and show my portfolio.

"On one of my long drives to New York ... I thought about how fun it would be to actually write a book, and how similar a short nonfiction book and a long magazine story were. The ideas for books started coming immediately. While in New York, a friend gave me the name of an agent and within a year, my agent was hustling me around introducing me to editors at various publishers where we emphasized nonfiction books. One editor studied a batch of my China photos, and I soon had a contract to introduce children to China in a book. A month later, another editor looked at my thoroughbred horse photos and began discussing what kind of horse book we could do. Boom, boom! Two books directly from magazine stories! Today, I still enjoy doing magazine work, but being a book journalist takes most of my time."

Two of Johnson's book projects stemmed from his interest in historical reenactments. When an editor proposed a book based on a famous Civil War battle illustrated with photographs of reenactors, his response was enthusiastic. Of the actual photography process he related: "At one point during the photographing of *The Battle of Gettysburg* at the largest-ever Civil War reenactment in 1988, I was very close to thousands of 'soldiers' facing each other in long lines and all shooting blanks at each other as fast as they could. The deafening, continuous noise and the strong, acrid smell of black powder smoke was almost overwhelming! For a few seconds, I was shocked to actually feel like I was witnessing the horrifying tragedy of a real battle. It was both exciting and very, very scary.

"We were extremely proud of *The Battle of Gettysburg* and followed up a few years later with *The Battle of Lexington and Concord,* published in 1992. Half of the illustrations in both books were photographed during actual reenactments for the public and the other half I staged. I have always been fascinated by the process of making movies, and here I was doing something very similar. I was dealing with actors, costumes, props, strict schedules, and even special effects. For one image in *The Battle of Lexington and Concord,* I gathered about thirty 'Redcoats' on a dirt road and directed them for an illustration of the British retreat from Concord to

*The Battle of
Lexington and Concord*

NEIL JOHNSON

Illustrated with the author's photographs, this history of a climactic battle in America's "War for Independence" captures the excitement and drama of the period.

Boston, which had been along that very dirt road in 1775. When I yelled, 'Action!,' there was a lot of running and shooting—all for a single still image. Then, we repeated the action twice to make sure I got just the image I wanted. I owe a lot to these 'living historians' for the help they gave me.

"Writing two history books made me realize how important historians are and how difficult their job can be. Numerous authors had already written about both battles in many books. As a historian, I had the responsibility to read as many of these [accounts] as I could and then compare the detailed descriptions which did not always agree with one another. There turned out to be certain information on Lexington and Concord that was accepted as American *history,* but was actually American *myth.* I also wanted to present the Americans and the British as real people, not as 'bigger-than-life' heroes and villains. It was also very important for me to remember that I was telling a *story* to my readers. My job was to bring these two war stories to life and make

the stories flow quickly and dramatically, so that learning about history was also an enjoyable experience.

"I am fascinated with the constant flow of drama and beauty in the world around me. My favorite topic is whatever subject I happen on that grabs my interest and flips on my curiosity switch. But it also has to catch my eye—like majestic hot air balloons in the sky or cowboys in the Rocky Mountains—for a subject to become one of my books. Luckily, there is an unending supply of interesting and visual topics in the world, and I hope to be asking questions about them and pointing my camera at them for many years to come. My goal is always to produce a book that I would enjoy reading, if I happened to see it in a library or bookstore. Working is a part of life and I feel very fortunate to absolutely love my work. But I do not get enough feedback. It is especially enjoyable then to give talks on what I do to groups of young readers, and find that they have read, enjoyed, and even learned something new about the world from my books."

JONES, Marcia Thornton 1958-

PERSONAL: Born July 15, 1958, in Joliet, IL; daughter of Robert Edwin (a federal government employee) and Thelma Helen (a homemaker; maiden name, Kuhljuergen) Thornton; married Stephen Walter Jones (an electrical engineer), July 19, 1980. *Education:* University of Kentucky, A.B., 1980; Georgetown College, M.A., 1987. *Politics:* Independent. *Religion:* Roman Catholic.

ADDRESSES: Home—3328 Otter Creek Dr., Lexington, KY 40515. *Office*—Mary Todd Elementary School, 551 Parkside Dr., Lexington, KY 40505.

CAREER: St. Leo Elementary School, Versailles, KY, teacher, 1980-81; Sayre School, Lexington, KY, teacher, 1981-87; Auditor of Public Accounts, Frankfort, KY, principle administrative specialist, 1991; Fayette County Public Schools, Lexington, teacher, 1991—. Chairperson of Sayre School Teacher Evaluation Revision Committee, 1984, and Sayre Lower School Evaluation Committee, 1986; Argus Publications, free-lance writer, 1988—; University of Kentucky, community education instructor, 1990; Fayette County Public Schools, workshop presenter, 1992.

MEMBER: Society of Children's Book Writers and Illustrators, Lexington Writers Critique Group.

AWARDS, HONORS: Sayre School Short Award for excellence in teaching, 1985.

WRITINGS:

WITH DEBBIE DADEY

Vampires Don't Wear Polka Dots, Scholastic, 1990.
Werewolves Don't Go to Summer Camp, Scholastic, 1991.
Santa Claus Doesn't Mop Floors, Scholastic, 1991.
Leprechauns Don't Play Basketball, Scholastic, 1992.
Ghosts Don't Eat Potato Chips, Scholastic, 1992.
Aliens Don't Wear Braces, Scholastic, 1993.
Frankenstein Doesn't Plant Petunias, Scholastic, 1993.
Genies Don't Chew Bubblegum, Scholastic, 1993.
Pirates Don't Wear Pink Sunglasses, Scholastic, 1993.

Contributing editor of *Kidstuff* magazine. Contributor to *Kicks* magazine.

WORK IN PROGRESS: A juvenile novel entitled *Cross Your Heart and Hope to Die.*

SIDELIGHTS: "There is magic in the written word," Marcia Thornton Jones told *SATA.* "My most vivid childhood memories involve reading well-crafted stories that took me places I never imagined possible. Other children collected baseball cards and Barbie dolls. I collected paper and pencils. I wanted to create magic for myself, but no one ever taught me how to write—or even where to begin. So my efforts were limited, and even then I felt the isolated frustration writers feel when they're not sure if their work is good or not.

"During high school and college, my writing became formal as I completed theme after theme. No one taught me how to write themes either, but my grades indicated a knack for writing—or at least for fooling professors! After graduating with high distinction from the University of Kentucky, I dedicated myself to the teaching profession. My favorite thing about teaching was having the opportunity to read to my students. The stories I read were not necessarily classic literature. Instead, I shared books that made me laugh and cry and want to keep reading even after the story ended.

"I dreamed of having my name on books like these, but writing takes a great deal of self-confidence and discipline! Then I met Debbie. Debbie Dadey and I taught at the same private school. Once, while working out in the weight room, we talked about our mutual dream of being published authors. We looked at each other and said, 'What's stopping us?' We started writing during our lunch period the next day, and continued to write every day for the next two years with little success.

"Then one day we had a really rough teaching experience. It seemed as if we were invisible because the students totally ignored us. 'What would it take to get their attention?' we asked. 'I suppose we'd have to grow eight feet, sprout horns and blow smoke before they'd pay attention?' The more we talked, the sillier we became. So we decided to write a story about it. *Vampires Don't Wear Polka Dots,* a story about a really rotten group of students who suspect their new teacher is a vampire, was written in three weeks. Since then, we've published eight companion books. They weren't written as quickly, but they've all been fun!

"Writing is a big part of my life now. It is full of emotion, dreams, and hopes. It challenges me to snip the threads of every day life to weave something new and colorful. Most of all, writing is just plain old fun! That's the message I try to convey to writers at workshops and creative writing classes.

"Once upon a time, I read books that would take me to far away magical lands," Jones told *SATA.* "Now I *write* them!"

*   *   *

JORDAN, Don
See HOWARD, Vernon (Linwood)

*   *   *

JOSEPH, Anne
See COATES, Anna

K

KARL, Herb 1938-

PERSONAL: Born June 20, 1938, in Peekskill, NY; children: Bill, Joe. *Education:* Florida State University, B.A., 1962, M.A., Ph.D., 1971. *Politics:* Independent. *Religion:* Protestant.

ADDRESSES: Home—4350 West Kennedy Blvd., Tampa, FL 33609. *Office*—University of South Florida at St. Petersburg.

CAREER: Writer. *Palm Beach Post,* West Palm Beach, FL, reporter, 1959-60; Broward County Schools, Fort Lauderdale, FL, teacher, 1962-65; Florida State University, Tallahassee, FL, graduate assistant and instructor, 1965-71; University of South Florida at St. Petersburg, instructor, 1971—. *Military service:* U.S. Marine Corps., 1955-57; honorably discharged.

MEMBER: National Council of Teachers of English.

AWARDS, HONORS: The Toom County Mud Race was named a Delacorte Press Honor Book in 1991; a screenplay version won first place in the Florida Screenwriter's Competition in 1985.

WRITINGS:

The Toom County Mud Race, Delacorte, 1992.

Also author of screenplay *Deadly Deceits* with Ric Morales.

WORK IN PROGRESS: Inside Game, a young adult novel.

SIDELIGHTS: Herb Karl told *SATA:* "To me, both the writing and reading of fiction are adventures. As a writer, nothing is more satisfying than to watch my characters take over the story; they literally tell me what to write. Readers of fiction, I feel, are active participants in turning a writer's words into the sights, smells, sounds, and feelings that become the movie in our minds.

HERB KARL

"I wrote *The Toom County Mud Race* for every young adult male and female who would rather participate in an adventure than watch one on TV. Jackie Lee, Bonnie, and Snake are far from perfect teenagers. They confront the adult world—with all its deceits and ambiguities—head on. They aren't afraid to make choices, even though the choices they make aren't always the best ones. But they survive and grow."

FOR MORE INFORMATION SEE:

PERIODICALS

Publishers Weekly, January 1, 1992, p. 56.
School Library Journal, March, 1992, p. 256.
Voice of Youth Advocates, April, 1992, p. 30.

*   *   *

KEHRET, Peg 1936-

PERSONAL: Surname is pronounced "carrot"; born November 11, 1936, in LaCrosse, WI; daughter of Arthur R. (executive of Geo. A. Hormel Co.) and Elizabeth M. (a homemaker; maiden name, Showers) Schulze; married Carl E. Kehret (a player piano restorer), July 2, 1955; children: Bob C., Anne M. *Education:* Attended University of Minnesota, 1954-55. *Hobbies and other interests:* Reading, gardening, antiques, watching baseball and football, animals, cooking.

ADDRESSES: Office—c/o Cobblehill Books, 375 Hudson St., New York, NY 10014-3657. *Agent*—Emilie Jacobson, Curtis Brown Ltd., 10 Astor Place, New York, NY 10003.

CAREER: Writer, 1973—. Volunteer for The Humane Society.

MEMBER: Authors Guild, Society of Children's Book Writers, Mystery Writers of America.

AWARDS, HONORS: Forest Roberts Playwriting Award, Northern Michigan University, 1978, Best New Play of 1979, Pioneer Drama Service, and Best Plays for Senior Adults, American Theatre Association, 1981, all for *Spirit!;* Children's Choice Award, Children's Book Council and International Reading Association, 1988, and master list for Young Reader's Choice Award in Nevada and Oklahoma, all for *Deadly Stranger;* Service Award, American Humane Association, 1989; Recommended Books for Reluctant Young Adult Readers, American Library Association, 1989, for *The Winner,* and 1992, for *Cages;* named a Book for the Teen Age, New York Public Library, 1992, for *Cages,* and for *Winning Monologs for Young Actors;* Young Hoosier Book Award, Association for Indiana Media Educators, 1992, and master list for Young Reader's Choice Awards in Vermont, Illinois, Oklahoma, Nebraska, Iowa, West Virginia, and Missouri, all for *Nightmare Mountain;* Young Adults Choice Award, International Reading Association, 1992, for *Sisters, Long Ago;* Texas Lone Star list, 1992, for *Cages;* Pacific Northwest Writer's Conference Achievement Award, 1992.

PEG KEHRET

WRITINGS:

Wedding Vows: How to Express Your Love in Your Own Words, Meriwether Publishing, 1979, second edition, 1990.
Refinishing and Restoring Your Piano, Tab Books, 1983.

Also contributor to periodicals.

PLAYS

Cemeteries Are a Grave Matter, Dramatic Publishing, 1975.
Let Him Sleep 'till It's Time for His Funeral, Contemporary Drama Service, 1977.
Spirit!, Pioneer Drama Service, 1979.
Dracula, Darling, Contemporary Drama Service, 1979.
Charming Billy, Contemporary Drama Service, 1983.
Bicycles Built for Two (musical), Contemporary Drama Service, 1985.

FOR CHILDREN

Winning Monologs for Young Actors, Meriwether Publishing, 1986.
Deadly Stranger, Dodd, 1987.
Encore! More Winning Monologs for Young Actors, Meriwether, 1988.
The Winner, Turman Publishing, 1988.
Nightmare Mountain, Cobblehill Books, 1989.
Sisters, Long Ago, Cobblehill Books, 1990.
Cages, Cobblehill Books, 1991.
Terror at the Zoo, Cobblehill Books, 1992.

Acting Natural: Monologs, Dialogs, and Playlets for Teens, Meriwether Publishing, 1992.
Horror at the Haunted House, Cobblehill Books, 1992.
Night of Fear, Cobblehill Books, 1993.

Also author of children's book for Acropolis Books.

WORK IN PROGRESS: An autobiography concerning battle with polio.

SIDELIGHTS: Peg Kehret told *SATA:* "I have always loved to write. When I was small, my grandfather used to pay me three cents each to write stories for him. At the age of nine, I wrote, published, sold, and distributed a dog newspaper about all the dogs in my neighborhood. This was before we had photocopy machines, so I hand printed every copy of my dog newspaper. It went out of business after only a few weeks because I made one big mistake: in every issue the entire front page was devoted to *my* dog, while all the other dogs had small stories on the back page. People got tired of reading about B.J. and quit subscribing to my newspaper—and I learned that if I expect other people to read what I write, I must make it interesting to them. During my teen years, I wanted to be a writer or a veterinarian. I'm glad I chose writing,

In this second novel featuring Ellen and Corey Streater, the adventurous duo gets wrapped up in a mystery that involves a very active ghost and a plot against the local historical society. (Cover illustration by Stephen Marchesi.)

but two of the main characters in my books want to be veterinarians. Dogs, llamas, and elephants have played important parts in my books.

"I volunteer at the Humane Society. Each month, I write a Pet of the Month feature for a local newspaper, showcasing a Humane Society animal that needs a home. My husband and I also collect supplies for a senior citizen pet food bank and help with an annual fund-raising auction. (I donate signed copies of my books.) We have two dogs and a cat, all adopted from The Humane Society's shelter.

"For a long time, I had wanted to use my Humane Society experiences in a book and I finally did it in *Cages.* The book has a double dedication: all of the companion animals who have enriched my life, and the Humane Society and SPCA. I always give the first copy of each book to the person to whom it is dedicated. The first copy of *Cages* is in the library of the Seattle/King County Humane Society. Even though I write fiction, my books require a lot of research. For example, when I was writing *Cages,* I interviewed the head security officer of a large department store, a police officer, and a psychologist who serves on a juvenile court committee. For *Sisters, Long Ago,* my research included getting hypnotized. I published more than three hundred magazine stories, two adult books, and several plays before I began writing books for young people. As soon as I tried writing from a youthful point of view, I knew I had found my place in the writing world.

"When I was in the seventh grade, I got polio and was paralyzed from the neck down. The doctors told my parents that I would never walk again. Much to everyone's surprise, I made almost a complete recovery. I vividly remember the time when I got sick and my months in the hospital and my eventual return to school. Maybe that's why I enjoy writing books for young people; I recall exactly how it felt to be that age. I remember my friends and the books I liked and even what programs I listened to on the radio. When I write, it is easy for me to slip back in my imagination and become twelve years old again."

FOR MORE INFORMATION SEE:

PERIODICALS

Bulletin of the Center for Children's Books, July-August, 1987.
School Library Journal, October, 1989, p. 120; June, 1991, p. 126.
Voice of Youth Advocates, June, 1991, p. 97; October, 1992, p. 224.

*   *   *

KETTEMAN, Helen 1945-

PERSONAL: Born July 1, 1945, in Augusta, Georgia; daughter of Jack (a physician) and Mary Helen (a teacher; maiden name, Walker) Moon; married Charles Harry Ketteman, Jr. (an accountant), in 1969; children: William Gregory, Mark David. *Education:* Young Harris College, A.A., 1965; attended Georgia Southern College, 1965-66; Georgia State University, B.A., 1968.

ADDRESSES: Home—Dallas, TX. *Agent*—Ginger Knowlton, Curtis Brown Ltd., 10 Astor Pl., New York, NY 10003.

CAREER: Writer.

WRITINGS:

Not Yet, Yvette, Albert Whitman, 1992.
Aunt Hilarity's Bustle, Simon & Schuster, 1992.
The Christmas Blizzard, Scholastic, in press.
The Year of No More Corn, Orchard, in press.
One Baby Boy, Simon & Schuster, in press.

Also contributor to periodicals, including *Highlights for Children.*

WORK IN PROGRESS: "Many picture books."

SIDELIGHTS: Helen Ketteman told *SATA:* "I believe children should be exposed to books early and often. If children learn at an early age that books can be fun and entertaining, I think the battle with television and video games can be won. Readers that are created early will be lifelong readers."

*   *   *

KILLIEN, Christi 1956-

PERSONAL: Born December 27, 1956, in Tulsa, OK; daughter of Cloyse Edwin (an oil company executive) and Marie (a homemaker; maiden name, Austin) Overturf; married William F. Killien (a junior high school principal), December 20, 1980; children: Molly, Annie Rose, Austin. *Education:* Baylor University, B.A. (magna cum laude), 1978; attended Baylor Law School, 1978;

CHRISTI KILLIEN

attended University of Washington for graduate studies, 1979-80.

ADDRESSES: Office—Scholastic, 730 Broadway, New York, NY 10003. *Agent*—Ruth Cohen, P.O. Box 7626, Menlo Park, CA 94025.

CAREER: Writer. Taught middle school in Lake Stevens, WA, during the early 1980s. Workshop leader and writing conference presenter.

MEMBER: Authors Guild, Authors League of America, Society of Children's Book Writers and Illustrators, PEN.

AWARDS, HONORS: Putting on an Act was named a Recommended Book for Reluctant Young Adult Readers by the American Library Association, a Young Adult Choice by the International Reading Association's *Journal of Reading,* both 1988, and awarded the Volunteer State Book Award, 1990; *Rusty Fertlanger, Lady's Man* was named a Recommended Book for Reluctant Young Adult Readers by the American Library Association and was selected for the "Pick of the Lists" by *American Bookseller,* both 1988; *Fickle Fever* was selected as a Recommended Book for Reluctant Young Adult Readers by the American Library Association, 1988.

WRITINGS:

JUVENILE

Putting on an Act, Houghton, 1986.
All of the Above, Houghton, 1987.
Rusty Fertlanger, Lady's Man, Houghton, 1988.
Fickle Fever, Houghton, 1988.
Artie's Brief: The Whole Truth and Nothing But, Houghton, 1989.
The Daffodils, Scholastic, 1992.

OTHER

(With Sheila Bender) *Writing in a Convertible with the Top Down: A Unique Guide for Writers,* Warner Books, 1992.

WORK IN PROGRESS: An adult novel.

SIDELIGHTS: Known for realistic situations and a light sense of humor, Christi Killien's juvenile novels have won numerous awards for their ability to draw even reluctant young adults into the act of reading. Surprisingly, the author of six pre-teen novels and one adult nonfiction guide to writing told *SATA* she never thought of becoming a "real" writer until she finished college and began teaching junior high school. As a teacher, Killien spent many hours reading aloud to her appreciative students until suddenly it occurred to her "that I really didn't want to be teaching history; what I wanted to be doing was telling stories."

A voracious reader of biographies and historical novels as a youngster, Killien found an escape from the strain of her family life in books. Since her father's job required frequent relocations, young Killien often felt like an outsider and, as a result, became a keen observer of those around her. "My two brothers and one sister handled these moves better than I did. I was kind of a rebellious teenager. Writing my feelings helped me through some of the crises of this time, though," she recalled in an essay for *SATA*. Writing, in fact, helped Killien to discover her identity. "I was saying, 'I feel these things and that's real and that's who I am.' That's the way I kept hold of some sense of myself."

Her memorable adolescent years are part of the reason she is able to write from the perspective of her young protagonists, Killien explained in an interview with *SATA*. "I still have that person, that twelve-year-old, in me somewhere and I can very easily feel that again. Certain periods of my life are accessible to me and others aren't. I know some friends of mine remember being five or six very clearly and those are my picture-book writer friends. That isn't a time period that is very clear to me emotionally whereas the emotions of early adolescence and high school years are very clear," she said.

Killien's books are often heavily autobiographical, she told *SATA*. "Over the years, I have realized that what begins story writing for me is something from my own life. It is some detail, some incident, some observation that snags me. It is an external event, but it triggers something deep inside me." The external events that spark book ideas can vary widely, she said. "In *Rusty Fertlanger, Lady's Man,* I started with a newspaper article about a boy in Seattle who was paired with a girl at one of his wrestling meets, and a book entitled *How to Draw Comics the Marvel Way*," she recalled. "These two ideas tumbled around in my head for a couple of months. I was snagged by the unhappy picture of that young boy in the paper. I ended up writing a story that explored my feelings about the 'masculine' image that our comic book, TV, Barbie doll culture teaches us." Another novel, *The Daffodils,* was sparked by a friend's comment: "My eleven-year-old daughter wants to wear a bra, so I'm letting her, but only on Wednesdays." The comment excited Killien, and she had to write about it, she told *SATA,* because she "couldn't forget it."

One deeply personal incident in Killien's life that inspired a book was the suicide of her youngest brother in 1986. "In *Artie's Brief: The Whole Truth and Nothing But,* I started with the feelings I had when my own brother committed suicide, and I paired them with my law background," said Killien, who attended law school for a short time. Although Killien based the story on her own feelings, she had to make changes in order to keep it from becoming *too* personal. "I wanted the protagonist to be a boy largely because I wanted to remove him from me. That was part of the way I leapt off the lily pad of personal experiences," she explained. "There are certain choices that I make that remove the story from me, that free me from the autobiography." In *The Daffodils,* for example, Killien made her protagonist, Nicole, the daughter of a single parent father in order to "get her away from *me* as a sixth grade girl with bra troubles."

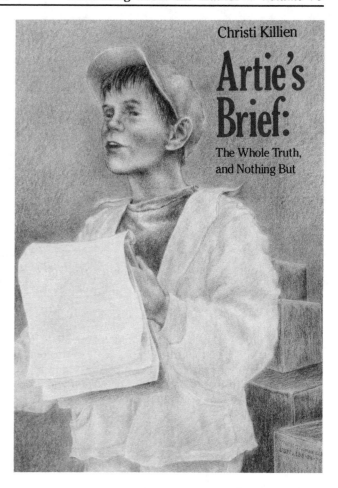

Inspired by both his brother's troubles and a need to see justice done, aspiring lawyer Artie tries to help his disaster-prone classmate Gilbert Flowers. (Cover illustration by Pam Johnson.)

Killien's first published book, *Putting on an Act,* is also very autobiographical, she told *SATA*. The plot deals with fifteen-year-old Skeeter McGee, a bright girl who enjoys dime-store romance novels as much as the plays of William Shakespeare. At the outset of the story, Skeeter is happy fantasizing about her imaginary romance with Campbell Lancaster, the school's basketball star, until she finds out that her pen-pal of many years, Terry, is moving to town and will be attending her school. Skeeter's problem is that she has written Terry many letters describing her "boyfriend" in great detail: "I had told her all about a date, which I had totally made up, of course, in which Campbell had taken me to a movie and then to McDonald's," Skeeter remembers. "McDonald's isn't exactly an enchanting setting, but I had to be realistic. I told her about how I had gotten our order since Campbell was in the rest room. When he came back to the table, I had decided to do an imitation of a McDonald's person, like one I had read about in *Popularity High,* a Tender Moments romance. I said, 'One cheese quarter, two Macs, two fries and a coupla Cokes, sir,' and then I stuck a fry in Campbell's mouth. 'Taste good?' I asked. He swallowed the fry and said, 'It's okay. But this tastes even better.' And he had leaned

Nicole learns a lot about friendship and teamwork after she devises a plan to motivate the members of her champion softball team, the Daffodils. (Cover illustration by Aleta Jenks.)

over and kissed me, several times. I had actually written that to Terry! Pretty far out. But very romantic."

Skeeter's sticky situation and the plan she devises to save face when Terry moves to town are fictional, Killien said, but the character is very much a reflection of the author's own personality. "*Putting on an Act* will always be one of my favorites because it was the first and because it's about this idea, this sense of who I really am. I think that question, of discovering what's important to you and who you really are is something that I write about all the time. For me, there is always this sense of reflection and of self-discovery."

Writing about different aspects of herself is how Killien found what she calls her "voice," she told *SATA*. "Voice has to do with where you are speaking from," she explained, "and what's absolutely clear and interesting to yourself. I knew I had found my voice with *Putting on an Act* when I got a lot of response on that book that I hadn't before." Killien maintains that her best writing, and best reviews, develop from her humorous streak although she said she never thinks about making particular scenes funny while she's writing them. "I just think in terms of something I enjoy that's giving me pleasure as I'm writing it. A humorous situation where things

don't quite match up—that's where the writing really takes off for me," she said.

Killien continued the adventures of Skeeter McKee in a sequel entitled *Fickle Fever* because she felt the conclusion of the first book offered "too pat an ending for what it was really like to be in an adolescent love relationship." At the start of the novel, Skeeter finally has a real boyfriend. However, she soon finds that she cannot remain interested in just one boy and so begins a series of crushes on just about every boy she knows. With each new crush, she adopts the interests of the object of her desire. Bowling, cars and kites are just a few of the hobbies Skeeter pretends to adore in order to catch a new boy's eye. But with each new crush comes disappointment. Her discovery of the fleeting nature of infatuation is a real source of dismay for Skeeter, who muses: "Love is forever ... until the next day. This seemed to be the theme of my life. It was downright scary." As Skeeter learns about love, she also learns about the importance of maintaining her own identity. Killien said the story gave her an opportunity to explore the phenomenon of adapting one's personality in order to attract another person. "It's a question of 'am I really interested in this or am I just trying to further a relationship with someone I care about?' At what point are you really doing something because it is interesting to you? This seems to be a problem especially when you

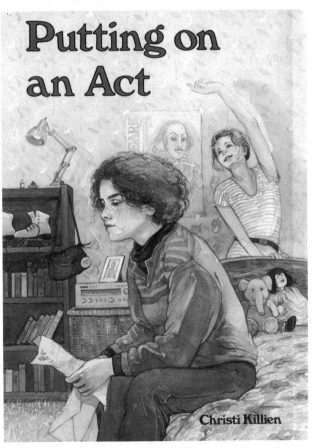

Skeeter's tall tales get her into trouble when her pen pal Terry moves to town. (Cover illustration by Diane de Groat.)

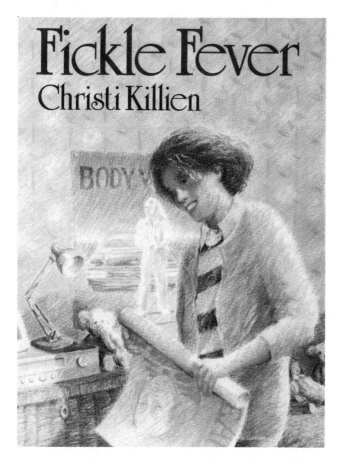

When her romance with Terry begins to get a little stale, Skeeter begins looking for "true love" in other places—with surprising results. (Cover illustration by Mary Kubricht.)

are young and you're trying out all kinds of things and so it seemed to me that it would be a problem for Skeeter," Killien explained.

Although Killien has no other sequels planned, she does intend to continue writing in the humorous style that she knows so well. "Trying to write about what you don't know is deadly," she said. Her advice to aspiring writers is to remember that "bad writing is the key to good writing. When I say bad writing, I mean writing that doesn't work for a reader. You start with just a raw incident or description and then get an honest response from people about where it affects them emotionally. Then ask your trusted readers where they want to hear more and listen to yourself about where you want to hear more and just go from there. You'll end up with a piece that's good."

WORKS CITED:

Killien, Christi, *Putting on an Act,* Houghton, 1986.
Killien, *Fickle Fever,* Houghton, 1988.

—Sketch by Cornelia A. Pernik

KISH, Eleanor M(ary) 1924-
(Ely Kish)

PERSONAL: Born Eleanor Mary Kiss, March 17, 1924, in Newark, NJ; legally changed surname to Kish, 1973; daughter of Eugene Kiss (a painter, decorator, and actor) and Teresa Bittman. *Education:* Essex County (New Jersey) Vocational School in Productive Art, 1942; Institute of Fine Art, Newark, New Jersey; studied under Ejnar Hansen and Julian Ritter; attended Institute del Alliende, Mexico, 1949-51.

ADDRESSES: Office—RR 1, Box 87C, Hammond, Ontario K0A 2A0, Canada. *Agent*—Huguette Vrancken, RR 1, Lavigne Rd. 1863, Hammond, Ontario K0A 2A0, Canada.

CAREER: Artist, paleoartist, and sculptor. *Exhibitions:* Kish's works have been exhibited in numerous galleries and museums throughout Canada and the United States; her murals are included in permanent collections of several museums, including the Canadian Museum of Nature, Ottawa; the New Mexico Museum of Natural History, Albuquerque; and the National Museum of Natural History, Smithsonian Institution, Washington, DC.

AWARDS, HONORS: Parents' Choice Award, 1992, for *The Tiny Perfect Dinosaur Book, Bones, Egg & Poster: Presenting Leptoceratops.*

ELY KISH

Kish's skill as a paleoartist—a painter of dinosaurs and prehistoric landscapes—is evident in this volume about the lifestyle and eating habits of a small herbivore. (Illustration from *The Tiny Perfect Dinosaur: Presenting Leptoceratops,* by John Acorn and D. Russell.)

ILLUSTRATOR:

Dale A. Russell, *An Odyssey in Time: The Dinosaurs of North America,* University of Toronto Press, 1989.

UNDER NAME ELY KISH

Dale A. Russell, *A Vanished World: Dinosaurs of Western Canada,* National Museum of Natural Sciences, 1977.
John Acorn and D. Russell, coauthors, *The Tiny Perfect Dinosaur Book, Bones, Egg & Poster: Presenting Leptoceratops,* Andrews & McMeel, 1991, published as *The Tiny Perfect Dinosaur Book and Bones—Leptoceratops,* Somerville House, 1991.
Jennifer A. Kirkpatrick, *Dinosaur Babies* (part of "Pop-Ups" series edited by Jane H. Buxton), National Geographic Society, 1991.

Contributor of paintings to several books, including *Dinosaurs: An Illustrated History,* Hammond, 1983; *Wonder and Mystery of Dinosaurs in Art,* Gakken, 1990; *Encyclopedia of Dinosaurs,* Beekman House, 1990; and *Thread of Life: The Smithsonian Looks at Evolution,* by Roger Lewin, Smithsonian Institution Press, 1982. Contributor of paintings to television productions and periodicals, including *Art Impression, Canadian Geographic, Equinox, Horizon, Ottawa Revue, Ranger Rick,* and *Wild Life Art News.*

WORK IN PROGRESS: The Book of Life, Century/Random House, expected to be published in 1993; *Dinosaur Posterbook,* Benedikt Taschen Verlag.

SIDELIGHTS: World-renowned artist Ely Kish is one of the few famed paleoartists—a painter of dinosaurs and prehistoric landscapes—in the world and the only woman in that class. It wasn't until 1974, however, after years of exhibiting the many still lifes, portraits, landscapes, and cityscapes painted in her unique realistic style in galleries throughout Canada and the United States, that she was introduced to the world of prehistory and dinosaurs. Invited to paint an Indian mural for the reopening of the National Museum of Man in Ottawa, Canada, Kish met paleobiologist Dr. Dale Russell, who needed to create a dinosaur slide show and asked Kish for help. Finding her art and technique the ideal medium for translating his knowledge of dinosaurs into visual form, Russell asked her to illustrate his book *A Vanished World: The Dinosaurs of Western Canada.* Thus began her illustrious career as a paleoartist. More recently, the two collaborated on *The Tiny, Perfect Dinosaur Book, Egg, Bones & Poster,* the first children's book illustrated by Kish.

One of seven children, Kish grew up in a poor section of Newark, New Jersey. She recalled her childhood for Suzanne Kingsmill in an article for *Canadian Geographic:* "They would shoot tommy guns across the street at each other. We'd lie on our bellies ... watching the shooting and knife fights. It was quite a neighborhood." In school, she refused to take traditional "girls'" courses like home economics and was the only girl in carpentry class. Encouraged by a school principal who recognized her artistic talents, Kish attended a technical high school where she took nothing but industrial arts courses; she also took four years of evening art courses.

After graduation, Kish traveled throughout the United States and Mexico for fifteen years, earning her living at a variety of jobs, including painting billboards, designing greeting cards, and various construction-related jobs, all the while continuing her work as a painter of landscapes, portraits, and nature. She began using a masculine name, Ely, a shortened version of Eleanor, feeling that this would alleviate problems she encountered in the male-dominated world of fine arts. In the late 1950s she moved to Canada and became a Canadian citizen.

When Dr. Russell commissioned Kish to illustrate *A Vanished World,* she was able to quit her job at a display company and devote all her time to painting. She told Kingsmill, "That was the first time I had a chance to paint for my living." Her paintings for *A Vanished World* established her as a top-ranking paleoartist and led to her commissions to paint murals depicting prehistoric life at several other museums around the world.

After many years as a realist painter creating works of art directly from nature, Kish has developed new artistic approaches to create her prehistoric subjects. "For a woman who has painted from living models most of her life, the limits imposed by her dinosaur art highlight her adaptability, patience, and professionalism," notes Kingsmill. In order to make her images as scientifically accurate and realistic as possible, she first sculpts the skeletons of her subjects in papier mache, then forms their muscles and flesh from a variety of materials, consulting with science experts and studying actual fossils throughout this stage to ensure accuracy. Kish then uses the models as a guide for both her preliminary pencil drawings and her oil paintings; they enable her to see exactly how contours should be shaded and how light should reflect off each individual creature.

Kish told Kingsmill that her imagination allows her to envision how creatures she's never actually seen behave during various activities: "I'm the dinosaur. I dream of what I'd do, how I would eat, how I would feed my baby and how I would protect myself. Once you get acquainted with the animal, then you can imagine it turning, moving."

WORKS CITED:

Kingsmill, Suzanne, "Recreating the World of Dinosaurs," *Canadian Geographic,* April/May, 1990, pp. 17-27.

FOR MORE INFORMATION SEE:

PERIODICALS

Canadian Geographic, October/November, 1990.
Museum & Arts Washington, July/August, 1990.
Washington Post, April 12, 1990, p. C1.

*　　*　　*

KISH, Ely
See KISH, Eleanor M(ary)

*　　*　　*

KUNJUFU, Jawanza 1953-

PERSONAL: Born June 15, 1953, in Chicago, IL; son of Eddie and Mary (Snyder) Brown; married June 1, 1985; wife's name, Rita (an administrator); children: Walker Smith, Shik. *Education:* Attended Morgan State University and Towson State University, 1973; Illinois State University, B.A., 1974; attended Union Graduate School, 1980-84.

ADDRESSES: Home—12 Willow Brook Trail, Crete, IL 60417. *Office*—African American Images, 9204 Commercial, Chicago, IL 60617.

CAREER: African American Images, Chicago, IL, consultant, 1980—. Consultant to twenty school districts; member of the board of directors for ten organizations.

JAWANZA KUNJUFU

MEMBER: Affiliated with twenty-five professional organizations.

WRITINGS:

(With Haki R. Madhubuti) *Black People and the Coming Depression,* Institute of Positive Education, c. 1975.

Children Are the Reward of Life: Parent/Teacher Guidelines for Maximizing Black Children's Potential, Afro-American Publishing Co., c. 1982.

Countering the Conspiracy to Destroy Black Boys, Afro-American Publishing Co., Volume 1, c. 1983, Volume 2, c. 1986, Volume 3, 1990.

Developing Positive Self-Images and Discipline in Black Children, African American Images, c. 1984.

Motivating and Preparing Black Youth to Work, African American Images, c. 1986.

Lessons from History: A Celebration in Blackness, African American Images, c. 1987.

To Be Popular or Smart: The Black Peer Group, African American Images, c. 1988.

A Talk with Jawanza: Critical Issues in Educating African American Youth, African American Images, c. 1989.

Also author of *Black Economics,* 1991; author and executive producer of *Up against the Wall,* a film for young people, and coauthor with Lady Jane Hubbard of screenplay novelization, both for African American Images.

SIDELIGHTS: Jawanza Kunjufu told *SATA:* "I have been exposed to excellent teachers and role models who have given me high expectations. As president of African American Images, a communications company based in Chicago, Illinois, I am constantly on the lecture circuit conducting over thirty different workshops, addressing students, parents, teachers, community residents, and churches.

"I have been a guest on *The Oprah Winfrey Show, Tony Brown's Journal, Sally Jessy Raphael,* and the BET network and have had numerous articles written about my work appearing in *Essence* and *Ebony* magazines. I am executive director of the African American Images Talent Center, designed to identify and develop our children's talents and motivate them to start their own businesses. I am also executive producer of a full-feature movie titled *Up against the Wall,* starring Marla Gibbs. The movie, now available on videocassette, is about peer pressure. I give full credit for my accomplishments to Jesus Christ, who is first in my life; my wife, who happens to be my best friend; and my two sons."

L

LATHROP, Francis
See LEIBER, Fritz (Reuter, Jr.)

* * *

LAWRENCE, Lynn
See GARLAND, Sherry

* * *

LECOURT, Nancy (Hoyt) 1951-

PERSONAL: Surname is pronounced "le-coor"; born May 3, 1951, in Glendale, CA; daughter of Franklyn (a history professor) and Laurie (a medical technologist; maiden name, Chapman) Hoyt; married Patrick Pierre Lecourt (a teacher), June, 1973; children: Sebastian Joseph, Peter Alexander. *Education:* Loma Linda University, B.A. (English), 1973, B.A. (French), 1973, M.A., 1974. *Politics:* Democrat. *Religion:* Seventh-Day Adventist.

ADDRESSES: Home—345 McReynolds Dr., Angwin, CA 94508. *Office*—English Department, Pacific Union College, Angwin, CA 94508.

CAREER: Loma Linda University, Riverside, CA, instructor, 1974-78; Pacific Union College, Angwin, CA, assistant professor, 1979-81 and 1984—, English department chair, 1991—; writer. St. Helena Public Library, member of board of trustees, 1989-92.

MEMBER: Society of Children's Book Writers.

WRITINGS:

Rainbow (picture book), illustrated by Betty Wind, Review & Herald, 1980.
Abracadabra to Zigzag (picture book), illustrated by Barbara Lehman, Lothrop, 1991.
Teddy, the Better-Than-New Bear, illustrated by Bobbi Tull, Pacific Press Publishing Association, in press.

WORK IN PROGRESS: Ishi: A Biography of the Last Unacculturated Native North American (working title).

SIDELIGHTS: Nancy Lecourt told *SATA:* "I wrote my first book, *Rainbow,* with my first baby sitting on the table beside me, dozing in his little yellow chair. He was only a few weeks old. I had been asked to write a Bible story at the second-grade reading level. I found the challenge of trying to tell a story in a limited vocabulary rather fun—sort of like writing poetry."

NANCY LECOURT

122

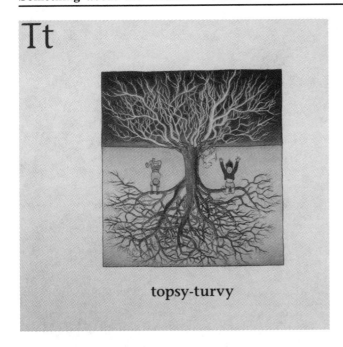

The illustrations in *Abracadabra to Zigzag* highlight the humor Lecourt sees in words that "double themselves." (Illustration by Barbara Lehman.)

"The similarity of picture books to poetry became even clearer with my next book, *Abracadabra to Zigzag*. The text could not be more spare. I prefer picture books—[Maurice] Sendak's are a good example—in which the text is clean and bare. Like poetry, they hint and distill in order to engage the reader. In a picture book, of course, one purpose is to leave room for the pictures to work—or perhaps I should say dance—with the text in a delightful wholeness.

"This is some of what I hope happens in *Abracadabra to Zigzag*. In many ways it is a poem; it is unified only by sound, not by meaning. I had noticed that English was full of words that doubled themselves: 'knickknack,' 'hunky-dory,' 'jiggery pokery.' I found these words amusing, and wondered if there might not be one for every letter of the alphabet.

"I think that one of the most interesting things about this book, from an adult point of view, is the way the editor and illustrator worked to give it unity. The carnival theme, the dog, the colors—these work in counterpoint to the variety of the text.

"My third book, *Teddy, the Better-Than-New Bear*, was written for a religious publishing house. I tried to find a way to incorporate the religious idea—about the resurrection—into the story in such a way that it was as nondidactic as possible. I hope I succeeded.

"I am excited about the manuscript I am currently at work on. The current title is rather awkward, and may not survive: *Ishi: A Biography of the Last Unacculturated Native North American*. My father is a California historian, and he introduced me to Ishi when I was a teenager. However, I only recently realized, with chil-

dren of my own, that this story is not really accessible to elementary school children.

"The story of Ishi is very powerful in many ways: his life with his tribe, the years of hiding, the massacre of his people, and his ability to adjust to a new life—all these make fascinating reading. I hope to tell this story as pure biography for middle-grade children—with all the photographs."

*   *   *

LEIBER, Fritz (Reuter, Jr.) 1910-1992 (Francis Lathrop)

OBITUARY NOTICE —See index for *SATA* sketch: Born December 25, 1910 (some sources say December 24), in Chicago, IL; died of a stroke, September 5, 1992, in San Francisco, CA. Author. Best known for his fantasy series centered on the adventures of Fafhrd and the Grey Mouser—including *Swords and Deviltry*—Leiber is remembered as a preeminent writer of science fiction, fantasy, and horror. His works deal with the terror that lurks beneath the facade of everyday, urban reality, and his prose style is characterized by vivid language and satire. His horror novel *Conjure Wife* has been called a modern masterpiece, and his science fiction novels *The Big Time* and *The Wanderer* both won Hugo awards. In total, Leiber amassed six Hugos, three Nebula awards, two World Fantasy awards, and the World Fantasy Life Award. His extensive catalogue of prose and poetry includes *Our Lady of Darkness, The Knight and Knave of Swords,* and *Gummitch and Friends.*

OBITUARIES AND OTHER SOURCES:

BOOKS

Who's Who in America, 46th edition, Marquis, 1990.

PERIODICALS

Chicago Tribune, September 10, 1992, section 3, p. 14.
Los Angeles Times, September 11, 1992, p. A26.
New York Times, September 11, 1992, p. D16.
Times (London), September 28, 1992, p. 15.

*   *   *

LEVY, Constance 1931-

PERSONAL: Born May 8, 1931, in St. Louis, MO; daughter of Samuel (a clothing store proprietor) and Esther (a homemaker; maiden name, Seigel) Kling; married Monroe D. Levy (a physicist), February 15, 1953; children: Robert, Carol Levy Charles, Kenneth, Donald, Edward. *Education:* Washington University (St. Louis, MO), B.A., 1952, M.A., 1974. *Politics:* Independent. *Religion:* Jewish.

ADDRESSES: Home—58 Frontenac Estates, St. Louis, MO 63131.

CAREER: Webster Groves School District, Webster Groves, MO, teacher, 1952-53; Ritenour School District, St. Louis, MO, teacher, 1953-54; Washington

University, St. Louis, supervisor of student teachers, 1974-75; Missouri Arts Council, "Writers in the Schools" program, St. Louis, children's poet, 1975-81; Harris-Stowe State College, St. Louis, adjunct instructor of children's literature, 1980-82. Free-lance poet in schools, 1981-92; member of commission board, Brodsky St. Louis Jewish Library, 1989—; guest speaker in schools and educational conferences, 1991—.

MEMBER: Chicago Children's Reading Roundtable.

WRITINGS:

I'm Going to Pet a Worm Today and Other Poems, Macmillan, 1991.

Work represented in several periodicals and anthologies, including _Cricket, Instructor,_ and _Puddle Wonderful._

WORK IN PROGRESS: A second book of poems for children.

SIDELIGHTS: "I'm both a new author and an old one," Constance Levy told _SATA,_ "a grandmother with a first book published in 1991 and an 'old,' occasionally published poet with poems in teacher's educational journals, _Cricket_ magazine, and anthologies.

"I would never have wondered about how I became a poet except that children I meet as a visiting poet frequently ask that question. And the only answer I can provide, for them and for myself, is that I don't really know, but I think I always was. As a child I was drawn to poetry and loved hearing my mother recite poems for me that she learned when she was young. It always seemed that the poem I read or listened to was speaking to me. I could see it and feel it. The words made music and danced and played games with each other and stirred my senses. I have never stopped loving poetry, especially poetry for children. Poems are habit forming, you know. Once you have a good taste of a flavor that suits you, you want more and more, and the pleasures stay with you always.

"My writing years began, as I recall, the day I was able to write the words, at around age six; [I was] at my creative best from ages six through ten or eleven. It was so easy then. Poems seemed to turn themselves on and bubble and flow onto the paper. The wonderful feeling of getting a poem 'right' nourished my spirit then as it does now. Through high school and college I enjoyed reading poetry but did little writing. Becoming a primary grade teacher and then a mother helped turn the spigot back on. Of course, it has never again been so easy to please myself or catch the 'flow' as it was in those early years when children all possess that special magic. I work slowly now and I'm a stern editor of my own work, often working and reworking even a small poem until it begs for mercy, and I have to put it aside for another time.

"Many years after that 'magic' time of childhood, when I received my master's degree in education, I was

CONSTANCE LEVY

determined to do my part to keep that magic from fading and to use it to enrich the educational process. Instead of becoming a reading specialist as planned, I became a poet in the schools for the Missouri Arts Council and engaged children and teachers in poetry workshops. It was obvious that children of all abilities thrived on this kind of reading, writing and talking in poetry workshops. Teachers who continued incorporating poetry in the curriculum were enthusiastic and well rewarded for their efforts. After leaving the Arts Council program, I continued as a free-lance poet in the schools, and am continuing to share poetry now as a published poet. I still go into the schools as an author and teach occasional workshops. I sometimes feel that I am a 'Johnny Appleseed' for poetry (a 'Connie' Appleseed?).

"When you read a poet's work, you peek inside her or him, and I am no exception. As a writer I reveal myself in my poems, not intentionally, but because poetry is a natural expression of what the poet thinks, feels and observes. It is me as silly, thoughtful, wondering, playing, discovering. If curiosity really 'killed,' I'd be long gone, because I like to poke around to find the how and why of things, never tire of watching bugs go about their bug business and, yes, I really did 'pet' a worm. I love the out of doors and am constantly discovering and rediscovering it, as children do. I feel a special rapport with children and especially enjoy writing about the kinds of things they respond to, ordinary things that adults sometimes don't really 'see' for all our modern distractions.

"_I'm Going to Pet a Worm Today_ is about a world I find fascinating: birds, bugs, worms, sunrise, sunsets, rain, green peas, web-spinners, butterflies that I have been nose to nose with, hummingbirds that amaze, water that wants to return to the ocean, growing things and eating things, beautiful things, wonderings. They are both new and old, written by the young mother that I once was and the grandmother (I still *feel* young) I am now. Some are even a bit raucous, such as 'Rah, Rah, Peas!' which, when I present it in person, the children and I (and even teachers in their workshops) perform as cheerleaders, making up our own appropriate gestures and asides. All this follows my explanation of how I always loved eating fresh, raw peas right from the pods, and describing the pods. Some children don't even know how peas grow! Introducing other poems, I might share stories of my butterfly experiences, an ant I observed trying to carry a large feather, how an acorn becomes an oak (we sometimes act that one out, too), why I wrote 'Weeds' and what made it fun for me, or whatever I think that a particular group would be interested in. The children (and adults) enjoy the sharing of observations, feelings and sometimes technique, all of which serves to bring them closer to my poems and how poetry is made, and stimulates them to write their own. My poems are 'me' and I want them to be 'them' and to feel free to play with ideas and words and join in the 'game' of language.

"Sometimes, with the older children, I discuss the book publishing process and my own saga of attempts, the years of trying, the hopes and disappointments. After a number of ego-crushing rejections over the years (poetry doesn't sell, some said) fortune smiled upon me in the person of the much loved and respected publisher/editor Margaret K. McElderry, who accepted the book in July of 1990, for publication in September of 1991. Some very nice reviews followed, all of which made me feel tremendously grateful. With the second book being readied for publication I'm again being extremely careful crossing streets—I want to be here to see it on the shelves."

*   *   *

LEWIS, Barbara A. 1943-

PERSONAL: Born April 16, 1943, in Salt Lake City, UT; daughter of Val C. (a railroad clerk) and Ruby (Christiansen) Anderson; married Lawrence Guy Lewis (a math professor and owner of a software consulting company), December 19, 1964; children: Michael, Andrea, Christian, Samuel. *Education:* University of Utah, B.S., 1965; Utah State Board of Education Gifted Endorsement, 1988. *Politics:* "Demo-Republicat." *Religion:* Church of Jesus Christ of Latter-Day Saints (Mormon).

ADDRESSES: Home—Salt Lake City, UT. *Office*—Jackson Elementary, 750 West Second N., Salt Lake City, UT 84116.

CAREER: Unionville School, Monroe County, IN, elementary teacher, 1965-67; Jackson Elementary, Salt Lake City, UT, teacher, 1986—. Speaker at over sixty seminars, workshops, and conferences, including Utah Association for Gifted Children, Association of Supervision and Curriculum Development, and keynote speaker at Brigham Young University and Michigan State Gifted and Talented Conference.

MEMBER: Society of Children's Book Writers, Salt Lake Teachers Association, Utah Education Association, National Education Association, Utah Association for Gifted Children, National Association for Gifted Children, Association of Supervision and Curriculum Development, National Council for Social Studies, Phi Kappa Phi.

AWARDS, HONORS: Short story contest first place award, *Ensign,* 1973; Utah Arts Council Literary Contest, honorable mention in juvenile novel category, 1984, for *Icky in the Mountain Mystery,* and second place, 1986, for *Peak of Friendship;* Excellence in Education Recognition Award, *Deseret News,* 1988; Recognition Award for Outstanding Teaching, Utah Association for Gifted Children, 1989; Professional Best Leadership Award, *Learning Magazine,* 1991; Light of Learning Award, Utah State Board of Education, 1991; Award for Excellence in Educational Journalism, Educational Press Association of America, 1991; Gold Medal Award, Susan Kovalik and Associates, and Reading Magic Award, *Parenting,* both 1991, Children's Books of Distinction Award, Hungry Mind, and Best Books for Teen Age citation, New York Library System, both 1992, all for *The Kid's Guide to Social Action;* Salt Lake Education Foundation grant; thirty local and state awards for Jackson projects and seven national awards, including two President's Youth Environment Awards, Take Pride in America Award, and two National Community Problem Solving Awards.

WRITINGS:

The Kid's Guide to Social Action, Free Spirit, 1991.
Kids with Courage, Free Spirit, 1992.
A Teacher's Guide to Kids with Courage, Free Spirit, 1992.

Author of short stories, including "Lilies Grow Wild." Author of unpublished juvenile novels, *Icky in the Mountain Mystery* and *Peak of Friendship.* Contributor of education articles to journals, including *Instructor, Scholastic, Social Education, Learning, Educational Leadership, Congressional Record,* and *Earth Care Annual.* Also contributor to magazines, including *Utah Holiday, Ensign, Latter-Day Woman,* and *Science of the Mind.*

ADAPTATIONS: "Lilies Grow Wild" was adapted into a movie by Brigham Young University Films, 1978.

WORK IN PROGRESS: Inspirational stories of young people with faith, completion expected in 1993.

SIDELIGHTS: Barbara A. Lewis told *SATA:* "When my sixth graders discovered a hazardous waste site three blocks from Jackson Elementary, they flew into action. They grew concerned that dangerous chemicals from the 50,000 barrels that were stockpiled might leak down into the groundwater. They researched that hazardous chemicals could cause brain damage, birth defects, cancer, and other diseases, and they didn't want to drink these toxic substances.

In *Kids with Courage,* **Barbara A. Lewis profiles teens who get involved in social issues, such as Charles Carson, who distributes posters encouraging race relations.** (Photograph by Karen Stallwood.)

"In the beginning, health officials told them there was nothing to do, and they brushed the children away like pesky flies. Although officials were generous with information, they truly believed nothing could be done. At that time there were 152 sites awaiting investigation in Utah, and there was no money to begin the huge investigation. But the students continued on their project anyway, hitting the community with zillions of phone calls, speeches, letters, petitions, surveys, proposals. Television and newspaper reporters grew fascinated with these 'pre-teen toxic avengers' and followed them closely.

"As a result of their efforts, all 50,000 barrels were removed within one year. It was an impressive story for a bunch of kids from one of the lowest income schools in Utah. Jackson also has the second largest minority population of any school in Utah. While the children made a great contribution to the State, inwardly they learned how to better control their personal lives. They grew confident, important, powerful. I decided these 'social-action' skills should be taught in school. I knew that in my school career I had never learned how to petition, much less how to lobby for improvements. The very thought of speaking to the State Legislature would probably have made me break out in hives as a

youngster. But I had learned with my students that improving your world could be as simple as walking up to officials with power and speaking to them.

"So I wrote *The Kid's Guide to Social Action* for young people, in a simple-to-read style that even adults could understand. I used to say it was aimed at fifth grade through high school. But I have received reports from all ages of people who use it, so I have amended my target audience. I now say it is directed at anyone who is interested in social action, kindergarten through death.

"In the process of writing *The Kid's Guide to Social Action,* I met many young people who were engaged in making a difference. Some were involved in fighting for kids' rights. Some were trying to save elephants and wetlands. Others were fighting crime in schools. And some had performed acts of heroism, like saving their friends and family from fire or drowning. I said to myself, 'These kids are performing courageous acts which I doubt even adults could have accomplished so well.' So I wrote a second book, *Kids with Courage,* which consists of eighteen biographies of young people who have stood up for what they believed, spoken out, or reached out until someone listened.

"I was not an activist as a child. Growing up in Salt Lake City as a Mormon girl, I developed faith, believing that with God's help and agreement, a person could accomplish anything that she needed to do. And I still believe that. But mostly, I spent my warm summer days engaged in activities like hiking to Timpanogas Cave, playing paper dolls, football, or simply daydreaming beneath star-studded skies with neighborhood friends. I enjoyed drawing, especially ordinary people, and as an adult, I have continued with this interest. I also wrote as a child, but I didn't write many exciting things. I kept journals for eight to ten paper dolls. My personal journal was stuffed full of details of my childhood: games, experiences, stories I had written, faded prom roses, invitations, photographs, secret letters, napkins—even jewelry. It grew to eight inches deep with an expandable binder. In college I affectionately labeled it my 'Treasures of Trash' book, and with a crimson face, I hid it in an obscure box in a spidery corner of my parents' basement.

"Following the birth of our first child, I rediscovered my obese journal and pulled it out from hiding. I now read it with pleasure, because I realize it is rich in details of my growing up as a Mormon girl, with great-grandparents who were polygamists, who rode the pony express, and lived in earthen dugouts while trying to make the 'desert blossom as the rose'. It's the story of my youthful experiences in the rugged Rocky Mountains, 4,500 feet above sea level, floating on my back in the Great Salt Lake, attending church firesides, and following old Mormon pioneer, handcart trails in East Canyon, searching for my roots.

"I obtained a degree in elementary education, partly because my older sister, Pat, set the example, but mostly I loved children. I married Larry, my college sweetheart. And after teaching two years in Unionville, Indiana, I retired temporarily when our first child was born. After twenty years of raising children, I returned to the classroom, rusty and insecure. I asked myself, 'Why is it that most of what I teach is imaginary? Memorizing what other people have done? There must be a way to connect school to real life.' That began my process of teaching kids to think and solve problems.

"My students never feel like they have to solve the world's problems. They only attack problems in which they have some interest. They have creative solutions, because—unlike adults—kids don't know all the reasons why something won't work. I think of children as the last major minority. No one really represents their viewpoints. Adults might say that the parents of the children represent their views. But, before women obtained the right to vote, they were told their husbands represented their ideas. What's the difference? I believe only young people can represent their views. Children need to learn to be responsible, caring citizens before they're eighteen years old, before they grow either apathetic or intimated by the idea. So that's why I wrote *my books*. This is the age of the kid."

* * *

LIPPINCOTT, Gary A. 1953-

PERSONAL: Born September 2, 1953, in Woodstown, NJ; son of Lynn (an E. I. Du Pont employee) and Arden (a homemaker; maiden name, McTyre) Lippincott; married Wendy L. Warner (a horse trainer and riding instructor), October 6, 1979; children: Ian W., Aja W. *Education:* Maryland Institute, College of Art, B.F.A., 1975. *Hobbies and other interests:* Playing piano, composing music, magic, scuba diving.

ADDRESSES: Home and office—131 Greenville Rd., Spencer, MA 01562.

CAREER: Free-lance illustrator, 1984—.

MEMBER: Western Massachusetts Illustrators Group, Arts Worcester, Worcester Artist Group.

ILLUSTRATOR:

Jacob and Wilhelm Grimm, *The Fisherman and His Wife,* Troll, 1988.
Mem Fox, *With Love at Christmas,* Abingdon Press, 1988.
Daniel Cohen, *Ancient Egypt,* Doubleday, 1990.
Bruce Coville, *Jeremy Thatcher-Dragon Hatcher,* Harcourt, 1991.
Bruce Coville, *Jennifer Murdley's Toad,* Harcourt, 1992.
Mark Twain, *The Prince and the Pauper,* David Godine, 1993.

By describing the political process for her readers, Lewis hopes to encourage more young people to get involved in matters that are important to them.

GARY A. LIPPINCOTT

SIDELIGHTS: Gary A. Lippincott told *SATA:* "I started drawing at an early age. Before 'settling' on becoming an illustrator, I had many unusual careers in mind, such as a magician, actor, make-up artist, clown, animator, etc. I am inspired by American animated films producer Walt Disney, fantasy illustrators the Hildebrandt brothers, and illustrator Alan Lee."

FOR MORE INFORMATION SEE:

PERIODICALS

Booklist, March 15, 1990, p. 1444; May 15, 1991; March 15, 1992, p. 1357.
Publisher's Weekly, January 19, 1990.
School Library Journal, April, 1990, p. 30; May, 1991, p. 91.
Voice of Youth Advocates, June, 1991, p. 106.

*   *   *

LOH, Morag 1935-

PERSONAL: Born March 3, 1935, in Melbourne, Australia; daughter of Joseph Keilty (a teacher) and Flora Fulton (a homemaker; maiden name, Gillies) Foster; married Tim Loh (a consultant surgeon and medical acupuncturist), 1958; children: Su-lin, Mei-lin. *Education:* Melbourne University, B.A., 1954, diploma of

education, 1955, graduate studies, 1972. *Politics:* Independent. *Religion:* Agnostic.

ADDRESSES: Office—c/o Orchard Books, 95 Madison Ave., New York, NY 10016.

CAREER: Office of Multicultural Affairs, Department of Prime Minister and Cabinet, Canberra, Australian Capital Territory, writer and editor, 1987-88; State Library of Victoria, Melbourne, curator of photography, 1988-92; Victorian Ministry for the Arts, writer in residence in the cities of Melbourne, Shepparton, and Gippsland, in Victoria, Australia, 1990-91; lecturer and writer. Member of Advisory Council on Multicultural Affairs, 1987-90, Council for the Arts, and Ministerial Advisory Committee on Multicultural Affairs.

MEMBER: Amnesty International, Australian Society of Authors, Oral History Association of Australia, Union of Australian Women, Australia-East Timor Association, Victorian Writers' Centre, Victorian Centre for Photography, Victorian Community Writers Inc., Royal Historical Society of Victoria, Victorian Women's Trust.

AWARDS, HONORS: Picture book shortlist, Children's Book Council of Australia, 1988, and notable children's book citation, American Library Association, 1989, both for *Tucking Mommy In.*

WRITINGS:

FOR CHILDREN

Growing Up in Richmond, Richmond Community Education Centre, 1979.
Children in Australia: An Outline History, Oxford University Press, 1980, revised edition coauthored with Suzane Fabian, 1989.

MORAG LOH

People and Stories from Indo-China, Indo-China Refugee Association, 1982.

Stories and Storytellers from Indo-China, Hodja Educational Resources Cooperative, 1985.

(With Fabian) *Australian Children through Two Hundred Years,* Kangaroo Press, 1985.

The Kinder Hat, illustrated by Donna Rawlins, Hyland House, 1985.

Tucking Mommy In, illustrated by Rawlins, Ashton Scholastic, 1987.

(With Fabian) *All in a Day's Work: A Focus on Teenagers,* Oxford University Press, 1990.

FOR ADULTS

(With Wendy Lowenstein) *The Immigrants,* Hyland House, 1977, Penguin, 1978.

With Courage in Their Cases: Thirty-five Italian Immigrant Workers and Their Families in Australia, Filef, 1980.

The Changemakers: Ten Significant Australian Women, Jacaranda, 1983.

Sojourners and Settlers: Chinese in Victoria, 1948-1985, Victorian Government China Advisory Committee, 1985.

(Editor with Christine Ramsay) *Survival and Celebration: Women in Chinese Settlement in Australia, 1856-1986,* Raya Gallery (Melbourne), 1986.

Dinky-di: The Contributions of Chinese Immigrants and Australians of Chinese Descent to Australia's Defence Forces and War Efforts, 1899-1988, Australian Government Publishing Service, 1989.

Sojourners and Settlers from Japan in Victoria, 1897-1991, State Library of Victoria, 1991.

Also contributor to encyclopedias, including *The Australopedia* and *The Australian People,* and to books, including *Double Time: Women in Victoria, 150 Years,* edited by Marilyn Lake and Farley Kelly, Penguin, 1985. Contributor of articles and reviews to periodicals and journals, including *Meanjin, Hemisphere, Journal of the Royal Historical Society of Victoria, Australian Book Review, Australian Society, Australian Historical Studies, Youth Studies Bulletin,* and *Gippsland Heritage Journal.* Coeditor of *The Oral History Association of Australia Journal,* 1979-80.

WORK IN PROGRESS: Garden Boy, a novel for teenagers about a young boy of immigrant parents, growing up in a small farming community on the eve of the 1939-45 war (World War II); *Patience and Persistence: The Union of Australian Women in Victoria, 1950-1992,* coauthored with Fabian; researching the history of practitioners of Chinese traditional medicine in Victoria and the settlement of Chinese immigrants in Gippsland, 1850-1990s.

SIDELIGHTS: Morag Loh told *SATA:* "The first nine years of my life were spent in rural Victoria. There were few playmates outside of school and books were my most constant companions. The highlights of the year were holidays spent in Melbourne among my father's large, lively family, where books, newspapers, and journals cluttered the sitting room and conversation

seemed endless. A love of books and of storytelling engendered in those early years has never left me.

"I did not begin writing, however, until my children were at school and I'd resumed a teaching career at an inner city high school. There, I found that the traditions and experiences of my mostly immigrant students were nowhere represented—not in books, theatre, or films. Yet they and their families had interesting stories to tell and perspectives of Australia very different from those in popular currency. In the mid 1970s, following [American interviewer and writer] Studs Terkel's example, I became an oral historian, recording, transcribing, and editing for publication aspects of immigrant experience, including the experiences of children and adolescents. I was, in many ways, dealing with life stories similar to my own—I was born in Australia of immigrant parents, my husband was an immigrant, we lived outside Australia for a number of years and our younger daughter, born in Britain, was technically an immigrant.

"By the late 1970s it occurred to me that the experiences of young people in general, though represented in fiction, were absent from history books. So, with Suzane Fabian, I began to write books documenting something of the history of children in Australia. In the course of this work I became interested in the use of photographs and illustrations as documents.

"In 1984 Donna Rawlins, who had illustrated some of my oral histories, suggested that we work as author and illustrator on a picture book. We produced *The Kinder Hat* and *Tucking Mommy In.* Both stories had their origins in experiences shared by my children and me. During the past few years, while working mainly as a curator of photography, I have been preparing, little by

When their mother has a hard time staying awake, two little girls decide to help her get ready for bed. (Cover illustration by Donna Rawlins.)

little, to tackle writing a novel. Drawing on my own experiences and those of friends and of years of research into the history of immigrants and their descendants in Australia, I hope to produce a novel about a boy of immigrant parents growing up in a small farming community in the 1930s. I'm both nervous and eager to begin."

M

MAARTENS, Maretha 1945-

PERSONAL: Born June 22, 1945, in Bloemfontein, South Africa; daughter of Matthys Johannes (a policeman) and Jacoba Danilina (a homemaker; maiden name, Diederichs) Strydom; married Joachim Hendrik Maartens (a minister of the Dutch Reformed Church), January 24, 1970; children: Danila, Naomi. *Education:* University of Stellenbosch, B.A. (with honors); received secondary teacher's diploma. *Politics:* National Party. *Religion:* Protestant.

ADDRESSES: Home and office—17 Naval Rd., Bloemfontein, South Africa.

CAREER: Author, 1970—. Served as a lecturer at University of Stellenbosch for three years. Public speaker; active in church.

AWARDS, HONORS: Recipient of the Sanlam Award for Youth Literature, the Credo Award, and the F.A.K. Prestige Award.

WRITINGS:

IN AFRIKAANS

Lea, Lea, Makro Boeke, 1975.
Stormvoel, Haum, 1975.
Koms van die wolf, Tafelberg (Kaapstad), 1978.
Die Midas-seisoen, Tafelberg, 1980.
Een Ligjaar, J. P. Van Der Walt, 1982.
My Dik Boek, Tafelberg, 1982.
Vrymoedige Gesprek Met God, Tafelberg, 1982.
Ons Mooiste Kersfees, Cum-Boeke, 1983.
Voor Die Oog Van Hierdie Son, Tafelberg, 1983.
Swart Griet Is Vas, Tafelberg, 1984.
Moedhou, Maria, Dis Donkermaan, J. P. Van Der Walt, 1984.
Om Waarlik te Leef, Daan Retief (Pretoria), 1984.
'N Pakkie Mieliepitte (title means "Sidwell's Seeds"), Tafelberg, 1984.
Die Sakmense, Tafelberg, 1985.
Rowe Val Af, Tafelberg, 1985.
Die Huisdagboek, NGK-Uitgewers (Transvaal), 1986.

MARETHA MAARTENS

Verste Grens, Folio-Uitgewers, 1986.
Om Kinders Groot te Maak, Daan Retief, 1986.
Oud Genoeg Vir Nagbriewe, Lux Verbi, 1987.
Oor Die Nek van die Draak, Tafelberg, 1988.

Vlug Van Die Eden-Mens, Daan Retief, 1988.
Here, Dis Ek, Magriet, Bybelkor, 1988.
Goue Fluit, My Storie Is Uit, Tafelberg, 1988.
Op Filippa se Planeet, J. P. Van Der Walt, 1989.
Mooi Loop, Meisiekind, Bybelkor, 1989.
'N Pot Vol Winter, Haum, 1989.
Geagte Mej. Snob: 'N Jeugverhaal Oor Serebraal Gestremde Kinders, Daan Retief, 1992.

IN ENGLISH TRANSLATION

Is Gideon dan'n Swartskaap?, illustrated by Alida Carpenter, Daan Retief, 1989, English translation by Madeleine van Biljon published as *Black Sheep?,* Daan Retief, 1989.
Die Inkvoel, Tafelberg, 1987, English translation by van Biljon published as *Paper Bird: A Novel of South Africa,* Clarion, 1989.

OTHER

Contributor to periodicals.

ADAPTATIONS: A film based on *Pot Vol Winter* was released in May, 1992.

WORK IN PROGRESS: A book on teenage sex.

SIDELIGHTS: Maretha Maartens told *SATA:* "I sometimes say to my husband [a minister of the Dutch Reformed Church] that we do not live in a house: we live in an institution. We actually run it. Our private lives are inundated by telephone calls from the congregation, catering for church functions, people coming for counselling, teenage activities, boyfriends, kids turning up for psychometric testing by our elder daughter, beggars on our doorstep, street children turning up for bread and coffee or soup and coffee, people staying for the night. We live right in the centre of the country: people travel from Cape Town to Johannesburg and come for bed and breakfast.

"My husband and I have been married for twenty-two years. We live like any ordinary family. (Ordinary?) We are *happy* (which is not quite so ordinary). Because home base is secure, I can write as much as I do. I travel a lot: about 1250 miles per week. I am a public speaker at conferences and in schools. I know this country because I travel so much. I know its vastness, its splendour, its plains and mountains and people.

"We are fiercely independent. Hennie, my husband, is always experimenting with new approaches in his congregation. Danila, who is twenty-one, is getting married to an academic twenty years her senior on December 5, 1992. Naomi, who is sixteen, has just returned from Germany, where she studied for six months as an exchange student. She attended the Theodor Heuss Gymnasium in Dattelu, Kreis Recklinghausen. I myself have visited the Angolese border in wartime, Zimbabwe under its black government, America, the Scandinavian countries, Europe (including 'East Germany'), and the Namib desert. We love travelling, are against apartheid, cherish friendships with people of all races, and believe in family life.

"I grew up in a small town called Petrusburg. My father bought me a portable typewriter; I discovered that my brain was located within that typewriter. I started writing as a child. My dad and later my husband were my real motivators. I wrote a lot of stories for magazines, mainly to keep the family alive while my husband was studying to become a minister. I progressed to novels for adults, books for young people, books on prayer, marriage, dying, happiness, sickness, sex, etc. I love writing and I consider books for teenagers the toughest books to write. I battle with these manuscripts. I love them and hate them; I curse them and I always vow to myself that I'll never ever again get involved in stories about teenage sex, divorcing parents, heavy petting, race relationships, overcoming hardships, etc. I always break my vows."

Maartens examines the topic of race relations in *Paper Bird: A Novel of South Africa,* in which ten-year-old Adam must support his siblings and his recently widowed, pregnant mother by selling newspapers. When political activists declare a strike, Adam must choose between his family's income and its safety. "*Paper Bird* did not come easily," Maartens related. "I cursed the manuscript a lot. It wasn't difficult to portray Adam's life; I just had to look around me. I just had to walk the streets of Bloemfontein. *Paper Bird* is an honest account

Because he must work to support his family, Adam faces his fear and makes the dangerous trip between the black township of Phameng and the city of Bloemfontein. (Cover illustration by Paul Morin.)

of life in South Africa, but more could have been said. Which would have made the story sadder." A *Publishers Weekly* reviewer commented, "Maartens's account of the desperate situations created by the social injustice of her homeland is striking and painful." Carolyn Phelan, writing in *Booklist,* concluded, "While the setting may be South African, the depiction of the effects of poverty and the threat of violence have universal significance, transcending race or place."

"Fortunately, things are changing in South Africa," Maartens added. "A new kind of book is waiting to be born: a book about children sharing life as equals. I do hope I will have the privilege to write that book."

WORKS CITED:

Review of *Paper Bird: A Novel of South Africa, Publishers Weekly,* July 12, 1991.
Phelan, Carolyn, review of *Paper Bird: A Novel of South Africa, Booklist,* September 15, 1991.

FOR MORE INFORMATION SEE:

PERIODICALS

Kirkus Reviews, August 1, 1991.
School Library Journal, October, 1991.

*   *   *

*   *   *

MANNING-SANDERS, Ruth 1895(?)-1988

PERSONAL: Born in 1895 (some sources say 1888), in Swansea, Wales; died October 12, 1988, in Penzance, Cornwall, England; daughter of a minister; married George Manning-Sanders (an artist and writer; died, 1952); children: Joan (an artist), David. *Education:* Attended Manchester University.

CAREER: Poet and novelist prior to World War II; author of books for children, 1948-88. Worked for two years with Rosaire's Circus, England.

AWARDS, HONORS: Blindman International Poetry Prize, 1926, for *The City.*

WRITINGS:

FOR ADULTS

The Pedlar and Other Poems (verse), Selwyn & Blount, 1919.
Karn (verse), Leonard and Virginia Woolf, 1922.
Pages from the History of Zachy Trenoy (verse), Christophers, 1923.
The City (poem), Dial, 1927.
Circus Book (nonfiction), Collins, 1947, published in America as *The Circus,* Chanticleer Press, 1948.
The West of England (nonfiction), B. T. Batsford, 1949.
The River Dart (nonfiction), Westaway Books, 1951.
Seaside England (nonfiction), B. T. Batsford, 1951.

ADULT FICTION

The Twelve Saints, E. J. Clode, 1926.
Selina Pennaluna, Christophers, 1927.
Waste Corner, Christophers, 1927, E. J. Clode, 1928.
Hucca's Moor, Faber & Gwyer, 1929.
The Crochet Woman, Coward-McCann, 1930.
The Growing Trees, Morrow, 1931.
She Was Sophia, Cobden-Sanderson, 1932.
Run Away, Cassell, 1934.
Mermaid's Mirror, Cassell, 1935.
The Girl Who Made an Angel, Cassell, 1936.
Elephant: The Romance of Laura (short stories), F. A. Stokes, 1938.
Children by the Sea, illustrated by Mary Shepard, Collins, 1938, published in the United States as *Adventure May Be Anywhere,* F. A. Stokes, 1939.
Luke's Circus, Collins, 1939, Little, Brown, 1940.
Mystery at Penmarth, illustrated by Susanne Suba, McBride, 1941.
Mr. Portal's Little Lions, Hale, 1952.
The Golden Ball, Hale, 1954.
Melissa, Hale, 1957.

FOR CHILDREN

Swan of Denmark: The Story of Hans Christian Andersen, illustrated by Astrid Walford, Heinemann, 1949, McBride, 1950, later edition published as *The Story of Hans Andersen, Swan of Denmark,* Dutton, 1966.
The English Circus, Laurie, 1952.
Peter and the Piskies: Cornish Folk and Fairy Tales, illustrated by Raymond Briggs, Oxford University Press, 1958, Roy, 1966.
Circus Boy, illustrated by Annette Macarthur-Onslow, Oxford University Press, 1960.
Red Indian Folk and Fairy Tales, illustrated by C. Walter Hodges, Oxford University Press, 1960, Roy, 1962.
Animal Stories, illustrated by Macarthur-Onslow, Oxford University Press, 1961, Roy, 1962.
A Book of Giants, illustrated by Robin Jacques, Methuen, 1962, Dutton, 1963.
The Smugglers, illustrated by William Stobbs, Oxford University Press, 1962.
A Book of Dwarfs, illustrated by Jacques, Methuen, 1963, Dutton, 1964.
A Book of Dragons, illustrated by Jacques, Methuen, 1964, Dutton, 1965.
Damian and the Dragon: Modern Greek Folk-Tales, illustrated by William Papas, Roy, 1965.
The Crow's Nest, illustrated by Lynette Hemmant, Hamish Hamilton, 1965.
Slippery Shiney, illustrated by Constance Marshall, Hamish Hamilton, 1965.
The Extraordinary Margaret Catchpole, Heinemann, 1966.
A Book of Wizards, illustrated by Jacques, Methuen, 1966, Dutton, 1967.
A Book of Mermaids, illustrated by Jacques, Methuen, 1967, Dutton, 1968.
The Magic Squid, illustrated by Eileen Armitage, Methuen, 1968.

Stories from the English and Scottish Ballads, illustrated by Trevor Ridley, Dutton, 1968.

A Book of Ghosts and Goblins, illustrated by Jacques, Methuen, 1968, Dutton, 1969.

The Glass Man and the Golden Bird: Hungarian Folk and Fairy Tales, illustrated by Victor G. Ambrus, Roy, 1968.

The Spaniards Are Coming!, illustrated by Jacqueline Rizvi, Heinemann, 1969, Watts, 1970.

Jonnikin and the Flying Basket: French Folk and Fairy Tales, illustrated by Ambrus, Dutton, 1969.

A Book of Princes and Princesses, illustrated by Jacques, Methuen, 1969, Dutton, 1970.

Gianni and the Ogre, illustrated by Stobbs, Methuen, 1970, Dutton, 1971.

A Book of Devils and Demons, illustrated by Jacques, Dutton, 1970.

A Book of Charms and Changelings, illustrated by Jacques, Methuen, 1971, Dutton, 1972.

A Choice of Magic, illustrated by Jacques, Dutton, 1971.

A Book of Ogres and Trolls, illustrated by Jacques, Methuen, 1972, Dutton, 1973.

A Book of Sorcerers and Spells, illustrated by Jacques, Methuen, 1973, Dutton, 1974.

A Book of Magic Animals, illustrated by Jacques, Methuen, 1974, Dutton, 1975.

Stumpy: A Russian Tale, illustrated by Leon Shtainmets, Methuen, 1974.

Grandad and the Magic Barrel, illustrated by Jacques, Methuen, 1974.

Old Dog Sirko: A Ukrainian Tale, illustrated by Shtainmets, Methuen, 1974.

Sir Green Hat and the Wizard, illustrated by Stobbs, Methuen, 1974.

Tortoise Tales, illustrated by Donald Chaffin, Nelson, 1974.

Ram and Goat, illustrated by Jacques, Methuen, 1974.

A Book of Monsters, illustrated by Jacques, Methuen, 1975, Dutton, 1976.

Young Gabby Goose, illustrated by J. Hodgson, Methuen, 1975.

Scottish Folk Tales, illustrated by Stobbs, Methuen, 1976.

Fox Tales, illustrated by Hodgson, Methuen, 1976.

The Town Mouse and the Country Mouse: Aesop's Fable Retold, illustrated by Harold Jones, Angus & Robertson, 1977.

Robin Hood and Little John, illustrated by Jo Chesterman, Methuen, 1977.

Old Witch Boneyleg, illustrated by Kilmeny Niland, Angus & Robertson, 1978.

The Cock and the Fox, illustrated by Jenny Williams, Angus & Robertson, 1978.

Boastful Rabbit, illustrated by Hodgson, Methuen, 1978.

Folk and Fairy Tales, illustrated by Jacques, Methuen, 1978.

RUTH MANNING-SANDERS

A Book of Marvels and Magic, illustrated by Jacques, Methuen, 1978.

The Haunted Castle, illustrated by Niland, Angus & Robertson, 1979.

A Book of Spooks and Spectres, illustrated by Jacques, Dutton, 1979.

Robin Hood and the Gold Arrow, illustrated by Chesterman, Methuen, 1979.

Oh Really, Rabbit!, illustrated by Hodgson, Methuen, 1980.

A Book of Cats and Creatures, illustrated by Jacques, Dutton, 1981.

Hedgehog and Puppy Dog Tales, Methuen, 1982.

Tales of Magic and Mystery, illustrated by Christopher Quaile, Methuen, 1985.

EDITOR

A Bundle of Ballads, illustrated by Stobbs, Oxford University Press, 1959, Lippincott, 1961.

Birds, Beasts, and Fishes, illustrated by Rita Parsons, Oxford University Press, 1962.

The Red King and the Witch, illustrated by Ambrus, Oxford University Press, 1964, Roy, 1965.

The Hamish Hamilton Book of Magical Beasts, illustrated by Briggs, Hamish Hamilton, 1965, published in the United States as *A Book of Magical Beasts,* T. Nelson, 1970.

A Book of Witches, illustrated by Jacques, Methuen, 1965, Dutton, 1966.

Festivals, illustrated by Briggs, Heinemann, 1972, Dutton, 1973.

A Cauldron of Witches, illustrated by Scoular Anderson, Methuen, 1988.

SIDELIGHTS: Ruth Manning-Sanders began publishing verse and fiction in her early years and continued right up until her death in 1988. Much of her early work was aimed at adults; but after her artist husband's untimely death in 1952, she turned to books for children and released some sixty titles over thirty years. She was best known for her tales of circus life and her retellings of folktales from all over the world.

Manning-Sanders was born in Swansea, Wales, the youngest daughter of a minister. She grew up in Cheshire in a happy home full of books, and she and her sisters were encouraged to exercise their active imaginations by writing and performing plays. During the summers the family moved to the Highlands of Scotland. There the young girls were allowed to roam freely in the rugged countryside.

When Manning-Sanders grew up, she attended Manchester University, specializing in English literature and Shakespearean studies. While still a student she met and married George Manning-Sanders, an artist and writer from Cornwall. From the outset theirs was an unusual union—they spent the early years of their married life touring Great Britain in a horse-drawn caravan. While George Manning-Sanders painted, Ruth worked with a circus and wrote poetry. Many of her experiences as an employee of Rosaire's Circus found their way into her

In *A Book of Ghosts and Goblins,* **Manning-Sanders presents tales of people facing frightening hauntings and evil spectres.** (Illustration by Robin Jacques.)

books including *The Circus, The English Circus,* and *Circus Boy.*

In a review of *The English Circus,* a *Saturday Review* critic wrote: "No one even faintly interested in the circus—its history, traditions, and bizarre personalities—can fail to be interested in this detailed tribute.... [Manning-Sanders] more often than not manages to bring to life the glories of 'the art that eternally contemplates the proud enchantment of its own perfection.'"

After the birth of their two children, Ruth and George Manning-Sanders settled down a bit. Ruth earned a significant reputation as a poet and novelist for adults, and her daughter Joan followed in the family footsteps and became an artist.

World War II and the death of her husband soon thereafter brought a change to Manning-Sanders's career. Before the war she had written almost exclusively for adults. After the war she turned to writing for children and produced a great number of works. Beginning with a biography of Hans Christian Andersen, she went on to collect and rewrite folk and fairy tales from every part of the world, taking great care to preserve each story's original flavor and tone. In a series with titles beginning *A Book of ...,* she introduced English-speaking readers to dragons, dwarfs, witches, magicians, giants, sorcerers, and magic animals from every imaginable culture. *Junior Bookshelf* correspondent M. S. Crouch noted of Manning-Sanders: "Her personal preference seems to have been for the humorously bizarre, and she had a liking for dragons, ogres and other grotesques. She liked humble, unheroic heroes, simple people keeping their end up by means of cunning and persistence."

At the time of her death, Manning-Sanders had just released a collection of witch stories, and more than twenty-five of her books were still in print. Crouch claimed that the author never lost her touch for poetry, producing work with subtle rhythms and melodies. "Every present-day story-teller must be in her debt," the critic continued. "Her work is peculiarly suited to the domestic, one-to-one story-telling session. It forges a link between speaker and hearer whose strength is best appreciated in the home rather than the hall and the classroom."

Crouch concluded: "For many long-lived writers, death is followed by eclipse. I hope that publishers will [continue to re-release Manning-Sanders's] priceless treasury of folk-tales. We would all be the poorer for their loss."

WORKS CITED:

Crouch, M. S., "Ruth Manning-Sanders," *Junior Bookshelf,* February, 1989, pp. 7-9.
Review of *The English Circus, Saturday Review,* April 3, 1954.

FOR MORE INFORMATION SEE:

PERIODICALS

Times Literary Supplement, November 14, 1952; September 28, 1973; July 23, 1982.

OBITUARIES:

PERIODICALS

Times (London), October 13, 1988.*

*　　*　　*

MARSH, James 1946-

PERSONAL: Born July 27, 1946, in Yorkshire, England. *Education:* Received national diploma in design (NDD) and college diploma from Batley College of Art and Design, 1966.

ADDRESSES: Home—21 Elms Rd., London SW4 9ER, England.

CAREER: Free-lance illustrator. Director of Artbank International (an illustration agency and library) and lecturer in the United Kingdom, the United States, and Canada. *Exhibitions:* Group exhibitions include European Illustration Annual Exhibitions, United Kingdom, 1975-89; London Arts Council, Fairfields Hall, London, England, 1976; Association of Illustrators Annual Exhibitions, United Kingdom, 1977-92; Lock Means Key, Copenhagen, Denmark, 1979; Meccanorma Silver Awards, London, 1982; Aberdeen Gallery, California, 1982; The Cow Book, New York, 1983; Time, Benson & Hedges, Hamilton Gallery, London, 1984; From Claxton to Chloe, The British Council World Tour, 1985-86; Images, Aberystwyth Arts Centre, Wales, 1986; The Art

JAMES MARSH

of the Beatles, Liverpool, England, 1987, Japan tour, 1987-88, and Cologne, Germany, 1988; Alter Images, A.O.1 Gallery, London, 1989; Six of the Best, England, Scotland, and Wales tour, 1989-90; Reactor Christmas Shows, Toronto, Canada, 1989-91; Green Pieces (Artbank), Fonts and Fowler Gallery, 1990; Illustrator and the Environment (United Nations), Society of Illustrators Museum of American Illustration, United States, 1990-91; Opening Show, Lustrare Gallery, New York, 1990-91; Power, Benson & Hedges, Mall Galleries, London and tour, 1991-92; and Children's Books, Society of Illustrators, New York, 1991.

MEMBER: Association of Illustrators (founder member).

AWARDS, HONORS: Design and Art Directors Association Award (United Kingdom), 1975; Society of Publication Designers Award (United States), 1981; Meccanorma Silver Award (United Kingdom), 1982; Bomac Batten National Magazine Award (Canada), 1984; Art Directors Club Magazine Award (United States), 1984 and 1987; Communications Arts Awards (United States), 1984, 1985, 1986, 1987, 1990, 1991, 1992; Print Certificates of Excellence (United States), 1985 and 1986; Creative Forum Diploma (Norway), 1987; Art Directors Club of Toronto Award (Canada), 1988; TMA Communications Award (United Kingdom), 1989; Strategia "Oscar" Award (Italy), 1989; the twenty-seventh and thirty-first Society of Illustrators Inc. Awards (United States).

WRITINGS:

Bizarre Birds and Beasts, Dial, 1991.
From the Heart, Dial, 1993.

Contributor of illustrations to numerous books and periodicals.

WORK IN PROGRESS: Birds of a Feather, illustrated proverbs with verse.

SIDELIGHTS: James Marsh is a free-lance artist and children's author and illustrator known for the bold colors, natural and mythical images, and surreal perspectives in his work. As a young man, Marsh attended Batley College of Art and Design in England, intending to become a graphic designer. After graduation in the 1960s, he designed album covers at two record companies in London, and went on to illustrate for magazines and books. *Communication Arts* contributor Michael Kaplan commented about Marsh's early work: "While he now dismisses that work, those early jobs provided him with a foundation for the brightly colored, graphically rich illustrations that have become his trademark."

Marsh has gone on to a highly successful career in advertising illustration and publishing work, listing among his clients, *Time, Atlantic Monthly, The Sunday Times, The Observer,* Bantam Books, Random House, Penguin, London Transport, British Airways, Chevrolet, and Mitsubishi. His work has been exhibited worldwide. In 1991 he published his first picture book, *Bizarre Birds and Beasts,* which he has followed with *From the Heart.* Kaplan noted, "James Marsh closes in on the illustrator's grail: recognition as a fine artist. It's a quality with which he aims to imbue all of his work."

Marsh's whimsical sense of humor and love for natural subjects are evident in this illustration of a happy amphibian.

Marsh has maintained a devout interest in artistic freedom. He told Kaplan, "I like to do illustration projects that ultimately stand on their own as paintings. When that ends up being the case, it's usually because I've had the creative freedom to use the images that I desire. It means they're a bit more inspired than the typical illustration with a pure commercial usage. There's a lot more personal input, and that imparts the piece with the best of both worlds."

Marsh told *SATA:* "Anthropomorphic images constantly occur in my work. Ever since I was a young child I can remember seeing faces in things, such as wallpaper patterns, shadows, folds in fabric, buildings, rocks, trees, light switches, etc. I am still the same today. Whenever I am on a holiday, I wander around with a camera and like to look at things through the camera's eye, recording the place, but not in the normal holiday snapshot way. I tend to take slides of plants, textures, and details of buildings, but invariably, I see anthropomorphic images to record. These images are not intended to be used literally, it's merely my way of viewing the world and this filters through and comes out in my work.

"Double entendres also figure in my life. I love images that have two meanings. Recently I have been taking this a stage further from just the visual image and have been combining it with words, playing with them in the same way I do with an illustration. The results can be seen in my two books, *Bizarre Birds and Beasts* and *From the Heart.*"

WORKS CITED:

Kaplan, Michael, "James Marsh," *Communication Arts,* May/June, 1991.

*   *   *

MATLOFF, Gregory 1945-

PERSONAL: Born March 2, 1945, in Brooklyn, NY; son of Simon (a dentist) and Eudice (a legal secretary; maiden name, Strom) Matloff; married Janet Schneider, 1967 (divorced, 1985); married Constance Bangs (an artist and curator), August 8, 1986. *Education:* Queens College of the City University of New York, B.A., 1965; New York University, M.S., 1969, Ph.D., 1976; doctoral study at Wesleyan University, 1969-70. *Politics:* Democrat. *Religion:* Jewish.

ADDRESSES: Home and office—417 Greene Ave., Brooklyn, NY 11216. *Agent*—Richard Curtis, 171 East 74th St., New York, NY 10021.

CAREER: New York University, New York City, postdoctoral researcher in department of applied science, 1975-78; National Aeronautics and Space Administration (NASA), Greenbelt, MD, consulting scientist, 1978-81; City of New York Department of Parks and Recreation, consulting astronomer, 1986-91. Environmental Science and Services Co., Long Island City, NY, consulting environmental scientist, 1981—; City University of New York, New York City, adjunct assistant

Gregory Matloff provides tips for city-bound stargazers in *The Urban Astonomer.*

professor of physics, 1981—; State University of New York, New York City, adjunct professor of physics, 1992—. Aerospace engineer, 1965-69; Wesleyan University, research astronomer, 1969-70; New School of Social Research, faculty member, 1992—. Voluntary environmental consultant to community of Brooklyn, NY, 1980-84.

MEMBER: American Institute of Aeronautics and Astronautics, Optical Society of America, American Association for the Advancement of Science, British Interplanetary Society (fellow), Planetary Society, Astronomy Society of Pacific, New York Academy of Sciences.

AWARDS, HONORS: Gregory Matloff was dubbed an ecumenical knight of Malta, 1986; *The Starflight Handbook* was named one of the best books for young adults by the New York Public Library, 1991.

WRITINGS:

(With E. Mallore) *The Starflight Handbook,* drawings by C. Bangs, Wiley, 1989.
The Urban Astronomer, drawings by Bangs, Wiley, 1991.
Telescope Power, drawings by Bangs, Wiley, in press.

Assistant editor, *Physics Today,* 1970-71; contributor of more than fifty scientific papers to professional journals.

WORK IN PROGRESS: Research on extra-solar space-flight and search for extraterrestrial intelligence, in collaboration with scientists at Alena Spatiale (in Turin, Italy).

SIDELIGHTS: Gregory Matloff told *SATA:* "Scientific research is exciting and can be made accessible to readers of all ages. It is important to return to the roots of the scientific endeavor and involve the reader as a participant, not merely as a spectator. As well as that, fine art and poetry can be used to communicate scientific ideas."

*   *   *

MAYER, Mercer 1943-

PERSONAL: Born December 30, 1943, in Little Rock, AR; married; wife's name, Gina; children: (previous marriage) Arden, Jessie, Len; (current marriage) Benjamin, Zebulon. *Education:* Studied at the Honolulu Academy of Arts and the Art Students League. *Hobbies and other interests:* Guitar playing, painting, walking in the woods, sitting by the river, and messing around with computers and multimedia.

ADDRESSES: Home—Bridgewater, CT.

CAREER: Author and illustrator of children's books; Angel Entertainment, White Plains, NY, co-owner, 1983—. Worked as an art director for an advertising agency, 1965. *Exhibitions:* Illustrations for Jane Yolen's *The Bird of Time* and Jan Wahl's *Margaret's Birthday* were included in American Institute of Graphic Arts 1971-72 Children's Book Show.

AWARDS, HONORS: Citation of Merit, Society of Illustrators Annual National Exhibit, 1970, for *A Boy, A Dog, and A Frog,* 1975, for *What Do You Do with a Kangaroo?,* and 1976, for *Frog Goes to Dinner;* Children's Book Award, American Institute of Graphic Arts, 1971, for *A Special Trick;* Brooklyn Art Books for Children citation, 1973, for *A Boy, a Dog, and a Frog,* 1975, for *What Do You Do with a Kangaroo?,* and 1977, for *Frog Goes to Dinner;* International Books for Children Award, Association for Childhood Education, 1974, for *A Boy, a Dog, and a Frog;* Best Books of the Year citation, Child Study Association, 1974, for *You're the Scaredy-Cat;* Best Illustrated Books of the Year citation, *New York Times,* Ten Best Books citation, *Learning,* and Irma Simonton Black Award, Bank Street College of Education, all 1977, all for *Everyone Knows What a Dragon Looks Like;* Brooklyn Art Books for Children Award, 1977, for *Frog Goes to Dinner;* Michigan Young Readers Award, 1982, for *Beauty and the Beast;* California Young Reader Medal, 1983, for *Liza Lou and the Yeller Belly Swamp.*

WRITINGS:

SELF-ILLUSTRATED

A Boy, a Dog, and a Frog, Dial, 1967.

MERCER MAYER

There's a Nightmare in My Closet, Dial, 1968, published
    in England as *There's a Nightmare in My Cupboard*,
    Dent, 1976.
Terrible Troll, Dial, 1968.
If I Had..., Dial, 1968.
I Am a Hunter, Dial, 1969.
Frog, Where Are You?, 1969.
A Special Trick, Dial, 1970.
The Queen Always Wanted to Dance, Simon & Schuster,
    1971.
A Silly Story, Parents Magazine Press, 1972.
Frog on His Own, Dial 1973.
Bubble, Bubble, Parents Magazine Press, 1973.
Mrs. Beggs and the Wizard, Parents Magazine Press,
    1973, reprinted as *The Wizard Comes to Town*,
    Rainbird Productions, 1973.
A Frog and a Friend, Golden Press, 1974.
What Do You Do with a Kangaroo?, Four Winds, 1974.
Two Moral Tales, Four Winds, 1974.
Two More Moral Tales (contains *Just a Pig at Heart* and
    Sly Fox's Folly), Four Winds, 1974.
Walk, Robot, Walk, Ginn, 1974.
You're the Scaredy-Cat, Parents Magazine Press, 1974.
Frog Goes to Dinner, Dial, 1974.
One Monster after Another, Golden Press, 1974.
Just for You, Golden Press, 1975.
The Great Cat Chase: A Wordless Book, Four Winds,
    1975.
Professor Wormbog in Search of the Zipperump-a-Zoo,
    Golden Press, 1976.

Liza Lou and the Great Yeller Belly Swamp, Parents
    Magazine Press, 1976.
Ah-Choo, Dial, 1976.
Four Frogs in a Box, Dial, 1976.
Hiccup, Dial, 1976.
Just Me and My Dad, Golden Press, 1977.
Oops, Dial, 1977.
*Professor Wormbog's Gloomy Kerploppus: A Book of
    Great Smells (And a Heart-Warming Story, Besides)*,
    Golden Press, 1977.
Mercer's Monsters, Golden Press, 1977.
How the Trollusk Got His Hat, Golden Press, 1979.
Herbert the Timid Dragon, Golden Press, 1980.
East of the Sun and West of the Moon, Four Winds,
    1980.
*Professor Wormbog's Cut It, Glue It, Tape It, Do-It
    Book*, Golden Press, 1980.
Professor Wormbog's Crazy Cut-Ups, Golden Press,
    1980.
Play with Me, Golden Press, 1982.
Malcolm's Race, Scholastic, 1983.
Gator Cleans House, Scholastic, 1983.
Too's Bracelet, Scholastic, 1983, reprinted as *Little
    Sister's Bracelet*, Green Frog, 1983.
Sweatmeat's Birthday, Scholastic, 1983, reprinted as
    Bun-Bun's Birthday, Green Frog, 1983.
Possum Child Goes Shopping, Scholastic, 1983.
Bat Child's Haunted House, Scholastic, 1983.
Little Critter's Day at the Farm, Scholastic, 1984.
Little Critter's Holiday Fun, Scholastic, 1984.
Little Monster's Moving Day, Scholastic, 1984.
Little Monster's Sports Fun, Scholastic, 1984.
Astronaut Critter, Simon & Schuster, 1986.
Cowboy Critter, Simon & Schuster, 1986.
Fireman Critter, Simon & Schuster, 1986.
Policeman Critter, Simon & Schuster, 1986.
Sailor Critter, Simon & Schuster, 1987.
Doctor Critter, Simon & Schuster, 1987.
Construction Critter, Simon & Schuster, 1987.
The Pied Piper of Hamelin, Macmillan, 1987.
There's Something in My Attic, Dial, 1988.
Just Shopping with Mom, Golden Press, 1989.
When I Grow Up, Golden Press, 1991.
Thrills and Spills, Delmar, 1991.
A Monster Followed Me to School, Golden Press, 1991.
Where's My Sneaker, Green Frog, 1991.
Where's My Frog, Green Frog, 1991.
Where's Kitty, Green Frog, 1991.
Little Critter's Little Red Riding Hood, Green Frog,
    1991.
Little Critter's Hansel and Gretel, Green Frog, 1991.
Little Critter's Jack and the Beanstalk, Green Frog,
    1991.
What a Bad Dream, Golden Press, 1992.
Little Critter's Shapes, Green Frog, 1992.
Little Critter's Numbers, Green Frog, 1992.
Little Critter's Colors, Green Frog, 1992.
I am Helping, Green Frog, 1992.
I am Hiding, Green Frog, 1992.
I am Playing, Green Frog, 1992.
I am Sharing, Green Frog, 1992.
Little Critter's Read It Yourself Storybook, Golden
    Press, 1993.

16 sixteen

Sixteen is sixteen fish.

Little Monster caught one. How many fish are left in the lake?

In his self-illustrated "Little Monster" series, Mayer teaches basic themes and ideas using colorful characters and humor.

Also author of *The Little Drummer Mouse,* recorded by Mayer for audio cassette, Caedmon, 1987. Mayer produced an animated video based on *Just Me and My Dad* in 1992.

Mayer's work, *There's a Nightmare in My Closet,* has been translated into French.

"LITTLE MONSTER" SERIES

Little Monster's Word Book, Golden Press, 1977.
Little Monster at Home, Golden Press, 1978.
Little Monster at School, Golden Press, 1978.
Little Monster at Work, Golden Press, 1978.
Little Monster's Alphabet Book, Golden Press, 1978.
Little Monster's You-Can-Make-It Book, Golden Press, 1978.
Little Monster's Bedtime Book, Golden Press, 1978.
Little Monster's Counting Book, Golden Press, 1978.
Little Monster's Neighborhood, Golden Press, 1978.
Mercer Mayer's Little Monster's Library (set of six books), Golden Press, 1978.
Little Monster's Mother Goose, Golden Press, 1979.
Little Monster's Scratch and Sniff Mystery, Golden Press, 1980.

"LITTLE CRITTER" SERIES

The New Baby, Golden Press, 1983.
When I Get Bigger, Golden Press, 1983.
I Was So Mad, Golden Press, 1983.
All by Myself, Golden Press, 1983.
Me Too!, Golden Press, 1983.
Just Grandma and Me, Golden Press, 1983.

Just a Snowy Day, Golden Press, 1983.
Just Me and My Puppy, Golden Press, 1985.
Just Grandpa and Me, Golden Press, 1985.
Just Go to Bed, Golden Press, 1985.
Just Me and My Babysitter, Golden Press, 1986.
Just Me and My Little Sister, Golden Press, 1986.
Little Critter's Bedtime Storybook, Golden Press, 1987.
Just a Mess, Golden Press, 1987.
Baby Sister Says No!, Golden Press, 1987.
Little Critter's Little Sister's Birthday, Golden Press, 1988.
Little Critter's The Picnic, Golden Press, 1988.
Little Critter's Staying Overnight, Golden Press, 1988.
Little Critter's This Is My House, Golden Press, 1988.
Little Critter's The Trip, Golden Press, 1988.
Little Critter's These Are My Pets, Golden Press, 1988.
I Just Forgot, Golden Press, 1988.
Just My Friend and Me, Golden Press, 1988.
Happy Easter, Little Critter, Golden Press, 1988.
Little Critter's This Is My Friend, Golden Press, 1989.
Little Critter's Christmas Book, Golden Press, 1989.
Merry Christmas, Mom and Dad, Golden Press, 1989.
Little Critter's the Fussy Princess, Golden Press, 1989.
Little Critter's Play with Me, Golden Press, 1989.
Mercer Mayer's Little Critter at Play, Golden Press, 1989.
Mercer Mayer's Little Critter's Day, Golden Press, 1989.
Just a Daydream, Golden Press, 1989.
Just a Nap, Golden Press, 1989.
Just Camping Out, Golden Press, 1989.
Just a Rainy Day, Golden Press, 1990.
Just Me and My Mom, Golden Press, 1990.
Just Going to the Dentist, Golden Press, 1990.
Little Critter's This Is My School, Golden Press, 1990.
Two-Minute Little Critter Stories, Golden Press, 1990.
Little Critter at Scout Camp, Golden Press, 1991.
Just Me and My Little Brother, Golden Press, 1991.

"TINK! TONK! TALES" SERIES

Tinka Bakes a Cake, Bantam, 1984.
Tuk Takes a Trip, Bantam, 1984.
Tink Goes Fishing, Bantam, 1984.
Teep and Beep Go to Sleep, Bantam, 1984.
Trouble in Tinktonk Land, Bantam, 1985.
The Tinktonks Find a Home, Bantam, 1985.
Tonk Gives a Magic Show, Bantam, 1985.
Zoomer Builds a Racing Car, Bantam, 1985.

WITH GINA MAYER

Rosie's Mouse, Golden Press, 1992.
This Is My Family, Golden Press, 1992.
The New Potty, Golden Press, 1992.
Just Me and My Cousin, Golden Press, 1992.
Just a Thunderstorm, Golden Press, 1993.
A Very Special Critter, Golden Press, 1993.
It's Mine, Golden Press, 1993.
Just a Gum Wrapper, Golden Press, 1993.
That's Not Fair, Golden Press, 1993.
Just Like Dad, Golden Press, 1993.
Just Me & My Bicycle, Golden Press, 1993.
Just Too Little, Golden Press, 1993.
Going to the Races, Golden Press, 1993.
Just Say Please, Golden Press, 1993.

Taking Care of Mom, Golden Press, 1993.
This Is My Body, Golden Press, 1993.

WITH MARIANNA MAYER

Mine, Simon & Schuster, 1970.
A Boy, a Dog, a Frog, and a Friend, Dial, 1971.
Me and My Flying Machine, Parents Magazine Press, 1971.
One Frog Too Many, Dial, 1975.
There's an Alligator under My Bed, Dial, 1987.

ILLUSTRATOR

John D. Fitzgerald, *The Great Brain,* Dial, 1967.
Liesel M. Skorpen, *Outside My Window,* Harper, 1968.
George Mendoza, *The Gillygoofang,* Dial, 1968.
Sidney Offit, *The Boy Who Made a Million,* St. Martin's, 1968.
G. Mendoza, *The Crack in the Wall, and Other Terribly Weird Tales,* Dial, 1968.
Sheila LaFarge, *Golden Butter,* Dial 1969.
J. D. Fitzgerald, *More Adventures of the Great Brian,* Dial, 1969.
Kathryn Hitte, *Boy, Was I Mad!,* Parents Magazine Press, 1969.
Mildred Kantrowitz, *Good-bye Kitchen,* Parents Magazine Press, 1969.
Warren Fine, *The Mousechildren and the Famous Collector,* Harper, 1970.
Jean R. Larson, *Jack Tar,* M. Smith, 1970.

Appelard the farmer adopts a strange little creature named Liverwurst in Mayer's story about a unique friendship, *Appelard and Liverwurst.* **(Cover illustration by Steven Kellogg.)**

Barbara Wersba, *Let Me Fall before I Fly,* Atheneum, 1971.
Jane H. Yolen, *The Bird of Time,* Crowell, 1971.
Jan Wahl, *Margaret's Birthday,* Four Winds, 1971.
J. D. Fitzgerald, *Me and My Little Brain,* Dial, 1971.
Candida Palmer, *Kim Ann and the Yellow Machine,* Ginn, 1972.
J. Wahl, *Grandmother Told Me,* Little, Brown, 1972.
J. D. Fitzgerald, *The Great Brain at the Academy,* Dial, 1972.
Mabel Watts, *While the Horses Galloped to London,* Parents Magazine Press, 1973.
J. D. Fitzgerald, *The Great Brain Reforms,* Dial, 1973.
B. Wersba, *Amanda Dreaming,* Atheneum, 1973.
J. D. Fitzgerald, *Return of the Great Brain,* Dial, 1974.
J. D. Fitzgerald, *The Great Brain Does It Again,* Dial, 1975.
John Bellairs, *The Figure in the Shadows,* Dial, 1975.
Jay Williams, *Everyone Knows What a Dragon Looks Like,* Four Winds, 1976.
J. Williams, *The Reward Worth Having,* Four Winds, 1977.
Marianna Mayer, reteller, *Beauty and the Beast,* Four Winds, 1978.
Nancy Garden, reteller, *Favorite Tales from Grimm,* Four Winds, 1982.
(With Gail E. Haley, Laurel Schindelman, and Gary Parker) E. L. Konigsburg, *Altogether, One at a Time,* Macmillan, second edition, 1989.

OTHER

(Editor) *The Poison Tree and Other Poems,* Scribner, 1977.
Appelard and Liverwurst, illustrated by Steven Kellogg, Four Winds, 1978.
Liverwurst Is Missing, illustrated by S. Kellogg, Four Winds, 1982.
(Reteller) Charles Perrault, *The Sleeping Beauty,* Macmillan, 1984.
Whinnie the Lovesick Dragon, illustrated by Diane Dawson Hearne, Macmillan, 1986.
(Reteller) Charles Dickens, *A Christmas Carol: Being a Ghost Story of Christmas,* Macmillan, 1986.

ADAPTATIONS: A Boy, a Dog, and a Frog was adapted for film by Gary Stempleton and released by Phoenix Films; *There's a Nightmare in My Closet* was adapted for film by Gary Stempleton and released by Phoenix Films, 1987; *There's Something in My Attic* was adapted for film and released by Phoenix/BFA Films, 1990.

SIDELIGHTS: Popular children's author Mercer Mayer is well-known for his versatility, humor, and artistic skill. Noted as one of the first creators of wordless picture books, Mayer also writes and illustrates nonsense fiction, fantasy, and folktales. In both his writing and illustrating, Mayer emphasizes the unconventional; his language can be simple or sophisticated, while his illustrations run the gamut of artistic styles. Despite his notoriety, Mayer is still a bit surprised that his works are so popular with young readers. "I find it quite odd to be included amongst authors. For it is hard to conceive of myself as one. I tell stories with pictures, and quite often

book explores a boy and a dog's attempt to capture a frog from a pond. During their pursuit, the boy and the dog fall in the water, the boy nets his dog instead of the frog, and the frog displays various emotions from amusement to irritation. Eventually defeated, the boy and the dog abandon their conquest and retreat home. The lonely frog follows them home and voluntarily becomes their friend. *Young Readers Review* contributor Robert Cohen described the illustrations as "wonderfully graphic and informative," and in her review for *School Library Journal,* Elinor Cullen suggested that *A Boy, a Dog, and a Frog* is "good reading readiness material."

Mayer has repeated the success of *A Boy, a Dog, and a Frog* with a number of colorful volumes. *There's a Nightmare in My Closet,* written and illustrated by Mayer, contains a humorous story about a young boy confronting the monsters in his nightmares who are hiding in his closet. While the young boy is sleeping in bed, a monster with big ears, large droopy eyes, and buck teeth apprehensively tiptoes out of the boy's closet and sits at the end of the boy's bed. When the boy wakes up and finds the nervous monster hovering over him, he tries to shoot the ugly creature with his toy gun. The beast becomes frightened and begins to cry. Fearful that his parents might wake up, the boy invites the distressed creature to sleep with him. Before the monster and the

Written by Mayer and his former wife Marianna, *A Boy, a Dog, a Frog, and a Friend* relates—without text—the further adventures of four pals whose ingenuity gets them out of a number of scrapes.

I even add words," he noted in an essay for the *Fourth Book of Junior Authors.* "I am now at home with what I do. Children's books are a good place to call home."

Because his father was in the navy, Mayer moved around a great deal as a child. The family eventually settled in Hawaii, where Mayer attended Theodore Roosevelt High School; upon graduation, he continued his studies at the Honolulu Academy of Arts. In 1964, Mayer moved to New York City for instruction at the Art Student's League. Over time, he began to put together an art portfolio, which he hoped to use to land illustration jobs. Unfortunately, Mayer had little luck. He related in the *Fourth Book of Junior Authors:* "I pounded the streets of New York and received a polite smile everywhere I went. Finally I received some good advice from an art director. He told me to throw my portfolio away because it was so bad." Although initially upset by this evaluation, Mayer decided to take the advice; in his spare time, he began to refine his sketching. Mayer soon quit his job with an advertising agency in order to peddle his artwork to various publishers. Eventually, he was able to secure a number of illustration contracts.

Mayer published his first picture book, *A Boy, a Dog, and a Frog,* in 1967. Without words this award-winning

"Go away, Nightmare, or I'll shoot you," I said.

A little boy decides to face his fears instead of running away from them in Mayer's self-illustrated *There's a Nightmare in My Closet.*

The evil fairy gets her comeuppance in Mayer's self-illustrated retelling of *Sleeping Beauty*.

boy fall asleep together, the boy contemplates, "I suppose there is another nightmare in my closet, but my bed's not big enough for three." In a review for *Young Readers Review,* Phyllis Cohen described *There's a Nightmare in My Closet* as "a magnificently funny book" with "superb illustrations."

Award-winning *Liza Lou and the Yeller Belly Swamp* is another picture book featuring a child's interactions with monsters. Liza Lou, a young black girl, is asked to deliver sweet potatoes to her grandmother who lives across the Yeller Belly Swamp. During her trek through the swamp, she runs into ugly swamp creatures, but with different strategies, she eludes her attackers. *Booklist* contributor Betsy Hearne lauded Mayer for his illustrations that "show forceful proportion, lively expression, and energetic color." Mary Agnes Taylor, a reviewer for *The Reading Teacher,* regarded *Liza Lou and the Yeller Belly Swamp* to be "a good-natured spoof that should amuse readers young and old."

As a writer and illustrator, Mayer created three distinct series of children's books for select publishers. One of his series stars Little Monster, a childlike reptilian with wings and large ears. The first book in the series, *Little Monster's Word Book,* uses friendly monsters to explore numerous words on various topics for children. Barbara Karlin, writing in *West Coast Review of Books,* praised *Little Monster's Word Book* as "a book with which a lot of little people are going to spend many happy hours." Mayer told *SATA* that his Little Critters series is the most successful with fifty million books in print.

In spite of his own busy writing schedule, Mayer has found time to illustrate books for a number of other authors. His pictures for Marianna Mayer's retelling of Mme. Leprince de Beaumont's *Beauty and the Beast* were applauded by P. Gila Reinstein in her *Dictionary of Literary Biography* review as having a "wealth of detail" that is "full and lavish." And Bonita Brodt, writing in the *Chicago Tribune,* called Mayer's adaptation of Charles Dickens' *A Christmas Carol* a "wonderful interpretation because it makes the tale accessible to young children and also remains true to the older ones as well." In summing up Mayer's success, Reinstein notes: "Reflecting the world from the child's point of view has been a hallmark of [Mayer's] work from the beginning of his career, and whatever changes come in his approach to children and their books, the honesty and emotional intensity that are essential to his work will remain unchanged."

WORKS CITED:

Brodt, Bonita, review of *A Christmas Carol, Chicago Tribune,* December 7, 1986, section 14, p. 3.
Cohen, Phyllis, review of *There's a Nightmare in My Closet, Young Readers Review,* June, 1968, p. 10.
Cohen, Robert, review of *A Boy, a Dog, and a Frog, Young Readers Review,* December, 1967, p. 12.
Cullen, Elinor, review of *A Boy, a Dog, and a Frog, School Library Journal,* October, 1967, p. 165.
Hearne, Betsy, review of *Liza Lou and the Yeller Belly Swamp, Booklist,* September 1, 1976, p. 40.
Karlin, Barbara, review of *Little Monster's Word Book, West Coast Review of Books,* September, 1977, p. 55.
Mayer, Mercer, essay in *Fourth Book of Junior Authors,* edited by Doris De Montreville and Elizabeth D. Crawford, Wilson, 1978, pp. 259-60.
Reinstein, P. Gila, essay in *Dictionary of Literary Biography,* Volume 61: *American Writers for Children since 1960: Poets, Illustrators, and Nonfiction Authors,* Gale, 1987, pp. 208-09.
Taylor, Mary Agnes, review of *Liza Lou and the Yeller Belly Swamp, The Reading Teacher,* Vol. 30, No. 8, May, 1977, pp. 947-48.

FOR MORE INFORMATION SEE:

BOOKS

Contemporary Literary Criticism, Volume 11, Gale, 1979, pp. 159-76.

PERIODICALS

Booklist, November 1, 1980, p. 407.
New York Times Book Review, November 26, 1967, p. 62; May 1, 1977; May 25, 1980; January 4, 1981; August 16, 1987; November 29, 1987.

*   *   *

McCALL SMITH, Alexander 1948-

PERSONAL: Born August 24, 1948, in Chipinga, Zimbabwe; son of Sandy (a public prosecutor) and Daphne (Woodall) McCall Smith; married Elizabeth Parry (a medical practitioner and writer), September 4, 1982; children: Lucy Ishbel, Emily Rose. *Education:* University of Edinburgh, LL.B., 1971, Ph.D., 1979. *Religion:* Episcopalian. *Hobbies and other interests:* Wind instruments.

ADDRESSES: Home—Edinburgh, Scotland, Great Britain. *Agent*—Murray Pollinger, 222 Old Brompton Rd., London SW5 0BZ, England.

CAREER: Southern Methodist University, Dallas, Texas, visiting professor of law, 1988; University of Edinburgh, reader in law and associate dean of law faculty; writer.

WRITINGS:

FICTION; FOR CHILDREN

The White Hippo, illustrated by Michael Clifford, Hamish Hamilton, 1980.
The Little Theatre, illustrated by Peter Rush-Jansen, Macdonald, 1982.
The Perfect Hamburger, illustrated by Laszlo Acs, Penguin Books, 1982.
Mike's Magic Seeds, illustrated by Kate Shannon, Corgi, 1988.
Alix and the Tigers, illustrated by Jon Miller, Corgi, 1988.
Film Boy, illustrated by Joanna Carey, Methuen, 1988.
Uncle Gangster, illustrated by Carey, Methuen, 1989.
Akimbo and the Elephants, illustrated by Mei Yim Low, Methuen, 1990.
Suzy Magician, illustrated by Alison Darke, Corgi, 1990.
The Ice Cream Bicycle, illustrated by Stephanie Ryder, Viking, 1990.
Children of Wax, Canongate, 1989, Interlink Books, 1991.
The Five Lost Aunts of Harriet Bean, illustrated by Jean Baylis, Blackie & Son, 1990.
Jeffrey's Joke Machine, illustrated by Robert Bartelt, Blackie & Son, 1990, Puffin, 1992.
The Tin Dog, illustrated by Jon Riley, Corgi, 1990.
The Spaghetti Tangle, illustrated by Elke Counsell, Methuen, 1991.
Akimbo and the Lions, illustrated by Low, Methuen, 1992.
The Princess Trick, illustrated by Katinka Kew, Blackie & Son, 1992.
Springy Jane, illustrated by Counsell, Blackie & Son, 1992.
Calculator Annie, illustrated by Riley, Corgi, 1992.
The Doughnut Ring, illustrated by Glenys Ambrus, Hamish Hamilton, 1992.

Also author of *Marzipan Max,* 1991.

FOR ADULTS

(Editor with Tony Carty) *Power and Manoeuvrability,* Q Press, 1978.
(Editor with wife, Elizabeth McCall Smith) *All about Drinking,* W. & R. Chambers, 1986.
(Editor with E. McCall Smith) *So You Want to Try Drugs,* W. & R. Chambers, 1986.
All about Drink and Drug Abuse, Macmillan, 1990.
(Editor with Elaine Sutherland) *Family Rights: Family Law and Medical Advances,* Edinburgh University Press, 1990.
(With J. K. Mason) *Law and Medical Ethics,* Butterworths, 1990.
(With K. Frimpong) *The Criminal Law of Botswana,* Juta, 1992.

(With D. Sheldon) *Scots Criminal Law,* Butterworths, 1992.

OTHER

On the Road (for young adults), W. & R. Chambers, 1988.

Author of short stories and broadcast plays for British Broadcasting Corporation (BBC).

McCall Smith's works have been translated into Japanese, German, Welsh, and Caracan.

WORK IN PROGRESS: Akimbo and the Crocodile Man and *Who Invented Peanut Butter?,* both to be published by Methuen in 1993; *The Muscle Machine,* to be published by Hamish Hamilton in 1993.

SIDELIGHTS: Alexander McCall Smith is the author of numerous adventure books for children. Among them are *The Perfect Hamburger* and *The Spaghetti Tangle,* both of which involve an effort to improve a certain food. In the author's 1982 work, *The Perfect Hamburger,* which a *Times Educational Supplement* contributor called "an engaging tale," a boy becomes determined to create the world's best hamburger seasoning, in order to prevent a giant fast-food chain from taking over a local eatery. *The Spaghetti Tangle,* published in 1992, concerns John and Nicky, two children living with their Aunt Rebecca. As a result of a lost love years ago, Aunt Rebecca now lives on nothing but raw cabbage, nuts, onion rings, and carrot juice, and serves John and Nicky the same. Craving chips and cake, the youngsters go to a restaurant, but cannot afford these items. Luckily, an understanding waiter allows them to sample spaghetti. John and Nicky then become caught up in a spaghetti sauce competition, and eventually tour a spaghetti factory. A romance develops between the factory owner and Aunt Rebecca when she invents carrot-flavored spaghetti. A *Junior Bookshelf* critic found *The Spaghetti Tangle* fast-paced and entertaining.

McCall Smith told *SATA:* "A number of my books are set in Africa, and in these I try to convey to children some of the special feeling of the African landscape. In my recent "Akimbo" books (*Akimbo and the Elephants* and *Akimbo and the Lions*), I have introduced ecological themes, attempting to convey the fragility of wildlife."

WORKS CITED:

Review of *The Spaghetti Tangle, Times Educational Supplement,* April 27, 1984, p. 27.

FOR MORE INFORMATION SEE:

PERIODICALS

Junior Bookshelf, February, 1992, p. 23.

McDONOUGH, Yona Zeldis 1957-

PERSONAL: Born June 26, 1957, in Chadera, Israel; daughter of Chayym (a writer) and Malcah (a painter; maiden name, Brightman) Zeldis; married Paul A. McDonough (a photographer), November 2, 1985; children: James Redden. *Education:* Vassar College, A.B., 1979; Columbia University, M.A., 1982. *Religion:* Jewish.

ADDRESSES: Home—1623 Second Avenue, New York, NY 10028.

CAREER: Free-lance writer.

MEMBER: American Society of Journalists and Authors, Society of Children's Book Illustrators, National Writers Union.

WRITINGS:

Coping with Social Situations, Rosen Press, 1984.
Beauty, Fitness, and Fashion, Rosen Press, 1987.

WORK IN PROGRESS: A picture-book of women from the Bible for Greenwillow.

SIDELIGHTS: Author Yona Zeldis McDonough told *SATA:* "In the past, I wrote books for young adults with

YONA ZELDIS McDONOUGH

great verve and interest, partly because I always felt connected to the adolescent in me. Now that I have a child—he's just turned one—I find I am interested in going back even further, and have been working on manuscripts for very young children.

"My father is a writer and my mother a painter. I learned about discipline and organization from him and about creativity and spontaneity from her. Right now, I'm collaborating with my mother on a project. It's a book about Biblical heroines for which I am writing the text and she is doing the illustrations. We read the Bible together and spend hours talking about the stories; what they mean, why they're important. It's been wonderful working with her—I highly recommend joining forces with your mother!"

*   *   *

McKISSACK, Fredrick L(emuel) 1939-

PERSONAL: Born August 12, 1939, in Nashville, TN; son of Lewis Winter and Bessye (Fizer) McKissack; married Patricia Carwell (a writer), December 12, 1964; children: Fredrick Lemuel, Robert and John (twins). *Education:* Tennessee Agricultural and Industrial State University (now Tennessee State University), B.S., 1964. *Politics:* Independent. *Religion:* Methodist. *Hobbies and other interests:* Collecting antique model ships, gardening, spending time with pet cat, Kit.

ADDRESSES: Home—5900 Pershing Ave., St. Louis, MO 63112. *Office*—225 South Meramec Ave., #206, Clayton, MO 63115.

CAREER: Worked as a civil engineer for city and federal governments, 1964-74; owner of general contracting company in St. Louis, MO, 1974-82; writer, 1982—; co-owner with Patricia C. McKissack of All-Writing Services. *Military service:* U.S. Marine Corps, 1957-60.

AWARDS, HONORS: C. S. Lewis Silver Medal award, Christian Educators Association, 1985, for *Abram, Abram, Where Are We Going?;* Jane Addams Children's Book Award, Women's International League for Peace and Freedom, and Coretta Scott King Award, both 1990, both for *A Long Hard Journey: The Story of the Pullman Porter;* Coretta Scott King Honor Award, 1993, for *Sojourner Truth: Ain't I a Woman?*

WRITINGS:

Fredrick Douglass: A Biography, Children's Press, 1986.
History of the Civil Rights Movement, Children's Press, 1986.

FOR CHILDREN; WITH WIFE, PATRICIA C. McKISSACK

Look What You've Done Now, Moses, illustrated by Joe Boddy, David Cook, 1984.
Abram, Abram, Where Are We Going?, illustrated by Boddy, David Cook, 1984.
Cinderella, illustrated by Tom Dunnington, Children's Press, 1985.

Country Mouse and City Mouse, illustrated by Anne Sikorski, Children's Press, 1985.
The Little Red Hen, illustrated by Dennis Hockerman, Children's Press, 1985.
The Three Bears, illustrated by Virginia Bala, Children's Press, 1985.
The Ugly Little Duck, illustrated by Peggy Perry Anderson, Children's Press, 1986.
When Do You Talk to God? Prayers for Small Children, illustrated by Gary Gumble, Augsburg, 1986.
King Midas and His Gold, illustrated by Dunnington, Children's Press, 1986.
Frederick Douglass: The Black Lion, Children's Press, 1987.
A Real Winner, illustrated by Quentin Thompson and Ken Jones, Milliken, 1987.
The King's New Clothes, illustrated by Gwen Connelly, Children's Press, 1987.
Tall Phil and Small Bill, illustrated by Kathy Mitter, Milliken, 1987.
Three Billy Goats Gruff, illustrated by Dunnington, Children's Press, 1987.
My Bible ABC Book, illustrated by Reed Merrill, Augsburg, 1987.
The Civil Rights Movement in America from 1865 to the Present, Children's Press, 1987, 2nd edition, 1991.
All Paths Lead to Bethlehem, illustrated by Kathryn E. Shoemaker, Augsburg, 1987.
Messy Bessey, illustrated by Richard Hackney, Children's Press, 1987.
The Big Bug Book of Counting, illustrated by Bartholomew, Milliken, 1987.
The Big Bug Book of Opposites, illustrated by Bartholomew, Milliken, 1987.
The Big Bug Book of Places to Go, illustrated by Bartholomew, Milliken, 1987.
The Big Bug Book of the Alphabet, illustrated by Bartholomew, Milliken, 1987.
The Big Bug Book of Things to Do, illustrated by Bartholomew, Milliken, 1987.
Bugs!, illustrated by Martin, Children's Press, 1988.
The Children's ABC Christmas, illustrated by Kathy Rogers, Augsburg, 1988.
Constance Stumbles, illustrated by Dunnington, Children's Press, 1988.
Oh, Happy, Happy Day! A Child's Easter in Story, Song, and Prayer, illustrated by Elizabeth Swisher, Augsburg, 1989.
God Made Something Wonderful, illustrated by Ching, Augsburg, 1989.
Messy Bessey's Closet, illustrated by Hackney, Children's Press, 1989.
James Weldon Johnson: "Lift Every Voice and Sing," Children's Press, 1990.
A Long Hard Journey: The Story of the Pullman Porter, Walker & Co., 1990.
Taking a Stand against Racism and Racial Discrimination, F. Watts, 1990.
W. E. B. DuBois, F. Watts, 1990.
The Story of Booker T. Washington, Children's Press, 1991.
Messy Bessey's Garden, illustrated by Martin, Children's Press, 1991.

Frederick Douglass
The Black Lion
by Patricia and Fredrick McKissack

Among the many historically-based books written by Fredrick McKissack is this volume about the famous abolitionist, lecturer, and writer. (Cover illustration by Len W. Meents.)

From Heaven Above, Augsburg, 1992.

FOR CHILDREN; "GREAT AFRICAN AMERICANS" SERIES; WITH PATRICIA C. McKISSACK

Carter G. Woodson: The Father of Black History, illustrated by Ned Ostendorf, Enslow, 1991.
Frederick Douglass: Leader against Slavery, illustrated by Ostendorf, Enslow, 1991.
George Washington Carver: The Peanut Scientist, illustrated by Ostendorf, Enslow, 1991.
Ida B. Wells-Barnett: A Voice against Violence, Enslow, 1991.
Louis Armstrong: Jazz Musician, illustrated by Ostendorf, Enslow, 1991.
Marian Anderson: A Great Singer, Enslow, 1991.
Martin Luther King, Jr.: Man of Peace, Enslow, 1991.
Mary Church Terrell: Leader for Equality, illustrated by Ostendorf, Enslow, 1991.
Mary McLeod Bethune: A Great Teacher, illustrated by Ostendorf, Enslow, 1991.
Ralph J. Bunche: Peacemaker, Enslow, 1991.
Jesse Owens, Enslow, 1992.
Langston Hughes, Enslow, 1992.
Sojourner Truth, Enslow, 1992.
Zora Neale Hurston: Writer and Storyteller, Enslow, 1992.
Satchel Paige, Enslow, 1992.
Sojourner Truth: Ain't I a Woman?, Scholastic, 1992.
Madam C. J. Walker: Self-Made Millionaire, Enslow, 1992.

OTHER

Also contributor with Patricia C. McKissack to *The World of 1492,* edited by Jean Fritz, Holt, 1992; author with P. C. McKissack of "Start Up" series for beginning readers, four volumes, Children's Press, 1985; editor with P. C. McKissack of "Reading Well" series and "Big Bug Books" series, both for Milliken.

WORK IN PROGRESS: A history of the West African kingdoms from 1000-1500, A.D.

SIDELIGHTS: Fredrick L. McKissack once said, "A lot of people wonder how a general contractor can become a writer. The two occupations are not that far removed. I render the service for which I am paid, but writing is much more satisfying than construction work because of the wonderful children I have met. It's an enjoyable experience, and it's also one I've come to love." Please see Patricia C. McKissack's essay in this volume for Sidelights from an interview with Patricia and Fredrick McKissack.

*   *   *

McKISSACK, Patricia C. 1944-
(L'Ann Carwell)

PERSONAL: Born August 9, 1944, in Nashville, TN; daughter of Robert (a civil servant) and Erma (a civil servant) Carwell; married Fredrick L. McKissack (a writer), December 12, 1964; children: Fredrick Lemuel, Robert and John (twins). *Education:* Tennessee Agricultural and Industrial State University (now Tennessee State University), B.A., 1964; Webster University, M.A., 1975. *Politics:* Independent. *Religion:* Methodist. *Hobbies and other interests:* Gardening.

ADDRESSES: Home—5900 Pershing Ave., St. Louis, MO 63112. *Office*—All-Writing Services, 225 South Meramec, #206, Clayton, MO 63115.

CAREER: Junior high school English teacher in Kirkwood, MO, 1968-75; Forest Park College, St. Louis, MO, part-time instructor in English, 1975—. Children's book editor at Concordia Publishing House, 1976-81, and Institute of Children's Literature, 1984—; instructor at University of Missouri—St. Louis, 1978—; co-owner with Fredrick L. McKissack of All-Writing Services. Educational consultant on minority literature.

MEMBER: Society of Children's Book Writers.

AWARDS, HONORS: Helen Keating Ott Award, National Church and Synagogue Librarians Association, 1980, for editorial work at Concordia Publishing House; C. S. Lewis Silver Medal awards, Christian Educators Association, 1984, for *It's the Truth, Christopher* and 1985, for *Abram, Abram, Where Are We Going?;* Jane Addams Children's Book Award, Women's International League for Peace and Freedom, and Coretta Scott King Award, both 1990, both for *A Long Hard Journey: The Story of the Pullman Porter;* Newbery Honor Award and Coretta Scott King Author Award, both 1993, both

Fredrick McKissack with his wife and collaborator Patricia C. McKissack.

for *The Dark-Thirty: Southern Tales of the Supernatural;* Coretta Scott King Honor Award, 1993, for *Sojourner Truth: Ain't I a Woman?*

WRITINGS:

FOR CHILDREN

(Under name L'Ann Carwell) *Good Shepherd Prayer,* Concordia, 1978.

(Under name L'Ann Carwell) *God Gives New Life,* Concordia, 1979.

Ask the Kids, Concordia, 1979.

Who Is Who?, Children's Press, 1983.

Martin Luther King, Jr.: A Man to Remember, Children's Press, 1984.

Paul Lawrence Dunbar: A Poet to Remember, Children's Press, 1984.

Michael Jackson, Superstar, Children's Press, 1984.

Lights Out, Christopher, illustrated by Bartholomew, Augsburg, 1984.

It's the Truth, Christopher, illustrated by Bartholomew, Augsburg, 1984.

The Apache, Children's Press, 1984.

Mary McLeod Bethune: A Great American Educator, Children's Press, 1985.

Aztec Indians, Children's Press, 1985.

The Inca, Children's Press, 1985.

The Maya, Children's Press, 1985.

Flossie and the Fox, illustrated by Rachel Isadora, Dial, 1986.

Our Martin Luther King Book, illustrated by Isadora, Child's World, 1986.

Who Is Coming?, illustrated by Clovis Martin, Children's Press, 1986.

Give It with Love, Christopher: Christopher Learns about Gifts and Giving, illustrated by Bartholomew, Augsburg, 1988.

Speak Up, Christopher: Christopher Learns the Difference between Right and Wrong, illustrated by Bartholomew, Augsburg, 1988.

A Troll in a Hole, Milliken, 1988.

Nettie Jo's Friends, illustrated by Scott Cook, Knopf, 1988.

Mirandy and Brother Wind, illustrated by Jerry Pinkney, Knopf, 1988.

Monkey-Monkey's Trick: Based on an African Folk-Tale, illustrated by Paul Meisel, Random House, 1989.

Jesse Jackson: A Biography, Scholastic, 1989.

(With Ruthilde Kronberg) *A Piece of the Wind and Other Stories to Tell,* Harper, 1990.

No Need for Alarm, Milliken, 1990.

A Million Fish—More or Less, illustrated by Dena Schutzer, Knopf, 1992.

The Dark-Thirty: Southern Tales of the Supernatural, illustrated by Brian Pinkney, Knopf, 1992.

FOR CHILDREN; WITH HUSBAND, FREDRICK L. McKISSACK

Look What You've Done Now, Moses, illustrated by Joe Boddy, David Cook, 1984.

Abram, Abram, Where Are We Going?, illustrated by Boddy, David Cook, 1984.

Cinderella, illustrated by Tom Dunnington, Children's Press, 1985.

Country Mouse and City Mouse, illustrated by Anne Sikorski, Children's Press, 1985.

The Little Red Hen, illustrated by Dennis Hockerman, Children's Press, 1985.

The Three Bears, illustrated by Virginia Bala, Children's Press, 1985.

The Ugly Little Duck, illustrated by Peggy Perry Anderson, Children's Press, 1986.

When Do You Talk to God? Prayers for Small Children, illustrated by Gary Gumble, Augsburg, 1986.

King Midas and His Gold, illustrated by Dunnington, Children's Press, 1986.

Frederick Douglass: The Black Lion, Children's Press, 1987.

A Real Winner, illustrated by Quentin Thompson and Ken Jones, Milliken, 1987.

The King's New Clothes, illustrated by Gwen Connelly, Children's Press, 1987.

Tall Phil and Small Bill, illustrated by Kathy Mitter, Milliken, 1987.

Three Billy Goats Gruff, illustrated by Dunnington, Children's Press, 1987.

My Bible ABC Book, illustrated by Reed Merrill, Augsburg, 1987.

The Civil Rights Movement in America from 1865 to the Present, Children's Press, 1987, 2nd edition, 1991.

All Paths Lead to Bethlehem, illustrated by Kathryn E. Shoemaker, Augsburg, 1987.

Messy Bessey, illustrated by Richard Hackney, Children's Press, 1987.

The Big Bug Book of Counting, illustrated by Bartholomew, Milliken, 1987.

The Big Bug Book of Opposites, illustrated by Bartholomew, Milliken, 1987.

The Big Bug Book of Places to Go, illustrated by Bartholomew, Milliken, 1987.

The Big Bug Book of the Alphabet, illustrated by Bartholomew, Milliken, 1987.

The Big Bug Book of Things to Do, illustrated by Bartholomew, Milliken, 1987.

Bugs!, illustrated by Martin, Children's Press, 1988.

The Children's ABC Christmas, illustrated by Kathy Rogers, Augsburg, 1988.

Constance Stumbles, illustrated by Dunnington, Children's Press, 1988.

Oh, Happy, Happy Day! A Child's Easter in Story, Song, and Prayer, illustrated by Elizabeth Swisher, Augsburg, 1989.

God Made Something Wonderful, illustrated by Ching, Augsburg, 1989.

Messy Bessey's Closet, illustrated by Hackney, Children's Press, 1989.

James Weldon Johnson: "Lift Every Voice and Sing," Children's Press, 1990.

A Long Hard Journey: The Story of the Pullman Porter, Walker & Co., 1990.

Taking a Stand against Racism and Racial Discrimination, F. Watts, 1990.

W. E. B. DuBois, F. Watts, 1990.

The Story of Booker T. Washington, Children's Press, 1991.

Messy Bessey's Garden, illustrated by Martin, Children's Press, 1991.

From Heaven Above, Augsburg, 1992.

FOR CHILDREN; "GREAT AFRICAN AMERICANS" SERIES; WITH FREDRICK L. McKISSACK

Carter G. Woodson: The Father of Black History, illustrated by Ned Ostendorf, Enslow, 1991.

Frederick Douglass: Leader against Slavery, illustrated by Ostendorf, Enslow, 1991.

George Washington Carver: The Peanut Scientist, illustrated by Ostendorf, Enslow, 1991.

Ida B. Wells-Barnett: A Voice against Violence, Enslow, 1991.

Louis Armstrong: Jazz Musician, illustrated by Ostendorf, Enslow, 1991.

Marian Anderson: A Great Singer, Enslow, 1991.

Martin Luther King, Jr.: Man of Peace, Enslow, 1991.

Patricia McKissack's *Mirandy and Brother Wind* tells the tale of a young girl who becomes convinced that she will dance with the wind at an upcoming party. (Illustration by Jerry Pinkney.)

Mary Church Terrell: Leader for Equality, illustrated by Ostendorf, Enslow, 1991.

Mary McLeod Bethune: A Great Teacher, illustrated by Ostendorf, Enslow, 1991.

Ralph J. Bunche: Peacemaker, Enslow, 1991.

Jesse Owens, Enslow, 1992.

Langston Hughes, Enslow, 1992.

Sojourner Truth, Enslow, 1992.

Zora Neale Hurston: Writer and Storyteller, Enslow, 1992.

Satchel Paige, Enslow, 1992.

Sojourner Truth: Ain't I a Woman?, Scholastic, 1992.

Madam C. J. Walker: Self-Made Millionaire, Enslow, 1992.

OTHER

Also contributor with Fredrick L. McKissack to *The World of 1492,* edited by Jean Fritz, Holt, 1992; author with F. L. McKissack of "Start Up" series for beginning readers, four volumes, Children's Press, 1985; editor with F. L. McKissack of "Reading Well" series and "Big Bug Books" series, both for Milliken. Writer for preschool series "L Is for Listening," broadcast by KWMU-Radio, 1975-77. Author of radio and television scripts. Contributor of articles and short stories to magazines, including *Friend, Happy Times,* and *Evangelizing Today's Child.*

WORK IN PROGRESS: "A book about the McKissack family and several biographies about great African-Americans."

SIDELIGHTS: Authors of historical fiction and biographies for children, Patricia and Fredrick McKissack's lives were shaped by one of the most optimistic eras in American history—the 1960s. "We're Kennedy products, and we were very idealistic," Pat told *Something about the Author* interviewer Deborah A. Stanley. "That was the period in which African Americans were really looking up, coming out of darkness, segregation, and discrimination, and doors were beginning to open—ever so slightly, but still opening." Their *Civil Rights Movement in America from 1865 to the Present* and *Martin Luther King, Jr.: Man of Peace,* together with almost one hundred other books, are the result of their experiences during that era.

The two were married in 1964, the same year they graduated from Tennessee State University in Nashville. Fred had served in the Marine Corps for three years before starting college, so although he was older, they finished school at the same time. "I had known him practically all my life," Pat told Stanley. "We grew up in the same town, where every family knew every other family, but he was five years older and you just didn't date boys who were five years older than you. When I was fifteen and he was twenty that just would have been forbidden. But suddenly I was twenty and he was twenty-five and it was perfectly okay." On their second date, Fred proposed and Pat accepted. They were married four months later. "All of our friends said it wouldn't last six months. They said it was ridiculous, and our families were a bit concerned," Pat remem-

bered. "But we just knew. We talked all the time and we still do. We have always had a very, very close relationship from the first date we had. We just had so much fun together that we knew."

One thing Pat and Fred discovered they had in common was a love of literature. Both recalled reading Ayn Rand's *Fountainhead, Atlas Shrugged,* and *Anthem,* as well as Aldous Huxley's *Brave New World* and other novels of similar futuristic themes. "We were talking about the future," Pat noted. Other influences included Julius Lester, an author known for his historically accurate, heroic depictions of black characters. Lester had graduated in 1960 from Fisk University, also in Nashville. "We all knew Julius," Fred recalled. "One way or another, we all knew him. I remember we were all discussing him."

While the era was filled with hope and opportunities, "at the same time it was a time of violent change, it really was," Fred related. "Life actually changed. In a sense we climbed from the Old South to the New South. We went from segregated schools to integrated situations." "Our generation was the first to do it," Pat added. "I remember when Fred took me to dinner at Morrison's. I was nervous as a flea because a sit-in had occurred only a few years earlier, and there had been people putting shotguns at young people's heads and saying, 'If you sit here we will blow you away.' And that happened to Fred" when he joined a sit-in at a Woolworth department store. The visit to Morrison's

McKissack explores the career of this famous educator and college president in a 1985 volume. (Cover illustration by Len W. Meents.)

---

was among many firsts for the McKissacks; after years of seeing them only from the outside, the two finally entered a Kentucky Fried Chicken restaurant, a Shoney's, a McDonald's, and a Hardee's. When Pat's younger brother got a job at Shoney's, Pat realized that "things were opening up. And we were very proud that we were the first generation to come through that."

For the McKissacks, the ugliest experiences of the '60s and '70s were the Vietnam War and the "white backlash" to the Civil Rights Movement. They found the television footage at that time, the first ever shown of American soldiers in combat, profoundly disturbing. "That was horrible for us to watch—the body bags coming back in," Pat related. "I was a young mother—I had three little boys—and I said, 'My God, I hope we never have to go through anything this nonsensical again.' When Desert Storm came [in the fall of 1990], those memories flooded back." The assassinations of John F. Kennedy and his brother Robert, Martin Luther King, Jr., Medgar Evers, and Malcolm X, along with church bombings and innumerable other violent incidents, all served to temper the McKissacks' positive attitude. "Just as blacks experienced white resistance to equality during Reconstruction, there was another backlash to the Civil Rights Movement of the 1960s," Pat commented. "By 1980 blacks were once again on the defense, trying to safeguard their and their children's rights."

The McKissacks acknowledge that what they lived through is difficult for today's children to understand; their goal is to write in such a way that the past comes alive for their young readers. "The reason that we write for children," Fred remarked, "is to tell them about these things and to get them to internalize the information, to feel just a little of the hurt, the tremendous amount of hurt and sadness that racism and discrimination cause—for all people, regardless of race."

One of Pat's first writing projects was a biography of Paul Lawrence Dunbar, written for her class of eighth-grade English students in Kirkwood, Missouri. "The school was twenty-five percent black and I wanted to teach about an African American writer who I had come to know and appreciate when I was growing up, by the name of Paul Lawrence Dunbar," Pat recalled. When she began researching Dunbar, "I couldn't find a biography, so I wrote his biography myself for my students." She also sought information on Langston Hughes and James Weldon Johnson, both of whom she and Fred later wrote about. Many more biographies have followed.

James Weldon Johnson: "Lift Every Voice and Sing" "makes Johnson come alive for young readers," Jeanette Lambert commented in *School Library Journal.* Readers learn that Johnson was the author of "Lift Every Voice and Sing," the song recognized as the African American national anthem, and also was the first African American to pass the bar in Florida, was principal of the first black high school in Jacksonville,

McKissack and her husband collaborated on this Coretta Scott King award-winning book that profiles the difficult lives of Pullman train porters.

Florida, and served as executive secretary of the NAACP.

In a review of the McKissacks's *Ida B. Wells-Barnett: A Voice against Violence, Marian Anderson: A Great Singer, Martin Luther King, Jr.: Man of Peace,* and *Ralph J. Bunche: Peacemaker,* Phyllis Stephens noted that the authors present each of the subjects as people with convictions so strong that "not even a racially biased society could provide effective obstacles to deter them" from achieving their dreams. "A revealing book," *W. E. B. DuBois* "should entice readers to seek more information about this complex man," Lydia Champlin remarked in *School Library Journal. Voice of Youth Advocates*'s Bruce Lee Siebers recommended *W. E. B. DuBois* as "a good addition to African American history and biography collections."

The McKissacks find writing therapeutic. "It's a kind of freedom," Pat said. "Writing has allowed us to do something positive with our experiences although some of our experiences have been very negative. We try to enlighten, to change attitudes, to form new attitudes—to build bridges with books." While they have produced close to one hundred books, "It's a big world and we are just two writers," Pat remarked. "We cannot possibly represent 30 million African Americans. We cannot, *we cannot* get out all the information there is to know about African Americans." This is one reason the McKissacks encourage other black writers to share their experiences and opinions in books. Another reason is their acknowledgement that their perspective is not necessarily representative of all blacks. "Others have a right to their opinions and should be heard as well," Pat commented. "Fred and I represent Pat and Fred McKissack, but we in no way reflect all the ideas, all the emotions, all the feelings, all the experiences that African Americans have had in this country. More blacks need to write; they need to have a voice as well."

They stress the importance of both parenting and teaching. "It's quite interesting how your youth shapes how you think in the future," Pat remarked. "The things that are happening to you now will affect how you parent, how you will function in your work, and how you will treat your neighbors." She stresses that intervention at this crucial time in a young person's development must help to provide a strong foundation for his or her future. "When I do a workshop with teachers, I always say, 'Someone in your class might be the person who has the cure for cancer. The cure for AIDS is sitting in someone's classroom right now. The solution for world hunger can be found by someone sitting in a classroom. You do not know whether you will be the person to touch that person. So, therefore, you have to respect and treat all of these students with an equal measure of concern.'" Fred agreed: "You don't know who's going to be the puzzle part that you need. The solutions to all these problems are somewhere between kindergarten and Ph.D. I wonder who they are."

WORKS CITED:

Champlin, Lydia, review of *W. E. B. DuBois, School Library Journal,* January, 1991, p. 103.
Lambert, Jeanette, review of *James Weldon Johnson: "Lift Every Voice and Sing,"* School Library Journal, February, 1991, p. 79.
McKissack, Fredrick, and Patricia McKissack, interview with Deborah A. Stanley, August 21, 1992.
Siebers, Bruce Lee, review of *W. E. B. DuBois, Voice of Youth Advocates,* October, 1990, p. 248.
Stephens, Phyllis, review of *Ida B. Wells-Barnett: A Voice against Violence, Marian Anderson: A Great Singer, Martin Luther King, Jr.: Man of Peace,* and *Ralph J. Bunche: Peacemaker, School Library Journal,* November, 1991, p. 111.

FOR MORE INFORMATION SEE:

PERIODICALS

Booklist, March 1, 1992, p. 1270; April 15, 1992, p. 1525.
Interracial Books for Children Bulletin, Number 8, 1985, p. 5.
School Library Journal, February, 1992, pp. 83, 103.

—*Sketch by Deborah A. Stanley*

McLAUGHLIN, Frank 1934-
(Paul Bertolet)

PERSONAL: Born March 28, 1934, in Philadelphia, PA; son of Frank (a telephone lineman) and Helen (a homemaker; maiden name, Sinnickson); married Ruth Deacon (a nurse), November 11, 1961; children: Frank III, Paul, Matthew, Rachel. *Education:* St. Joseph's University, B.S., 1956; Villanova University, M.A., 1963. *Politics:* Independent.

ADDRESSES: Home—18 Whaleback Ter., Ringwood, NJ 07456. *Office*—Department of English, Fairleigh Dickinson University, Teaneck, NJ.

CAREER: Haverford High School, Avertown, PA, English teacher and track coach, 1959-62; Monmouth Regional High School, New Shrewsbury, NJ, English department chair, 1962-66; Monmouth College, West Long Branch, NJ, assistant professor, 1967-69; Brookdale Community College, Lincroft, NJ, director of humanities, 1969-71; Fairleigh Dickinson University, Teaneck, NJ, professor of English, 1971—. *Media and Methods,* founder and editor, 1966-80. *Military service:* U.S. Army, 1956-58, private first class.

MEMBER: National Council of Teachers of English.

WRITINGS:

The Mediate Teacher, National Textbook, 1975.
(Co-author) *Focus on Literature* (six-volume high school literature series), Houghton, 1980.
Yukon Journey, Scholastic, 1991.

Contributor to periodicals, including *Media and Methods, Writing!,* and *Yukon Reader.* Also author of short stories under pseudonym Paul Bertolet.

WORK IN PROGRESS: Runner's Song (a novel); a sequel to *Yukon Journey,* tentatively titled *The Boy Who Loved Wolves.*

SIDELIGHTS: Frank McLaughlin told *SATA:* "I've always wanted to be a writer, but teaching has paid the bills and has been a rewarding career. In the last three years I have written two novels and am on my way to achieving my goals: writing fiction and becoming a full-time writer. It took me years to overcome my self-doubt; I am a good model to illustrate it's never too late to pursue your dream."

*   *   *

MEIDELL, Sherry 1951-

PERSONAL: Born May 6, 1951, in Logan, UT; daughter of Clyde and Renae (Fuhriman) McBride; married David Meidell (a seminary teacher), January 28, 1977; children: James, Luke, Peter, Nathan, Matthew. *Education:* Attended Utah Technical College, 1971-73. *Religion:* Church of Jesus Christ of Latter Day Saints (Mormon).

SHERRY MEIDELL

ADDRESSES: Home—West Bountiful, UT.

CAREER: Worked as a commercial artist, Salt Lake City, UT, 1973-77; illustrator.

MEMBER: Society of Children's Book Writers.

ILLUSTRATOR:

Barbara Williams, *ABC's of Uniforms and Outfits,* Winston-Derek, 1992.

Has also illustrated covers for *Friend* magazine.

WORK IN PROGRESS: Merry Christmas Mouse, a picture book; research on shoemakers.

SIDELIGHTS: Sherry Meidell told *SATA:* "When I was growing up, if I was not playing Cowboys and Indians, I had a book in my lap, or I had a pencil in my hand drawing a picture. I was very disappointed in school when I outgrew the books with illustrations. After high school, I took a commercial arts course from Utah Technical College, and after graduating, I worked in Salt Lake City as a commercial artist.

"For the last fourteen years, I have lived with my husband and five growing boys. I've spent a lot of time with snakes and turtles and cub scouts. Raising tadpoles

and watching snakes eat rosy red feeder fish in the bath tub may have caused a certain loss of brain cells which allowed me to think that I could write and illustrate picture books.

"*ABC's of Uniforms and Outfits* is the first book I've illustrated. I came up with an idea for each of the illustrations from Aa Astronaut until I came to Xx X-ray Technician. How could I make an illustration of an X-ray technician look anything but boring? But, after visiting the X-ray lab and talking to the X-ray technician, it became one of my favorite illustrations in the entire book. I have a great love for picture books and hope to contribute many more efforts in writing and illustrating."*

*   *   *

MERRIAM, Eve 1916-1992

PERSONAL: Born July 19, 1916, in Philadelphia, PA; died of cancer, April 11, 1992, in New York, NY; married Waldo Salt; children: Guy Michel, Dee Michel (sons). *Education:* Attended Cornell University; University of Pennsylvania, A.B., 1937; graduate study at University of Wisconsin, Madison, and Columbia University. *Hobbies and other interests:* Travel, swimming, walking, folk dancing, group singing, the city in winter, the ocean in the summer, the theatre, frequenting public libraries and secondhand bookstores.

ADDRESSES: Home—101 West 12th St., New York, NY 10011. *Agent*—Marian Reiner, 20 Cedar St., New Rochelle, NY 10801.

CAREER: Author, poet, and playwright. Copywriter, 1939-42; radio writer, mainly of documentaries and scripts in verse for Columbia Broadcasting System, Inc., and other networks, and conductor of weekly program on modern poetry for station WQXR, New York City, 1942-46; *PM,* New York City, daily verse columnist, 1945; *Deb,* New York City, feature editor, 1946; *Glamour,* New York City, fashion copy editor, 1947-48; freelance magazine and book writer, 1949—; City College of the City University of New York, teacher of courses in creative writing, 1965-69. Bank Street College of Education, attached to field project staff, 1958-60. Public lecturer, 1956-92. Director of *Out of Order* (play), by Janet Neipris, produced in New York, 1982.

MEMBER: Authors Guild, Dramatists Guild Council.

AWARDS, HONORS: Yale Younger Poets Prize, 1946, for *Family Circle; Collier's* Star Fiction Award, 1949, for "Make Something Happen"; William Newman Poetry Award, 1957; grant to write poetic drama, Columbia Broadcasting System, Inc., 1959; *New York Times* best illustrated award, 1970, for *Finding a Poem;* National Council of Teachers of English Awards, 1970 and 1981, for excellence in poetry for children; Obie Award, *Village Voice,* 1976, for play *The Club;* Parents' Choice Award, 1985, for *Blackberry Ink: Poems; New York Times* best illustrated award, 1987, for *Halloween ABC.*

EVE MERRIAM

WRITINGS:

CHILDREN'S BOOKS

The Real Book about Franklin D. Roosevelt, illustrated by Bette J. Davis, Garden City, 1952, revised edition, Dobson, 1961.

The Real Book about Amazing Birds, illustrated by Paul Wenck, Garden City, 1955, revised edition, Dobson, 1960.

The Voice of Liberty: The Story of Emma Lazarus, illustrated by Charles W. Walker, Farrar, Straus, 1959.

A Gaggle of Geese, illustrated by Paul Galdone, Knopf, 1960.

Mommies at Work, illustrated by Beni Montresor, Knopf, 1961.

What's in the Middle of a Riddle?, illustrated by Murray Tinkelman, Collier, 1963.

The Story of Benjamin Franklin, illustrated by Brinton Turkle, Four Winds, 1965.

Small Fry, illustrated by Garry MacKenzie, Knopf, 1965.

(Translator) Hana Doskocilova, *Animal Tales,* illustrated by Mirko Hanak, Doubleday, 1971.

(Translator) Dick Bruna, *Christmas,* illustrated by Bruna, Doubleday, 1971.

Bam! Zam! Boom!: A Building Book, illustrated by William Lightfoot, Walker, 1972.

(Editor with Nancy Larrick) *Male and Female under Eighteen: Frank Comments from Young People about Their Sex Roles Today,* Avon, 1973.

Ab to Zogg: A Lexicon for Science-Fiction and Fantasy Readers, illustrated by Albert Lorenz, Atheneum, 1977.

Daddies at Work, illustrated by Eugenie Fernandez, Simon & Schuster, 1989.

Wise Woman and Her Secret, Simon & Schuster, 1991.

Train Leaves the Station, illustrated by Dave Gottlieb, Holt, 1992.

Goodnight to Annie: An Alphabet Lullaby, illustrated by Carol Schwartz, Hyperion, 1992.

CHILDREN'S POETRY

There Is No Rhyme for Silver (Junior Literary Guild selection), illustrated by Joseph Schindelman, Atheneum, 1962.

Funny Town, illustrated by Evaline Ness, Macmillan, 1963.

It Doesn't Always Have to Rhyme, illustrated by Malcolm Spooner, Atheneum, 1964.

Don't Think about a White Bear, illustrated by Tinkelman, Putnam, 1965.

Catch a Little Rhyme (also see below), illustrated by Imero Gobbato, Atheneum, 1966.

Independent Voices, illustrated by Arvis Stewart, Atheneum, 1968.

Finding a Poem (Junior Literary Guild selection), illustrated by Seymour Chwast, Atheneum, 1970.

I Am a Man: Ode to Martin Luther King, Jr., illustrated by Suzanne Verrier, Doubleday, 1971.

Out Loud (also see below), illustrated by Harriet Sherman, Atheneum, 1973.

Rainbow Writing, Atheneum, 1976.

The Birthday Cow, illustrated by Guy Michel, Knopf, 1978.

A Word or Two with You: New Rhymes for Young Readers, illustrated by John Nez, Atheneum, 1981.

If Only I Could Tell You: Poems for Young Lovers and Dreamers, illustrated by Donna Diamond, Knopf, 1983.

Jamboree: Rhymes for All Times, illustrated by Walter Gaffney-Kessell, Dell, 1984.

A Book of Wishes for You, C. R. Gibson, 1985.

Blackberry Ink: Poems, illustrated by Hans Wilhelm, Morrow, 1985.

Fresh Paint: New Poems, woodcuts by David Frampton, Macmillan, 1986.

A Sky Full of Poems, illustrated by Gaffney-Kessell, Dell, 1986.

Halloween ABC, illustrated by Lane Smith, Macmillan, 1987.

You Be Good and I'll Be Night: Jump-on-the-Bed Poems, illustrated by Karen Schmidt, Morrow, 1988.

Chortles: New and Selected Wordplay Poems, illustrated by Sheila Hamanaka, Morrow, 1989.

A Poem for a Pickle: Funnybone Verses, illustrated by Hamanaka, Morrow, 1989.

The Singing Green, illustrated by Kathleen C. Howell, Morrow, 1992.

CHILDREN'S FICTION

What Can You Do with a Pocket?, illustrated by Sherman, Knopf, 1964.

Do You Want to See Something?, illustrated by Abner Graboff, Scholastic, 1965.

Miss Tibbett's Typewriter, illustrated by Rick Schreiter, Knopf, 1966.

Andy All Year Round: A Picture Book of Four Seasons and Five Senses, illustrated by Margo Hoff, Funk & Wagnalls, 1967.

Epaminondas, illustrated by Trina S. Hyman, Follett, 1968, published as *That Noodle-Head Epaminondas*, Scholastic, 1972.

Project 1-2-3, illustrated by Sherman, McGraw, 1971.

Boys and Girls, Girls and Boys, illustrated by Sherman, Holt, 1972.

Unhurry Harry, illustrated by Gail Owens, Four Winds, 1978.

Good Night to Annie, illustrated by John Wallner, Four Winds, 1980.

The Christmas Box (picture book), illustrated by David Small, Morrow, 1985.

The Birthday Door (picture book), illustrated by Peter J. Thornton, Morrow, 1986.

Where Is Everybody? (picture book), illustrated by Diane deGroat, Simon & Schuster, 1989.

Fighting Words (picture book), illustrated by Small, Morrow, 1991.

ADULT BOOKS

Emma Lazarus: Woman with a Torch (biography), Citadel, 1956.

Figleaf: The Business of Being in Fashion (nonfiction), illustrated by Burmah Burris, Lippincott, 1960.

After Nora Slammed the Door: American Women in the 1960's, the Unfinished Revolution, World, 1964.

Man and Woman: The Human Condition, Research Center on Woman, 1968.

(Editor and author of introduction) *Growing Up Female in America: Ten Lives* (also see below), Doubleday, 1971.

A Conversation against Death (also see below), photographs by Anna K. Moon, Center for Thanatology Research & Education, 1991.

ADULT POETRY

Family Circle, Yale University Press, 1946.

Tomorrow Morning, Twayne, 1953.

Montgomery, Alabama, Money, Mississippi, and Other Places (pamphlet in poetry), Cameron, 1956.

The Double Bed from the Feminine Side, Cameron, 1958, M. Evans, 1972.

The Trouble with Love, Macmillan, 1960.

Basics: An I-Can-Read-Book for Grownups, illustrated by Robert Osborn, Macmillan, 1962.

The Inner City Mother Goose (also see below), photographs by Lawrence Ratzkin, Simon & Schuster, 1969.

The Nixon Poems, illustrated by John Gerbino, Atheneum, 1970.

A Husband's Notes about Her: Fictions, Macmillan, 1976.

Thinking of You, illustrated by Judith Sutton, C. R. Gibson, 1991.

ADULT PLAYS

Inner City (musical; based on *The Inner City Mother Goose*), music by Helen Miller, produced on Broadway, 1971.

(With Paula Wagner and Jack Hofsiss) *Out of Our Father's House* (based on *Growing Up Female in America: Ten Lives;* produced in New York, 1975), Samuel French, 1975.

The Club (produced in New York, 1976), Samuel French, 1976.

At Her Age, Samuel French, 1979.

Dialogue for Lovers: Sonnets of Shakespeare Arranged for Dramatic Presentation (produced in New York, 1980), Samuel French, 1981.

And I Ain't Finished Yet (produced in New York, 1981), Samuel French, 1982.

Plagues for Our Time, music by Tom O'Horgan, produced in New York, 1983.

(And director) *Woman Alive: Conversation against Death* (libretto), music by Patsy Rogers, produced in New York, 1983.

Street Dreams, music by Miller, produced in New York, 1984.

Also author of television play *We the Women*, 1975.

OTHER

Also author of *The Words and Music of My Mother*, and of "Make Something Happen." Adapter of *Catch a Little Rhyme*, 1976, and *Out Loud*, 1988, into sound recordings. Contributor to anthologies, including *Believe and Make-Believe*, Dutton, 1957, and *Let's Read More Stories*, Garden City, 1960. Contributor to *Equality, Identity, and Complementarity: Changing Perspectives of Man and Woman*, edited by Robert H. Amundson, Research Center on Woman, 1968. Also contributor to periodicals, including *Nation, New Republic, Saturday Evening Post, Ladies' Home Journal, True, Saturday Review, Digest, New York Times Magazine, Diplomat, Learning 85, New York Magazine, Ms., Washington Post*, and *Village Voice*. Merriam's manuscripts are housed in the Kerlan Collection, University of Minnesota, Minneapolis, the de Grummond Collection, University of Southern Mississippi, Hattiesburg, and the Schlesinger Library, Radcliffe College, Cambridge, MA.

ADAPTATIONS: The Inner City Mother Goose was adapted for stage as *Sweet Dreams* by John Broswell and produced Off-Broadway, 1984.

SIDELIGHTS: Eve Merriam wrote poetry for people of all ages, but she paid special attention to making poetry accessible to children. She also wrote picture books for young readers, as well as biographies of famous people, including President Franklin D. Roosevelt and Emma Lazarus. In addition to her writings for children, Merriam was the author of successful plays for adults, including *The Club* and *Out of Our Father's House*. To all of her work, for children and adults, she brought a sense of social conscience, embracing causes such as feminism and racial equality. But to her children's poetry, for which she is most famed, she brought a sense of the fun of words. As Myra Cohn Livingston declared in *Twentieth-Century Children's Writers:* "Eve Merriam's versatility is astounding. A keen observer of contemporary life, she brings to her poetry a fresh outlook on all phases of the modern world, its delights as well as absurdities. Agile and penetrating, she beguiles her readers with a variety of rhythms, rhymes, and forms attuned to the spirits of the young. Her craftsmanship is exemplary."

Merriam was born July 19, 1916, in Philadelphia, Pennsylvania. From an early age she loved poetry, both light verse and narrative poems; she enjoyed reciting such works as "The Highwayman" and "Gunga Din." Merriam also loved the complex verses of the lyrics of Gilbert and Sullivan musicals, which she went to see often as a child. Almost equally early in her life, she began writing her own poetry. By the time she was in high school, her poems became more serious efforts—emotive verse published in the school magazine and political and social satire in the weekly school newspaper. Nevertheless, Merriam once recalled in *SATA:* "It never occurred to me that someday I might like to *be* a writer. I just wrote. I think one is chosen to be a poet. You write poems because you must write them; because you can't live your life without writing them."

After high school, Merriam first attended college at Cornell University; then she obtained her bachelor's degree at the University of Pennsylvania. She did some graduate study at both the University of Wisconsin and at Columbia University; while at the latter she decided to quit school and become a copywriter. She explained the decision to Patricia McLaughlin in the *Pennsylvania Gazette:* "I was a poet, and it's hard to figure out what to do to make a living when you're a poet.... I was reading Dorothy Sayers [author of the Lord Peter Wimsey whodunits]—I liked her a lot, and I knew that she had worked in an advertising agency, and I knew that Carl Sandburg had worked in an advertising agency, so I thought, well, that sort of makes sense for a poet, because who can use words more economically? But I didn't have any experience."

Meanwhile, Merriam had already written a successful radio script, and, as she told McLaughlin, "it just *happened* ... that the boss of this advertising agency had heard my radio script the night before I went into the agency. And he was something of a snob, so I think he liked the idea that I was a poet and that I had done something 'cultural'—as it were—so he hired me." She thus served as a copywriter for a few years, though a somewhat unorthodox one—for instance, she once refused to write an ad for a hair rinse on the grounds that the product was not good for people.

From copywriting Merriam went on to editing, for magazines such as *Deb* and *Glamour;* at the latter she served as a fashion copy editor. She also continued writing poetry; she wrote a verse column for the New York magazine *PM,* and in 1946 she won the Yale Younger Poets Prize for her first volume of verse, *Family Circle.* As Merriam reminisced in *SATA:* "At

that time the contest was for a book of poems awarded to someone under thirty years old. The first time I entered, I didn't win. I tried again and again for four more years until I won it. The year that I won it, Archibald MacLeish was the judge. He had been my hero. When I went away to college, I slept with a copy of his *Conquistador* under my pillow so that no one could steal it.... I remember being absolutely thrilled. I was very excited by his work."

In 1960, Merriam published her first book for children, *A Gaggle of Geese.* A picture book, it illustrates unusual group terms for about forty animals, fish, and birds, presenting "a shrewdness of apes," for example. Several critics have commented that her enthusiasm for word play and unique words is evident in *A Gaggle of Geese.* Ellen Lewis Buell in the *New York Times Book Review* noted that Merriam took an adult diversion and made it accessible for young readers, writing that children would "get a lot of fun out of the sound and rhythm of the phrases." "Stimulating and fun," concluded Margaret Sherwood Libby in *Lively Arts and Book Review.*

The sequel to *A Gaggle of Geese, Small Fry,* was published in 1965 and follows the same idea of introducing young readers to unique words, but focuses on those for baby animals. A "joey" is the term for a young kangaroo, but what about a farrow, or an eyas? Curiosity

In *Where Is Everybody?,* **Merriam uses a host of animals to introduce the alphabet to young readers.** (Cover illustration by Diane de Groat.)

draws the reader in, and Merriam uses poetry to connect the terms presented. Reaction to this book was mixed, as a reviewer in *Science Books: A Quarterly Review* explained, calling *Small Fry* a "colorful yet over-embellished little book." The verse was labeled by several reviewers as nonsense, and a contributor to *Virginia Kirkus' Service* commented that "irrelevant and pretty meaningless verses" might cause adult readers to "gag." But, this book was not written for grown-ups, and Guernsey Le Pelley in the *Christian Science Monitor* recommended that it "should be bought only for the education of children." Merriam appeals to younger audiences with these two books, making reading and learning an enjoyable experience.

Continuing to write for younger audiences, Merriam published her first book of poetry for children in 1962, *There Is No Rhyme for Silver*. This book, very well received, was the first in what would become a trilogy—*It Doesn't Always Have to Rhyme* and *Catch a Little Rhyme* round out the set. A devoted wordmonger, Merriam plays with syllables in these books, rather than words as a whole as in *A Gaggle of Geese*. Using word sounds, rhythm, alliteration, and assonance, she is able to "provide the reader with the special musical effects of poetry," as Laura M. Zaidman explained in the *Dictionary of Literary Biography*. *There Is No Rhyme for Silver* contains poems that invite the audience to participate in the poetry, with Zena Sutherland in the *Bulletin of the Center for Children's Books* calling it a "light and pleasant collection of poems." Margaret Sherwood Libby, writing in *Books,* was more expressive, praising the melody of the poems and the sound effects of "certain words," concluding that this volume is "crazy, but enjoyably so."

The other two volumes of the trilogy compliment the first. *It Doesn't Always Have to Rhyme* presents readers with the basic elements of poetry, such as metaphor and simile. Silence Buck Bellows in the *Christian Science Monitor* exclaimed that the verse "romps along like uninhibited brook water, inviting a child to adventure." The final volume, *Catch a Little Rhyme*, was written for an even younger audience than the first two. A reviewer in *Virginia Kirkus' Service* remarked on Merriam's "special flair for the humor small children enjoy," and another reviewer in *Publishers Weekly* noted that while all three volumes should be read aloud, "this one shouts to be shared." Zaidman commended Merriam's ability in general to "make poetry fun as well as instructional without sounding pedantic." These and other poetry volumes are part of Merriam's crusade to help children enjoy, be knowledgeable about, and, if so inclined, write poetry.

Merriam remembered the delights of childhood and recreated the feelings and moods for her older readers, while allowing her younger readers to identify with her work. In *Blackberry Ink: Poems,* she touches on topics and feelings small children would readily recognize, such as favorite foods, eating sun-ripened berries, and wanting to keep something new unused and fresh. Critics were generally positive in their reviews, praising

POEMS BY EVE MERRIAM

PICTURES BY HANS WILHELM

In this poetry collection, Merriam touches on topics and feelings familiar to young readers, such as favorite colors and the desire to keep things new and fresh. (Cover illustration by Hans Wilhelm.)

Merriam's style. Sutherland commented on the "sunny quality" of the poems, and a reviewer in *Publishers Weekly* noted Merriam's ability to turn everyday things into "rollicking amusements." Susan Scheps, writing in *School Library Journal,* concluded that *Blackberry Ink* was sure to appeal to young readers' sense of humor and to "provide many moments of pleasure."

Both in her poetry and in her other works, including those for children, Merriam often dealt with social issues, such as feminism, sexual equality, pacifism, ecology, and racial equality. Noting injustices in American society, she once commented in *SATA:* "I think the Civil Rights situation, certainly the race situation is better than it was.... People are aware, and while there still may be only tokenism in some fields, you do see Blacks, Asian, and all sorts of people in situations you wouldn't have before. Although I still think there is a great way to go, I don't think we will ever go back to the kinds of chauvinism we had in an earlier period."

Merriam was also optimistic about social equality. Citing her loneliness as both a young feminist and poet, she applauded the strides made in the arena of sexual equality. As she once explained to *SATA,* "That's why I love the women's movement because it's brought me comradeship. No one could be happier than I at the

Cats are closing in their claws.

**Merriam's love for creating unique imagery with words
is evident in works such as *Goodnight to Annie*.**
(Illustration by John Wallner.)

proliferation of the women's movement and women's
writing.... To grow up in a world where there is much
more equality and much less hypocrisy between the
sexes, where there is openness and frankness is good."

Merriam's 1968 volume *Independent Voices* includes
poems about admirable figures of various races and
sexes, including Elizabeth Blackwell, the first woman
doctor in the United States, and black leader Frederick
Douglass. While many reviewers criticized her presentation and verse, they respected her effort. Ethel L. Heins
in *Horn Book* commented that the poetry "varies in ...
quality and emotional impact." A *Kirkus Service* reviewer voiced a similar opinion and concluded that "each of
the portraits is bloated and seven at a blow is too
much." A reviewer in *Publishers Weekly* speculated on
the positive side, commenting that Merriam selected
and portrayed American historical figures many young
adults could identify with—characters able to jump
"out of the history books and into the hearts of all young
people."

Merriam wrote several other books that expressed her
social consciousness and concerns. In 1971, she published the children's poem *I Am a Man: Ode to Martin
Luther King, Jr.*, a brief account of King's life and
philosophy. A "distinctive poem," as a *Publishers*

Weekly reviewer called it, it was noted by many critics
for its frequent lack of concrete, in-depth details.
Margaret Riddell in *School Library Journal* commented
that *I Am a Man* is "an idealistic summary." "The lines,
suggestive variously of image and event, here and there
fleetingly touch,..." wrote a reviewer in *Kirkus Reviews*. Merriam's socially conscious picture books for
children include *Mommies at Work* and *Boys and Girls,
Girls and Boys*, which provide non-stereotypical role
models and sex roles. Zaidman noted: "Depicting
equality in relationships between the sexes is important
for Merriam, as evidenced by poems which show both
girls and boys with similar needs and the same feelings."

Merriam, however, explored these issues in more than
just poetry and prose. After Merriam's adult poetry
work *The Inner City Mother Goose* (a book of updated
nursery rhymes) was adapted as a stage play and
produced on Broadway in 1972, she became interested
in writing plays herself. One of her most successful was
The Club, which features characters who belong to an
exclusive men's club at approximately the turn of the
century and sit around telling derogatory jokes about
women—but the characters are played by actresses
rather than actors. Produced Off-Broadway, the play
won a total of ten Obies in 1976, including one for the
author. Though Merriam became more involved in
playwriting and other theatrical matters later in her life,
including direction, she continued to write books of
poetry and prose for children.

Merriam wrote until her death in 1992, appealing to all
ages with her love of the English language, her sense of
fun, and her ability to invite readers into her works. Her
extensive literary range encompassed children's picture
books to feminist tracts, child audiences to addressing
adult interests. As Zaidman explained, "Eve Merriam's
excellence in poetry has given her readers a better
appreciation for a wide range of topics expressing the
varieties of a child's experiences, and her insights into
the way in which children should approach poetry have
greatly influenced the ability of parents and teachers to
help them enjoy it. By inviting two generations of
readers into her world of words, Eve Merriam has
greatly enriched children's poetry."

WORKS CITED:

Bellows, Silence Buck, review of *It Doesn't Always Have
    to Rhyme, Christian Science Monitor,* May 7, 1964,
    p. 6B.
Review of *Blackberry Ink: Poems, Publishers Weekly,*
    May 17, 1985, pp. 117-18.
Buell, Ellen Lewis, "Company Words," *New York Times
    Book Review,* August 7, 1960, p. 26.
Review of *Catch a Little Rhyme, Publishers Weekly,*
    April 4, 1966, p. 62.
Review of *Catch a Little Rhyme, Virginia Kirkus'
    Service,* January 15, 1966, p. 54.
Heins, Ethel L., review of *Independent Voices, Horn
    Book,* April, 1969, pp. 182-83.
Review of *I Am a Man: Ode to Martin Luther King, Jr.,
    Kirkus Reviews,* March 1, 1971, p. 240.

Review of *I Am a Man: Ode to Martin Luther King, Jr.,* *Publishers Weekly,* May 10, 1971, p. 43.
Review of *Independent Voices, Kirkus Service,* October 19, 1968, p. 1170.
Review of *Independent Voices, Publishers Weekly,* October 21, 1968, p. 51.
Le Pelley, Guernsey, review of *Small Fry, Christian Science Monitor,* May 6, 1965, p. 2B.
Libby, Margaret Sherwood, review of *A Gaggle of Geese, Lively Arts and Book Review,* March 5, 1961, p. 35.
Libby, review of *There Is No Rhyme for Silver, Books,* November 11, 1962, p. 2.
Livingston, Myra Cohn, essay in *Twentieth-Century Children's Writers,* edited by Tracy Chevalier, 3rd edition, St. James Press, 1989, pp. 675-77.
McLaughlin, Patricia, "Found: Eve Merriam," *Pennsylvania Gazette,* April, 1978, pp. 17-21.
Merriam, Eve, comments in *Something about the Author,* Volume 40, Gale, 1985, pp. 141-49.
Riddell, Margaret, review of *I Am a Man: Ode to Martin Luther King, Jr., School Library Journal,* May, 1971, p. 68.
Scheps, Susan, review of *Blackberry Ink: Poems, School Library Journal,* September, 1985, p. 122.
Review of *Small Fry, Science Books: A Quarterly Review,* December, 1965, p. 158.
Review of *Small Fry, Virginia Kirkus' Service,* March 1, 1965, p. 232.
Sutherland, Zena, review of *Blackberry Ink: Poems, Bulletin of the Center for Children's Books,* June, 1985, p. 191.
Sutherland, review of *There Is No Rhyme for Silver, Bulletin of the Center for Children's Books,* December, 1962, p. 63.
Zaidman, Laura M., "Eve Merriam," *Dictionary of Literary Biography,* Volume 61: *American Writers for Children since 1960: Poets, Illustrators, and Nonfiction Authors,* Gale, 1987, pp. 224-33.

FOR MORE INFORMATION SEE:

BOOKS

Baskin, Barbara H., and Karen H. Harris, *Books for the Gifted Child,* Bowker, 1980, pp. 192-95.
Children's Literature Review, Volume 14, Gale, 1988, pp. 187-204.

PERIODICALS

Bulletin of the Center for Children's Books, October, 1985; October, 1986; December, 1987.
Children's Literature Association Quarterly, winter, 1981, p. 45.
Language Arts, November-December, 1981, pp. 957-64; October, 1986, pp. 594-600.
New York Times Book Review, May 17, 1987, pp. 46-47; March 26, 1989, p. 19.
Wilson Library Bulletin, May, 1986, pp. 45-46.

OBITUARIES:

PERIODICALS

Publishers Weekly, April 27, 1992, p. 32.*

—Sketch by Terrie M. Rooney

MIKAELSEN, Ben(jamin John) 1952-

PERSONAL: Born November 24, 1952, in La Paz, Bolivia; son of John (a radio engineer) and Luverne (Wold) Mikaelsen; married Melanie Troftgruben (a flight nurse), June, 1980. *Education:* Attended Concordia College, Moorhead, MN, 1971-72, and Bemidji State University, Bemidji, MN, 1975-79. *Religion:* Protestant. *Hobbies and other interests:* Horseback riding, parachute jumping, motorcycle travel, sled dog racing, flying airplanes, scuba diving, bears.

ADDRESSES: Home and office—233 Quinn Creek Rd., Bozeman, MT 59715. *Agent*—Sandra Choron, 4 Myrtle St., Haworth, NJ 07641.

CAREER: Owner of awards and office supplies business, Bozeman, MT, 1980-84; owner of woodworking business, Bozeman, MT, 1984-85; writer, 1985—. *Military service:* U.S. Army, 1973-75, Arlington, VA; corporal; received Joint Service Commendation Medal.

MEMBER: Society of Children's Book Writers, Hellgate Writers, Montana Authors' Coalition.

AWARDS, HONORS: Spur Award from the Western Writers of America, Inc., and Children's Book Award from the International Reading Association, both 1991, both for *Rescue Josh McGuire.*

WRITINGS:

Rescue Josh McGuire, Hyperion Books, 1991.
Sparrow Hawk Red, Hyperion Books, in press.

Rescue Josh McGuire has been translated into Danish.

SIDELIGHTS: Ben Mikaelsen's award-winning first novel, *Rescue Josh McGuire,* has been widely praised for its fast-paced adventure, its detailed depictions of the Montana wilderness, and its engaging portrait of a wild bear cub. Mikaelsen, who says he draws the "soul" of each of his novels from real experience, is no stranger to bears, the wilderness, or adventure. The author has had the unique experience over the past nine years of raising a 600-pound black bear named Buffy at his home in the mountains of Bozeman, Montana. Beyond this, Mikaelsen told *SATA* that over the years he has been involved in many adventures, including "a 1,600 mile cross-country horseback trip from Minnesota to Oregon, over 800 parachute jumps, nine years of raising and studying bears, racing sled dogs, playing horse polo, building a log house, private and commercial pilot training, extensive scuba diving, and worldwide travel." Although his personal adventures have entailed courage and endurance and his fiction is engaging for its action and suspense, Mikaelsen's adventure stories are not of the rugged "man versus nature" variety. Rather, they make an appeal for peaceful coexistence between the natural and social worlds. In *Rescue Josh McGuire,* to be kind and gentle in a sometimes inhumanely bureaucratic society is the greatest act of courage.

Ben Mikaelsen and Buffy

Mikaelsen says he remembers his childhood from the viewpoint of a social outsider. In his early youth he lived in Bolivia, where "being raised as a minority helped me understand the self-doubt and desperate lack of self-worth many children face while growing up." Because his parents worked too far from the schools for their six children to commute, Mikaelsen and a younger brother were placed in a boarding school apart from their older siblings, permanently weakening the family bonds, according to the author. In an interview with *SATA,* Mikaelsen said his boarding school was a rigid place, where "English matrons held a solid seat of law, all the way down to strappings if you didn't do things right." When Mikaelsen returned to the United States at the age of thirteen, he found that schoolmates could be equally harsh and demanding. "In Bolivia," he told *SATA,* "we wore uniforms—saddle shoes with high bobby socks and leather knickers with a kind of blouse-type shirt. So the first day of school in the United States, I dressed up in my best go-to-school clothes. I learned early how cruel kids can be."

Although his feelings of being an outsider lasted throughout high school, Mikaelsen is positive about his childhood experiences. "Being ostracized," he told *SATA,* "contributed to writing in the sense that a piece of paper became my friend. I was one of those kids that laid awake at night dreaming *before* I went to sleep. I would always forget the things I was dreaming about the next morning so I realized that if I was to capture them, I would have to put them on paper. I never thought of myself as a writer, but I enjoyed writing poetry. Back then if you were a male writing poetry you were a sissy, so I never showed anybody. That was just my own secret. A lot of my writings for many, many years came that way."

Despite his feelings of self-doubt within the social world, Mikaelsen was an adventurer even as a child. "I was always the kid that took the dare, always the one that would climb up the telephone pole or the flag pole. I remember once when my group of friends was cliff-diving, rather than take the chance of failing in front of other kids, I swam across the lake and, all by myself, I got up the courage and dived off this cliff. Somebody heard that Ben dove off that twenty-foot rock and that just led from one thing to another. Pretty soon it was twenty-five feet, then thirty feet, then thirty-five feet and then it was heights no other kid would even jump off of. All of a sudden it struck me that this was the very, very first time in my life when somebody said 'gosh, that's neat.' My whole body had a hunger for that attention, so I started doing other things . . ."

By the time he was in college, Mikaelsen was sky-diving. "I was able to parachute into the homecoming game and bring in the game football and things like that. Kids would say 'wow, that's pretty neat,' and I felt like a hero, with more positive attention than I'd ever received in my life." In college Mikaelsen also received encouragement about his writing for the first time. "My first language was Spanish," Mikaelsen told *SATA.* "At five years old I could not speak English very well. I always

had trouble with grammar, with spelling, with word mechanics. I was always told that that was what writing was, and because I was so poor at these things, I thought I could not be a writer." Mikaelsen recalled that in his first year of college his English professor called him to the front of the room to comment on a paper he had written, telling him immediately that his grammar skills were those of a seventh or eighth grader. With much fear Mikaelsen asked his professor if he should drop the class. Mikaelsen remembers the professor's words: "'Oh no, no, no. I just finished reading two hundred and fifty essays and out of that only one made me laugh and cry and that was yours. You're a writer.'" Mikaelsen told *SATA,* "That was the first time that somebody let me know that this was something special. Then I was anxious to sit down with the tutor and work on grammar and word mechanics, although I'm still terrible with that."

Mikaelsen soon discovered that being a writer required just as much courage as being an adventurer. "There is so much more to writing than I ever dreamed," he told *SATA.* "I know when I first started sitting over the cliff at twenty feet above the water with nobody around, I looked down and this monster was facing me, saying 'you can't do it.' I said 'I can' and I jumped into the monster's face. It's the same monster that looked at me when I wanted to make my first parachute jump, and the same one I saw later when we made a cross-country horseback trip from Minnesota to Oregon in 1976. Now, when I'm writing at 2:00 in the morning, halfway through a book, I'm doubting my premise for the book, I'm doubting my story line, I'm doubting myself. It's that same identical monster that I have to jump in the face of. I began, finally, to realize that being a successful writer isn't just putting the good words down, it's facing that monster."

Mikaelsen, whose childhood home in Bolivia had been high upon a fourteen-thousand-foot plateau in the Andes mountain range between Bolivia and Peru, grew up with a deeply ingrained love of mountains. Consequently, in 1980 he and his wife moved to the mountains of Bozeman, Montana. In 1984, the couple adopted Buffy, a declawed black bear cub, from a wild game farm. The adoption entailed a huge commitment. Mikaelsen told *SATA:* "We have probably twenty thousand dollars invested in Buffy's facility with its pond and playground and eating area, denning area, and waste area. I spend about three to four hours a day with him when he's out of hibernation, and a half hour or forty-five minutes a day when he's in hibernation, and that's still not enough time. Buffy gets better care than most children—that's what an animal needs, and that's the only reason Buffy and I have the relationship we do, because of that tremendous amount of time."

Mikaelsen learned quickly that keeping a wild animal in captivity is not like raising a household pet. Buffy had been used in laboratory research before Mikaelsen adopted him. "I don't know what had been done with him in research," Mikaelsen told *SATA,* "but it hadn't been good. He was very, very distrusting and insecure.

One minute he would cuddle with me and hug my side as if I was the only thing he had in life, and the next minute a car horn or something would scare him and he would turn around and bite me as hard as he could. The first couple of months I started raising him like you would a dog and I wasn't having any luck. He was getting more independent and more angry. So then I started raising him like a child. I would give him his food in a bottle instead of a dish, and cuddle him in my arms as he drank it. I would go out and put him to bed every night and let him fall asleep in my lap. If I heard him crying then I would go out and sleep with him the rest of the night. When I started doing that I immediately had luck.

"I learned a real important lesson with Buffy, and that's that you never tame a wild animal. Buffy is not a tame animal. If something threatens him, he is a six-hundred-and-some pound very, very dangerous animal. My wife and I are the only two people that can come into his facility. If a stranger were to come into his facility without me along, he would most likely attack him. But when Buffy comes into the house (and he comes into the house a lot), he's visiting. A stranger could come in the house and Buffy would just be as friendly as all get out. But even after a half hour of playing with him in the house, if the stranger went into Buffy's facility, he'd lay his ears back. You're dealing with really deep instincts.

"I used to think I owned Buff and that I'm his master and he should do what I say. Having that attitude almost got me killed. He would get violent when I tried to rule him. Then I finally said, 'Hold it, I'm not his master, neither is he mine, but we're friends, we're going to coexist.' To this day we have the most wonderfully equal relationship. We have rules between us. If he violates the rule, I will punish him. A lot of times I will just withhold my love from him, or I'll give him a good sharp swat on the nose. He won't even think of retaliating because he knows it's a punishment. If I were to give him the same swat unprovoked, he would probably turn around and bite me. So it's very much a matter of fairness. Likewise if I violate the rules. Say I want to play and I jump on his back and he shrugs me off because he's preoccupied. If I do that a couple of times he'll turn around and he'll very forcefully take me down to the ground and put his paw on my chest and he'll put his mouth, which is huge, completely around my head. He won't bite down, but it's like a wall just closed around me. If I want to keep struggling like a fool, he'll keep going; he's trying to communicate to me to quit it. If I relax and say 'Buffy, I'm sorry,' then he'll pick me up and dust me off and lick my nose to make sure that everything is all right and that I've forgiven him.

"What I really want to impress here, is that I don't own Buffy. Buffy and I have a relationship that is deeper than you can ever imagine. Buffy trusts me incredibly, and now when people ask me if I really trust him, well, yes, I do, because he trusts me." Learning to understand and respond to Buffy's needs rather than to try to control him, Mikaelsen told *SATA*, was a big lesson in life. A former bear hunter himself, Mikaelsen realized while raising Buffy that he had previously been enjoying wildlife from a very limited perspective. "Any appreciation I had of a wild animal ceased at the moment I killed it. Now I feel like I've come to appreciate and understand and be amazed by the complexity of Buffy's existence." Among Mikaelsen's dedications in *Rescue Josh McGuire*, is one to "'Buffy,' a 500-pound black bear who taught me to have respect and be gentle."

When it became known that Mikaelsen was successfully raising Buffy, the Fish and Game Department in Bozeman brought him other orphaned black bear cubs. Mikaelsen took care of some of these orphans while the department decided what to do with them. Since there were few viable alternatives, the orphaned cubs were sometimes then destroyed. Although Montana has laws against shooting a mother bear with a cub, the laws are unenforceable, and during spring hunting many mother bears are shot and killed when their cubs have momentarily wandered away. Mikaelsen blames spring bear hunting for the hundreds of orphaned cubs in Montana every season, and he has become active in his state, promoting more sportsman-like hunting laws. The strength of his feelings about this issue triggered his first published novel. "There was one pair of cubs," he told *SATA*. "I spent probably a week trying to save their lives, staying up all night to bottle feed them. They ended up being destroyed because they couldn't find a good home. I think that was the point when I said, 'Hold it, let's make it the premise of a book.'"

Rescue Josh McGuire begins with the senseless killing of a mother bear by thirteen-year-old Josh's alcoholic father, Sam. Although Sam will not admit that the bear he shot was a mother, Josh, who witnesses the killing, goes back to the scene during the night and finds the orphaned cub. Bringing the cub, whom he names Pokey, back home with him, Josh sets up a room for him in the barn and, despite Pokey's unpredictable biting, the two develop a very close and affectionate relationship. Relations in Josh's home, on the other hand, are severely strained. The previous year, Josh's brother Tye was killed in a car accident. Sam, devastated by the loss, has taken to heavy drinking and, while drunk, he is abusive to his wife and his surviving son. Pokey, who is a reminder to Sam of his unacknowledged error in killing the mother bear, is doomed to almost certain death when Sam notifies the game warden of his existence. Sam tells Josh that there is no alternative but for Pokey to be delivered into the hands of medical researchers.

After thinking it over, Josh decides he cannot accept the fate that adults have devised for Pokey. Borrowing his brother's motocross cycle, he rides off in the night—with Pokey in a box on the cycle rack and his dog, Mud Flap, on the cycle's gas tank—to the mountains north of Yellowstone Park, seventy miles from his home. Josh leaves behind a note: "I can't let Pokey die so I'm running away. I'll come home when I can keep Pokey and when nobody can hunt bears anymore." After they arrive on the mountain trail, a ferocious summer

After his alcoholic father kills a mother bear, young Josh decides to rescue the bear's orphaned cub—a decision that leads to a wild adventure in the wilderness. (Cover illustration by Stephen Marchesi.)

blizzard breaks out, severely testing the boy's survival skills. In the days that follow, the three experience extremes of cold, deprivation, loneliness, and danger, as well as some triumphs and happy times together.

Much of the novel is divided between Josh's adventures in the mountains and the initially unsuccessful efforts of the search and rescue team to find him. When Mud Flap is badly wounded in a bear attack, Josh must overcome his distrust of the adult world in order to contact his friend Otis for help. Otis is a gruff ex-wildlife biologist who at one time had become so frustrated with the bureaucracies that were supposed to protect wildlife that he gave up trying to change the laws. Becoming a recluse, Otis has kept civilization at arm's length and spends most of his time tending to wounded wild animals. Josh, one of the only people with whom Otis interacts, has helped him out with the animals. Otis agrees to help Mud Flap, but when he drives out to pick her up, he is unknowingly followed by the police, leading to Josh's eventual rescue.

After getting into a serious motorcycle accident in the night, Josh stands in need of rescue but, thinking that he has been deceived by his friend, he continues to try to elude the search and rescue party. What Josh has not

understood is the way his disappearance into a deadly storm has raised the interest of the media. During his absence his intention to change wildlife laws has received national coverage. In the events that follow Josh's rescue, the reader sees that the actions of a fairly naive young boy who only wants to do what is right can be an effective counter to the injustices of hypocritical bureaucracies, a complacent social world, and even to his father's alcoholism.

Josh's point of view is limited, as any child's would be, and at the same time, clear and optimistic. Mikaelsen told *SATA* that he had written half of *Rescue Josh McGuire* before he could find a way to save Pokey's life. "It was a problem I was not able to solve as an adult. With this problem I needed a child's point of view. Children see the world in a black and white format. They don't understand politics, they don't understand bureaucracy, they don't understand budget. Looking at it through Josh's point of view as just this precious little life that's going to die if I don't do something—it's just that simple. As an adult, I would have had to let the cub go and let it get killed. A child doesn't understand that you have to."

In contrast to Josh's naivete is the character Otis's cynicism. Otis, having spent many years fighting city hall about wildlife laws, gave up on people. Understanding the politics of the situation, unlike Josh, Otis is initially overwhelmed by its absurdity: "He was tasting again the very poison that had wasted thirty years of his life. Man created government and built big buildings and arbitrated until he thought of himself as God. Was it a committee's decision how much pollution a million dollars was worth? Were animals something to be budgeted like tax dollars?" But now, in awe of young Josh's integrity in living up to his beliefs against an array of powerful forces, Otis is spurred back into action against ruling powers.

Josh, Pokey, Mud Flap, and Otis all encounter some extremely harsh and unfair experiences. Although the outcome of the novel is highly positive, Mikaelsen does not paint a particularly rosy picture of the American way. "I am one of those people that believe if you don't reveal the world's shortcomings, you slam the door on learning. If we try to teach kids that all bureaucracy is right and not questionable, then we eliminate any chance of improving upon the deficiencies that bureaucracies have. Likewise with parents. If a child can never look at a parent and say, 'Maybe my parent is wrong, maybe what they're doing isn't right,' then the parents' ways can never be improved upon."

Mikaelsen did a great deal of research for *Rescue Josh McGuire*. "When I write about issues, I get an overwhelming sense of responsibility. If I write about an issue wrongly, I do as much harm as I do good. So when I decided that I was going to take on spring bear hunting and alcoholism—gosh! I've spent time with people that were in rehab, I went up to the part of the country where much of the novel takes place and, with my wife, spent the whole week camping up in there, laying it all out for authenticity. I also went down to the Bozeman Search and Rescue Department. I knew some of the members, and they actually sat down with me and drew a format and helped me choreograph Josh's rescue."

For Mikaelsen, writing takes place in life and experience as well as in an author's mind. Living his books by actively entering into the adventures he writes about is, according to the author, "a fun way to keep from getting to be a mole. I think writers tend to get reclusive. I don't find the actual writing of a book healthy. I have to spend too many hours by myself. Whenever I finish a rough draft, I just clear out and head down to some water hole somewhere and sit, trying to get away from the computer terminal, away from being a human mole."

Mikaelsen continued: "My next book, *Sparrow Hawk Red,* is an adventure story about a young boy who lives among the homeless in Mexico. Now, how in the world am I going to know what it's like to be homeless in Mexico living up here in Montana? So I actually went down and spent several weeks in a variety of places all the way from Tucson to Tijuana to Ensenada to Nogales to Mexicali. There was one point where I was standing around looking at the homeless children, thinking, 'This is really good for me to stand around and look at the homeless and feel guilty.' And then I thought, 'Baloney, I have no more idea of what it's like to be hungry and cold than the man on the moon.' One afternoon I was getting a taco, and pulled my billfold out and I thought, 'Those homeless children don't have a billfold.' So I put that away and the next day I came back with no billfold, just a T-shirt and jeans. For the next three days I just lived among the homeless and I got very hungry. I wasn't willing to eat out of a garbage can the way I saw a lot of them do, but I did eat some pretty wretched food that made me sick. I also slept on gravel in the alleys at night with a piece of cardboard over me. I was fortunate enough that three days later I could just walk back across the border to a motel and my clean clothes and a hot shower. I had a feeling at that point what it was like to be homeless—at least I've seen that look in their eyes and I can write about it.

"I can go to libraries and get a lot of my research, but I've never found the soul of my story in a library. Not until I was laying awake at 4:00 in the morning trying to bottle-feed a cub that was almost starved to death. In that struggle—the little critter struggling for life—I discovered the soul of my novel. Or when I was among the homeless and I saw that look of hopelessness in some little kid that hasn't had a decent meal in three years and is almost naked except for his dirty underpants. When I actually felt the hunger and cold and looked into his eyes, that's where I found the soul for that story. For my new book, I worked for a month at a dolphin facility. I went out and helped find a dolphin who was caught in a shrimp net, and I also got involved in a whale stranding. That is when I found the soul of my story."

Mikaelsen interacts not only with his issues and settings, but, on a different level, with his child protagonists as well. "I try to imagine a child walking through the real world beside me. Then that character comes alive for me. What's wonderful then is that it's just like having a best friend—you can never predict what your best friend will do next. In *Rescue Josh McGuire,* for instance, the part of the book where Josh had his motorcycle accident was not in my plans. While I was writing, Josh did just what Josh would do in the circumstances: he rode his cycle too fast in the dark. I put my cursor back and erased two paragraphs and I tried to write him continuing up the hill. But again, he went into the ditch, this time getting hurt even worse, and I realized that my character had come alive and I had to let him do what he wanted to do. And it made a much better end."

For all his understanding and respect for children, Mikaelsen did not set out to become a children's writer. *Rescue Josh McGuire* was written as an adult novel; it was his publisher who suggested it be promoted for young adults. Mikaelsen said that this "taught me a real good lesson, that there is no difference in an adult book and a children's book except that the main character is a child. I realized that I can write what I want, as complexly and to whatever issues I wish. In fact, I can do anything I want, looking through a child's point of view."

Mikaelsen, who has not forgotten the challenges he faced as an insecure teenage boy, seeks to empower the children with whom he has contact. "Now I go into a school system as an author-in-residence and I realize that every kid gets teased for something. Sometimes it's just that they're off a farm and they still have the smell of manure on their shoes or sometimes their parents cut their hair funny. When I talk to the kids I say, 'Okay, the differences aren't a weakness, the differences are what make you special. That's what has made me an author; that's what has made me able to write a book. So what you do is take your differences and highlight them.'" Mikaelsen's books also aim at offering children new possibilities. "In all my writing I try to help children discover that they count. I want to take a child on a journey that changes their emotions, attitudes, and perspective. Children are the future. Children's literature offers a sobering but exciting chance to effect that future, environmental or social. For this reason I enjoy writing to issues.

"The secret to happiness," Mikaelsen concluded, "has been described to me as doing whatever you do with a passion, to the best of your ability, and for others. Writing has given me this happiness."

WORKS CITED:

Mikaelsen, Ben, *Rescue Josh McGuire,* Hyperion, 1991.
Mikaelsen, Ben, telephone interview with Sonia Benson for *Something about the Author,* conducted October 9, 1992.

FOR MORE INFORMATION SEE:

PERIODICALS

Booklist, December 15, 1991, p. 758.
Bulletin of the Center for Children's Books, December, 1991, p. 100.
School Library Journal, February, 1992, p. 108.

—*Sketch by Sonia Benson*

*   *   *

MILLER, Jewel 1956-

PERSONAL: Born January 9, 1956, in Goshen, IN; daughter of Edwin (a minister) and Tressa (a homemaker; maiden name, Schrock) Knepp; married Mervin Miller (a farmer and truck driver), August 28, 1976; children: Jay, Marilyn, Phyllis, Sherri Lou. *Hobbies and other interests:* Quilting, photography, handcrafts, mothering.

ADDRESSES: Home—Route 3, Box 575, Macon, MS 39341.

CAREER: Writer and homemaker.

WRITINGS:

Whisper of Love: An Amish Romance on the Moonlit Prairie, Herald Press, 1991.

Contributor to periodicals, including *Family Life, Companions,* and *Partners.*

WORK IN PROGRESS: Love Forbidden, a romance.

SIDELIGHTS: Jewel Miller is the author of *Whisper of Love: An Amish Romance on the Moonlit Prairie,* a love story for younger audiences set in the early 1900s in an Amish community—a religious, agricultural sect whose members refrain from the use of modern technology. The work follows Maudie, the six-year-old protagonist, as she matures and eventually discovers love. Emphasizing the closeness of Maudie's family, Miller also shows the hard work the farmers must endure. *School Library Journal* contributor Jane Gardner Connor described Miller's writing as possessing "a nostalgic, affectionate tone."

Miller told *SATA:* "I don't remember learning to write, probably because I was born with a pencil in my hand. I didn't write the usual things child writers write, like journals and inner feelings and stuff like that. I always wrote real things; stories that I was sure would be published.

"When I was in the sixth grade, I sat right behind Robert Stewart. Robert didn't waste time on anything and became a banker when he grew up. One day I was engrossed in a good story and writing as fast as I could with a dull and grimy yellow pencil. Suddenly Robert turned around, looked at my paper out of the corner of his eye and sneered, 'Whatcha think yer doin'?'

"'Writin',' I whispered softly.

"'Well it don't look like nothin' but chickenscratch to me!' he answered disgustedly. And I ain't been doin' nothin' but chickenscratch ever since.

"Because of circumstances out of my control, I could not finish high school and had to go to work when I was sixteen. I married a farmer, Mervin Miller, when I was twenty and soon had three children in tow. I secretly dreamed of writing a book about my grandmother, but with the endless tasks of mothering and housekeeping and helping on the farm, my writing career was a mere fantasy. But often as I rocked our little ones to sleep, the characters and scenes grew and came to life until I felt they would burst forth without me, leaving me behind. I began reading English handbooks and books about how to write fiction and the works of really good writers. Then, without a typewriter, I began writing short stories and essays in longhand and sending them to various editors. To my delight, and surprise, they began accepting my work—and instructing me to type my manuscripts. Out of necessity I ignored them and continued writing in longhand, getting checks in the mail nonetheless. When my grandmother asked me to write some of her childhood stories for her, I knew the time had come to pursue the dream I had harbored since childhood. For three years I wrote in longhand and then my grandmother bought a word processor for me, and in less than a year the book was written and accepted by Herald Press, a publishing company that specializes in Amish life.

"I take no credit for realizing the book and fulfilling my dream because God, my husband, my grandmother, my mother, my editor, and so many other people contributed to it. I am just thrilled to be a part of this wonderful world of literature.

JEWEL MILLER

"There is much emphasis today on dreaming and realizing your dreams. But if we are totally honest we will admit that we are not in control of our destinies. Time and circumstances shape us and lead us in directions we hadn't planned to take. We must consider others and live responsibly; not oblivious to the rest of the world or recklessly denying ourselves, but living to glorify God. Only then will our dreams be fruitful and of any importance."

WORKS CITED:

PERIODICALS

Connor, Jane Gardner, review of *Whisper of Love, School Library Journal,* March, 1992.

* * *

MILLER, Maryann 1943-

PERSONAL: Born July 4, 1943, in Detroit, MI; daughter of Russell (a manufacturing manager) and Evelyn (a homemaker; maiden name, Gundrum) Van Gilder; married Carl Vincent Miller (a data processing professional), August 20, 1965; children: Anjanette, David, Michael, Paul, Danielle. *Education:* Attended South Macomb Community College, 1961-65, University of Houston, 1979-80, University of Texas at Dallas, 1982—, Collin County Community College, 1989-90. *Politics:* Independent. *Religion:* Roman Catholic. *Hob-*

MARYANN MILLER

bies and other interests: Painting, film, theatre, guitar, music.

ADDRESSES: Home—2704 Greywood, Plano, TX 75075.

CAREER: Author. Miller Wargo Productions, Dallas, TX, executive producer, 1982-84; *Plano* magazine, Plano, TX, staff writer and editor, 1983-86; Stephen Marro Productions, New York City, staff writer, 1983—; Catholic Foundation, Dallas, member of public relations staff, 1986—; Book Publishers of Texas, executive director, 1989-90. Music and hospital lay minister; St. Francis Outreach Center volunteer.

MEMBER: Greater Dallas Writer's Association (president, 1978-83; conference chair, 1983, 1986; treasurer, 1990—).

AWARDS, HONORS: Detroit News Scholastic Writing Award, 1958, for short story "The Cost of Freedom"; Golden Pen Award, University of Houston, 1980, for short story "Going Back," and 1981, for screenplay "A Question of Honor"; honorable mention, *Short Story Digest,* 1992, for "Maybe Someday."

WRITINGS:

Coping with Cults, Rosen Publishing, 1990.
Coping with a Bigoted Parent, Rosen Publishing, 1992.
Coping with Weapons and Violence in School and on Your Streets, Rosen Publishing, 1992.

WORK IN PROGRESS: Bunker Knows, a screenplay for Stephen Marro Productions; research on domestic violence; *One Small Victory,* an adult novel.

SIDELIGHTS: Maryann Miller told *SATA:* "Reading was one of my favorite pastimes as a child. By the time I was in the sixth grade, I had read everything available in the children's section of our local library, and had to get special permission to read books from the adult section. My favorite place to read was in the branches of the huge elm tree in our back yard.

"By the time I was ten years old, I knew I wanted to be a writer. I wanted to capture the magic of words and books for others. The subjects of my earliest short stories were animals, primarily horses, and I felt like I made a major breakthrough when I wrote my first story about people as a senior in high school. After that, my interest in writing about people and life experiences grew. I studied psychology and sociology in college and discovered a real fascination with what makes people do the things they do. That realization eventually led me in the direction of journalism.

"My first professional work was as a columnist for a large suburban newspaper just outside of Dallas. I wrote about family life, in a humorous style, and the column was titled 'It's Not All Gravy.' That column ran for six years and introduced me to a concept of 'talking on paper.' Using that same concept I went on to write a regular column for the viewpoints department of the

Miller explores the destructive nature of cults in this volume aimed at teens and their parents.

Texas Catholic newspaper. I have always been concerned about social issues, and this was a wonderful outlet for ideas and opinions. As my free-lance writing career developed in the 1980s, I discovered that most of the articles and stories I sold were done in a personal commentary style, so obviously I'd mastered that technique. But I was also a good journalist who loved to do research, and those two professional strengths aided me considerably in taking on my first book assignment.

"A long time ago I learned never to say 'no' to an opportunity, so when a business associate told me about a publisher who was looking for a writer to do a book about destructive cults, I called the publisher. At the time I didn't know much about the subject beyond a few headlines in newspapers, but I said, 'Sure, I can do this book.' The result was *Coping with Cults,* which is aimed for the teen market as part of a series published by Rosen Publishing in New York. It was a 1990 release, and since then I've written *Coping with a Bigoted Parent* and *Coping with Weapons and Violence in School and on Your Streets.*

"My books are for and about young people, and a good deal of my research involves interviewing teens and talking to them in informal discussion groups. Subse-

quently, I have met many bright, interesting young people who have much to say to and about our world. These books deal with serious life problems many teens face and I feel a special obligation to give them something beyond the intellectual considerations. As an active lay minister in our church, I have learned that people facing problems need to know someone out there cares. I have tried to be personally sensitive to that in my writing as well as introducing readers to lots of other people who care about these life issues and are trying to do something to help.

"I can't say I enjoy writing these books, not like I enjoy writing fiction, but I feel good about doing them. Each book is another opportunity to 'talk on paper' to a whole lot of readers, and maybe something I say will make a difference in their lives."

*   *   *

MORAY WILLIAMS, Ursula 1911-

PERSONAL: Born April 19, 1911, in Petersfield, Hampshire, England; daughter of Arthur (an archaeologist and tutor in classics) and Mabel (a teacher; maiden name, Unwin) Moray Williams; married Conrad (Peter) Southey John (an aircraft engineer), September 28, 1935, (died, 1974); children: Andrew, Hugh, Robin, James. *Education:* Privately educated at home by governess; attended finishing school in France, 1927-28, and the Winchester College of Art, Winchester, England, 1928-29. *Religion:* Church of England. *Hobbies and other interests:* Gardening, traveling, sewing.

ADDRESSES: Home—Court Farm House, Beckford near Tewksbury, Gloucestershire, England. *Agent*—Curtis Brown Ltd., 162-168 Regent St., London W1R 5TA, England.

CAREER: Author and illustrator of books for children, 1931—. Former Justice of the Peace, Worcestershire-Evesham bench; chairman of Evesham Juvenile Panel, 1972-75; deputy chairman of Adult Bench, 1975-81. Former governor of County High School, Evesham; former governor of Vale of Evesham School for Educationally Subnormal Children. President of Women's British Legion, 1974—; former presiding member of Mothers Union. Founder of children's writing competitions in Cheltenham, England, the Outer Hebrides, and New Zealand. Has given talks about books at school libraries in the United Kingdom, New Zealand, and Australia.

MEMBER: National Book League, West Country Writers Association, Cheltenham Literary Festival Society.

AWARDS, HONORS: Spring Book Festival middle honor, 1971, for *The Three Toymakers.*

WRITINGS:

SELF-ILLUSTRATED CHILDREN'S BOOKS

Jean-Pierre, A. & C. Black, 1931.

URSULA MORAY WILLIAMS

For Brownies: Stories and Games for the Pack and Everybody Else, Harrap, 1932.
Grandfather (verse), Allen & Unwin, 1933.
The Pettabomination (also see below), Search Publishing, 1933, revised edition, Lane, 1948.
Autumn Sweepers, and Other Plays for Children, A. & C. Black, 1933.
More for Brownies, Harrap, 1934.
(Illustrator with sister, Barbara Moray Williams) *Kelpie, the Gipsies' Pony,* Harrap, 1934, Lippincott, 1935.
Anders and Marta, Harrap, 1935.
Adventures of Anne, Harrap, 1935.
Sandy-on-the-Shore, Harrap, 1936.
The Twins and Their Ponies, Harrap, 1936.
Tales for the Sixes and Sevens, Harrap, 1937.
Dumpling: The Story of a Pony, Harrap, 1937.
(Illustrator with B. Moray Williams) *Elaine of La Signe,* Harrap, 1937, published as *Elaine of the Mountains,* Lippincott, 1939.
Gobbolino, the Witch's Cat, Harrap, 1942, abridged edition, Puffin, 1965.
The Good Little Christmas Tree (also see below), Harrap, 1943, published with illustrations by Jane Paton, Hamish Hamilton, 1970.
The House of Happiness (also see below), Harrap, 1946.

The Three Toymakers, Harrap, 1946, Thomas Nelson, 1971, published with illustrations by Shirley Hughes, Hamish Hamilton, 1976.
Malkin's Mountain, Harrap, 1948, Thomas Nelson, 1971, revised edition illustrated by Hughes, Hamish Hamilton, 1976.
The Story of Laughing Dandino, Harrap, 1948.
Pettabomination (play; adapted from her book of the same title), Samuel French, 1951.
The Good Little Christmas Tree (play; adapted from her book of the same title), Samuel French, 1951.
The House of Happiness (play; adapted from her book of same title), Samuel French, 1951.
The Binklebys at Home, Harrap, 1951.
The Binklebys on the Farm, Harrap, 1953.
Secrets of the Wood, Harrap, 1955.
Grumpa, Brockhampton Press, 1955.
Goodbody's Puppet Show, Hamish Hamilton, 1956.
The Golden Horse with a Silver Tail, Hamish Hamilton, 1957.
Hobbie, Brockhampton Press, 1958.
The Moonball, Hamish Hamilton, 1958, Morrow, 1960.
O for a Mouseless House!, Chatto & Windus, 1964.

CHILDREN'S BOOKS

(With husband, Peter John) *Adventures of Boss and Dingbatt,* photographs by John, Harrap, 1937.
Adventures of the Little Wooden Horse, illustrated by Joyce L. Brisley, Harrap, 1938, Lippincott, 1939.
Adventures of Puffin, illustrated by Mary Shillabeer, Harrap, 1939.
Peter and the Wanderlust, illustrated by Jack Matthew, Harrap, 1939, illustrated by Henry C. Pitz, Lippincott, 1940, revised edition published as *Peter on the Road,* Hamish Hamilton, 1963.
Pretender's Island, illustrated by Brisley, Harrap, 1940, Knopf, 1942.
A Castle for John-Peter, illustrated by Eileen A. Soper, Harrap, 1941.
Jockin the Jester, illustrated by B. Moray Williams, Chatto & Windus, 1951, Thomas Nelson, 1973.
The Noble Hawks, Hamish Hamilton, 1959, published as *The Earl's Falconer,* illustrated by Charles Geer, Morrow, 1961.
The Nine Lives of Island Mackenzie, illustrated by Edward Ardizzone, Chatto & Windus, 1959, published as *Island Mackenzie,* Morrow, 1960.
Beware of This Animal, illustrated by Paton, Hamish Hamilton, 1964, Dial, 1965.
Johnnie Tigerskin, illustrated by Diana Johns, Harrap, 1964, Duell, Sloane, & Pearce, 1966.
High Adventure, illustrated by Prudence Seward, Thomas Nelson, 1965.
The Cruise of the "Happy-Go-Gay," illustrated by Gunvor Edwards, Hamish Hamilton, 1967, Meredith Press, 1968.
A Crown for a Queen, illustrated by Hughes, Meredith Press, 1968.
The Toymaker's Daughter, illustrated by Hughes, Hamish Hamilton, 1968, Meredith Press, 1969.
Mog, illustrated by Faith Jaques, Allen & Unwin, 1969.
Boy in a Barn, illustrated by Terence Dalley, Thomas Nelson, 1970.

Johnny Golightly and His Crocodile, illustrated by Jaques, Chatto & Windus, 1970, Harvey House, 1971.

Traffic Jam, illustrated by Robert Hales, Chatto & Windus, 1971.

Man on a Steeple, illustrated by Mary Dinsdale, Chatto & Windus, 1971.

Mrs. Townsend's Robber, illustrated by Gavin Rowe, Chatto & Windus, 1971.

Out of the Shadows, illustrated by Rowe, Chatto & Windus, 1971.

Castle Merlin, Thomas Nelson, 1972.

A Picnic with the Aunts, illustrated by Jaques, Chatto & Windus, 1972.

The Kidnapping of My Grandmother, illustrated by Mike Jackson, Heinemann, 1972.

Children's Parties, and Games for a Rainy Day, Corgi Books, 1972.

Tiger-Nanny, illustrated by Edwards, Brockhampton Press, 1973, Thomas Nelson, 1974.

The Line, illustrated by Barry Wilkinson, Puffin, 1974.

Grandpapa's Folly and the Woodworm-Bookworm, illustrated by Jaques, Chatto & Windus, 1974.

No Ponies for Miss Pobjoy, illustrated by Pat Marriott, Thomas Nelson, 1975.

Bogwoppit, illustrated by Hughes, Thomas Nelson, 1978.

Jeffy, the Burglar's Cat, illustrated by David McKee, Andersen Press, 1981.

Bellabelinda and the No-Good Angel, illustrated by Glenys Ambrus, Chatto & Windus, 1982.

The Further Adventures of Gobbolino and the Little Wooden Horse, illustrated by Pauline Baynes, Penguin/Puffin, 1984.

Spid, illustrated by McKee, Andersen Press, 1985.

Grandma and the Ghowlies, illustrated by Susan Varley, Andersen Press, 1986.

Paddy on the Island, illustrated by Tor Morisse, Andersen Press, 1987.

OTHER

Contributor to numerous anthologies and magazines, including *Puffin Post, Marshall Cavendish Storyteller Magazine, Cricket, USA,* and *Lady.* Moray Williams's books have been translated into over thirteen languages.

ADAPTATIONS: Gobbolino, the Witch's Cat was recorded on Delyse Records, 1967, Storyteller Cassettes, 1982-83; *The Three Toymakers, Bogwoppit, The Nine Lives of Island Mackenzie, Paddy on the Island, Jeffy, the Burglar's Cat,* and *Gobbolino, the Witch's Cat* were adapted for the British Broadcasting Company children's program, *Jackanory.*

SIDELIGHTS: Ursula Moray Williams is a well-known and prolific writer of children's literature. She published her first book at the age of twenty, and in the following decades she has completed dozens more, many of which are self-illustrated. She is known for her fanciful tales which have enchanted readers of all ages and nationalities with their strong sense of humor and direct, realistic dialogue. As a testament to the universal appeal of her work, Moray Williams's books have been translated into

languages as diverse as Icelandic and Japanese, and her classic *Adventures of the Little Wooden Horse* has been in print in England continuously for over fifty years.

Ursula Moray Williams was born on April 19, 1911, ten minutes after her identical twin sister, Barbara. After the end of World War I, the family moved from Petersfield, England, to a sprawling home in the more rural area between Southampton and Winchester. Their new house was called a "folly" because the owner who had it built 150 years previously had wanted an elegant and opulent manor home like others that were fancied in that era. However, his money did not match his ambitions, and it was never quite finished.

Still, it proved to be a wonderful playground for the imagination of the two girls. They would roam through the mostly unused rooms of the mansion by day, playing games and sports. At night, they amused themselves by telling each other stories, switching the narration back and forth when one got tired of telling the story. "For years we had to go to bed so early that of course we could not sleep," mused Moray Williams in the *Something about the Author Autobiography Series* (*SAAS*). "So we used those precious hours for telling stories, breaking off in turn to toss the thread to one another: 'Now You!' 'Now you!' I can't remember any occasion when the other twin changed the plot too violently." They began illustrating some of the stories they told and would present these books to each other on their birthday and on Christmas morning.

Having been educated primarily by a governess until they were seventeen, Moray Williams and her twin were sent by their family to a finishing school in France so that they could become more worldly. It was there that

Moray Williams uses the French landscape as a backdrop for the adventures of Marta, a beautiful and heartless doll. (Illustration by Shirley Hughes.)

In *Johnnie Golightly and His Crocodile,* Moray Williams tells the whimsical story of a unique friendship. (Cover illustration by Faith Jacques.)

Moray Williams began to write without her sister's help. "The scenery and countryside were so beautiful they made a great impression on me, and I slowly began to write independently," she commented in *SAAS.* Later, she was to use the French landscape for the background of several of her books, including *The Three Toymakers, The Toymaker's Daughter,* and *Malkin's Mountain.* These books follow the follies of a beautiful, but often heartless, doll named Marta.

Returning home to England, the twins attended the Winchester College of Art. This suited Barbara quite well, but after a year Ursula quit and stayed with her parents to write children's books. Working diligently, she published her first book, *Jean-Pierre,* in 1931. Moray Williams also did all the illustrations for it. After finishing *Jean-Pierre* she continued to write, encouraged by her uncle, Sir Stanley Unwin, a publisher. In 1935, she met Conrad Southey John, who had been in the Royal Air Force. After a false start where John courted her cousin, the two fell in love, married, and moved to a flat in a London suburb. Around the same time, Moray Williams's twin sister married and settled in Iceland.

While pregnant with her first child, Moray Williams wrote what was to become her best-known book, *Adventures of the Little Wooden Horse.* This fantasy folktale offers a look at the relationship between good and evil

through the wanderings of the main character, a quiet little horse. The author's second son was born in 1940, at the beginning of World War II. The family moved to Beckford, where, with the help of neighbors, Moray Williams was relieved of the child care for a few hours each day. "The great advantage of having the children taken out in the afternoons was the freedom it gave me to write for at least two hours every day, without which I don't think I would be writing now," she commented in *SAAS.* During this time she wrote *The Good Little Christmas Tree* and *Gobbolino, the Witch's Cat,* a story about the adventures of an unhappy witch's cat. These books were both to become popular favorites with young children.

After the war, the family moved to Court Farm, a large country estate that would allow them to garden and had plenty of room for the family, now increased to four young boys. Not long after they had settled into the new abode, Moray Williams found herself launching on another adventure—she took a fishing trawler to Iceland with her two eldest sons to visit her twin sister. They arrived in time for the midnight sun and witnessed the eruption of the volcano Helka. She later wrote about their adventures in *Golden Horse with a Silver Tail,* which is a description of a typical Icelandic pony—chestnut coat with flaxen mane and tail.

Moray Williams has traveled all over the English-speaking world to give speeches and talks to schoolchildren. Often, she is questioned on how she gets her ideas for stories. "My ideas just come, I never plan them, and always find something inside trying to get out! I still write better when time is a little short!," she once commented. She continued in *SAAS* that "when winter comes, I dive into my imaginary bag and pull out the outline of a plot. It may have been brooding there all summer, or it may be a flash of an idea that I know will make a book."

Moray Williams's husband died in 1974, but she has continued to live in the old farmhouse and write her books. There is an essence of her own childhood in some, such as *The Twins and Their Ponies,* which draws on experiences of her pony-mad youth. *Grandpapa's Folly and the Woodworm Bookworm,* an Edwardian style book, was inspired by the ornate but non-functional library from the "folly" in which she grew up.

Many of Moray Williams's books are noted for their sense of fun. For example, *Jeffy, the Burglar's Cat* finds Miss Amity's thieving instincts thwarted by her do-gooding cat; *Bogwoppit* follows a courageous young heroine clashing with some mischievous marsh dwellers; and *Spid* chronicles the adventures of a charming eight-legged spider. Several of her books have also been made into television programs.

Throughout her prolific career, Moray Williams has endeavored to produce lively, fun books with amusing characters and exciting plots. To her credit, she boasts nearly seventy books, many of which are still in print or are being adapted into other media. Winifred Whitehead summed up Moray Williams's career in *Twentieth-Century Children's Writers,* saying that she "is an inventive as well as prolific writer, and in their different ways her books are well-written; pleasantly intriguing, and occasionally achieve a haunting power and a delightfully sharp and witty observation of the foibles of mankind."

WORKS CITED:

Moray Williams, Ursula, essay in *Something about the Author Autobiography Series,* Volume 9, Gale, 1990, pp. 235-250.
Whitehead, Winifred, "Ursula Moray Williams," *Twentieth-Century Children's Writers,* 3rd edition, St. James Press, 1989, pp. 696-698.

FOR MORE INFORMATION SEE:

PERIODICALS

Horn Book, August, 1969; October, 1969; August, 1971.
New York Times Book Review, May 7, 1967.
Saturday Review, May 13, 1967; June 15, 1968; August 16, 1969; January 23, 1971.
Times Literary Supplement, June 17, 1965; June 6, 1968; December 11, 1970; November 3, 1972; December 8, 1972; July 7, 1978.

*   *   *

MOSS, Jeff(rey)

PERSONAL: Born in New York, NY; son of an actor and a writer; married; children: one son. *Education:* Received degree from Princeton University. *Hobbies and other interests:* Theatre.

ADDRESSES: Home—New York, NY.

CAREER: Columbia Broadcasting System (CBS), New York City, began as production assistant for television program *Captain Kangaroo,* became writer for *Captain Kangaroo;* Children's Television Workshop, New York City, head writer and composer/lyricist for *Sesame Street,* beginning in 1969, currently staff writer for *Sesame Street;* children's book author in New York City, c. 1989—. Composer and lyricist for film *The Muppets Take Manhattan,* Tri-Star, 1984; contributor of music and lyrics to numerous *Sesame Street* song albums. *Military service:* U.S. Army.

AWARDS, HONORS: Emmy awards—outstanding achievement in a children's program, Academy of Television Arts and Sciences, both 1969, for music and lyrics for *Sesame Street* episode "This Way to Sesame Street" and writing for episode "Sally Sees Sesame Street"; Emmy award—individual achievement in a children's program, Academy of Television Arts and Sciences, 1973, for *Sesame Street;* Emmy awards—writing in a children's series, Academy of Television Arts and Sciences, 1982, 1983, 1984, 1985, 1986, 1987, 1988, 1989, and 1990, all for *Sesame Street;* Emmy awards—music composition in a children's program,

Academy of Television Arts and Sciences, 1982 and 1989, both for *Sesame Street;* Grammy awards—recording for children, National Academy of Recording Arts and Sciences, 1972, for *Sesame Street II,* 1980, for *The People in Your Neighborhood,* and 1984, for *The Muppets Take Manhattan—The Original Soundtrack;* Academy award nomination—original song score, Academy of Motion Picture Arts and Sciences, 1984, for *The Muppets Take Manhattan.*

WRITINGS:

The Butterfly Jar: Poems, illustrated by Chris Demarest, Bantam, 1989.
The Other Side of the Door: Poems, illustrated by Demarest, Bantam, 1991.
The Sesame Street Book of Poetry, illustrated by Bruce McNally, Random House/Children's Television Workshop, 1991.
Bob and Jack: A Boy and His Yak (picture book), illustrated by Demarest, Bantam, 1992.
The Sesame Street Songbook, Macmillan, 1992.

UNDER NAME JEFFREY MOSS

(With others) *The Sesame Street Treasury: Featuring Jim Henson's Sesame Street Muppets,* illustrated by Tom Cooke and others, Random House/Children's Television Workshop, 1973.
(With Norman Stiles and Daniel Wilcox) *The Sesame Street ABC Storybook: Featuring Jim Henson's Muppets,* illustrated by Peter Cross and others, Random House, 1974.
(With Emily Perl Kingsley and David Korr) *The Sesame Street Book of Fairy Tales: Featuring Jim Henson's Muppets,* illustrated by Joe Mathieu, Random House, 1975.
Oscar's Book, illustrated by Michael Gross, Western Publishing, 1976.

JEFF MOSS

People in Your Neighborhood, illustrated by Richard Brown, Western Publishing/Children's Television Workshop, 1983.

People in My Family, illustrated by Carol Nicklaus, Western Publishing/Children's Television Workshop, 1983.

(With others) *The Songs of Sesame Street in Poems and Pictures: Featuring Jim Henson's Sesame Street Muppets,* illustrated by Normand Chartier, Random House/Children's Television Workshop, 1983.

Author of book, music, and lyrics for two musical plays, both produced by the Princeton Triangle Club; contributor of poems to anthologies, including *Free to Be . . . a Family,* by Marlo Thomas et al., Bantam, 1990.

WORK IN PROGRESS: Zoo Fantasy, a screenplay for Francis Ford Coppola.

SIDELIGHTS: "I think my main goals in whatever I do are to entertain the audience, and to teach them a little bit, leave them a tiny bit better off than when I found them," Jeff Moss said in an interview with *Something about the Author* (*SATA*). Moss—the original head writer and composer/lyricist for the groundbreaking children's television series *Sesame Street*—has penned many of the program's best known songs, including "Rubber Duckie" and "The People in Your Neighborhood." More recently, he has published two volumes of poetry for young people, *The Butterfly Jar* and *The Other Side of the Door,* and a story in verse, *Bob and Jack: A Boy and His Yak.* In both his television work and his books, the award-winning writer has succeeded in making children and their parents laugh while they gain some new insight into themselves and the world around them.

Although he only recently became a parent, Moss believes that his childlike perspective arises from observing children, as well as from his strong memories of his own childhood. But more important, he commented, "I don't look at writing for children as that different than writing for anybody else. The emotions that you write about are for the most part the same as you would write about for anybody. You just do it with a vocabulary of experience that children will understand." Moss also derives inspiration from watching adults, for, as he explained, "All of us have a great deal of the child left in us, and some of us show it more than others."

Moss began writing poetry and music at an early age. His father, an actor, and his mother, who had been a writer for a time, filled their home with recordings of classical music and Broadway show tunes. The young Moss studied piano and read a great deal. During a road trip with his father at the age of eight or nine, he discovered crossword puzzles for the first time and felt as though they had been created for him. On the subject of words, Moss told *SATA,* "I have always loved them and I still love them. When I'm sitting around, I play with them in my head, the way other people think about—I don't know—cars. I think a certain amount of that is just born into you. I think I would love words no matter what I did for a living—if I were a factory worker, or a doctor, or whatever."

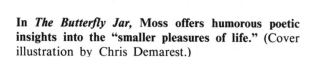

In *The Butterfly Jar,* Moss offers humorous poetic insights into the "smaller pleasures of life." (Cover illustration by Chris Demarest.)

Remembering a party he held for the publication of his first collection of poetry, *The Butterfly Jar,* in 1989, Moss recalled, "My stepson, who was then ten or eleven, somehow had found this old box of stuff from when I was six years old, and found, in fact, a little poem I had written, along with a drawing that I had done to go with it. And he said that he could see very clearly, even when I was six, why I had become a writer—and also why I had not become an illustrator."

As a teenager, Moss realized that his peers were not interested in the kinds of music he had studied. He continued composing, but added rock 'n' roll songs to his repertoire. In college, he became involved with the Princeton Triangle Club, a student-run musical comedy group which toured major theatres throughout the country. Moss wrote the book, music, and lyrics for two Princeton Triangle reviews, and also appeared in them.

After graduating from Princeton, Moss was offered two positions with Columbia Broadcasting System (CBS) television. One was in the news department, and the other was for the children's program, *Captain Kangaroo.* He told *SATA,* "I hadn't seen *Captain Kangaroo,* and I had seen the news, so I said, 'let me try *Captain Kangaroo.*'" This show—which appeared from 1955 to 1984—was the longest-running children's series in television history. Moss worked as a production assistant for less than a year before leaving to serve in the army. Six months later, he returned to the show as a writer, and stayed on for two years. He decided at that point to leave television and do some "serious" writing.

Some of Moss's colleagues at *Captain Kangaroo* were also leaving CBS, hoping to start a new children's series on public television. The idea that would become *Sesame Street* had begun to take shape in the minds of a number of artists and educators in the mid-1960s. Included in the group were Joan Ganz Cooney, who served as the executive director of the Children's Television Workshop, Gerald S. Lesser, who chaired the board of advisors, famed puppeteer Jim Henson, musical director Joe Raposo, and many others. They all shared the belief that television could be a positive influence in the lives of preschoolers. Their goal—one which had never been successfully accomplished—was to create a television program which would be entertaining to young children, and which would also introduce some basic educational concepts.

Moss was invited to join the effort as head writer and composer/lyricist. Although he initially refused the offer, the others continued to pester him. Finally, Moss agreed to come to the studio to see for himself what they were trying to do, "and I saw two things. What they were trying to do was wonderful. But it was a strangely financed thing. Because it was public money, they paid very, very low salaries to everybody, but there was a lot of money available, so that whatever you wrote could get produced tremendously well. Plus, half the cast was black. This was in 1969, and it meant a lot to me back

then. And it was only going to be for six months, and I said, 'well, let me see.'"

Moss has since spent more than two decades as a writer and composer for the series, producing *Sesame Street* books and records as well as creating some of the show's most memorable characters and songs. In *Children and Television: Lessons from Sesame Street,* Gerald S. Lesser refers to the original *Sesame Street* artists' contributions as "different forms of creative genius." The show's educational focus has evolved a great deal over the years; while the earlier episodes stress reading and math skills, the later ones deal more with emotional and social issues. The program's content—based on the findings of an ongoing research team which observes preschoolers watching television—includes a variety of different kinds of segments. Brief animated sketches are linked with neighborhood scenes by a connection with certain letters and numbers, or by a visual or conceptual theme. The street itself appears several times throughout each episode, and its residents—who come from diverse racial and ethnic backgrounds—invite viewers to become a part of their safe, accepting world. In addition, there are segments which introduce the viewer to environments which he or she may not have the opportunity to visit.

I DON'T WANT TO LIVE ON THE MOON

I'd like to visit the moon
On a rocket ship high in the air.
Yes, I'd like to visit the moon,
But I don't think I'd like to live there.
Though I'd like to look down at the earth from above,
I would miss all the places and people I love.
So although I might like it for one afternoon
I don't want to live on the moon.

I'd like to travel under the sea,
I could meet all the fish everywhere.
Yes, I'd travel under the sea,
But I don't think I'd like to live there.
I might stay for a day if I had my wish,
But there's not much to do when your friends are all fish,
And an oyster and clam aren't real family,
So I don't want to live in the sea.

I'd like to visit the jungle, hear the lion roar,
Go back in time and meet a dinosaur.
There are so many strange places I'd like to be,
But none of them permanently.

So if I should visit the moon,
I will dance on a moonbeam and then
I will make a wish on a star,
And I'll wish I was home once again.
Though I'd like to look down at the earth from above,
I would miss all the places and people I love.
So although I may go, I'll be coming home soon,
'Cause I don't want to live on the moon.

Written originally as a song for the popular children's television program *Sesame Street,* "I Don't Want to Live on the Moon" features Moss's trademark humor and sensitivity. (Illustration by Demarest.)

Among *Sesame Street*'s strongest attractions for both young children and adults are the "Muppets," which are part marionette and part puppet. Created by Jim Henson and his associates, the Muppets were transformed—by a combination of the puppeteers' skills and the writers' words and songs—from lifeless objects into highly realistic characters, many of whom express a full range of human emotions. The brightly-colored animals and monsters—which talk and sing like people—have the dual ability to charm children with their cute, fuzzy quality and captivate adults with their irreverent yet innocent humor.

The Muppets have played a major role in Moss's experience as a *Sesame Street* writer. He considers them to be "a lot more real than the great majority of characters on television. A lot of them have a little more depth and interest to them than, say, a lot of the sitcoms." Moss explained that even if the puppeteer is in plain sight, the Muppet seems so real that the viewer will often forget that the person is there. When children visit the studio, they often talk only to the Muppet, and are barely aware of the puppeteer's presence. "And the kid will send back the message the next day: 'say hi to the Count for me—and the Count's friend,' and that will be the puppeteer." Moss himself once asked Frank Oz, the master puppeteer who plays Miss Piggy, "'how did you get her to do that expression without moving or changing the eyes?' The answer is if you slow down the film and look at it, she really isn't changing her expression, you just believe that she is because they are all so wonderful at what they do."

By coming up with ideas for characters, just as a fiction writer would do, Moss contributed to the development of two important Muppets—Cookie Monster and Oscar the Grouch—and paved the way for countless others. In the early days of the program, according to Moss, all the monster Muppets were scary, and none of them talked. One day, Moss picked up the monster Muppet which he called "Boggle Eyes," and wondered what it would be like as a humorous character—perhaps with a childlike obsession. When the writer shared his idea, he was told to try it out, but not to give the creature too much to say. At Cookie Monster's debut rehearsal, the Muppet said just two words: "milk" and "COOOOOOOO-KKKKKKIEEEEEEEEE." The reaction was extremely favorable; as Moss told *SATA,* "Everybody fell off their chairs, and I went back and wrote some more. Obsessive characters are always interesting."

Moss is perhaps best known for the many songs he composed for the *Sesame Street* Muppets. His most famous song, written for the Ernie character, is a tribute to bath toys and special friends: "Rubber Duckie, you're the one/ you make bath time lots of fun/ Rubber Duckie, I'm awfully fond of you." Another favorite, "I Love Trash," was inspired by lovable green monster Oscar the Grouch, who lives in a garbage can with Slimey, a pet worm created by Moss, and detests sunshine, pleasantness, and people. From the beginning, Moss was

One of Moss's memorable contributions to *Sesame Street* was "Rubber Duckie," a song about the joys of bathtime. (Illustration from *The Sesame Street Songbook* by David Prebenna.)

infinitely pleased with the way in which his musical scores were translated into Muppet performances. "The first song I wrote—which was very early on, of course, the second week I came to work—was called "Five People in My Family." I remember going there and watching it taped. I think if a writer sees something that he does performed, and it's eighty percent of what he wants it to be, you're just very, very happy. That was the first song I'd written, and Joe [Raposo] arranged it, and I went and saw it done, and said, 'gee, that's about 103 percent.' A total pleasure."

By the mid-1970s, *Sesame Street* had gained worldwide popularity. While still remaining faithful to their beginnings, the Muppets began moonlighting as stars of their own syndicated prime-time series, *The Muppet Show.* Their success in this endeavor would lead to three major motion pictures, *The Muppet Movie, The Great Muppet Caper,* and *The Muppets Take Manhattan.* Moss would receive both an Academy award nomination and a Grammy award for the soundtrack to *The Muppets Take Manhattan.* Also in the mid-1970s, Moss stopped writing for television in order to concentrate on composing songs for *Sesame Street* record albums. He later returned to the program as a staff writer, and is now contributing about three months out of every year to the series. "They're nice enough to let me do pretty much what I want, whenever I want," he said of the current *Sesame Street* staff, "and it's still a lot of fun. It's a wonderful home base—it's like a family."

Moss's main activity now is writing books of humorous rhymed verse. The author stresses that his poems—like his work for *Sesame Street*—are intended not simply for children, but for families. It is important to him that his work be enjoyable to all ages, "with the family as the target and the children the bull's-eye." Moss explained this with a comparison to his work for *Sesame Street*: "If the subject's about the letter *D,* you're not going to have a thirty year old say, 'Oh, thank God this show about the letter *D* is on,' but you will have the thirty year old be able to watch the television set and say, 'hey, that's a real entertaining bit about the letter *D,'* and the poems are more like that."

When Moss began writing poetry on his own, he was not intending to publish a collection. Though he had been writing for children's television for many years, he had no children of his own at the time, and was unacquainted with contemporary literature for young people. But he was asked to write a few poems for an anthology, "and I really enjoyed it. And the next time I had a free period in my schedule, I said, 'well, let's see if I can do a few more.' I didn't know where it would lead, and then I had a half a dozen. I said, 'well, let's keep going,' and then I was about a third of the way through and I said, 'well, I think I'll just keep going until I have a book.'"

In terms of a unifying concept for the work, Moss told *SATA,* "I think I had an idea for 'The Butterfly Jar,' which was just one of the poems, and then when I had written that, it seemed like that was what the book was about, as much as anything else." The title poem portrays the world of the imagination in a very poignant way: "And there are things inside my head / Waiting to

be thought or said / Dreams and jokes and wonderings are / Locked inside, like a butterfly jar." The poem sets the stage for other cleverly rhymed, energetic pieces—ranging in tone from the very silly to the very serious—which look at commonplace, universal situations from a young person's perspective.

In *The Butterfly Jar,* Moss continues to communicate the values he supported as a *Sesame Street* writer. His funny situations and wordplay work together with Chris Demarest's whimsical illustrations to illuminate a range of feelings with which most people can identify. "Meeting Strangers" is narrated by a shy monster character who epitomizes the fear of not being liked or accepted by others. "They act like I'm a monster / When I'm the one who's new. / They never smile at me and say, / Why, hi there, how are you?" In "This and That," Moss picks up on the visual format *Sesame Street* uses to illustrate simple concepts. The poem demonstrates the notion of relative size by contrasting large, bold type with smaller, lighter type. Comprised of short, repeated sounds, the poem is both fun to look at and fun to read aloud. "I Don't Want to Live on the Moon," which was recorded as a song on a *Sesame Street* album, celebrates the joy of visiting new places, as well as the comfort of returning home. "Though I'd like to look down at the earth from above, / I would miss all the places and people I love. / So although I might like it for one afternoon / I don't want to live on the moon."

Moss told *SATA* of his experience with the poem "Grandma's Kisses": "When I wrote it, I thought, 'This is very personal—the way my grandma used to try to kiss me when I was a kid.' Well, it turns out that every child in the world has somebody who wants to kiss them in a very wet, juicy way, whom they don't want to be kissed by." The author added, "You don't really realize you're speaking to as many people as you are, and that's always fun—to be surprised. I go to a school or a convention or wherever and I say, 'Is there anybody here who has somebody who really loves to kiss them but they're not really crazy about being kissed by?' And they start squealing and eight hundred hands go up, so you've really touched a nerve."

Reviewers found *The Butterfly Jar* interesting and enjoyable, although one felt that some of the pieces might be more successful in performance than they are in print. Barbara S. McGinn, writing in *School Library Journal,* called the poems "slightly wacky" and "fun-to-read." A *New York Times Book Review* contributor termed the book "an appealing collection." Several critics compared *The Butterfly Jar* to Shel Silverstein's book *Where the Sidewalk Ends,* on account of its design, which leaves a lot of white space on each page. However, *Booklist* contributor Kathryn LaBarbera found Moss's work "more optimistic and less irreverent" than that of Silverstein. Moss told *SATA,* "I'm pleased that they put me in the league with somebody who is as much an institution as [Silverstein] is. I think my poems have a little bit more to do with day-to-day real living than his."

Moss's 1991 book, *The Other Side of the Door,* which is illustrated by Demarest and similar in format to *The*

Moss explores more complicated—and somewhat darker—themes in his poems for *The Other Side of the Door*. (Cover illustration by Demarest.)

Butterfly Jar, may be viewed as a more adventurous collection. Whereas the cover of *The Butterfly Jar* presents a light, carefree scene, *The Other Side of the Door* has a more daring, mysterious look. The title piece promises that "I can be a different me," and "there's no place I can't explore," for "everything can happen, / on the other side of the door." In the poem "Pictures of Grampa," a child describes the death of a grandfather, and the grandmother's subsequent journey from grief to recovery. The poem "Babies" promotes acceptance of new siblings by offering a different way of looking at things: "Even your teacher who's so smart at school / Would lie in her playpen and gurgle and drool. / So love your new sister and please don't forget / Even *you* were once tiny and noisy and wet." And "Bad Mood" portrays an experience everyone has had: "Please don't write, please don't phone, / Please just leave me alone / In this big deep dark hole that I've dug." Toward the end of *The Other Side of the Door,* Moss begins to experiment with form. His poems imitate other types of short texts with which children are familiar, such as a multiple choice question and a letter. There is also a word game in which the reader completes the poem by choosing words to fill in the blanks.

Bob and Jack: A Boy and His Yak, Moss's 1992 publication, is a story written in verse that spans an entire life cycle in its celebration of friendship. As a child, Jack shares many adventures with Bob, his pet yack. But when it comes time for Jack to leave for college, the two begin a separation process that is completed when Bob dies. Jack goes on to marry and start a family, and eventually gives his daughter a pet yak of her own. A *Publishers Weekly* reviewer appreciated the book's "eminent readability and sweet message."

Moss's recent projects provide certain pleasures that were lacking in his work for television, he told *SATA*. With book writing, "you know you're going directly to your audience. There is nothing in between, so you don't have to take into consideration a performer." In addition, there's "a different kind of excitement to hear somebody read your stuff out loud. I've been in a house where the kid didn't know that I wrote the book, and will say to his mother, 'Read me to sleep with *The Butterfly Jar,*' which is the absolute pleasure. It's not the same as television, because with television, you're not in the room, for the most part, when anybody's watching. Even though a couple million people may be watching, you're not with them. The books are so personal, so one-on-one—I mean I can read to a kid or go out to sign books or whatever, and you're coming into direct contact with somebody, you've spoken to them. It's a true pleasure.

"Where I've been luckiest is—it happened twice—to be in a bookstore where somebody is buying your book, or to hear somebody singing your song. To know people are getting a kick out of what you've done; they don't know who you are, but they know that you've done it—and it's very rewarding. I think kids are the one audience that's straightforward and honest in their reaction to everything. So you know that if you're doing well with them, they're not just saying it to be nice."

WORKS CITED:

Review of *Bob and Jack: A Boy and His Yak, Publishers Weekly,* October 19, 1992, p. 75.
Review of *The Butterfly Jar, New York Times Book Review,* March 4, 1990, p. 33.
LaBarbera, Kathryn, review of *The Butterfly Jar, Booklist,* February 1, 1990, p. 1093.
Lesser, Gerald S., *Children and Television: Lessons from Sesame Street,* Vintage Books, 1974, p. 240.
McGinn, Barbara S., review of *The Butterfly Jar, School Library Journal,* July, 1990, p. 86.
Moss, Jeff, telephone interview with Joanna Brod for *Something about the Author,* conducted August 27, 1992.

FOR MORE INFORMATION SEE:

PERIODICALS

Detroit Free Press, November 18, 1992.
Kirkus Reviews, November 15, 1989, p. 1674.
School Library Journal, March, 1984, p. 148.

—Sketch by Joanna Brod

N

NELSON, Peter N. 1953-

PERSONAL: Born February 8, 1953, in Minneapolis, MN; son of Newell N. (an economist) and Lois (a homemaker and secretary; maiden name, Jacobson) Nelson; married Diane Porcella, July 8, 1989. *Education:* Graduated cum laude and received B.A.s in both English and art from St. Olaf College, 1975; University of Iowa, M.F.A., 1979. *Politics:* Independent. *Hobbies and other interests:* "In my spare time I play with my dog, work in the garden, paint or draw, and I sometimes play piano in a country-western dance band."

ADDRESSES: Agent—Alice Martell, 555 Fifth Ave., New York, NY 10017.

CAREER: Free-lance journalist, 1981—. Teacher of creative writing at Rhode Island School of Design and St. Lawrence University.

AWARDS, HONORS: Michener Fellowship; Rhode Island State Arts Council grant for fiction, 1985; Massachusetts Artists Foundation Fellowship in playwriting, for *Crazytime;* Edgar Award nomination, Mystery Writers of America, 1992, for *Scarface.*

WRITINGS:

YOUNG ADULT NOVELS

Sylvia Smith-Smith, Crosswinds, 1987.
Fast Lane West, Simon & Schuster, 1991.
Night of Fire, Simon & Schuster, 1991.
Scarface, Simon & Schuster, 1991.
Deadly Games, Simon & Schuster, 1992.
Dangerous Waters, Simon & Schuster, 1992.
Double Dose, HarperCollins, 1992.
First to Die, HarperCollins, 1992.

OTHER

Real Man Tells All (collected columns), Viking, 1987.
Marry Like a Man, New American Library, 1992.

Also author of the screenplay *Crazytime.* Contributor of the "His" column to *Mademoiselle.* Contributor to

PETER N. NELSON

periodicals, including *Esquire, Harpers, New England Monthly, Redbook,* and *Special Report.*

SIDELIGHTS: Peter N. Nelson told *SATA:* "I was born on the eighth of February, 1953, in Minneapolis, Minnesota, the second of four children. My father, Newell N. Nelson, worked as an economist for General Mills until retiring in 1987. My mother, Lois, was a mother and later a secretary until she retired in 1989.

"I attended Washburn High School, in Minneapolis, and later St. Olaf College, in Northfield, Minnesota, majoring in art and English, bachelor degrees cum laude, 1975, my studies including a year at St. Peter's College in Oxford, England. I taught English and studied poetry at the University of Arizona, in Tucson, from 1976 to 1977, but transferred to the University of Iowa Writers' Workshop, in Iowa City, where I finished an M.F.A. in poetry in 1979. By the time I finished my degree, I was writing only fiction. In 1981, I received a James Michener Fellowship, an award given to promising first novelists, and moved to Portland, Oregon.

"The grant, which lasted a year and a half, bought me the time to establish myself as a free-lance writer. My very first publication appeared in *Esquire* in 1982, after which I moved to Providence, Rhode Island, where I taught creative writing at the Rhode Island School of Design (briefly), while making frequent trips to New York City to find magazine work. I continued to write both fiction and nonfiction throughout the 1980s. In 1992, I taught creative writing at St. Lawrence University in Canton, New York.

"My nonfiction has appeared in the Chicago *Tribune, Elle, Esquire, Glamour, Mademoiselle, Men's Life, Mother Jones, New England Monthly, Northwest Orient, Outside, Rolling Stone,* and other magazines, and for two years I wrote the 'His' column for *Mademoiselle,* those columns collected in a volume called *Real Man Tells All.*

"My fiction has appeared in *Esquire, Harpers, Iowa Review, Northwest Orient, Playboy, Redbook,* and *Seventeen.* My short stories appearing in *Seventeen* were collected in a volume named after the title character, Sylvia Smith-Smith, a girl whose mother had the same last name as her father but refused to take it when they married. Simon & Schuster has published the next five books of the series *Night of Fire, Fast Lane West, Scarface, Deadly Games* and *Dangerous Waters,* as well as a reprint of the original volume. HarperCollins has published a second series of young adult novels. *First to Die, Double Dose,* and *Third Degree* are the titles of the first three books. Three more are scheduled for 1993, and the series has been optioned by Viacom Productions as a possible television series.

"Sylvia Smith-Smith was based on a real girl I knew named Marah who hated anchovies. One night at dinner, when Marah was perhaps twelve years old, her stepfather and I tried to get her to eat a single anchovy. We each took a ten dollar bill from our wallets and laid the money on the table before her—hers for the consumption of a mere hairy fish. She refused, though twenty dollars is a lot of money for a twelve year old, even today. I admired her gumption so much that I wanted to put it into a story, and so Sylvia was born.

"How the career writing Sylvia Smith-Smith stories and books (as well as other young adult material) came about is equally accidental. I sold the first Sylvia story to *Seventeen* magazine. After it was published, my agent

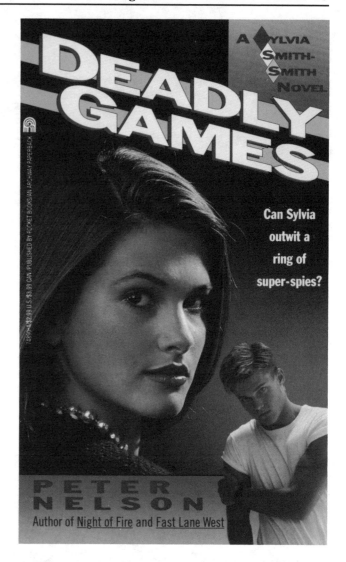

Sylvia Smith-Smith's trip to Oxford University becomes especially exciting when she becomes involved with computer genius Freddy St. Claire and a ring of spies.

called to say *Seventeen* really liked it and wondered if I had any more Sylvia stories. I said I did not. My agent, sounding puzzled, thought I did and advised me that, if I did, I should send them to *Seventeen.* I thought, well, 'duh' . . . and said I would. If I were to write another. I had no plans to do so. Several months later the fiction editor from *Seventeen* called and said, 'I don't want to pressure you, but the story is scheduled for March, and we need to know what it's about so we can get the art department started.' 'What *what's* about?' I asked. They had thought they'd assigned another Sylvia story, commissioned one, I should say, but my agent (my first one—I've since gotten another, for obvious reasons) had failed to accurately convey the message. 'Give me a week,' I told the fiction editor. I wrote one story, wasn't thrilled with it, wrote a second which I liked better, all in a week, mailed them both, and *Seventeen* bought them both. Three stories became a series, which became a book, which became a series of books . . .

"You never know, do you?"

NICKELL, Joe 1944-

PERSONAL: Born December 1, 1944, in Lexington, KY; son of James Wendell (a postmaster) and Ella Kathleen (a secretary and bookkeeper; maiden name, Turner) Nickell. *Education:* University of Kentucky, B.A., 1967, M.A., 1982, Ph.D., 1987. *Hobbies and other interests:* Collecting antique writing materials.

ADDRESSES: Home—P.O. Box 67, West Liberty, KY 41472. *Office*—1215 Office Tower, University of Kentucky, Lexington, KY 40506-0027.

CAREER: Volunteers in Service to America (VISTA), Washington, DC, volunteer worker in Carroll County, GA, 1967-68; stage magician, 1968-73; private investigator, 1973-75; Dawson City Museum, Dawson City, Yukon Territory, Canada, museologist, 1975-76; freelance investigative writer, 1976—; University of Kentucky, Lexington, technical writing instructor, 1980—.

MEMBER: Historical Confederation of Kentucky (member of executive committee, 1988—), Committee for the Scientific Investigation of Claims of the Paranormal (technical consultant, 1984-88; member of the executive council, 1988).

AWARDS, HONORS: Committee for the Scientific Investigation of Claims of the Paranormal fellow, 1988.

WRITINGS:

FOR CHILDREN

The Magic Detectives, self-illustrated, Prometheus Books, 1989.
Wonderworkers! How They Perform the Impossible, self-illustrated, Prometheus Books, 1991.

FOR ADULTS

Inquest on the Shroud of Turin, Prometheus Books, 1983.
(With John F. Fischer) *Secrets of the Supernatural,* Prometheus Books, 1988.
Pen, Ink & Evidence: A Study of Writing and Writing Materials for the Penman, Collector, and Document Detective, University Press of Kentucky, 1990.
Ambrose Pierce Is Missing and Other Historical Mysteries, University Press of Kentucky, 1992.
(With Robert A. Baker) *Missing Pieces: How to Investigate Ghosts, UFOs, Psychics, and Other Mysteries,* Prometheus Books, 1992.

Contributor to periodicals, including *Popular Photography, Journal of Police Science and Administration,* and *Skeptical Inquirer.*

WORK IN PROGRESS: Several articles and books.

SIDELIGHTS: Joe Nickell told *SATA:* "My background as a stage magician and private investigator naturally helped prepare me for my avocation of investigating strange mysteries—particularly such allegedly 'paranormal' topics as ghosts, Unidentified Flying Objects (UFOs), psychic powers, and the like. Since the late 1970s I have been associated with the Committee for the Scientific Investigation of Claims of the Paranormal (CSICOP), a scientific group founded by such scientists as Carl Sagan and Isaac Asimov. I soon became, in turn, Technical Consultant, Fellow, and member of the Executive Council.

"At our annual conference in 1987 in Pasadena, California, Dr. Sagan spoke about CSICOP's important message of critical thinking (that is, of careful, rational thought as opposed to superstitious, prejudicial, or other emotionally held beliefs.) He challenged us to direct our message not just to adults but to children as well. As a consequence, I was inspired to combine my former work of entertaining children as a magician and of writing books about the paranormal—the result being, thus far, two books that assist young readers in learning to discern between scientific and pseudoscientific concepts.

"*The Magic Detectives* (1989) features thirty paranormal mysteries embedded with clues; children about ages nine to fifteen are encouraged to try to solve each mystery before reading the solution actually reached by paranormal investigators. Cases include 'The Haunted Stairs,' 'The Vanished Tanker,' 'The Visions of Nostradamus,' and 'The Mummy's Curse.' *The Magic Detectives* was recommended by the *Journal of the Center for Children's Books.*

JOE NICKELL

"*Wonderworkers!* (1991) narrates the life stories of ten persons alleged to have magical powers, while making occasional, interesting digressions to explain how particular feats were actually accomplished. Included are biographies of 'The Man Who Walked through Walls' (Harry Houdini), 'The Human Magnet' (Lulu Hurst), 'The Sleeping Prophet' (Edgar Cayce), and 'Psychic Detective' (Peter Hurkos).

"From the feedback I have gotten from teachers, parents, and children themselves, it appears that children not only learn from these books, but also enjoy them."

* * *

NUGENT, Nicholas 1949-

PERSONAL: Born March 30, 1949, in Whitstable, Kent, England; son of Oliver (an attorney) and Mary Tudor (Witty) Nugent; married Duong Xuan (an interpreter), June 18, 1976; children: Benjamin, Timothy. *Education:* Queens' College, Cambridge University, B.A., 1971, M.A., 1974.

ADDRESSES: Home—16 Richmond Rd., West Wimbledon, London, SW20 0PQ, England. *Office*—BBC World Service, Bush House, London, WC2B 4PH, England.

CAREER: Broadcast journalist. Associated with the United Nations Children's Fund, beginning in 1971; associated with BBC World Service since 1974, began working in Thai language service, currently senior commentator in Eastern Service Topical Unit.

WRITINGS:

News from the Front, Macmillan, 1990.
World in View: India, Heinemann, 1990.
Rajiv Gandhi: Son of a Dynasty, BBC Books, 1990, revised, 1991.
World in View: Pakistan and Bangladesh, Heinemann, 1992.

SIDELIGHTS: "My writing and career as a broadcast journalist were strongly influenced by going to live and work in India straight from school," Nicholas Nugent told *SATA.* "I spent several months teaching at the famous Doon School, a boys' boarding school situated in the foothills of the Himalayan mountains, before returning to Britain to take my degree. I studied law, including Islamic law, but my main interest was in foreign affairs.

"After graduating I went to work for UNICEF in Indonesia, subsequently becoming liaison officer for Eastern Indonesia, including the Spice Islands. After traveling extensively through southeast Asia, I joined the BBC World Service, working firstly in its Thai

NICHOLAS NUGENT

language service and later in its Indonesian and Malay services. I now run the Eastern Service Topical Unit, which specializes in reporting from and political analysis of the region embracing Iran, Afghanistan, Pakistan, India, Sri Lanka, Bangladesh, Nepal, and Burma. In my time, I have reported for the BBC from Tehran to Tokyo, including from the important posts of Delhi and Singapore. One of my most challenging assignments was being flown into captured Iraqi territory by the Iranians during the Iran-Iraq war. I have also spent some time reporting on British affairs, and helping to run the BBC's network of foreign correspondents.

"My book writing is a sideline. My first book, *News from the Front,* aimed at children, tells of the life of an international radio reporter, and is based on my own experiences. I then accepted commissions to write firstly on India and then on Pakistan and Bangladesh for Heinemann Children's Reference "World in View" series of countries of the world. I know all three countries well. During periods spent reporting from India, I started writing a biography of Rajiv Gandhi. I had seen him come to power less than ten hours after his mother, Indira Gandhi, was assassinated in 1984, and was to see him assassinated too as he was on the verge of returning as prime minister of the world's most populous democracy. The resulting book shows how one family has dominated Indian politics for more than forty years."

P-Q

PARISH, Margaret Cecile 1927-1988
(Peggy Parish)

PERSONAL: Born in 1927, in Manning, SC; died November 19, 1988, of a ruptured aneurysm, in Manning, SC; daughter of Herman and Cecil (Rogers) Parish. *Education:* University of South Carolina, B.A., 1948; graduate study at George Peabody College for Teachers (now of Vanderbilt University), 1950.

CAREER: Writer. Also worked as a teacher in Oklahoma, Kentucky, and Texas; worked as an instructor in creative dancing, 1948-52, and in advertising; Dalton School, New York City, elementary school teacher for fifteen years. Children's book reviewer, "Carolina Today" television show, National Broadcasting Corp. (NBC) affiliate, Columbia, SC.

MEMBER: Authors Guild, Authors League of America, Delta Kappa Gamma.

AWARDS, HONORS: School Library Journal named *Dinosaur Time* one of the best books of the year, 1974; Garden State Children's Book Award, State of New Jersey, 1977, for *Dinosaur Time,* 1980, for *Teach Us, Amelia Bedelia,* and 1988; Palmetto State Award, 1977; Milner Award, City of Atlanta, 1984; Keystone State Children's Book Award, State of Pennsylvania, 1986.

WRITINGS:

UNDER NAME PEGGY PARISH

My Golden Book of Manners, illustrated by Richard Scarry, Golden Press, 1962.
Good Hunting, Little Indian, illustrated by Leonard Weisgard, Young Scott Books, 1962, revised edition published as *Good Hunting, Blue Sky,* illustrated by James Watts, Harper, 1988.
Let's Be Indians, illustrated by Arnold Lobel, Harper, 1962.
Willy Is My Brother, illustrated by Shirley Hughes, W. R. Scott, 1963.
Amelia Bedelia, illustrated by Fritz Siebel, Harper, 1963.

PEGGY PARISH

Thank You, Amelia Bedelia, illustrated by Siebel, Harper, 1964.
The Story of Grains: Wheat, Corn, and Rice, Grosset, 1965.
Amelia Bedelia and the Surprise Shower, illustrated by Siebel, Harper, 1966.
Key to the Treasure, illustrated by Paul Frame, Macmillan, 1966.
Let's Be Early Settlers with Daniel Boone, illustrated by Lobel, Harper, 1967.
Clues in the Woods, illustrated by Frame, Macmillan, 1968.
Little Indian, illustrated by John E. Johnson, Simon & Schuster, 1968.

A Beastly Circus, illustrated by Peter Parnall, Simon & Schuster, 1969.

Jumper Goes to School, illustrated by Cyndy Szekeres, Simon & Schuster, 1969.

Granny and the Indians, illustrated by Brinton Turkle, Macmillan, 1969.

Ootah's Lucky Day, illustrated by Mamoru Funai, Harper, 1970.

Granny and the Desperadoes, illustrated by Steven Kellogg, Macmillan, 1970.

Costumes to Make, illustrated by Lynn Sweat, Macmillan, 1970.

Snapping Turtle's All Wrong Day, illustrated by Johnson, Simon & Schuster, 1970.

Sheet Magic: Games, Toys, and Gifts from Old Sheets, illustrated by Sweat, Macmillan, 1971.

Haunted House, illustrated by Frame, Macmillan, 1971.

Come Back, Amelia Bedelia, illustrated by Wallace Tripp, Harper, 1971.

Granny, the Baby, and the Big Gray Thing, illustrated by Sweat, Macmillan, 1972.

Play Ball, Amelia Bedelia, illustrated by Tripp, Harper, 1972.

Too Many Rabbits, illustrated by Leonard Kessler, Macmillan, 1974.

Dinosaur Time, illustrated by Lobel, Harper, 1974.

December Decorations: A Holiday How-To Book, illustrated by Barbara Wolff, Macmillan, 1975.

Pirate Island Adventure, illustrated by Frame, Macmillan, 1975.

Good Work, Amelia Bedelia, illustrated by Sweat, Morrow, 1976.

Let's Celebrate: Holiday Decorations You Can Make, illustrated by Sweat, Morrow, 1976.

Teach Us, Amelia Bedelia, illustrated by Sweat, Morrow, 1977.

Hermit Dan, illustrated by Frame, Macmillan, 1977.

Mind Your Manners!, illustrated by Hafner, Greenwillow, 1978.

Zed and the Monsters, illustrated by Galdone, Doubleday, 1979.

Beginning Mobiles, illustrated by Sweat, Macmillan, 1979.

Amelia Bedelia Helps Out, illustrated by Sweat, Greenwillow, 1979.

Be Ready at Eight, illustrated by Kessler, Macmillan, 1979.

I Can, Can You?, four volumes, illustrated by Hafner, Greenwillow, 1980 (published in England as *See and Do Book Bag,* four volumes, MacRae, 1980).

Amelia Bedelia and the Baby, illustrated by Sweat, Greenwillow, 1981.

No More Monsters for Me!, illustrated by Simont, Harper, 1981.

Mr. Adams's Mistake, illustrated by Owens, Macmillan, 1982.

The Cats' Burglar, illustrated by Sweat, Greenwillow, 1983.

Hush, Hush, It's Sleepytime, illustrated by Leonid Pinchevsky, Western Publishing, 1984.

Amelia Bedelia Goes Camping, illustrated by Sweat, Greenwillow, 1985.

Merry Christmas, Amelia Bedelia, illustrated by Sweat, Greenwillow, 1986.

The Ghosts of Cougar Island, Dell, 1986.

Amelia Bedelia's Family Album, illustrated by Sweat, Greenwillow, 1988.

Scruffy, illustrated by Kelly Oechsli, Harper, 1988.

OTHER

Contributor of book reviews to newspapers. A collection of Parish's manuscripts is housed at the Kerlan Collection, University of Minnesota, Minneapolis.

ADAPTATIONS: Amelia Bedelia, Thank You, Amelia Bedelia, Come Back, Amelia Bedelia, and *Play Ball, Amelia Bedelia* have been adapted as film strips.

SIDELIGHTS: "Children have always been my life," Peggy Parish once commented, "so writing stories for children came naturally." The author of over 40 books for children, Parish wrote mysteries, craft books, and the popular "Amelia Bedelia" series. Parish's books sold over 7 million copies.

Amelia Bedelia, a maid who takes everything she is told literally, appeared in eleven books for young readers. Amelia's literal mindedness comes from reading cookbooks, where you must do exactly what it says. When

Parish's "Amelia Bedelia" series highlights the antics of a housekeeper who interprets the meanings of words literally—often with hilarious results. (Cover illustration by Wallace Tripp.)

Amelia is told to make a sponge cake, she uses real sponges in the recipe. When asked to stuff the Christmas stockings, she fills them with turkey dressing. When requested to dust the furniture, Amelia sprinkles dust on everything. ("At my house we undust the furniture," she says. "But each to his own way.")

According to Nancy Palmer in *School Library Journal*, "Amelia Bedelia is a model of well-intentioned mishap.... [She] has become such an institution and a welcome splash of comedy on the easy-reading shelf that one forgives the slightly patronizing domestic set-up." In the course of her adventures, Amelia goes camping (and "pitches the tent" right into the woods), plays baseball (running home after hitting the ball out of the park), and teaching school (yelling "hey, roll!" when the lesson plan says to call roll).

Enormously popular with beginning readers, the Amelia Bedelia books also teach that words can have several meanings. "Young children struggling to master odd usages will find enormous pleasure in Amelia Bedelia's misinterpretations," Judith Gloyer stated in *School Library Journal*. Writing in the *New York Times Book Review*, Cynthia Samuels noted: "No child can resist Amelia and her literal trips through the minefield of the English language—and no adult can fail to notice that she's usually right when she's wrong. Both parents and children can learn, as well, from Amelia's kind employers. Mr. and Mrs. Rogers always come to understand Amelia's confusion and to admit that the language, not the user, is the culprit."

"The things I have Amelia Bedelia do," Parish explained to Richard I. Ammon in *Teacher*, "must be plausible. When I was writing *Good Work, Amelia Bedelia* I thought of having her make a sponge cake in her own inimitable way. So, I spent one afternoon in the kitchen snipping pieces of a sponge into a cake batter. I didn't know whether it would get gooey, burn up or do what I hoped—stay like a sponge. Fortunately, the sponge stayed like a sponge and that's the way it is in the book."

To celebrate Amelia Bedelia's twenty-fifth "birthday" in 1988, her many readers were encouraged to send birthday greetings to Amelia through special mailboxes installed in bookstores and libraries across the country. Paulette C. Kaufmann, director of children's book marketing for Greenwillow, told Edwin McDowell in the *New York Times* about the celebration: "The contents of those mailboxes have been arriving daily— thousands of letters and drawings from children who have read and loved books about Amelia Bedelia."

In addition to her "Amelia Bedelia" series, Parish published a series of novels highlighting the adventures of siblings Liza, Bill, and Jed. First introduced in the author's 1968 work, *Key to the Treasure*, the three sleuths continue to follow treasure hunts and solve mysteries in four other books. *Clues in the Woods* involves the disappearance of several items from Liza, Bill, and Jed's house, including a puppy, a sweater, and

In this thriller, Liza, Bill and Jed move into a house that is reportedly haunted by the ghost of a previous owner. (Cover illustration by Paul Frame.)

some food. The three read of a group of runaway children in the area; to find out whether the children are the thieves, Liza, Bill, and Jed set a trap in the woods. In *Haunted House*, Liza, Bill, and Jed's family move into a house believed to be haunted by the ghost of its original owner. The children receive a series of mysterious coded messages, and decipher each one. The notes eventually lead the children into the woods, where they find a surprise gift and solve the mystery. Though *Library Journal* found *Haunted House*'s characters and plot weak, many reviewers felt that readers would enjoy the challenge of cracking the various codes.

Parish was also the author of a number of illustrated nonfiction books introducing young readers to basic crafts. Her 1970 work *Costumes to Make* contains step-by-step instructions for creating simple outfits suitable for plays or masquerade parties. The costumes suggested include biblical, historical, and storybook characters, as well as animals and Halloween spooks. *School Library Journal* contributor Mary I. Purucker commented that *Costumes to Make* will "enjoy a long welcome" on library shelves. In *Sheet Magic: Games, Toys, and Gifts from Old Sheets*, a work geared toward children ages six to nine, Parish demonstrates ways in which discarded bed sheets may be reused for sack races, blindman's

Bunny, Bunkins, and Judy Trudy surprise a thief in Parish's _The Cats' Burglar_. (Illustration by Lynn Sweat.)

bluff, tug-of-war, pin-the-nose-on-the-clown, indoor hopscotch, and other activities. The author includes directions for playing each game. Parish also explains how to use sheets to make toys and gifts, such as flags, parachutes, stuffed animals, dolls and doll clothing, mobiles, and aprons. Some of these may be embellished using braids and embroidery. Reviewers appreciated the author's detailed but easy to follow instructions, as well as illustrator Lynn Sweat's clear drawings and diagrams. Parish's other craft books include _December Decorations: A Holiday How-To Book, Let's Celebrate: Holiday Decorations You Can Make,_ and _Beginning Mobiles._

WORKS CITED:

Ammon, Richard I., "Amelia Bedelia: Sense, Stuff and Nonsense," _Teacher,_ May-June, 1980, pp. 41-43.

Gloyer, Judith, review of _Merry Christmas, Amelia Bedelia, School Library Journal,_ October, 1986, p. 111.

McDowell, Edwin, obituary for Peggy Parish, _New York Times,_ November 22, 1988.

Palmer, Nancy, review of _Amelia Bedelia Goes Camping, School Library Journal,_ May, 1985, p. 107.

Purucker, Mary I., review of _Costumes to Make, School Library Journal,_ September, 1970, p. 106

Samuels, Cynthia, review of _Amelia Bedelia Goes Camping, New York Times Book Review,_ March 10, 1985, p. 29.

FOR MORE INFORMATION SEE:

BOOKS

Children's Literature Review, Volume 22, Gale, 1990, pp. 152-169.

Norby, Shirley, and Gregory Ryan, _Famous Children's Authors,_ Dennison, 1988.

PERIODICALS

Bulletin of the Center for Children's Books, July-August, 1985, p. 213.

Kirkus Reviews, July, 1968, p. 691; January 15, 1971, pp. 52, 743; July 15, 1986, p. 1123; August 1, 1988, p. 1154.

Library Journal, May 15, 1971, p. 1821.

Publishers Weekly, July 23, 1979, pp. 159-160; December 23, 1988.

School Library Journal, January, 1989.

*   *   *

PARISH, Peggy
  See PARISH, Margaret Cecile

*   *   *

PHIPSON, Joan
  See FITZHARDINGE, Joan Margaret

*   *   *

QUINN, Patrick 1950-

PERSONAL: Born March 31, 1950, in St. Paul, MN; son of Joseph (a businessman) and Irene (a salesperson; maiden name, Costello) Quinn; married Mary Catherine Hren (an entrepreneur), December 27, 1975; children: Kelly, Gavin. _Education:_ University of Minnesota, M.S., 1976. _Politics:_ "I'm for it!" _Religion:_ "I'm for it!" _Hobbies and other interests:_ Songwriting, playing the guitar, basketball, golf, movies, select television shows, camping, history, biking.

ADDRESSES: Home—14160 Rolling Oaks Circle N.E., Prior Lake, MN 55372.

CAREER: New Prague Community Schools, New Prague, MN, speech and language pathologist, 1975—; writer. Basketball coach and guest lecturer at schools.

MEMBER: Minnesota Education Association.

WRITINGS:

(And illustrator) _Matthew Pinkowski's Special Summer,_ Kendall Green Publications, 1991.

WORK IN PROGRESS: "_The Fourth Sign of Spring,_ expected to be completed in the summer of '92. A deaf Native American boy rediscovers his heritage in north-

PATRICK QUINN

ern Minnesota in an adventure with his great-grandfather."

SIDELIGHTS: Patrick Quinn told *SATA:* "My motivation for writing is the enchanting enjoyment of the creative process. In addition to writing, I also enjoy painting and sketching.

"The actual catalyst for writing my first book was a car pool. One of the women in the car pool, Peggy, in addition to being a language arts teacher, is a writer. When she talked about her writing I was always coming up with suggestions for short stories or articles. Finally, Sandy, the other woman in the car pool, turned around and said to me in a somewhat scolding tone, 'You've got so many ideas, why don't you write?' It was one of those suggestions, among thousands one receives in a lifetime, that for some reason registers. I decided to see if I could write a novel. I was fortunate to have Peggy as a car pool partner and friend. She helped me tremendously with encouragement and in teaching me writing fundamentals. She also edited my manuscript a couple of times before I began sending it to publishers.

"The actual setting up of the plot and characters and the pacing and writing of dialogue don't come that hard for me. I really don't know why. I think I've been creative since childhood. I used to write and draw little 'Flintstones' comic books of my own design. I had a pretty vivid fantasy world. It was a world of cowboys and

horses and heroics and saving people's lives. I seem to remember having names for my shoes and I pretended to talk to them so they would help me run faster. My friends and I didn't play Superman; we *were* Superman. On Friday nights I would go to bed with my cowboy clothes on—holsters, six shooters, and red kerchief (and my cowboy boots if I could get away with it)—and my black hat on the bedpost.

"For me the hardest part about writing is making myself sit down. I usually enjoy the writing once I get going. I write about an hour or two at a crack. It keeps my material fresher if I'm fresher. I don't have to write at any particular time. It doesn't seem to matter as long as it's quiet. I do write on a word processor now, but the first book was actually written longhand. Ugh.

"With regard to the illustrating, I've drawn since I can remember. My parents, although not particularly artistic, were very encouraging with lots of 'oohs' and 'ahs' over anything I'd draw. My third grade teacher, Mrs. Curtis, would allow students to get a piece of scratch paper and draw if they finished an assignment early. I must have drawn two or three hundred horses that year. By the fourth grade I was considered one of the best drawers in my class and I got to work on the religious

Over the course of one magical summer, Matthew Pinkowski learns some important lessons about his own hidden talents. (Cover illustration by Laura Stutzmann.)

friezes that we would put up in our classroom. I usually got to draw Jesus. That was the highest art honor. My high school had no art classes at all (all college prep), but I continued to draw for recreation. In college a friend gave me a set of paints and I have continued to paint since then. I took a drawing class in the architecture department from a young man from Czechoslovakia who didn't speak any English and made us draw gourds. I got tired of drawing gourds and started putting faces on them, and thus wasn't taken very seriously the rest of the quarter.

"Some basic things I keep in mind when I write are: Be entertaining. Write about something you know about. Write about something you feel strongly about. Be entertaining. Use humor—it's the highest form of entertainment. Don't be too preachy. Mix in lots of dialogue. Avoid cliches. Avoid the word 'really.' Use all the senses in describing. Bring your readers to some place or circumstance they wouldn't normally visit. Vary the sentence structure. Be entertaining.

"Some themes I like to hit on are relationships, fear and courage, spiritual wonder (without being preachy or referring to specific religions), finding one's strengths, accepting things that are beyond our control, learning from experiences, and looking at life, situations, and relationships from a fresh perspective. That, perhaps, is

the reason people create. Artists point out the mysteries and magic behind the mundane. I like that."

Matthew Pinkowski's Special Summer features the adventures of thirteen-year-old Matthew, who yearns for summer vacations because his learning disability makes schoolwork so difficult for him. His group of summer friends includes Tommy, also learning disabled, and Laura, a deaf girl visiting her overprotective aunt and uncle. Matthew's confidence builds when he and his friends solve a boat theft, leaving him more optimistic about returning to school. "It is pleasantly surprising to read a book about a coed group of teen friends where hormones have not yet completely taken over their bodies, minds, and souls," Susan R. Farber wrote in *Voice of Youth Advocates.* Christine A. Moesch, writing in *School Library Journal,* praised the book for its portrayal of Laura, and described the writing as "brisk" with a "slightly sophisticated humor" that children will enjoy.

WORKS CITED:

Farber, Susan R., review of *Matthew Pinkowski's Special Summer, Voice of Youth Advocates,* February, 1992, p. 374.

Moesch, Christine A., review of *Matthew Pinkowski's Special Summer, School Library Journal,* August, 1991, p. 168.

R

REEF, Catherine 1951-

PERSONAL: Born April 28, 1951, in New York, NY; daughter of Walter H. Preston, Jr. (an advertising executive) and Patricia Preziosi (a teacher; maiden name, Deeley); married John W. Reef (a physical scientist), March 13, 1971; children: John Stephen. *Education:* Washington State University, B.A., 1983. *Hobbies and other interests:* Reading, music, handicrafts.

ADDRESSES: Home and office—9942 Lake Landing Rd., Gaithersburg, MD 20879.

CAREER: Taking Care (a health education newsletter), Reston, VA, editor, 1985-90; children's book author, 1990—.

MEMBER: Society of Children's Book Writers.

WRITINGS:

Washington, DC, Dillon, 1990.
Baltimore, Dillon, 1990.
Albert Einstein: Scientist of the Twentieth Century, Dillon, 1991.
Arlington National Cemetery, Dillon, 1991.
Monticello, Dillon, 1991.
Ellis Island, Dillon, 1991.
Rachel Carson: The Wonder of Nature, Twenty-First Century Books, 1992.
Henry David Thoreau: A Neighbor to Nature, Twenty-First Century Books, 1992.
Jacques Cousteau: Champion of the Sea, Twenty-First Century Books, 1992.
Gettysburg, Dillon, 1992.
Mount Vernon, Dillon, 1992.
Benjamin Davis, Jr., Twenty-First Century Books, 1992.
Colin Powell, Twenty-First Century Books, 1992.

WORK IN PROGRESS: Buffalo Soldiers and *Civil War Soldiers,* books about African-Americans in the military; a new series on staying healthy.

CATHERINE REEF

SIDELIGHTS: Catherine Reef told *SATA:* "I grew up in Commack, New York, a flat, spreading Long Island town, during the 1950s and 1960s. It was a town where most people lived in clean, new split-level or ranch houses on treeless land that had been farmers' fields.

"My house was different. I lived in one of Commack's few old houses, a place with carved woodwork and a yard full of trees. That backyard seemed enormous, and it beckoned my friends and me to imaginative play. There was an ancient apple tree, bent-over and climber-

In this colorful biography, Reef explores the life of famed French undersea explorer Jacques Cousteau.

friendly, where we acted out stories of loss and rescue. There was a sky-high pine tree from which a tire hung on a rope. We often would swing, heads leaning back and faces pointing up through the branches, and imagine that we could fly.

"Sometimes I played indoors on my bedroom floor with my dolls and stuffed animals lined up in front of me. The game was school, and it could last for hours. The dolls and toys were the pupils, and I was their teacher.

"If there ever was an energetic teacher, I was she! I planned lessons and lectured to my students on science and geography. I taught them to form letters and numbers, and to add and subtract. I made all of their textbooks and work sheets by hand, and I completed every assignment for everyone in my class. Then I corrected all of the work and handed it back.

"I read to my class, too, because I loved to read stories and poems. Literature never meant more to me than when I was a child. Dr. Seuss's books were among my early favorites, and I read them so often that I committed them to memory. (I can still recite long sections of *The Cat in the Hat* and *Happy Birthday to You!*) I loved the poems of English fiction writer and playwright A. A. Milne and turned my favorites into songs. I delighted in the silly, unreal characters of American journalist and playwright L. Frank Baum's Oz stories.

"Books brought scenes and characters to life in my imagination. They expressed wonder, love, humor, and sorrow. They taught me that language is a powerful tool.

Words are an artist's medium. Like clay, they can be molded into something beautiful.

"I also wrote poems and stories of my own. Some high-school boys I knew printed a small newspaper. How proud I was when they published one of my stories—the all-but-forgotten 'I Am a Dishwasher'!

"I kept on reading and writing as I got older, but I developed other interests as well. As a teenager I loved to draw with pastels, pencils, and charcoal. I acted in two school plays. I listened to music for hours at a time. I learned to knit and sew.

"And by the time I reached college, I had so many interests that I couldn't decide what to do—and so I did nothing. I felt bored with college and left after my first classes ended. I took a job as a secretary and soon got married.

"Then, nearly a decade later, when I was 28 years old and the mother of a young son, I decided that I wanted an education. I was finally ready to go to college. I still didn't know what to choose as a major, or main subject of study, but this time I didn't worry about it. I took classes in a variety of subjects, and I developed even more interests than I already had. I studied history, psychology, anthropology, and science. I also took courses in literature and writing, and I found that I liked writing best of all.

"Creating with the English language offered greater possibilities and deeper satisfaction than working with pastels or yarn or fabric. I realized, too, that my many interests stem from the fact that I love to learn—and so writing was right up my alley.

"To me, one of the best parts of writing nonfiction is doing the necessary research. I feel lucky to spend my time gathering information on the lives and work of famous people, learning about life in years gone by, talking with scientists and historians, and traveling to historic places.

"Writing lets me learn in other ways as well. As I organize and evaluate the facts that I have gathered, I gain insights into human nature and my own beliefs. I better understand the time in which I live by understanding times gone by. As I write, I continue to learn about using the language. I continue to become a more competent, more creative writer.

"I have always been interested in the human side of history. I prefer to read about how people lived and thought in the past than to memorize dates or pore over accounts of battles. I try, in my books, to bring the human stories in history to life. When I write about a famous person, whether it's George Washington, American government official Colin Powell, or French oceanographer Jacques Cousteau, I try to give a complete portrait of the person. I emphasize not just his or her outstanding accomplishments, but his or her activities outside of public life as well—how the person played as

GETTYSBURG

By Catherine Reef

Reef's desire to educate and inform readers through her writing is evident in this work about the site of one of the most important battles of the Civil War.

a child, what he or she was like as a parent, what kinds of hobbies the person enjoyed.

"I never became the classroom teacher that I pretended to be as a child, but I work as a teacher through my writing. For five years I wrote a newsletter about health for adults called *Taking Care.* My articles gave people information they needed to stay healthy. It was an interesting job that taught me a lot, but I wanted to do something more.

"When I tried writing a book for children, I liked it right away. Here was something that would enable me to keep on learning—about all kinds of subjects—for the rest of my life. By writing children's books, I could remain a teacher and share what I had learned with a very important group of readers.

"I enjoy thinking that my son, and the other children I know, will read what I write. I like to think about the many young people I've never met who will gain knowledge and pleasure from my books.

"But I also write for another person—the girl who climbed the crooked apple tree and read out loud to her dolls. I get to know her better as I think about what she

would like to read; at the same time, I get a deeper understanding of the woman I am today."

*   *   *

RIGGIO, Anita 1952-

PERSONAL: Born December 2, 1952, in Passaic, NJ; daughter of Frank Domenic (in business) and Clotilda (a homemaker; maiden name, Taranto) Riggio; married Roland George Axelson (an educator and administrator), July 19, 1975; children: Cloe, Lucas. *Education:* Attended Hartford Art School, 1970-72; University of Hartford, B.A., 1974. *Religion:* Christian. *Hobbies and other interests:* Playing piano, walking, reading, cooking for family and friends, gardening, flower arranging.

ADDRESSES: Home and office—503 Main St., Wethersfield, CT 06109. *Agent*—Kirchoff/Wohlberg, 866 United Nations Plaza, Suite 525, New York, NY 10017.

CAREER: American School for the Deaf, West Hartford, CT, art and language arts teacher, 1974-79; illustrator and writer, 1977—; National Broadcasting Company (NBC), CT, courtroom illustrator for WVIT news, 1983-85; Hartford College for Women, Hartford, CT, lecturer in writing and illustrating for children, 1983-85; University of Hartford Art School, West Hartford, CT, adjunct faculty member, 1985-89; Farmington Valley Arts Center, Farmington, CT, lecturer in illustration, 1986. Gives lectures and presentations on writing and illustrating children's books at schools, libraries, and organizations.

MEMBER: Society of Children's Book Writers and Illustrators (member of New England regional advisory board, 1990-92; New England regional coordinator, 1992—).

WRITINGS:

SELF-ILLUSTRATED; PICTURE BOOKS

Wake Up, William!, Atheneum, 1987.
Gert & Frieda, Atheneum, 1990.
A Moon in My Teacup, Boyds Mills, 1993.
Beware the Brindlebeast, Boyds Mills, in press.

ILLUSTRATOR

Margery Facklam, *I Go to Sleep* (picture book), Little, Brown, 1987.
Facklam, *I Eat Dinner* (picture book), Little, Brown, 1987.
Julie Schmidt, *The Apartment House* (picture book), Abingdon, 1988.
Elizabeth McHugh, *Beethoven's Cat,* Atheneum, 1988.
McHugh, *Wiggie Wins the West,* Atheneum, 1989.
Jamie Gilson, *Hobie Hanson, Greatest Hero of the Mall,* Lothrop, 1989.
Karen Waggoner, *Dad Gummit and Ma Foot* (picture book), Orchard Books, 1990.
Michelle Dionetti, *Coal Mine Peaches* (picture book), Orchard Books, 1991.
Bonnie Pryor, *Jumping Jenny,* Morrow, 1992.

ANITA RIGGIO

Pegi Deitz Shea, *Stitches* (picture book), Boyds Mills, in press.

WORK IN PROGRESS: Shake Hands with Happiness (tentative title), a picture book about "a malcontent who learns pencil tricks and encounters happiness along the way"; *Always Gert and Frieda* (tentative title), a sequel to *Gert and Frieda* in which Gert wins a trip around the world.

SIDELIGHTS: Anita Riggio told *SATA:* "I was raised in Clifton, New Jersey, the middle child of five. Our home was the hub of a large, extended Italian-American family, so I grew up, quite literally, at the center of a family teeming with fascinating characters of all attitudes, appearances, and demeanors. It was, undoubtedly, the child's keen observation of and loving interaction with these assorted relatives that contributed to my becoming an artist and writer as an adult. For included in this inexhaustible font of characters were Aunt Ellen, the spinster who played classical piano, and Uncle Jim, who played ragtime. A detective for the New Jersey State Troopers, Uncle Chet told great whodunits. Aunt Margaret, a thoroughly Irish in-law and former school principal, gently corrected our grammar with smiles and brownies. Aunt Alba had flaming red hair and always arrived hours late, with Uncle Augie, bald and round as a cue ball, in tow. Aunt Edie was an artist whose house smelled of turpentine and tomato sauce, and whose husband, Uncle Bob, was given to telling stories in some undefinable accent. Aunt Mary had an infectious laugh, told great jokes, and always called me 'Sarah Bernhardt.' And there were many others.

"Equally as significant to my becoming an illustrator was my great fortune in studying with one wonderful art teacher during my high school years. Sister Irene Marie taught me—in addition to technique—to trust my instincts as an artist. She gave me confidence; she taught me courage and resolve. At college, though, I floundered as an art major and graduated, finally, with a B.A. in theatre. Serendipity stepped in, and I found myself learning sign language and teaching English, and later, art to children at the American School for the Deaf in West Hartford, Connecticut.

"As a teacher I was finally introduced to the wonders of literature and art for children. By the time I married and had our daughter and son, my interest in children's books had blossomed into an abiding passion. With my children, I spent hours reading books, and steeped myself in the art of illustrators whose work I admired—in particular, Trina Schart Hyman, Charles Mikolaycak, Garth Williams, Paul Galdone, Margot Zemach, Hilary Knight, Maurice Sendak, and others.

"I wrote *Gert & Frieda* in celebration of a very special relationship that I share with my dear friend Alice, to whom it is dedicated. When the idea first came to me, I decided that I would model one character after Alice and the other after myself. Swell idea, but it didn't work, at first, because we are so much alike. It occurred to me then that other duos are comprised of two very distinct personalities: Rocky and Bullwinkle, Lucy and Ethel, Bert and Ernie. And so, too, Gert and Frieda: Frieda would moan, Gert would soothe; Frieda would be in crisis, Gert would be calm; Frieda had the questions, Gert had the answers. Sometimes.

"I loved *Dad Gummit and Ma Foot* from the moment I read it. For many reasons, this text is an illustrator's dream. Because it spans half a century, I had to age the characters from young lovers to crotchety old folks who had remained separate from one another for a lifetime because of a foolish quarrel.

"My wonderful mother-in-law, Alice Carlson Axelson, served as the model for Ma Foot. The minister emeritus of Immanuel Congregational Church in Hartford, Connecticut was the model for Dad Gummit. The art for the book was done in watercolor because I hoped the paintings would look like memory. The setting I chose is based on Collinsville, Connecticut, a factory town that manufactured hatchets and machetes during the Civil War. With the help of Margaret H. Perry, town librarian and historian, I found old photographs and postcards of the town that proved invaluable in authenticating the setting of my paintings. I also constructed a miniature church and several houses similar to those around the green in Collinsville. Costume research was done on several sweltering summer afternoons at the Connecticut Historical Society. And I found many wonderful period objects—most notably, Ma Foot's black stove—at the Canton Historical Museum in Collinsville.

"Although I did not write *Coal Mine Peaches,* the author's family history and experiences are remarkably like my own. My grandfather, like Michelle Dionetti's, worked as a 'slate picker' in a coal mine in Pennsylvania when he immigrated from Sicily. Additionally, he worked as a laborer, laying tracks for railroads. It was more than four years before he was able to send passage—in steerage—for his young wife and their baby daughter, whom my grandfather had never seen. Illustrating this book has become even more personal because my father and mother serve as the models for the grandfather and grandmother. My brother and sisters and nine-year-old son Lucas appear as Andrew, Aunt Louise, Uncle Dom, et al., and my daughter Cloe modelled for the narrator.

"*A Moon in my Teacup* took two years to write, but the initial images—childhood memories—came quickly, as palpable as the aroma of a neighborhood bakery. It happened like this: One evening I was playing the piano—Gershwin, Berlin, some show tunes. Then I began to play some sonatinas that I hadn't played since I was a child. All at once, the memory of playing those sweet sonatinas on Sundays in the parlor of my grandparents' house came flooding back. The memories were so strong that I was moved to leave the keyboard of the piano and go to the keyboard of the computer. *A Moon in my Teacup* began, then, as a series of Sunday visits

Members of Riggio's family served as models for her illustrations in Michelle Dionetti's *Coal Mine Peaches*.

throughout the year, strung together like beads on a necklace.

"One day, I shared an early version of this manuscript with one of my sisters, Maryellen. We talked at great length about making the journey to the bathroom at the top of the dark, spooky stairs, the footed porcelain tub, the soap that was the color of my grandmother's hairpins. We reminisced about the piles of Grandma's cookies, the smell of the old lace tablecloth, and about having tea from real china cups. 'Don't forget the lights in the teacups,' Maryellen reminded me. And so the mesmerizing reflection of the overhead chandelier became the 'moon' which leads the narrator, as the Christmas star led others long ago."

FOR MORE INFORMATION SEE:

PERIODICALS

Booklist, September 1, 1991.
Bulletin of the Center for Children's Books, September, 1991.
First for Women, January, 1991.
Hartford Courant, May 12, 1991, p. G1.
Horn Book, Jan-Feb, 1992, p. 56.
Kirkus Reviews, July 1, 1991.

*   *   *

ROBERTUS, Polly M. 1948-

PERSONAL: Surname is pronounced "row-bert-us"; born January 16, 1948, in Denver, CO; daughter of John Clinton Mohler (a journalist) and Dorothy May (Davis) Schell; married Jon D. Robertus (a professor of chemistry), August 28, 1971; children: David, Clare, Kate. *Education:* University of California, San Diego, B.A. (with honors), 1970; attending University of Texas at Austin, 1991—. *Politics:* "Reasonable."

CAREER: Writer. Girl Scout leader; member of neighborhood association board.

WRITINGS:

The Dog Who Had Kittens, Holiday House, 1991.

Contributor of stories to *Cricket.*

WORK IN PROGRESS: Teacup, a novel for children; poetry for young adults; reviews.

SIDELIGHTS: Polly M. Robertus told *SATA:* "I always wanted to be a writer, but for many years that's as far as I got. I didn't know how authors worked. I thought that I had to have the whole idea in my head before I started, and that I should start with 'Chapter One' and write in complete, perfectly grammatical sentences all the way to 'The End.' Now I know that I have to start writing in order to *discover* what I'm going to write about, and that I can do draft after draft after draft, each one representing a larger discovery of what a piece is to become.

POLLY M. ROBERTUS

"My book, *The Dog Who Had Kittens,* came about this way: One day I was casting about for an idea and decided to make a list of made-up titles without thinking about it very much as I went—just write fifteen or so titles very quickly. When I was done, I read back over the list just as I might look at titles on spines of books on a shelf. I was most surprised to see: 'The Dog Who Had Kittens.' I liked the sound of it, and immediately was reminded of an incident that I had entirely forgotten about.

"What had happened was that I'd gone to pick up my oldest daughter at her friend's house, and they'd invited me in to see their new kittens. When I got in, their little dog wouldn't let me anywhere near the kittens; he or she jumped in the box with them and barked at me. My daughter's friend said, 'Our dog is a better mother to those kittens than their own mother!'

"Well, I had already written a story that appeared in *Cricket* about a dog, a cat, and a bird, so I had my mother cat and my dog already, and I went to work. But after the dog became attached to the kittens I couldn't think how to end the story and had to put it away for a while. (I've discovered that there's an important difference between an interesting *incident* and a satisfying *story*). Then one day I got to thinking about just what *would* happen, over time, to those kittens. And I realized, of course! They would grow up and leave home! What would that do to poor Baxter?

"I started to write, and as I did, I got a very clear picture of the last scene of the book, Baxter and Eloise in the moonlit kitten box, comforting each other.

"I love writing. I'm finally accomplishing my dream of writing a lot, every day, without worrying of what the product will be. I trust the process and all my experience

as a human being, a reader, and a writer, to take care of the end result; I just show up and get to work."

*   *   *

RODENAS, Paula

PERSONAL: Born January 17, in New York, NY; daughter of Morton (an attorney) and Sophia (a homemaker; maiden name, Kronick) Peyser; married J. Alexander Rodenas (deceased), November 20, 1958; children: Jeffrey, Kenneth. *Education:* New York University, B.A.; attended William Smith College and University of Madrid.

ADDRESSES: Home—77 Crest Rd., Merrick, NY 11566.

CAREER: Writer, journalist, and columnist. Writes for several magazines, including *Chronicle of the Horse, Horseplay, Horse Directory,* and *Horsemen's Yankee Peddlar.* Worked four years in media relations for Belmont Horse Fair.

MEMBER: Press Club of Long Island.

AWARDS, HONORS: Press Club Awards; Gold Medal, Arpad Academy, for *The De Nemethy Years.*

WRITINGS:

The De Nemethy Years, Arco, 1983.
The Random House Book of Horses and Horsemanship, Random House, 1991.

Occasional columnist for *Newsday Sports.* Contributor to newspapers and magazines. News editor, *America's Equestrian.*

WORK IN PROGRESS: Pepe Goes to the Fair, based on a visit in 1983 to the Jerez Horse Fair in Spain, and previously published as a short story in *Carousel;* developing ideas for children's fiction.

SIDELIGHTS: Paula Rodenas told *SATA:* "As a child, I was an avid reader. I loved horses and devoured every book by Marguerite Henry and Walter Farley. I made up my mind that I wanted to write about horses. As an adult, I managed to write for equestrian newsletters and magazines, but did not publish my first book until 1983. Still, I wanted to write something specifically for children, so when the opportunity arose to do *The Random House Book of Horses and Horsemanship,* I jumped at it. I applied all the practical knowledge I had from years of riding, as well as research in libraries and stables, which I vastly enjoyed.

"I would very much like to write fiction for children, using foreign settings and experiences from my own travels. My work as a journalist has taken me to such places as Iceland, Spain, Holland, Ireland, and other countries, and I believe that, through the horses, children can learn a lot about other cultures.

"Although I love journalism, I believe that writers should not be 'typecast' like Hollywood actors. I believe that a writer should be able to reach adults and children and produce both fiction and non-fiction. Writing from experience is the best way to be successful. If you have a special area of interest, use it! I advise children to follow their interests by reading as much as possible, and I'd like to urge parents not to discourage them—reading of any kind is of value. Children depend too much on TV today. A book stretches the imagination, builds vocabulary and makes the reader *think.*"

S

SCOTTI, Anna
See COATES, Anna

*   *   *

SELDEN, George
See THOMPSON, George Selden

*   *   *

SERRAILLIER, Ian (Lucien) 1912-

PERSONAL: Born September 24, 1912, in London, England; son of Lucien and Mary (Rodger) Serraillier; married Anne Margaret Rogers, 1944; children: Helen, Jane, Christine Anne, Andrew. *Education:* St. Edmund Hall, Oxford, M.A., 1935. *Hobbies and other interests:* Mountain walking, skiing, swimming.

ADDRESSES: Home—Singleton, Chichester, Sussex PO18 0HA, England.

CAREER: Wycliffe College, Stonehouse, Gloucestershire, England, schoolmaster, 1936-39; Dudley Grammar School, Dudley, Worcestershire, England, teacher, 1939-46; Midhurst Grammar School, Midhurst, Sussex, England, teacher, 1946-61; writer.

AWARDS, HONORS: New York Times Best Illustrated Book citation, 1953, for *Florina and the Wild Bird;* Carnegie Medal commendation, 1956, Spring Book Festival Award, 1959, and Boys' Clubs of America Junior Book Award, 1960, all for *The Silver Sword.*

WRITINGS:

(Contributor) *Three New Poets: Roy McFadden, Alex Comfort, Ian Serraillier,* Grey Walls Press, 1942.
(Self-illustrated) *The Weaver Birds* (poems), Macmillan, 1944.
Thomas and the Sparrow (poems), illustrated by Mark Severin, Oxford University Press, 1946.
They Raced for Treasure, illustrated by C. Walter Hodges, J. Cape, 1946, simplified educational edi-

tion published as *Treasure Ahead,* Heinemann, 1954.
Flight to Adventure, illustrated by Hodges, J. Cape, 1947, simplified educational edition published as *Mountain Rescue,* Heinemann, 1955.
Captain Bounsaboard and the Pirates, illustrated by Michael Bartlett and Arline Braybrooke, J. Cape, 1949.
The Monster Horse (poems), illustrated by Severin, Oxford University Press, 1950.
There's No Escape, illustrated by Hodges, J. Cape, 1950, educational edition, Heinemann, 1952, Scholastic, 1973.
The Ballad of Kon-Tiki and Other Verses, illustrated by Severin, Oxford University Press, 1952.
Belinda and the Swans, illustrated by Pat Marriott, J. Cape, 1952.
(Translator with wife, Anne Serraillier) Selina Choenz, *Florina and the Wild Bird,* illustrated by Alois Carigiet, Oxford University Press, 1952.
(Editor with Ronald Ridout) *Wide Horizon Reading Scheme,* four volumes, Heinemann, 1953-55.
Jungle Adventure (based on a story by R. M. Ballantyne), illustrated by Vera Jarman, Heinemann, 1953.
(Translator) *Beowulf the Warrior,* illustrated by Severin, Oxford University Press, 1954, Walck, 1961.
The Adventures of Dick Varley (based on a story by Ballantyne), illustrated by Jarman, Heinemann, 1954.
Everest Climbed (poem), illustrated by Leonard Rosoman, Oxford University Press, 1955.
Making Good, illustrated by Jarman, Heinemann, 1955.
The Silver Sword, illustrated by Hodges, J. Cape, 1956, educational edition, Heinemann, 1957, Criterion, 1958, published as *Escape from Warsaw,* Scholastic, 1963.
Guns in the Wild (based on a story by Ballantyne), illustrated by Shirley Hughes, Heinemann, 1956.
Katy at Home (based on a story by Susan Coolidge), illustrated by Hughes, Heinemann, 1957.
Poems and Pictures, Heinemann, 1958.
(Contributor) Eleanor Graham, editor, *A Puffin Quartet of Poets: Eleanor Farjeon, James Reeves, E. V. Rieu,*

IAN SERRAILLIER

Ian Serraillier, illustrated by Diana Bloomfield, Penguin, 1958, revised edition, 1964.

Katy at School (based on a story by Coolidge), illustrated by Hughes, Heinemann, 1959.

The Ivory Horn (adaptation of *The Song of Roland,* an early 12th century *chanson de geste* sometimes attributed to Turoldus), illustrated by William Stobbs, Oxford University Press, 1960, educational edition, Heinemann, 1962.

The Gorgon's Head: The Story of Perseus, illustrated by Stobbs, Oxford University Press, 1961, Walck, 1962.

The Way of Danger: The Story of Theseus, illustrated by Stobbs, Oxford University Press, 1962, Walck, 1963.

The Windmill Book of Ballads, illustrated by Severin and Rosoman, Heinemann, 1962.

Happily Ever After, illustrated by Brian Wildsmith, Oxford University Press, 1963.

The Clashing Rocks: The Story of Jason, illustrated by Stobbs, Oxford University Press, 1963, Walck, 1964.

The Midnight Thief: A Musical Story, music by Richard Rodney Bennett, illustrated by Tellosa, BBC Publications, 1963.

The Enchanted Island: Stories from Shakespeare, illustrated by Peter Farmer, Walck, 1964, educational edition published as *Murder at Dunsinane,* Scholastic, 1967.

The Cave of Death, illustrated by Stuart Tresilian, Heinemann, 1965.

Fight for Freedom, illustrated by John S. Goodall, Heinemann, 1965.

Ahmet the Woodseller: A Musical Story, music by Gordon Crosse, illustrated by John Griffiths, Oxford University Press, 1965.

The Way of Danger [and] *The Gorgon's Head,* educational edition, Heinemann, 1965.

A Fall from the Sky: The Story of Daedalus, illustrated by Stobbs, Nelson, 1966, Walck, 1966.

The Challenge of the Green Knight, illustrated by Victor Ambrus, Oxford University Press, 1966, Walck, 1967.

Robin in the Greenwood, illustrated by Ambrus, Oxford University Press, 1967, Walck, 1968.

Chaucer and His World (nonfiction), Lutterworth, 1967, Walck, 1968.

The Turtle Drum (musical story), music by Malcolm Arnold, illustrated by Charles Pickard, BBC Publications, 1967, Oxford University Press, 1968.

Havelok the Dane, illustrated by Elaine Raphael, Walck, 1967 (published in England as *Havelok the Warrior,* Hamish Hamilton, 1968).

Robin and His Merry Men, illustrated by Ambrus, Oxford University Press, 1969, Walck, 1970.

The Tale of Three Landlubbers, illustrated by Raymond Briggs, Hamish Hamilton, 1970, Coward McCann, 1971.

Heracles the Strong, illustrated by Rocco Negri, Walck, 1970, illustrated by Graham Humphreys, Oxford University Press, 1971.

The Ballad of St. Simeon, illustrated by Simon Stern, F. Watts, 1970, Kaye and Ward, 1970.

A Pride of Lions (musical story; produced in Nottingham, England, 1970), music by Phyllis Tate, Oxford University Press, 1971.

The Bishop and the Devil, illustrated by Stern, Kaye and Ward, 1971, F. Watts, 1971.

Have You Got Your Ticket?, illustrated by Douglas Hall, Longman, 1972.

Marko's Wedding, illustrated by Ambrus, Deutsch, 1972.

The Franklin's Tale, Retold, illustrated by Philip Gough, Warne, 1972.

I'll Tell You a Tale: A Collection of Poems and Ballads, illustrated by Charles Keeping and Renate Meyer, Longman, 1973, revised edition, Kestrel Books, 1976.

Pop Festival (reader), illustrated by Hall, Longman, 1973.

Suppose You Met a Witch, illustrated by Ed Emberley, Little, Brown, 1973.

The Robin and the Wren, illustrated by Fritz Wegner, Longman, 1974.

How Happily She Laughs and Other Poems, Longman, 1976.

The Sun Goes Free (reader), Longman, 1977.

The Road to Canterbury, illustrated by John Lawrence, Kestrel Books, 1979.

All Change at Singleton: For Charlton, Goodwood, East and West Dean (local history), Phillimore, 1979.

(With Richard Pailthorpe) *Goodwood Country in Old Photographs,* Sutton, 1987.

Founder and editor with Anne Serraillier, New Windmill series of contemporary literature, published by Heinemann Educational Books.

ADAPTATIONS: The Silver Sword inspired a BBC-TV television series, 1957, and was dramatized as *The Play of the Silver Sword* by Stuart Henson, published by

Heinemann Educational Books, 1982, and produced in Oldham, England, 1983.

SIDELIGHTS: Ian Serraillier has tackled the ambitious task of interpreting some of world literature's classic stories for young audiences. Himself a poet, Serraillier also draws upon his knowledge of ancient Greek, Latin, and other archaic tongues to produce readable—and poetic—versions of old myths and ballads. Through Serraillier's efforts, the tales of Sir Gawain, Jason, Heracles, and Beowulf have become accessible to children who might otherwise never approach the original works.

A *Times Literary Supplement* reviewer notes that in his translations for children, Serraillier "has very skilfully succeeded in preserving colour, rhythm and phrase while presenting a more immediately comprehensible language." A *Junior Bookshelf* contributor likewise calls Serraillier "our finest poet writing for the young."

The author has also earned praise for his original writings, many of which draw upon his own experiences as a mountain climber in the Swiss Alps. The best known of Serraillier's novels for children is *The Silver Sword,* a World War II adventure that pits several

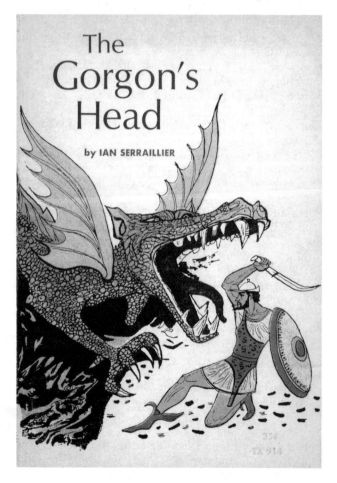

Serraillier's love for the classics led him to retell tales about figures from mythology such as noble Perseus and the evil Gorgon. (Cover illustration by William Stubbs.)

intrepid children against the rigors of nature and the violence of the German army. In his book *The Nesbit Tradition: The Children's Novel in England 1945-1970,* Marcus Crouch describes *The Silver Sword* as "a book which one cannot read without profound emotional response and personal involvement."

"I cannot remember a time when I did not want to become a writer," the author notes in *Something about the Author Autobiography Series (SAAS).* "I was always practising, even while I was still at school, where we were brought up on Latin and Greek and hardly any English—a dry and rather indigestible mixture it might seem today." The oldest of four children, Serraillier was born in London in 1912. His father died when the author was only seven, and his mother's own frail health often kept her in Switzerland where the mountain air helped to abate her asthma. From an early age Serraillier and his brother went to Brighton College, a boarding prep school in Sussex.

Serraillier's best memories of childhood center around his vacation-time visits to Switzerland. There he developed a passion for mountain climbing, going on an expedition to the Matterhorn when he was only sixteen. He also became an experienced downhill skier, and he explored the mountains in all sorts of weather—fair and foul.

Serraillier won a scholarship to St. Edmund Hall, Oxford University, where he studied classics and English literature. After graduating from college with a Master's degree in 1935, he became a schoolmaster. "For many years teaching was my livelihood, and most of my writing was done in school vacations," he remembered in the *Third Book of Junior Authors.* "Much as I enjoyed teaching, I had always wanted to be a writer, and I was glad when I was able to make it a full-time occupation."

As a teacher and a poet, Serraillier discovered that the best stories were those that had stood the test of time— Greek legends, folk tales, fairy tales, and ballads. He told the *Third Book of Junior Authors* that often these works "need reinterpreting for each generation, and I enjoy re-telling them whether in prose or in verse." Along with his volumes of original poetry, Serraillier began to produce books for children based on ancient English and Greek folklore. He also wrote a children's book about some of Shakespeare's plays.

"No one does retellings of ancient tales better than Mr. Serraillier," writes another *Junior Bookshelf* correspondent. "His versions have a quiet, timeless dignity, and he makes sense of ... complicated narrative." The *Times Literary Supplement* reviewer contends that the works could only have been accomplished "by someone who loves the whole body of early ballad, carol and lay and knows it intimately."

Serraillier won multiple awards, however, for an original novel he wrote, *The Silver Sword.* The work follows the fortunes of a group of Polish children who trek

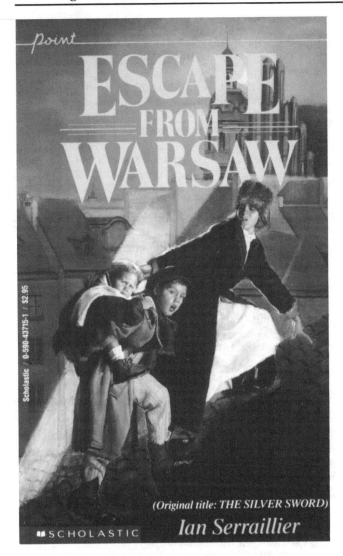

Based on actual events, Serraillier's novel follows three Polish siblings as they search war-torn Europe for their parents.

across the face of Europe in search of their parents. Based on a true story, *The Silver Sword* reveals the dangers and despair of war—and the violence—in a realistic fashion. Crouch states that the tale "was written without heroics, but the heroism and endurance of the children shone brightly in Serraillier's unobtrusively lovely prose." In *Written for Children: An Outline of English-Language Children's Literature,* John Rowe Townsend calls *The Silver Sword* "the one undeniably first-rate war book for children by a British author."

Today Serraillier lives and works in Sussex, England. "I no longer climb the Matterhorn, but am content with the view from lesser hills nearer to home," he remarked in *SAAS.* The author enjoys getting letters from his readers, among whom he can include his own children and grandchildren. Serraillier added in his autobiographical essay that when he is writing, he sometimes strikes "a really impossible patch" where his ideas seem to dry up altogether. If that happens, he said, "I give up for an hour or two and go for a walk or do a bit of cooking or spend time with family and friends. A phrase

I had been trying too hard to find when sitting at my typewriter may well pop into my head as I am making a caramel custard or mowing the lawn or sunbathing."

WORKS CITED:

Crouch, Marcus, *The Nesbit Tradition: The Children's Novel in England 1945-1970,* Ernest Benn, 1972, pp. 28-29.
Junior Bookshelf, December, 1967, p. 382.
Junior Bookshelf, August, 1971, p. 258.
Serraillier, Ian, essay in *Something about the Author Autobiography Series,* Volume 3, Gale, 1987.
Third Book of Junior Authors, H. W. Wilson, 1972, pp. 257-258.
Times Literary Supplement, November 30, 1967, p. 1139.
Townsend, John Rowe, *Written for Children: An Outline of English-Language Children's Literature,* Lippincott, 1974, p. 210.

FOR MORE INFORMATION SEE:

BOOKS

Children's Literature Review, Volume 2, Gale, 1976.

PERIODICALS

Kirkus Reviews, May 15, 1970.
New York Times Book Review, September 20, 1964; December 10, 1967.
Times Literary Supplement, November 19, 1954; November 28, 1963; November 24, 1966; July 2, 1971.*

*   *   *

SILSBE, Brenda 1953-

PERSONAL: Last name is pronounced "sillz-bee"; born October 10, 1953, in Terrace, British Columbia, Canada; daughter of Raymond A. (a worker in the forest industry) and Emma Ingrid Carolina (a secretary/receptionist; maiden name, Gustafson) Taft; married John Jesse Silsbe (a protection technologist), October 20, 1979; children: Anne Victoria, Jesse Raymond. *Education:* University of British Columbia, Bachelor of Education, 1977. *Politics:* "Noblesse oblige." *Religion:* "Love/every religion/no religion."

ADDRESSES: Home and office—R.R. 3, N. Eby and Orde, Terrace, British Columbia, Canada V8G 4R6.

CAREER: Affiliated with School District #88, Terrace, British Columbia, Canada, 1977-1980; free-lance writer, 1988—.

WRITINGS:

The Bears We Know, Annick Press, 1989.
Just One More Colour, Annick Press, 1991.

Also contributor to *Mackenzie King's Ghost,* by John Robert Colombo, Hounslow Press, 1991.

BRENDA SILSBE

SIDELIGHTS: Brenda Silsbe told *SATA:* "I was born and raised in the beautiful Skeena River Valley of northwestern British Columbia. Like many writers, I have loved books and writing all my life. In fourth grade, I wrote a series of stories about a girl named April O'Day. I cut pictures out of magazines and wrote the stories around the pictures. In sixth and seventh grade, I wrote 'chapter' books. Fortunately, I kept these chapter books and enjoy reading my earliest attempts at being an author.

"I was studying education at the University of British Columbia when the idea for my first book came to me. My future brother-in-law had built a house across the river. He and a few friends stayed there. One day my sister was talking to a little girl on the road. The little girl pointed to the house and said, 'I know who lives there.' 'Who lives there?' asked my sister. 'That's where the bears live,' she replied. When my sister told me what the little girl had said, I though it was very funny. My friends were just like a bunch of bears, living the way they wanted to, eating whatever and whenever they wanted. So I wrote a little story for them with simple illustrations. I liked the story and tucked it away with my poems and other writings.

"I graduated from university in 1977 with a Bachelor of Education and taught in Terrace, British Columbia for three years. I married John Silsbe in 1979 and had a daughter, Anne, in 1980, and a son, Jesse, in 1982. I quit teaching in 1980 to look after the children. All this time, the bear story waited in a drawer. Sometimes I pulled it out to show it to friends.

"When my youngest child started school, I decided to start sending what I wrote to publishers. I thought I was old enough to handle rejections. I also knew that I loved to write and that it would be wonderful to work at

something I really loved. I pulled out my writing and went through all the papers. The bear story was the only story that survived my critical weeding. I worked on the story and sent it off to Annick Press where it was read and accepted. You can find the name of my four 'bear' friends in the dedication at the beginning of the book.

"My second book came about when a friend of mine got cancer. I was so upset when I heard the news that I could hardly write. All my thoughts were gloom and doom. All I could think about was sickness and death. I wanted to write something for my friend but I couldn't think of anything to say. Finally, I told myself to forget about it and I started looking through the dictionary for interesting words. I saw the word 'paint' and suddenly a whole story popped into my head. It wasn't until I wrote out the story and worked on it a while that I realized that it was really about my friend. It wasn't about cancer and sickness and death. It was about faith, joy and survival. It was much better than anything I could think up about hospitals and illness. It was happy and hopeful and no matter what happened to the story, it would belong to my friend. I sent off the story and Annick Press accepted it for publication. It is dedicated to my friend who has since recovered and is very full of life!

"I hope to continue writing with the support of my husband and the encouragement of my children. From those wonderful first blue Dick and Jane readers to my desk of dreams, books and writing have been my lifelong companions—the best of companions."

*   *   *

SIMON, Seymour 1931-

PERSONAL: Born August 9, 1931, in New York, NY; son of David and Clara (Liftin) Simon; married Joyce Shanock (a travel agent), December 25, 1953; children: Robert Paul, Michael Alan. *Education:* City College (now City College of the City University of New York), B.A., 1953, graduate study, 1955-60. *Hobbies and other interests:* Reading history and poetry, collecting books and art, playing chess and tennis, traveling, listening to music, computers.

ADDRESSES: Home—4 Sheffield Rd., Great Neck, NY 11021.

CAREER: Writer. New York City public schools, science and creative writing teacher, 1955-79. *Military service:* U.S. Army, 1953-55.

MEMBER: Authors Guild, Authors League of America.

AWARDS, HONORS: Children's Book Showcase Award, Children's Book Council, 1972, for *The Paper Airplane Book;* National Science Teachers Association and Children's Book Council awards, 1972-88, for outstanding science books for children; Best Children's Science Book of the Year Award, New York Academy of Sciences, 1988, for *Icebergs and Glaciers;* Eva L. Gordon Award, American Nature Society, for contributions to children's science literature.

WRITINGS:

FOR CHILDREN

Animals in Field and Laboratory: Projects in Animal Behavior, McGraw, 1968.
The Look-It-Up Book of the Earth, Random House, 1968.
Motion, Coward, 1968.
Soap Bubbles, Hawthorn, 1969.
Weather and Climate, Random House, 1969.
Exploring with a Microscope, Random House, 1969.
Handful of Soil, Hawthorn, 1970.
Science in a Vacant Lot, Viking, 1970.
Science at Work: Easy Models You Can Make, F. Watts, 1971.
Chemistry in the Kitchen, Viking, 1971.
The Paper Airplane Book, Viking, 1971.
Science at Work: Projects in Space Science, F. Watts, 1971.
Science Projects in Ecology, Holiday House, 1972.
Science Projects in Pollution, Holiday House, 1972.
Science at Work: Projects in Oceanography, F. Watts, 1972.
From Shore to Ocean Floor: How Life Survives in the Sea, F. Watts, 1973.
The Rock Hound's Book, Viking, 1973.
A Tree on Your Street, Holiday House, 1973.
A Building on Your Street, Holiday House, 1973.
Projects with Plants, F. Watts, 1973.
Birds on Your Street, Holiday House, 1974.
Life in the Dark: How Animals Survive at Night, F. Watts, 1974.
Projects with Air, F. Watts, 1975.

SEYMOUR SIMON

Pets in a Jar: Collecting and Caring for Small Wild Animals, Viking, 1975.
Everything Moves, Walker & Co., 1976.
The Optical Illusion Book, Four Winds, 1976.
Life on Ice, F. Watts, 1976.
Ghosts, Lippincott, 1976.
Life and Death in Nature, McGraw, 1976.
Animals in Your Neighborhood, Walker & Co., 1976.
The Saltwater Tropical Aquarium Book: How to Set Them up and Keep Them Going, Viking, 1976.
What Do You Want to Know about Guppies?, Four Winds, 1977.
Beneath Your Feet, Walker & Co., 1977.
Space Monsters, Lippincott, 1977.
Look to the Night Sky, Viking, 1977.
Exploring Fields and Lots, Garrard, 1978.
Killer Whales, Lippincott, 1978.
About Your Lungs, McGraw, 1978.
Animal Fact/Animal Fable, Crown, 1979.
Danger from Below, Four Winds, 1979.
The Secret Clocks, Viking, 1979.
Meet the Giant Snakes, Walker & Co., 1979.
Creatures from Lost Worlds, Lippincott, 1979.
The Long View into Space, Crown, 1979.
Deadly Ants, Four Winds, 1979.
About the Foods You Eat, McGraw, 1979.
Meet Baby Animals, Random House, 1980.
Animals Nobody Loves, Random House, 1980.
Strange Mysteries, Four Winds, 1980.
Goony Birds, Bush Babies, and Devil Rays, Random House, 1980.
Mirror Magic, Lothrop, 1980.
Silly Animal Jokes and Riddles, McGraw, 1980.
Poisonous Snakes, Four Winds, 1981.
Mad Scientists, Weird Doctors, and Time Travelers, Lippincott, 1981.
About Your Brain, McGraw, 1981.
Strange Creatures, Four Winds, 1981.
Body Sense, Body Nonsense, Lippincott, 1981.
The Smallest Dinosaurs, Crown, 1982.
How to Be a Space Scientist in Your Own Home, Lippincott, 1982.
The Long Journey from Space, Crown, 1982.
Little Giants, Morrow, 1983.
Hidden Worlds: Pictures of the Invisible, Morrow, 1983.
Earth: Our Planet in Space, Four Winds, 1984.
Moon, Four Winds, 1984.
Dinosaur Is the Biggest Animal That Ever Lived, Harper, 1984.
Computer Sense, Computer Nonsense, Harper, 1984.
Chip Rogers, Computer Whiz, Morrow, 1984.
Shadow-Magic, Lothrop, 1985.
Soap Bubble Magic, Lothrop, 1985.
Meet the Computer, Harper, 1985.
How to Talk to Your Computer, Harper, 1985.
Your First Home Computer, Crown, 1985.
101 Questions and Answers about Dangerous Animals, Macmillan, 1985.
Bit and Bytes: A Computer Dictionary for Beginners, Harper, 1985.
The Basic Book, Harper, 1985.
Turtle Talk: A Beginner's Book of Logo, Harper, 1986.
The Largest Dinosaurs, Macmillan, 1986.

Icebergs and Glaciers, Morrow, 1987.
Volcanoes, Morrow, 1988.
How to Be an Ocean Scientist in Your Own Home, Harper, 1988.
Whales, Harper, 1989.
Oceans, Morrow, 1990.
Deserts, Morrow, 1990.
Earthquakes, Morrow, 1991.
Big Cats, Harper, 1991.
Space Words: A Dictionary, Harper, 1991.
Snakes, Harper, 1992.
Storms, Morrow, 1992.

"DISCOVERING" SERIES

Discovering What Earthworms Do, McGraw, 1969.
Discovering What Frogs Do, McGraw, 1969.
Discovering What Goldfish Do, McGraw, 1970.
Discovering What Gerbils Do, McGraw, 1971.
Discovering What Crickets Do, McGraw, 1973.
Discovering What Garter Snakes Do, McGraw, 1975.
Discovering What Puppies Do, McGraw, 1977.

"LET'S TRY IT OUT" SERIES

Let's Try It Out: Wet and Dry, McGraw, 1969.
Let's Try It Out: Light and Dark, McGraw, 1970.
Let's Try It Out: Finding out with Your Senses, McGraw, 1971.
Let's Try It Out: Hot and Cold, McGraw, 1972.
Let's Try It Out: About Your Heart, McGraw, 1974.

"EINSTEIN ANDERSON" SERIES

Einstein Anderson, Science Sleuth, Viking, 1980.
Einstein Anderson Shocks His Friends, Viking, 1980.
Einstein Anderson Makes up for Lost Time, Viking, 1981.
Einstein Anderson Tells a Comet's Tale, Viking, 1981.
Einstein Anderson Goes to Bat, Viking, 1982.
Einstein Anderson Lights up the Sky, Viking, 1982.
Einstein Anderson Sees through the Invisible Man, Viking, 1983.

"SPACE PHOTOS" SERIES

Jupiter, Morrow, 1985.
Saturn, Morrow, 1985.
The Sun, Morrow, 1986.
The Stars, Morrow, 1986.
Mars, Morrow, 1987.
Uranus, Morrow, 1987.
Galaxies, Morrow, 1988.
Neptune, Morrow, 1991.
Mercury, Morrow, 1992.
Venus, Morrow, 1992.
Our Solar System, Morrow, 1992.

SIDELIGHTS: Seymour Simon has been publishing science books for young readers since the late 1960s. In addition to many nonfiction titles on such diverse subjects as animal behavior and astronomy, he has also written fictional works that introduce children to science and computer principles, such as his "Einstein Anderson" and "Chip Rogers" books. Simon explained his motivation in an interview with Geraldine De Luca and Roni Natov for the *Lion and the Unicorn:* "It's very important to get kids to read science books from a very

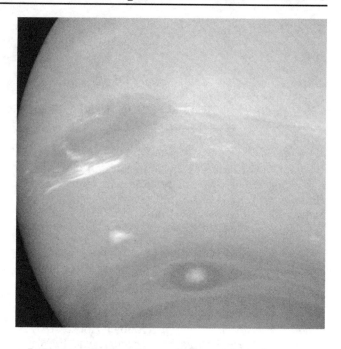

In *Neptune,* **Simon takes readers on a trip to the stormy planet.** (Photo from the Voyager mission by Jet Propulsion Lab/NASA.)

young age. If they're not reading books about science by the time they're twelve, you've probably lost them. When they grow up, they will view science with a great deal of fear and misinformation. Thus, if we want a literate citizenry, we have to start children on science books when they're young. They have no fear at a young age, and they will stay familiar with science all of their lives."

Simon was born August 9, 1931, in New York City. He recalled for De Luca and Natov: "I've always written—even while I was a high school student." He was also very interested in scientific topics while growing up. He attended the Bronx High School of Science, and became president of the Junior Astronomy Club at the American Museum of Natural History—projects he did in this capacity included grinding his own telescope lenses. Simon also enjoyed reading science fiction, which fueled his scientific interests.

After obtaining his bachelor's degree, Simon continued his education by doing graduate study at City College (now City College of the City University of New York). Between his undergraduate and graduate years, Simon served in the U.S. Army and married Joyce Shanock, a travel agent, on Christmas Day of 1953. His graduate work centered on animal behavior, and he later used the study and experience in many of his works for children about animals. After finishing his schooling, Simon became a teacher in the New York City public schools. He commented to De Luca and Natov: "After I began to teach, I decided to try to write while I was teaching. I sent some articles to *Scholastic* magazines and although they didn't accept the articles, the editor of one of the magazines asked me to come in and he gave me an assignment, which happened to be for an article about the moon. The editors were very interested that I taught science because they were having a very difficult time finding anyone who could write who also knew something about science."

Simon continued writing articles for *Scholastic* for a few years, then decided to write an entire book. He explained to De Luca and Natov: "Since my field in graduate school was mostly animal behavior, the first book that I wrote was called *Animals in Field and Laboratory: Science Projects in Animal Behavior.* I was teaching ninth grade then and a lot of kids in my classes were doing projects. I would tend to influence them to do work on animal behavior."

Since *Animals in Field and Laboratory* was published in 1968, Simon has written several books containing simple science experiments that younger readers can do themselves with minimal help from teachers or parents. Though many of his works focus on animals, others spotlight principles of physics or chemistry. Several encourage children to explore their own immediate environments to learn about science, such as *Science in a Vacant Lot* and *Chemistry in the Kitchen.* One of Simon's most acclaimed works is 1971's *The Paper Airplane Book,* in which he uses the examples of different paper airplanes to explain the principles of aerodynamics that make real airplanes work. Critic Zena Sutherland, writing in the *Bulletin of the Center for Children's Books,* called *The Paper Airplane Book* "an exemplary home demonstration book," noting that "the author uses the process approach, suggesting variations on the airplane and asking the reader to consider *why* a certain effect is obtained, or which change is most effective for a desired result." This approach is typical of Simon's books; he once explained: "It's questions like

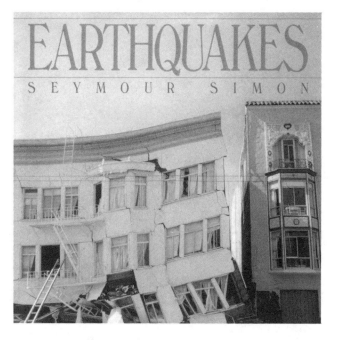

Simon explores the often devastating force of earthquakes in this pictorial study. (Cover photograph by Garry Gay.)

these that occur to me and that have been asked of me by children (both my own and in my science classes) that make me want to write science books. The books I write are full of such questions. Sometimes I'll provide an answer, but more often I'll suggest an activity or an experiment that will let a child answer a question by trying it out."

Simon retired from teaching to write full time in 1979. He told De Luca and Natov: "When I stopped teaching, I had published about forty or fifty books. But I found that I wanted to spend more time in selecting the types of books that I would do. I had been doing books that were very curriculum-oriented. They were not textbooks by any means, but they were books that were tied in with class work. What I really wanted was to write the kind of books that a kid might pick up in a library or in a bookstore, and I found that I needed more time to do that kind of book. My newer books are different from the earlier ones."

Some of Simon's later books are completely different from his earlier ones in that they are fiction. Always looking for ways to interest children in science, Simon uses an appealing character who adores bad puns and solves mysteries through his knowledge of science in his "Einstein Anderson" books. The series has been widely compared with the "Encyclopedia Brown" books of Donald Sobol. Similarly, in *Chip Rogers, Computer Whiz,* Simon has his protagonist solve mysteries with his computer, exposing his young readers to actual BASIC programming in the process. As he concluded in his interview with De Luca and Natov: "I'm going to continue to write imaginative books about science, and continue to present them in ways that I think are interesting or novel."

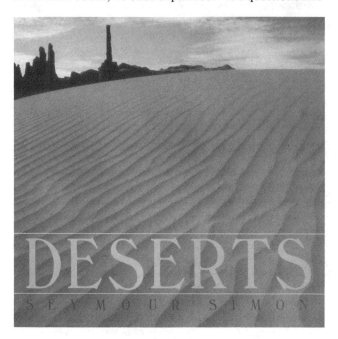

Simon's belief that children should be exposed to the wonders of science at an early age prompted the author to write books like *Deserts*. (Cover photograph by Chuck Place.)

The mysteries of the ocean depths were the focus of Simon's 1990 volume. (Cover photograph by Place.)

WORKS CITED:

De Luca, Geraldine and Roni Natov, "Who's Afraid of Science Books? An Interview with Seymour Simon," *Lion and the Unicorn,* Volume 6, 1982, pp. 10-27.

Sutherland, Zena, review of *The Paper Airplane Book, Bulletin of the Center for Children's Books,* May, 1972, p. 146.

FOR MORE INFORMATION SEE:

BOOKS

Children's Literature Review, Volume 9, Gale, 1985.
Sutherland, Zena, Dianne L. Monson, and May Hill Arbuthnot, *Children and Books,* 6th edition, Scott, Foresman, 1981, pp. 442-501.

PERIODICALS

Bulletin for the Center of Children's Books, November, 1976, p. 48.
Publishers Weekly, June 18, 1979, p. 93.
School Library Journal, September, 1975; pp. 111-112; September, 1981, p. 130; April, 1982, p. 63; January, 1983, p. 79; March, 1984, p. 151.
Science Books, May, 1973, p. 71; December, 1973, p. 257.
Science Books and Films, March-Aril, 1984, p. 216.*

* * *

SIMONT, Marc 1915-

PERSONAL: Born November 23, 1915, in Paris, France; first came to United States, 1927, but later went back to Europe with parents, returning to America, 1935; naturalized citizen, 1936; son of Josep (an illustrator on staff of *L'Illustration*) and Dolors (Baste) Simont; married Sara Dalton (a teacher of handicapped chil-

dren), April 7, 1945; children: Marc Dalton (Doc). *Education:* Studied art in Paris at Academie Ranson, Academie Julien, and Andre Lhote School, 1932-35, and in New York City at National Academy of Design, 1935-37. *Hobbies and other interests:* Country living, socializing, cigars, wine, skiing, soccer, and other sports.

ADDRESSES: Home—Town St., West Cornwall, CT 06796. *Office*—611 Broadway, New York, NY 10012.

CAREER: Artist and illustrator; since 1939 has worked in portraits, murals, sculpture, prints, and magazine and book illustration; translator and writer of children's books, 1939—. Advocate of community soccer in West Cornwall, CT. *Military service:* U.S. Army, 1943-46; produced visual aids; became sergeant.

MEMBER: American Veterans Commission, Authors League of America, Authors Guild.

AWARDS, HONORS: Tiffany fellow, 1937; Caldecott honor book citation, 1950, for *The Happy Day; Book World* Spring Book Festival Award, and Child Study Association Book Award, both 1952, both for *Jareb;* Caldecott Medal, 1957, for *A Tree Is Nice;* Steck-Vaughn Award, 1957, for *The Trail Driving Rooster;* citation of merit, Society of Illustrators, 1965; Best Book of the Season citation from the *Today Show,* 1972, for *Nate the Great;* National Book Award finalist, 1976, for *The Star in the Pail;* New York Academy of Sciences Children's Younger Book Award, 1980, for *A Space Story;* New Jersey Institute of Technology Award, 1981, for *Ten Copycats in a Boat and Other Riddles;* New York *Times* Outstanding Books citation, 1982, for *The Philharmonic Gets Dressed;* Garden State Children's Book Awards, 1984, for *Nate the Great and the Missing Key,* and 1985, for *Nate the Great and the Snowy Trail;* American Institute of Graphic Arts certificate of excellence; Jefferson Cup, 1985, for *In the Year of the Boar and Jackie Robinson;* Parents' Choice award, 1986, for *The Dallas Titans Get Ready for Bed.*

WRITINGS:

SELF-ILLUSTRATED

Opera Souffle: 60 Pictures in Bravura, Schuman, 1950.
Polly's Oats, Harper, 1951.
(With Red Smith) *How to Get to First Base: A Picture Book of Baseball,* Schuman, 1952.
The Lovely Summer, Harper, 1952.
Mimi, Harper, 1954.
The Plumber Out of the Sea, Harper, 1955.
The Contest at Paca, Harper, 1959.
How Come Elephants?, Harper, 1965.
Afternoon in Spain, Morrow, 1965.
(With members of staff of Boston Children's Medical Center) *A Child's Eye View of the World,* Delacorte, 1972.

TRANSLATOR

Federico Garcia Lorca, *The Lieutenant Colonel and the Gypsy,* Doubleday, 1971.

Francesc Sales, *Ibrahim,* illustrations by Eulalia Sariola, Lippincott, 1989.

ILLUSTRATOR

Emma G. Sterne, *The Pirate of Chatham Square: A Story of Old New York,* Dodd, 1939.

Ruth Bryan Owens, *The Castle in the Silver Woods,* Dodd, 1939.

Albert Carr, *Men of Power,* Viking, 1940.

Mildred Cross, *Isabella, Young Queen of Spain,* Dodd, 1941.

Charlotte Jackson, *Sarah Deborah's Day,* Dodd, 1941.

Richard Hatch, *All Aboard the Whale,* Dodd, 1942.

Dougal's Wish, Harper, 1942.

Meindert DeJong, *Billy and the Unhappy Bull,* Harper, 1946.

Margaret Wise Brown, *The First Story,* Harper, 1947.

Iris Vinton, *Flying Ebony,* Dodd, 1947.

Robbie Trent, *The First Christmas,* Harper, 1948, new edition, 1990.

Andrew Lang, editor, *The Red Fairy Book,* new edition, Longmans, Green, 1948.

Ruth Krauss, *The Happy Day,* Harper, 1949.

Krauss, *The Big World and the Little House,* Schuman, 1949.

Red Smith, *Views of Sport,* Knopf, 1949.

DeJong, *Good Luck Duck,* Harper, 1950.

MARC SIMONT

Krauss, *The Backward Day,* Harper, 1950.

James Thurber, *The Thirteen Clocks,* Simon & Schuster, 1951.

Marjorie B. Paradis, *Timmy and the Tiger,* Harper, 1952.

Alister Cooke, *Christmas Eve,* Knopf, 1952.

Miriam Powell, *Jareb,* Crowell, 1952.

The American Riddle Book, Schuman, 1954.

Elizabeth H. Lansing, *Deer Mountain Hideaway,* Crowell, 1954.

Jean Fritz, *Fish Head,* Coward, 1954.

Lansing, *Deer River Raft,* Crowell, 1955.

Fred Gipson, *The Trail-Driving Rooster,* Harper, 1955.

Julius Schwartz, *Now I Know,* Whittlesey House, 1955.

Janice May Udry, *A Tree Is Nice,* Harper, 1955.

Schwartz, *I Know a Magic House,* Whittlesey House, 1956.

Thomas Liggett, *Pigeon Fly Home,* Holiday House, 1956.

Chad Walsh, *Nellie and Her Flying Crocodile,* Harper, 1956.

Thurber, *The Wonderful "O",* Simon & Schuster, 1957.

Maria Leach, *The Rainbow Book of American Folk Tales and Legends,* World, 1958.

Alexis Ladas, *The Seal That Couldn't Swim,* Little, Brown, 1959.

James A. Kjelgaard, *The Duckfooted Hound,* Crowell, 1960.

Krauss, *A Good Man and His Wife,* Harper, 1962.

Schwartz, *The Earth Is Your Spaceship,* Whitlesey House, 1963.

David McCord, *Every Time I Climb a Tree,* Little Brown, 1967.

What To Do When There's Nothing To Do, Dell, 1967.

Charlton Ogburn, Jr., *Down, Boy, Down, Blast You!,* Morrow, 1967.

Janet Chenery, *Wolfie,* Harper, 1969.

Udry, *Glenda,* Harper, 1969.

Edward Fales, Jr., *Belts On, Buttons Down,* Dell, 1971.

McCord, *The Star in the Pail,* Little, Brown, 1975.

Beverly Keller, *The Beetle Bush,* Coward, 1976.

Karla Kuskin, *A Space Story,* Harper, 1978.

Faith McNulty, *Mouse and Time,* Harper, 1978.

McNulty, *How to Dig a Hole to the Other Side of the World,* Harper, 1979.

Alvin Schwartz, editor, *Ten Copycats in a Boat, and Other Riddles,* Harper, 1979.

McNulty, *The Elephant Who Couldn't Forget,* Harper, 1979.

Mitchell Sharmat, *Reddy Rattler and Easy Eagle,* Doubleday, 1979.

McCord, *Speak Up: More Rhymes of the Never Was and Always Is,* Little, Brown, 1980.

Marjorie Weinman Sharmat, *Chasing After Annie,* Harper, 1981.

Charlotte Zolotow, *If You Listen,* Harper, 1980.

Peggy Parish, *No More Monsters For Me!,* Harper, 1981.

Kuskin, *The Philharmonic Gets Dressed,* Harper, 1982.

Julie Delton, *My Uncle Nikos,* Crowell, 1983.

Mollie Hunter, *The Knight of the Golden Plain,* Harper, 1983.

Edward Davis, *Bruno the Pretzel Man,* Harper, 1984.

In his illustrations for Mollie Hunter's *The Three-Day Enchantment,* Simont emphasized the magical elements of the text.

Bette Bao Lord, *The Year of the Boar and Jackie Robinson,* Harper, 1984.
Joan W. Blos, *Martin's Hats,* Morrow, 1984.
John Reynolds Gardiner, *Top Secret,* Little, Brown, 1984.
Franklyn Mansfield Branley, *Volcanoes,* Crowell, 1985.
Hunter, *The Three Day Enchantment,* Harper, 1985.
Kuskin, *The Dallas Titans Get Ready for Bed,* Harper, 1986.
Branley, *Journey into a Black Hole,* Crowell, 1986.
Wendell V. Tangborn, *Glaciers,* Crowell, 1988, revised edition, Harper, 1988.
Sing a Song of Popcorn, Scholastic, 1988.
Zolotow, *The Quiet Mother and the Noisy Little Boy,* Harper, 1989.
Branley, *What Happened to the Dinosaurs?,* Harper, 1989.
Thurber, *Many Moons,* Harcourt, 1990.

ILLUSTRATOR; "NATE THE GREAT" SERIES BY MARJORIE WEINMAN SHARMAT

Nate the Great, Coward, 1972.
Nate the Great Goes Undercover, Coward, 1974.
Nate the Great and the Lost List, Coward, 1975.
Nate the Great and the Phony Clue, Coward, 1977.
Nate the Great and the Sticky Case, Coward, 1978.
Nate the Great and the Missing Key, Coward, 1981.
Nate the Great and the Snowy Trail, Coward, 1982.
Nate the Great and the Fishy Prize, Coward, 1985.
Nate the Great and the Boring Beach Bag, Coward, 1987.

Nate the Great Stalks Stupidweed, Coward, 1987.
Nate the Great Goes Down in the Dumps, Coward, 1989.
Nate the Great and the Halloween Hunt, Coward, 1989.
(By M. W. Sharmat and Craig Sharmat) *Nate the Great and the Musical Note,* Coward, 1990.
Nate the Great and the Stolen Base, Coward, 1992.

ADAPTATIONS: Nate the Great Goes Undercover and *Nate the Great and the Sticky Case* were made into films. The *Nate the Great* books were once optioned for a television series. An excerpt from *Nate the Great* was adapted and is on permanent display at the Museum of Science and Industry, Chicago, Illinois.

SIDELIGHTS: Marc Simont was born in 1915 in Paris, France, to parents from the Catalonian region of northern Spain. He attended schools in Paris, Barcelona, Spain, and New York City, because his parents kept traveling. Simont's father went to the United States after World War I and decided to become an American citizen. Because that process took five years, Simont lived with his grandfather in Barcelona. During this time he sketched bullfighters and taught himself to draw by studying *El Ginesello,* a picture book.

This repeated relocation affected his performance as a student. "I was always more concerned with what a teacher looked like than what he said, which didn't do my algebra any good," the illustrator explained in *More Junior Authors.* Simont didn't graduate from high school, although he became fluent in French, English, Spanish, and Catalonian. On the other hand, the traveling sharpened his skills as an observer—skills important for an artist. He studied art at the Academie Julian and the Academie Ranson in Paris, and in New York City at National Academy of Design. He also studied art with Andre Lohte, but he said his most important art teacher was his father, an illustrator for *L'Illustration* magazine. With a sister and two uncles also making a living as artists, he considers art the family trade.

When he returned to the United States, Simont worked odd jobs, painted portraits, and drew illustrations for advertising firms. Eventually he became an illustrator of picture books for children. Books by many notable children's writers, including James Thurber and Marjorie Weinman Sharmat, have been published with his illustrations. Simont illustrated Sharmat's book *Nate the Great,* featuring the boy detective who solves neighborhood mysteries, and has won several awards for books in the *Nate the Great* series; two were made into films, and the entire series was once optioned for a television series. His illustrations for Janice May Udry's *A Tree Is Nice* won the Caldecott Award in 1957, and he received Caldecott Honors for his pictures for Ruth Krauss's *The Happy Day.*

Critics have pointed out that Simont's illustrations are perfectly suited to the text in books by a variety of children's authors. George A. Woods comments in the *New York Times Book Review* about Karla Kuskin's *The Philharmonic Gets Dressed:* "Simont has not missed a beat. His musicians are a varied band in terms of age,

Simont received a Caldecott Honor for his illustrations in Ruth Krauss's *The Happy Day*.

Simont's drawings for Karla Kuskin's *The Philharmonic Gets Dressed* were praised by critics for both their variety and sense of humor.

race and physique. He conveys the awkward stance as well as the graceful pose, the little scenes and moments that are all around us—the hole in the sock, the graffiti inside the subway car as well as the advertising posters." Kenneth Marantz, writing about the same book in *School Library Journal,* notes that Simont's "ability to invest such convincing feelings of life using an almost cartoon-like simplicity is remarkable." *New York Times Book Review* contributor Nora Magid observes that Simont's illustrations in *How to Dig a Hole to the Other Side of the World* have terrific emotional power: "Simont's pictures break the heart. The child voyager is at once intrepid and vulnerable" as he takes an imaginary journey through the earth's crust to China. Other features of Simont's artistic style are a method of composition that gives continuity to the pictures in sequence, and humor that is inviting to readers of all ages.

"I believe that if I like the drawings I do, children will like them also," Simont told Lee Bennett Hopkins for *Books Are by People.* He continued, "The child in me must make contact with other children. I may miss it by ten miles, but if I am going to hit, it is because of the child in me."

WORKS CITED:

Hopkins, Lee Bennett, *Books Are by People: Interviews with 104 Authors and Illustrators of Books for Young Children,* Citation Press, 1969, pp. 267-269.
Magid, Nora, review of *How to Dig a Hole to the Other Side of the World, New York Times Book Review,* November 18, 1979, p. 320.
Marantz, Kenneth, review of *The Philharmonic Gets Dressed, School Library Journal,* August, 1982, p. 99.

Simont, Marc, in *More Junior Authors,* H. W. Wilson, 1963, pp. 186-187.
Woods, George A., review of *The Philharmonic Gets Dressed, New York Times Book Review,* October 17, 1982, p. 37.

FOR MORE INFORMATION SEE:

BOOKS

Caldecott Medal Books: 1938-1957, Horn Book, 1957.
Kingman, Lee, editor, *Newbery and Caldecott Medal Books: 1956-1965,* Horn Book, 1965.
Klemin, Diana, *The Art of Art for Children's Books,* Clarkson Potter, 1966.

PERIODICALS

Book World, November 5, 1972, p. 4.
Christian Science Monitor, November 11, 1971.
Horn Book, February, 1980, p. 140; April, 1983, p. 158; February, 1984, p. 54; June, 1984, p. 318; May/June, 1985, p. 326; November/December, 1986, p. 737; November/December, 1989, p. 788.
New York Times Book Review, October 31, 1965, p. 56; November 6, 1983, p. 43; May 20, 1984, p. 28; November 9, 1986, p. 40.
School Library Journal, August, 1984, p. 56; October, 1989, p. 100.
Science Books and Films, November/December, 1988, p. 95.
Time, December 4, 1978, p. 100; December 20, 1982, p. 79.*

* * *

SMALLS-HECTOR, Irene 1950-

PERSONAL: Born February 11, 1950, in Harlem, NY; daughter of Charles Smith and Mary Smalls; married Derek C. Hector, May 13, 1989; children: Jonathan, Kevin, Dawn, William, Derek. *Education:* Cornell University, B.A., 1971; New York University, M.B.A., 1974. *Hobbies and other interests:* Reading, shopping, traveling.

ADDRESSES: Agent—Liza Palitizer-Voges Kirchoff Wahlberg, 866 United Nations Plaza, New York, NY 10017-1811.

CAREER: Writer. Miss Black New York State, 1967-68; Smalls-Dawn Associates, marketing specialist, 1978-80; voice-over actress, 1988—.

MEMBER: Screen Actors Guild, American Federation of Television and Radio Artists, Society of Children's Book Writers, Cornell Black Alumni Association.

WRITINGS:

Irene and the Big, Fine Nickel, illustrated by Tyrone Geter, Little, Brown, 1991.
Jonathan and His Mommy, illustrated by Michael Hays, Little, Brown, 1992.
Dawn's Friends (textbook), illustrated by Geter, D. C. Heath, 1992.

WORK IN PROGRESS: Irene Jennie and the Christmas Masquerade: The Johnkankus, to be published in 1994 by Little, Brown; *Dawn and the Round Tuit,* to be published by Simon & Schuster in 1994; *Jenny Reen and the Jack Man Lantern,* to be published in 1995 by Atheneum; and *Hants, Hags, and Hoodoo.*

SIDELIGHTS: Irene Smalls-Hector told *SATA:* "I say that I wrote it, but in reality I just put my heart on the pages of *Jonathan and His Mommy.* It's the story of my son Jonathan and I and the walks we used to take when he was ages four-and-a-half to five. This book is for every adult who has ever loved a child and for every child who knows or remembers quiet talks, long walks, and smiles.

"My approach to writing children's books is that I write about what I know, what I see, and what I feel. I write very simple stories. I remember when I was five and I first learned how to read. My kindergarten teacher, Miss Abbott, would read and read to us. She read *God's Trombones* by James Weldon Johnson, *Little Brown Baby* by Paul Lawrence Dunbar. I remember not being particularly interested in learning how to read but I was very jealous of the sounds that my teacher would make. They were beautiful sounds, musical sounds. She opened up these books and out came these sounds. I simply wanted to make the sounds that she made. I [realize] now the wisdom of that very young teacher. She knew how to inspire children, not with pressure but with

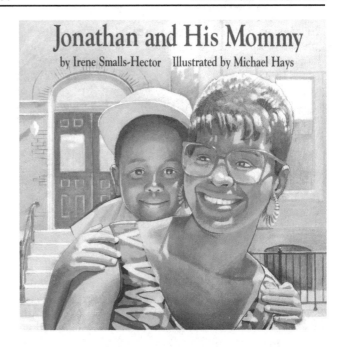

Smalls-Hector drew on her memories of the walks she took with her son when he was a young boy in order to write *Jonathan and His Mommy.* (Cover illustration by Michael Hays.)

pleasure. Wherever she is, I would like to thank kindergarten teacher Miss Abbott from P.S. 90 in Harlem, New York, around 1955.

"Another important element was that there was always music in my culture. My mother would give me cookies for dancing well to the latest songs. My teacher used that as a strength, the strong influence of music in black culture, and made the stories sing. When I write I still try to write musically, because it was the sounds of the words that moved me as a child. My stories almost always have songs or children's rhymes in them.

"*Dawn's Friends,* an early-reader Big Book text, contains the stories of my daughter Dawn's actual friends and what made each of them special. It was fun remembering her friends when she was two, when she was six, fourteen, etc. I tried to capture the texture of a child's friendship, the fast fun, funny fun, fat fun of childhood.

"In *Irene Jennie and the Christmas Masquerade: The Johnkankus,* I tell the story of a young slave girl to show the beauty and texture of slave life. The Johnkankus was an authentic slave Christmas celebration that the Africans brought over from Africa. All the songs in my stories are songs the slaves created and sang. The Johnkankus is colorful, historical, and poignant. At one point in the story the main character, even though a child, is faced with the horror of slavery and asks, 'Does God care about little colored girls?' The answer in the story is a resounding yes.

"I have just finished an African-American Halloween story that takes place during the time of slavery. Slavery was worse than probably any of us can imagine, but the

IRENE SMALLS-HECTOR

Africans who were enslaved created and sustained a culture, despite all the horror. They created songs, dances, and festivities that were uniquely African American. Unfortunately, because it wasn't written down, a great deal of that culture was almost lost. But aspects of slave culture still survive today in anecdotes and stories, in grandmothers' recipes, and most importantly in the Black Church.

"I am presently working on an African-American Thanksgiving story and a story about an African-American slave girl owned by an American Indian chief in the West."

* * *

SMITH, Jos(eph) A. 1936-

PERSONAL: Born September 5, 1936, in Bellefonte, PA; son of George Leonard (a barber) and Frieda Regina (a beautician; maiden name, Droege) Smith; married Nancy Clare Hutchison (a family counsellor), August 11, 1959 (divorced); married Charlotte Mitsua Honda (a dancer), July, 1972 (divorced); children: Kathryn (Kari) Anne, Joseph A., Emily Christian. *Education:* Attended Pennsylvania State University, summer sessions, 1955-60, New York University, New School for Social Research, Roscoe Center, and Wainright Center for Human Resources; received B.F.A. from Pratt Institute; graduate study at Pennsylvania State University, 1960-61, and Pratt Institute, 1961-62; studied at Institute for Mind Research. *Politics:* Democrat. *Religion:* Buddhist.

ADDRESSES: Home—159 John St., 6th Fl., New York, NY 10038-3511. *Office*—Pratt Institute, School of Art and Design, 200 Willoughby Ave., Brooklyn, NY 11205.

CAREER: Free-lance illustrator; Pratt Institute, School of Art and Design, Brooklyn, NY, professor of fine art, 1962—. Teacher of adult painting classes at Staten Island Museum, 1964; lecturer in drawing at Wagner College, 1965-66; teacher of a summer painting workshop for Art Alliance of Central Pennsylvania, 1969-71; teacher of the Visualization and Imagizing Workshop at Wainwright Center for Human Resources, 1975; visiting professor of fine arts at Richmond College, 1984; member of visual arts faculty at Stockton State College, Artist's and Teacher's Institute, and New Jersey Council on the Arts, summer sessions, 1987—; LaFont Painting Workshop, 1990; visiting artist at Art Institute of Chicago, 1990; visiting artist at Mississippi Art Colony, 1992. *Military service:* U.S. Army, became specialist 4.

EXHIBITIONS: Solo exhibitions include: Samuel S. Fleisher Art Memorial, Philadelphia, PA, 1961; Pratt Institute, Brooklyn, NY, 1962; Janet Nessler Gallery, New York City, 1963; Lehigh University, Bethlehem, Pennsylvania, 1964; Staten Island Museum, Staten Island, NY, 1966; Bloomsburg State College, Bloomsburg, PA, 1968; Parsons School of Design, New York City, 1971; Chambers Gallery, Pennsylvania State University, University Park, 1972; Bethel Gallery, Bethel, CT, 1978; Newhouse Gallery, Snug Harbor Cultural

JOS. A. SMITH

Center, Staten Island, 1982; The Visual Arts Gallery, Adirondak Community College, Glens Falls, NY, 1988. *Group exhibitions include:* Annual Summer Exhibitions, Pennsylvania State University, 1955-60; Annual American Watercolor Society Exhibition, New York City, 1965, 1967, and 1969; "Portraits for *Time,*" New York Society of Illustrators, New York City, 1979; "Aliens," Museum of the Surreal and Art Fantastique, New York City, 1981; Carlyle Gallery, New York City, 1982 and 1983; "Separate Realities," Circlework Visions Gallery, New York City, 1986; "The Original Art," Society of Illustrators Museum of American Illustration, New York City, 1991.

MEMBER: Princeton Zen Society.

AWARDS, HONORS: Dean's Medal, Pratt Institute, 1958; Mary S. Litt Award, American Watercolor Society, 1967; Juror's Choice Award, Pennsylvania State University, 1971; merit award from National Art Director's Club, 1971, New York Society of Illustrators, 1972, 1973, and 1975, American Institute of Graphic Arts, 1975, Bicentennial in Print, 1976, Art Directors Club of Metropolitan Washington, 1976, and Federal Design Council, 1976; first prize award in professional category, Pennsylvania State University, 1972; Staten Island Advance Award, Staten Island Museum, 1974; Purchase Prize in invitational section, Rutgers University, 1974; 1979 Andy Award of Merit, Advertising Club of New York; Print Club Purchase Award and merit award, University of Mississippi, 1991; *Jim Ugly* received the *Parents' Choice* Award from the Parents' Choice Foundation in 1992.

WRITINGS:

(And illustrator) *The Pen and Ink Book, Materials and Techniques for Today's Artist,* Watson-Guptill, 1992.

ILLUSTRATOR

Stan Steiner, *The Last Horse,* Holt, 1961.

Walter S. Carpenter and Philip Bluehouse, *Two Knots on a Counting Rope: A Navaho Counting Book,* Holt, 1964.

Katharine Carter (reteller), *Tales from Hans Christian Andersen,* Whitman Publishing, 1965.

Edward William Lane (reteller), *Tales from Arabian Nights,* Whitman Publishing, 1966.

The Sierra Club Survival Songbook, collected by Jim Morse and Nancy Mathews, Sierra Club, 1971.

Norman Borisoff, *Lily, The Lovable Lion,* Scholastic Inc., 1975.

MacKinly Kantor, *Andersonville,* Franklin Library, 1976.

Erica Jong, *Witches,* Abrams, 1981.

Joseph Conrad, *Heart of Darkness and Other Tales,* Franklin Library, 1982.

Bernard Evslin, *Hercules,* Morrow, 1984.

Deborah Hautzig (reteller), *The Wizard of Oz,* Random House, 1984.

Robin McKinley (reteller), *Tales from the Jungle Book,* Random House, 1985.

George MacDonald, *The Princess and the Goblin,* Grosset & Dunlap, 1985.

Barbara Ann Brennan, *Hand of Light,* Pleiades Books, 1987.

Susan Cooper, *Matthew's Dragon,* McElderry Books, 1991.

Helen V. Griffith, *"Mine Will," Said John,* Greenwillow, 1992.

Sid Fleischman, *Jim Ugly,* Greenwillow, 1992.

Lynne Reid Banks, *The Adventures of King Midas,* Morrow, 1992.

Jessie Haas, *Chipmonk!,* Greenwillow, 1993.

Haas, *Mowing,* Greenwillow, 1993.

Mary Serfozo, *Benjamin Bigfoot,* McElderry Books, 1993.

Cooper, *Danny and the Kings,* McElderry Books, 1993.

Diane Wolkstein, *Step by Step,* Morrow, 1993.

Contributor to periodicals, including *Time, Newsweek, New York Times, Harper's,* and *New Times.*

Author's collections are housed at Pennsylvania Academy of the Fine Arts, New York Stock Exchange, Lauren Rogers Museum, Library of Congress, Print Club at University of Mississippi, Rutgers University, Ministry of Education, Kassel Documenta Archive, Coeln Ludwig Museum, and Stuttgart Staatsgalerie Grafische Sammlung.

WORK IN PROGRESS: Illustrating various picture-books; "I am completing a set of drawings which will be used to illustrate the trial of Margaret Sanger, an advocate of birth control, for a television documentary written by Terese Svoboda to be shown on public television."

SIDELIGHTS: Jos. A. Smith told *SATA:* "I grew up in the town of State College, PA. Pennsylvania State University is located there. Although neither of my parents had had the opportunity to complete even grade school, they raised my brother and me to regard learning as the most important thing in our lives. It didn't matter what we wanted to do, they encouraged us. My brother is now chair of the industrial engineering department at Ohio State University, and I am a professor of fine art in the graduate fine art department and the undergraduate painting and drawing department at Pratt Institute in addition to my career as an artist.

"I was also fortunate to be asked by illustrator Richard Lindner to be his studio assistant while I was a student at Pratt Institute. As a result of this I had a rare opportunity to meet and listen to his friends when they visited him in his studio. These included painter Marcel Duchamp, actress Greta Garbo, artist Adja Yunkers, and cartoonist Saul Steinberg. Lindner was one of the most sensitive people I have ever known. He would stop work in the studio and we would go off for hours riding on all the elevated subway lines we could find in search of a certain red chimney that he had seen once years before, or we might go to Central Park Zoo and look at the eyes of the gorilla because of a wise expression he had. Lindner and Hobson Pittman (a painter on the faculty of the Pennsylvania Academy of the Fine Arts in Philadelphia who I studied with every summer at Pennsylvania State University until he retired and turned his studio workshops over to me) both had a profound influence on my life as an artist.

"Other important influences are related to my lifelong interest in drawing imagery from my unconscious for my drawings, sculptures, and paintings. I studied with Jean Houston at the Institute for Mind Research to learn non-drug techniques for inducing altered states. I joined the Princeton Zen Society to learn Zen meditation, and studied Jain meditation with Mouni Sri Chitrabanu, traditional shamanic trance techniques from the anthropologist Michael Harner and joined the Nyingmapa Lineage of the Tibetan Buddhists to learn their elaborate visualization techniques. I also studied biofeedback therapy and own and have used an electro-encephalogram (EEG) to record brainwave states evoked by these various methods, to understand them better. I use adaptations of all of these techniques to evoke imagery for my art, and occasionally incorporate some of the simpler forms in my art classes to enable other artists to be able to take advantage of them. Another of my lifelong interests is nature and the environment, and I have contributed my art to many environmental causes. One of the highpoints of my life in this area was spending one summer walking cross-country in East Africa, drawing people and photographing and filming wildlife. I have always had one or more pets, which usually included some snakes. At present I share my studio/loft, where I live, with a boa constrictor and a ball python."

FOR MORE INFORMATION SEE:

PERIODICALS

Publisher's Weekly, August 28, 1981, p. 386.
School Library Journal, September, 1984, p. 114; April, 1992, p. 113.

* * *

SOBOL, Donald J. 1924-

PERSONAL: Born October 4, 1924, in New York, NY; son of Ira J. and Ida (Gelula) Sobol; married Rose Tiplitz, 1955; children: Diane, Glenn (deceased), Eric, John. *Education:* Oberlin College, B.A., 1948; attended New School for Social Research, 1949-51. *Hobbies and other interests:* Travel, restoring antique cars, boating, fishing, scuba diving, gardening, tennis.

ADDRESSES: Home—Miami, FL. *Agent*—McIntosh & Otis, 310 Madison Ave., New York, NY 10017.

CAREER: Author of fiction and nonfiction for children. *New York Sun,* New York City, reporter, 1946-47; *Long Island Daily Press,* New York City, reporter, 1947-52; R. H. Macy, New York City, buyer, 1953-55; free-lance writer, 1954—. *Military service:* U.S. Army, Corps of Engineers, 1943-46; served in Pacific Theater.

MEMBER: Authors Guild, Authors League of America.

AWARDS, HONORS: Young Readers Choice Award, Pacific Northwest Library Association, 1972, for *Encyclopedia Brown Keeps the Peace;* Edgar Allan Poe Award, Mystery Writers of America, 1975, for entire body of work; Garden State Children's Book Award, 1977, for *Encyclopedia Brown Lends a Hand;* Aiken County Children's Book Award, 1977, for *Encyclopedia Brown Takes the Case;* Buckeye honor citation (grades 4-8 category), 1982, for *Encyclopedia Brown and the Case of the Midnight Visitor.*

WRITINGS:

JUVENILES

The Double Quest, illustrated by Lili Rethi, Watts, 1957.
The Lost Dispatch, illustrated by Anthony Palombo, Watts, 1958.
First Book of Medieval Man (nonfiction), illustrated by Rethi, Watts, 1959, revised edition published in England as *The First Book of Medieval Britain,* Mayflower, 1960.
Two Flags Flying (biographies of Civil War leaders), illustrated by Jerry Robinson, Platt, 1960.
A Civil War Sampler, illustrated by Henry S. Gilette, Watts, 1961.
The Wright Brothers at Kitty Hawk (nonfiction), illustrated by Stuart Mackenzie, T. Nelson, 1961.
(Editor) *The First Book of the Barbarian Invaders, A.D. 375-511* (nonfiction), illustrated by W. Kirtman Plummer, Watts, 1962.
(With wife, Rose Sobol) *The First Book of Stocks and Bonds* (nonfiction), Watts, 1963.

(Editor) *An American Revolutionary War Reader,* Watts, 1964.
Lock, Stock, and Barrel (biographies of American Revolutionary War leaders), illustrated by Edward J. Smith, Westminster, 1965.
Secret Agents Four, illustrated by Leonard Shortall, Four Winds, 1967.
(Editor) *The Strongest Man in the World,* illustrated by Cliff Schule, Westminster, 1967.
Two-Minute Mysteries, Dutton, 1967.
Greta the Strong, illustrated by Trina Schart Hyman, Follett, 1970.
Milton, the Model A, illustrated by J. Drescher, Harvey House, 1970.
More Two-Minute Mysteries, Dutton, 1971.
The Amazons of Greek Mythology, A. S. Barnes, 1972.
Great Sea Stories, Dutton, 1975.
Still More Two-Minute Mysteries, Dutton, 1975.
True Sea Adventures, T. Nelson, 1975.
(Editor) *The Best Animal Stories of Science Fiction and Fantasy,* Warne, 1979.
Disasters, Archway, 1979.
Angie's First Case, illustrated by Gail Owens, Four Winds, 1981.
The Amazing Power of Ashur Fine: A Fine Mystery, Macmillan Children's Book Group, 1986.

"ENCYCLOPEDIA BROWN" SERIES

Encyclopedia Brown: Boy Detective (also see below), illustrated by Leonard Shortall, T. Nelson, 1963.
Encyclopedia Brown and the Case of the Secret Pitch, illustrated by Shortall, T. Nelson, 1965.

DONALD J. SOBOL

Ashur Fine must use all of his extraordinary abilities when he finds himself in the middle of an international plot. (Cover illustration by Pistolesi.)

Encyclopedia Brown Finds the Clues, illustrated by Shortall, T. Nelson, 1966.

Encyclopedia Brown Gets His Man, illustrated by Shortall, T. Nelson, 1967.

Encyclopedia Brown Solves Them All, illustrated by Shortall, T. Nelson, 1968.

Encyclopedia Brown Keeps the Peace, illustrated by Shortall, T. Nelson, 1969.

Encyclopedia Brown Saves the Day, illustrated by Shortall, T. Nelson, 1970.

Encyclopedia Brown Tracks Them Down, illustrated by Shortall, T. Nelson, 1971.

Encyclopedia Brown Shows the Way, illustrated by Shortall, T. Nelson, 1972.

Encyclopedia Brown Takes the Case, illustrated by Shortall, T. Nelson, 1973.

Encyclopedia Brown Lends a Hand, illustrated by Shortall, T. Nelson, 1974.

Encyclopedia Brown and the Case of the Dead Eagles, illustrated by Shortall, T. Nelson, 1975.

Encyclopedia Brown and the Eleven: Case of the Exploding Plumbing and Other Mysteries, illustrated by Shortall, Dutton, 1976.

Encyclopedia Brown and the Case of the Midnight Visitor, illustrated by Lillian Brandi, T. Nelson, 1977, Bantam, 1982.

Encyclopedia Brown's Record Book of Weird and Wonderful Facts, illustrated by Sal Murdocca, Delacorte, 1979, illustrated by Bruce Degen, Dell, 1981.

Encyclopedia Brown Carries On, illustrated by Ib Ohlsson, Four Winds, 1980.

Encyclopedia Brown Sets the Pace, illustrated by Ohlsson, Dutton, 1981.

Encyclopedia Brown's Second Record Book of Weird and Wonderful Facts, illustrated by Degen, Delacorte, 1981.

Encyclopedia Brown's Third Record Book of Weird and Wonderful Facts, illustrated by Murdocca, Delacorte, 1981.

Encyclopedia Brown's Book of Wacky Crimes, illustrated by Shortall, Dutton, 1982.

Encyclopedia Brown (omnibus), illustrated by Shortall, Angus & Robertson, 1983.

Encyclopedia Brown's Book of Wacky Spies, illustrated by Ted Enik, Morrow, 1984.

Encyclopedia Brown's Book of Wacky Sports, illustrated by Enik, Morrow, 1984.

(With Glenn Andrews) *Encyclopedia Brown Takes the Cake!: A Cook and Case Book,* illustrated by Ohlsson, Scholastic, 1984.

Encyclopedia Brown and the Case of the Mysterious Handprints, illustrated by Owens, Morrow, 1985.

Encyclopedia Brown's Book of Wacky Animals, illustrated by Enik, Morrow, 1985.

Encyclopedia Brown's Book of the Wacky Outdoors, illustrated by Enik, Morrow, 1987.

Encyclopedia Brown's Book of Wacky Cars, illustrated by Enik, Morrow, 1987.

Encyclopedia Brown and the Case of the Treasure Hunt, illustrated by Owens, Morrow, 1988.

Encyclopedia Brown and the Case of the Disgusting Sneakers, illustrated by Owens, Morrow, 1990.

(With R. Sobol) *Encyclopedia Brown's Book of Strange but True Crimes,* Scholastic, 1992.

The Best of Encyclopedia Brown, illustrated by Ohlsson, Scholastic, in press.

Books from the "Encyclopedia Brown" series have been translated into thirteen languages and Braille.

OTHER

Author of syndicated column, "Two Minute Mysteries," 1959-68. Contributor of more than one hundred stories and articles to national magazines under a variety of pen names. Sobol's manuscripts are kept in the Kerlan Collection, University of Minnesota, Minneapolis, MN.

ADAPTATIONS: The Best of Encyclopedia Brown (includes "The Case of the Natty Nut," "The Case of the Scattered Cards," "The Case of the Hungry Hitchhiker," and "The Case of the Whistling Ghost"), was made into a filmstrip with cassette, Miller-Brody, 1977. Esquire Film Productions purchased the television and motion picture rights to the "Encyclopedia Brown" series; these rights were transferred to Howard David Deutsch Productions and Warner Brothers in 1979. *Encyclopedia Brown: Boy Detective* was filmed for Home Box Office in March, 1990. Books from the

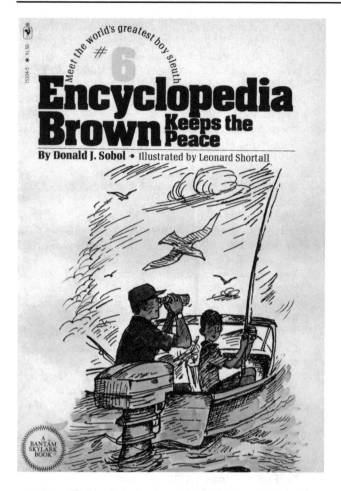

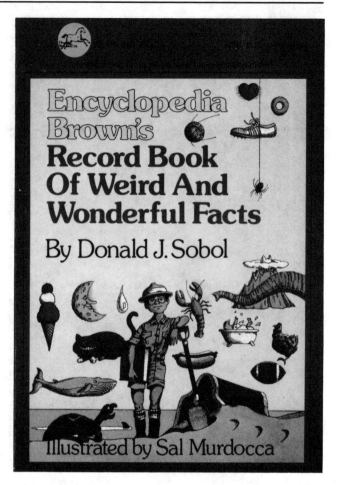

Full of the usual puns and verbal jokes, this "Encyclopedia Brown" mystery features the knowledgeable young detective using his vast store of information to help his father solve a tough case. (Cover illustration by Leonard Shortall.)

Sobol uses the ever-intrepid boy sleuth Encyclopedia Brown to introduce readers to fun facts in this 1979 work. (Cover illustration by Sal Murdocca.)

"Encyclopedia Brown" series have also been made into comic strips.

SIDELIGHTS: American children's mystery author Donald J. Sobol has kept schoolchildren on their toes since 1963 with the publication of the original Encyclopedia Brown book. *Encyclopedia Brown: Boy Detective* began the popular series, which has continued for over three decades. Over the years, Leroy "Encyclopedia" Brown, Sobol's young sleuth, has faced intriguing cases involving everything from dead eagles to disgusting sneakers. Solutions to each case are printed in the back of the book, but children are encouraged to try to solve the cases themselves.

The *Encyclopedia Brown* books each contain ten mysteries presented in readable sentences and enhanced with witty puns and other verbal jokes. It takes careful reading and a variety of methods—deductive reasoning, psychology, and careful observation of physical evidence—to solve the mysteries. "Complexity in writing style is not Sobol's intent, nor is it required for the success of these books," says Christine McDonnell in *Twentieth Century Children's Writers.* "Although the

stories are simply written, they are clever and fresh, and seldom obvious or easy to solve."

Ten-year-old Leroy Brown is called "Encyclopedia" because he is so smart that it seems he must have an entire set of encyclopedias crammed into his head. He is so adept at finding clues that he helps his father, the Chief of Police, solve criminal cases. "Readers constantly ask me if Encyclopedia Brown is a real boy. The answer is no," Sobol once told *SATA.* "He is, perhaps, the boy I wanted to be—doing the things I wanted to read about but could not find in any book when I was ten."

Sobol was born in 1924 in New York City, where he attended the Ethical Cultural Schools. During World War II, he served with the engineer corps in the Pacific, and after his discharge he earned a B.A. degree from Oberlin College. It wasn't until he took a short-story writing course in college that Sobol thought of becoming a writer, and even then he waited several years before making writing his profession. Sobol's first job was as a copyboy for the *New York Sun.* Later he became a journalist for the *Sun* and for the *Long Island Daily News.* "At the age of thirty I quit job-holding for good, married Rose Tiplitz, an engineer, and began to write full time," Sobol told *SATA,* adding that he has written more than sixty books since then.

For many years, Sobol has received letters from stumped young readers complaining that his mysteries have no proper explanation. These letters are often written by readers who have missed some significant detail. But in 1990, students in a Philadelphia school detected an actual error in the first *Encyclopedia Brown* book. The story about a trickster who bilks his classmates in an egg-spinning contest fails to explain how the cheater managed to get a boiled egg into the dozen before the contestants bought it at the grocery store. After the students wrote to Sobol asking for the explanation, he re-read the story for the first time in nearly thirty years. He admitted the solution should be more fully explained. "This is the first time in a couple of decades where it is really my fault," Sobol told Martha Woodall of the *Detroit Free Press.* "They are really smart kids." The teacher of the first- and second-graders who spotted the error said it has taught the students the importance of questioning the accuracy of what they read. She said they also learned that when something that is incorrect appears in print, there is something they can do about it. New editions including "The Case of

the Champion Egg-Spinner" will contain the revised version.

In addition to the boy detective series, Sobol has written many nonfiction books that required him to do extensive research on topics as varied as King Arthur's England (*Greta the Strong*) and Ancient Greece (*The Amazons of Greek Mythology*). His other nonfiction works include biographies of American military leaders of the Revolutionary and Civil Wars, in *Lock, Stock and Barrel* and *Two Flags Flying.* Sobol has also written an internationally syndicated newspaper feature, "Two-Minute Mystery Series," hundreds of articles and stories for adult magazines, historical books, and biographies. He is the editor of two history collections, *A Civil War Sampler* and *An American Revolutionary War Reader,* and the author of a book on stocks and bonds.

Sobol told *Pacific Northwest Library Association Quarterly,* "Outwitting you, the reader, is hard, but harder still is making you laugh. I try above all else to entertain.... I hope to be making children laugh for decades to come."

WORKS CITED:

McDonnell, Christine, *Twentieth Century Children's Writers,* St. Martin's Press, 1989, pp. 905-906.
Pacific Northwest Library Association Quarterly, winter, 1973, pp. 18-20.
Woodall, Martha, "Youngsters Outsmart Encyclopedia Brown," *Detroit Free Press,* February 12, 1991.

FOR MORE INFORMATION SEE:

BOOKS

Children's Literature Review, Volume 4, Gale, 1982, pp. 205-212.
Fourth Book of Junior Authors, Wilson, 1978, pp. 318-319.

PERIODICALS

Booklist, February 1, 1983, p. 27; May 1, 1984, p. 1254; March 1, 1991, p. 1382.
Christian Century, December 13, 1967, p. 1602.
Christian Science Monitor, October 5, 1967, p. 10; April 6, 1984, p. B7.
Fantasy Review, May, 1987, p. 795.
Horn Book Guide, July, 1990, p. 79.
New York Times Book Review, November 5, 1967, p. 44; November 11, 1979, pp. 56, 69.
People, March 12, 1990, pp. 17-18.
School Library Journal, February, 1982, p. 81; August, 1982, p. 107; April, 1984, p. 119; December, 1984, p. 103; April, 1985, p. 93; December, 1985, p. 95; November, 1986, p. 94; April, 1987, p. 104; January, 1988, p. 83; January, 1991, p. 97.
Science Fiction Chronicle, August, 1987, p. 53.
Young Readers' Review, November, 1967; November, 1968.

SCHOLASTIC BIOGRAPHY

Before the fact is the dream.

THE WRIGHT BROTHERS AT KITTY HAWK

In this biographical text, Sobol tells the colorful story of the Wright brothers and their attempts to build one of the first successful flying machines.

SONNENMARK, Laura A. 1958-

PERSONAL: Born August 24, 1958, in Virginia Beach, VA; daughter of Thomas Franklin (a general manager of a shipyard and retired from U.S. Navy) and Dolores Ann (Stewart) Austin; married Les Sonnenmark (a marine engineer), April 4, 1981; children: Daniel Austin. *Education:* University of Miami, B.S., 1979.

ADDRESSES: Home—Alexandria, VA. *Agent*—Natasha Kern, P. O. Box 2908, Portland, OR 97208-2908.

CAREER: Norwegian Caribbean Line, Miami, FL, personnel administrator, 1980; Miami-Dade Community College, Miami, English as a second language (ESL) instructor, 1981-83; Hyatt Regency Hotel, Miami, assistant personnel director, 1983; free-lance writer, Annapolis, MD, 1984-88; Annapolis *Capital,* Annapolis, columnist, 1988-90.

MEMBER: Washington Independent Writers; Society of Children's Book Writers.

WRITINGS:

Something's Rotten in the State of Maryland, Scholastic, 1990.
The Lie, Scholastic, 1992.

WORK IN PROGRESS: No Anchovies, a young adult novel about a mother-daughter relationship; researching life in colonial Maryland and seventeenth-century England for an adult historical saga.

SIDELIGHTS: Laura A. Sonnenmark told *SATA:* "My love of books comes from a childhood spent on a U.S. Naval Base in Yokosuka, Japan. We didn't have a television—my parents didn't bother to get one, for some reason—so we read books, lots and lots of books. Sometimes my brother and I would invent stories of our own.

"I never really intended to become a writer. I sort of fell into it. Sometimes, you know, life just happens to you when you aren't paying attention. Of course, I always enjoyed writing and was good at it in school. I was the poet laureate of my second grade class! But my older brother was going to be a writer, and I didn't want to get into a sibling rivalry with him. Besides, I don't think my parents could have survived the burden of worry if both their children had elected to become writers. As a career, writing isn't particularly lucrative, and it's quite difficult to achieve even a modicum of success.

"So I pursued other interests. Eventually my husband and I moved to Annapolis, Maryland, where I began a stint as the literary columnist for the local newspaper. I also taught Spanish briefly at a junior high school. It was while teaching that I first got the idea of writing a young adult novel, specifically, *Something's Rotten in the State of Maryland.*

"This might be a good place to mention that like Marie, the heroine of *Something's Rotten,* I also rewrote

LAURA A. SONNENMARK

Hamlet for an English assignment. I also got an A+. Unfortunately, that's where the similarity ends; the school didn't produce it, and there was no jock boyfriend nor any tyrannical, yet oh-so-intriguing director vying for my affection. You can see why I much prefer Marie's version of this story to mine.

"*The Lie* is a bit darker than my first novel. It's a tale of love-bordering-on-obsession, and it's set in Ocean City, Maryland. Nothing here parallels my own life, because, much to my everlasting regret, I'm not anywhere near as nervy as Norrie, the heroine.

"Right now I'm working on a new young adult novel. It's called *No Anchovies* and it's set among the 'summer people' of Maine.

"I didn't plan on writing young adult fiction, but now when I think about it, it seems like a perfectly natural and logical thing for me to do. It's a time in my life I remember with absolute vividness. Sometimes I feel like I never even left high school, like I'm still sixteen years old, hiding out in the body of an adult woman, about to be unmasked as a fraud at any moment.

"You see, high school is only three or four years of your life. That's a very tiny part of the average life span, and yet—everything you experience, everything you feel—

all of it stays with you forever. It's just something you never forget or entirely outgrow."

*   *   *

SUPREE, Burt(on) 1941-1992

PERSONAL: Born March 20, 1941, in New York, NY; died of an apparent heart attack, May 1, 1992, in Manhattan, NY; son of William and Sarah (Harris) Supree. *Education:* City College of the City University of New York, B.A., 1961. *Hobbies and other interests:* International travel, especially France (has also visited Scotland and the Outer Hebrides, South America, Central America, Japan, Cambodia, Nepal, and Afghanistan.)

CAREER: Village Voice, New York City, editor of entertainment listings, 1965-92, author of columns "Kids," 1973-92, and "Footlights," 1975-92. Associate professor at Sarah Lawrence College, 1971-76.

AWARDS, HONORS: Gold medal from Boys' Clubs of America, 1967, for *Mother, Mother, I Feel Sick, Send for the Doctor Quick, Quick, Quick;* Irma Simonton Black award from Bank Street College of Education, 1973, for *Harlequin and the Gift of Many Colors.*

WRITINGS:

(With Remy Charlip) *Mother, Mother, I Feel Sick, Send for the Doctor Quick, Quick, Quick,* illustrated by Charlip, Parents Magazine Press, 1966.

In *Bear's Heart,* Supree and co-author Ann Ross chronicle the life of a Cheyenne brave imprisoned on a military camp in Florida during the 1870s. (Cover illustration by Bear's Heart.)

(With Charlip) *Harlequin and the Gift of Many Colors,* illustrated by Charlip, Parents Magazine Press, 1973.

(With Ann Ross) *Bear's Heart: Scenes from the Life of a Cheyenne Artist of a Hundred Years Ago with Pictures by Himself,* afterword by Jamake Highwater, Lippincott, 1977.

Contributor to periodicals, including *St. Andrews Review* and *Weid.*

SIDELIGHTS: Burt Supree worked as a dancer, choreographer, and actor from 1963 to 1970, then switched to teaching courses and workshops designed to instruct theatre students in movement, sound, costuming, and "making things up." Supree's interest in costumes is evident in *Harlequin and the Gift of Many Colors,* described by Michael J. Bandler in *Washington Post Book World* as "an exquisite adaptation of the legend of the famed theatrical symbol." In the story, a poor boy named Harlequin wishes to attend an annual carnival, but cannot afford a costume. His friends each give him a scrap of their outfits; his mother sews them into a patchwork ensemble that transforms him into the most beautiful of the revelers.

Mother, Mother, I Feel Sick, Send for the Doctor Quick, Quick, Quick, Supree's first collaborative effort with Remy Charlip, shows what happens when a boy eats the wrong things—furniture, machinery, and other nonsensical foods. With illustrations emphasizing its design as a shadow play, "the book is useful because really good slapstick comes seldom," Alice Dalgliesh commented in *Saturday Review.*

In *Bear's Heart: Scenes from the Life of a Cheyenne Artist of One Hundred Years Ago with Pictures by Himself,* Supree chronicles the life of Bear's Heart, a Cheyenne imprisoned in a Florida military camp during an 1870s government roundup designed to crush Native Americans rebelling against the loss of their homeland. The story is told through Bear's Heart's drawings, made while in prison with pens, pencils, and paper provided by a kind lieutenant. A *Horn Book* reviewer described *Bear's Heart* as "a vivid pictorial record of the long, agonizing journey to St. Augustine [Florida] and of the captives' lives at the fort" and noted that the book's afterword, written by Jamake Highwater, provides valuable information for young readers. "The book arouses our sympathies and our consciences," Jean Mercier remarked in *Publishers Weekly.*

WORKS CITED:

Bandler, Michael J., "Harlequins, Dinosaurs, Ducks in the Bathtub," *Washington Post Book World,* July 8, 1973, p. 13.

Review of *Bear's Heart: Scenes from the Life of a Cheyenne Artist of One Hundred Years Ago with Pictures by Himself, Horn Book,* October, 1977, p. 545.

Dalgliesh, Alice, review of *Mother, Mother, I Feel Sick, Send for the Doctor Quick, Quick, Quick, Saturday Review,* April 16, 1966, p. 49.

Mercier, Jean, review of *Bear's Heart: Scenes from the Life of a Cheyenne Artist of One Hundred Years Ago with Pictures by Himself, Publishers Weekly,* May 16, 1977, p. 63.

FOR MORE INFORMATION SEE:

PERIODICALS

Bulletin of the Center for Children's Books, September, 1966, pp. 5-6; July-August, 1973, p. 167.
Children's Book Review, spring, 1975, p. 11.
New York Times Book Review, August 21, 1966, p. 20; March 11, 1973, p. 8.
Publishers Weekly, April 23, 1973, p. 62.
School Library Journal, May, 1966, p. 138; May, 1977, p. 73.*

OBITUARIES:

PERIODICALS

Los Angeles Times, May 10, 1992, p. A36.
New York Times, May 5, 1992, p. D31.

* * *

SUTCLIFF, Rosemary 1920-1992

OBITUARY NOTICE —See index for *SATA* sketch: Born December 14, 1920, in East Clanden, Surrey, England; died July 23 (one source says July 22), 1992. Author. Considered one of the greatest writers of children's literature, Sutcliff rooted her historical novels in scrupulous research, meaning them to be for both children and adults. She was acclaimed for her ability to bring past ages to life through a deep comprehension of historic details and to write about credible characters in vigorous prose. *The Mark of the Horse Lord* has often been called her masterpiece, and *The Lantern Bearers* won the Carnegie Medal in 1960. Sutcliff also wrote *The Eagle of the Ninth, Dawn Wind,* and *The Shining Company.*

OBITUARIES AND OTHER SOURCES:

BOOKS

Who's Who, 144th edition, St. Martin's, 1992.

PERIODICALS

Junior Bookshelf, October, 1992, pp. 181-84.
School Library Journal, September, 1992, p. 132.
Times (London), July 25, 1992, p. 17.

T–V

THOMPSON, George Selden 1929-1989
(George Selden)

PERSONAL: Born May 14, 1929, in Hartford, CT; died of complications from a gastrointestinal hemorrhage, December 5, 1989, in New York, NY; son of Hartwell Green (a doctor) and Sigrid (Johnson) Thompson. *Education:* Yale University, B.A., 1951. *Politics:* Independent. *Religion:* Independent. *Hobbies and other interests:* Archaeology, music.

CAREER: Writer of children's fiction, biographies, plays, and screenplays.

AWARDS, HONORS: Fulbright scholarship to Italy, 1951-52; Newbery Honor Book citation, 1961, and Lewis Carroll Shelf Award, 1963, both for *The Cricket in Times Square;* Christopher Book Award, 1969, for *Tucker's Countryside;* William Allen White Children's Book Award, 1978, for *Harry Cat's Pet Puppy.*

WRITINGS:

FOR CHILDREN; UNDER NAME GEORGE SELDEN

The Dog That Could Swim under Water: Memoirs of a Springer Spaniel, illustrated by Morgan Dennis, Viking, 1956.

The Garden under the Sea, illustrated by Garry MacKenzie, Viking, 1957, published as *Oscar Lobster's Fair Exchange,* illustrated by Peter Lippman, Harper, 1966.

The Cricket in Times Square, illustrated by Garth Williams, Farrar, Straus, 1960.

I See What I See!, illustrated by Robert Galster, Farrar, Straus, 1962.

The Mice, the Monks and the Christmas Tree, illustrated by Jan Balet, Macmillan, 1963.

Heinrich Schliemann, Discoverer of Buried Treasure (biography), illustrated by Lorence Bjorklund, Macmillan, 1964.

Sir Arthur Evans, Discoverer of Knossos (biography), illustrated by Lee Ames, Macmillan, 1964.

Sparrow Socks, illustrated by Lippman, Harper, 1965.

GEORGE SELDEN THOMPSON

The Children's Story (play; based on the novel by James Clavell), Dramatists Play Service, 1966.

The Dunkard, illustrated by Lippman, Harper, 1968.

Tucker's Countryside, illustrated by Williams, Farrar, Straus, 1969.

The Genie of Sutton Place (adapted from his television play of the same title, written with Kenneth Hever, produced by Westinghouse "Studio One"; also see below), Farrar, Straus, 1973.

Harry Cat's Pet Puppy, illustrated by Williams, Farrar, Straus, 1974.

Chester Cricket's Pigeon Ride, illustrated by Williams, Farrar, Straus, 1981.

Irma and Jerry, illustrated by Leslie H. Morrill, Avon, 1982.

Chester Cricket's New Home, illustrated by Williams, Farrar, Straus, 1983.

Harry Kitten and Tucker Mouse, illustrated by Williams, Farrar, Straus, 1985.

The Old Meadow, illustrated by Williams, Farrar, Straus, 1987.

Also author of unproduced film script based on the television play, "The Genie of Sutton Place," for Spoleto Productions.

ADAPTATIONS: The Cricket in Times Square was produced as a dramatized recording by Miller-Brody Productions in 1972, and was produced as an animated television show by the American Broadcasting Company (ABC) in 1973. Disney Studios holds an option on *The Genie of Sutton Place.*

SIDELIGHTS: With the debut of the beloved characters Harry Cat, Tucker Mouse, and Chester Cricket in his 1960 story, *The Cricket in Times Square,* George Selden Thompson created a trio of animal friends who have delighted readers for decades. Before his death in 1989, Thompson—who wrote under the name George Selden—offered readers six more books following their adventures, including *Tucker's Countryside, Harry Cat's Pet Puppy, Chester Cricket's Pigeon Ride, Chester Cricket's New Home, Harry Kitten and Tucker Mouse,* and *The Old Meadow. Dictionary of Literary Biography* contributor Lesley S. Potts explained the appeal of

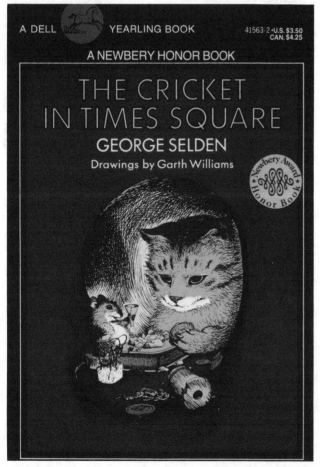

A DELL YEARLING BOOK   41563-2 •U.S. $3.50 CAN. $4.25

A NEWBERY HONOR BOOK

THE CRICKET IN TIMES SQUARE

GEORGE SELDEN

Drawings by Garth Williams

In this Newbery Honor Award-winning book, Chester the cricket gets some big-city survival tips from Harry Cat and Tucker Mouse. (Cover illustration by Garth Williams.)

Selden's animal friends: "Their all-too-human concerns and the give-and-take of their relationships lend complete credibility to the whimsical notion that a cat, a mouse, and a cricket could be the truest of friends.... Selden's clear and simple writing style provides insight into human frailties such as snobbery, greed, possessiveness, prejudice, ignorance, and vanity in a gently probing, yet affectionate, manner, without resorting to sentimentality."

"Like Chester Cricket," related Lee Bennett Hopkins in his *More Books by More People,* "George Selden was born in Connecticut—Hartford—and grew up there." As a child the author developed a love of nature, archaeology, and music. "I didn't have a particularly artistic home," Selden commented to Hopkins, "but I realized early that I wanted to be a writer. Both my brother and I had plenty of exposure to music, especially opera, through my mother. And it was my father, a doctor, who read a lot. I never had any idea that one day I'd write for children. I always liked children's literature, even as an adult." As a student at Yale University, Selden wrote for the literary magazine and was a member of the Elizabethan Club. He later won a Fulbright scholarship and went to Perugia and Rome, Italy, where he studied Latin and Greek.

When Selden returned to the United States after a year abroad it was with the determination to become a published writer. He decided to give himself three years to see whether he could make it in his chosen profession. "I started out as a playwright ...," Selden once told *Contemporary Authors New Revision Series* interviewer Jean W. Ross, "but I wasn't having too much success with my plays. A friend of mine who was employed at Viking at the time suggested that I write a children's book. I did and it was published, although I've disowned it now; it was the first one and I really don't like it too much. I'd always been interested in the field, but that got me *practically* interested. I began to think that I might be able to do something in it myself, and that's how I started." Although Potts similarly believed that Selden's first book, *The Dog That Could Swim under Water: Memoirs of a Springer Spaniel,* is not his best, the critic pointed out that its "theme of friends helping friends was to become a familiar one, more fully developed, in Selden's subsequent books.... [It also] shows the beginnings of a breezy, warm, and humorous style of writing."

Selden followed *The Dog That Could Swim under Water* with what Potts called "a prototype" for his later books, *The Garden under the Sea,* later reprinted as *Oscar Lobster's Fair Exchange,* which uses animal characters to satirize human behavior. Selden got the idea for his story from his stays at his family's summer house on Long Island Sound, where his familiarity with the coastal setting added believability to the book's narration. The story is about how Oscar organizes his friends to take human belongings from the shore of Long Island Sound as a response to vacationers who have been "stealing" rocks and shells from the beach; the sea creatures' adventures offer plenty of opportunities for humor and witty dialogue. Critics praised *The Garden under the Sea* for, as one *Virginia Kirkus' Service* reviewer wrote, "Selden's knowledge of the sea, and his ear for a humorous, salty tale."

Just as Selden was inspired to write *The Garden under the Sea* by his walks along the Long Island Sound beaches, the subways of New York City inspired him to write *The Cricket in Times Square.* One late night Selden was in the Times Square subway station when he heard the unexpected sound of a cricket's chirp, which reminded him of his former home in Connecticut. Immediately, a story rushed into his mind about a cricket who, like him, found himself in the hustle and bustle of New York City and was homesick for the countryside. To help the lost cricket, Selden invented a streetwise, materialistic mouse and a soft-spoken, kindly cat, and Chester, Tucker, and Harry were born.

In their first adventure, Chester accidentally arrives in Times Square after he sneaks into a picnic basket containing one of his favorite foods, liverwurst. Befriended by Harry and Tucker, who have taken up residence in a drainpipe, and a boy named Mario Bellini, Chester is discovered to possess a remarkable gift for music. Learning a wide variety of popular and classical tunes by listening to the radio, Chester—with the help of Harry and Tucker—saves the financially troubled newsstand that belongs to Mario's family by putting on a grand performance that makes Chester and the Bellinis famous. After saving the newsstand, however, Chester's homesickness gets the better of him and he returns to Connecticut.

The Cricket in Times Square is a unique work because, as Potts reported, it was "the first time ... an animal fantasy was located entirely in the big city." More importantly, critics praised the book for its well-drawn plot and lively characterization. One *New York Herald Tribune Book Review* critic pointed out that the author's earlier books "had the same excellent writing and original imaginative twist but they lacked the unified plot we have in [*The Cricket in Times Square*]. This is absolutely grand fun for anyone." And *Spectator* reviewer Benny Green called the book a "rare commodity, a children's book with subtle, vigorous and credible characterisations." Today, as Hopkins noted, *The Cricket in Times Square* is considered "a modern classic in children's literature."

Although Selden received many requests from readers for him to write a sequel to *The Cricket in Times Square,* he did not sit down to create a new adventure about these characters for almost a decade because he wanted to wait until another idea struck him that he felt would be worthy of Chester and his friends. Instead, he went on to write other works, such as two biographies and several more children's stories featuring new characters. His biographies, *Heinrich Schliemann, Discoverer of Buried Treasure* and *Sir Arthur Evans, Discoverer of Knossos,* were done by Selden because of his interest in archaeology. Schliemann was a pioneer in the science of

archaeology and discoverer of ancient Troy, and Evans discovered the remains of the Minoan civilization.

Like the author's earlier fiction, stories such as *Sparrow Socks, The Dunkard,* and *The Genie of Sutton Place* contain the usual Selden touches of satire and a focus on the importance of friendship. *The Dunkard* is a satirical picture book that spoofs the idea of show-and-tell days at school; *Sparrow Socks* relates how a group of sparrows help save a Scottish sock factory in gratitude for the socks that young Angus McFee has knitted them. In a somewhat more complex tale, Selden uses some of his knowledge of archaeology in *The Genie of Sutton Place* to add some realism to the story of how Tim enlists the help of a genie to prevent his aunt from taking his beloved dog Sam away. None of these books, however, have achieved the same amount of popularity as the Cricket stories. Even Selden's *Irma and Jerry,* a book with a premise that resembles that of *The Cricket in Times Square*—it involves a Connecticut animal (a dog this time) that ventures into New York City—was not nearly as successful.

Selden's favorite book about his well-known trio was the first sequel to *The Cricket in Times Square, Tucker's Countryside.* This was partly because it has to do with a

When the roof of his stump house falls in, Chester Cricket is forced to move in with his friends—with decidedly mixed results. (Cover illustration by Williams.)

subject that was very close to his heart: the conservation of nature. In this adventure, Harry and Tucker travel to Chester's home in a Connecticut meadow to save it from a building project. After *Tucker's Countryside,* Selden alternated the next five books of the series between Chester's home in the Old Meadow and Tucker's and Harry's New York City neighborhood. The books were generally well received by critics. For example, Margery Fisher praised *Harry Cat's Pet Puppy* in her *Growing Point* review for being "warm-hearted without being sentimental and full of a zippy dialogue." Only *Chester Cricket's Pigeon Ride* drew much negative response, largely because Selden adopted a picture book format in this case. Reviewers complained about the "slightness of the story line," as Potts reported. But Potts defended that "within its limitations as a pictorial essay, it succeeds very well."

Two years after the publication of his last Chester Cricket tale, *The Old Meadow,* Selden passed away in New York City. Though many will remember him for the Cricket stories, all of Selden's books share the same distinctive theme of friendship. "Implicit in Selden's friendship theme," observed Potts, "is the importance of understanding and caring between people of different backgrounds, beliefs, and temperaments. Whether the characters involved in a story are as incongruous as a

cat, a mouse, and a cricket or a boy, a dog-turned-man, and an Arabian genie, their differences are minimized and their common bond of humanity is stressed." Because of a shared concern for friendship and humanity, said Potts, Selden's stories "have been linked to the works of [*Charlotte's Web* author] E. B. White and Kenneth Graham," who wrote *The Wind in the Willows.* Like these writers, the critic declared, Selden has "assured him[self] a lasting place in children's literature."

WORKS CITED:

"A Connecticut Cricket," review of *The Cricket in Times Square, New York Herald Tribune Book Review,* November 13, 1960, p. 5.
Fisher, Margery, in a review of *Harry Cat's Pet Puppy, Growing Point,* April, 1978, p. 3291.
Review of *The Garden under the Sea, Virginia Kirkus' Service,* January 15, 1957, pp. 37-38.
Green, Benny, "Child Labour," *Spectator,* April 16, 1977, pp. 26-27.
Hopkins, Lee Bennett, *More Books by More People,* Citation Press, 1974, pp. 304-307.
Potts, Lesley S., "George Selden," *Dictionary of Literary Biography,* Volume 52: *American Writers for Children since 1960: Fiction,* Gale, 1986, pp. 325-333.
Thompson, George Selden, in an interview with Jean W. Ross, *Contemporary Authors New Revision Series,* Volume 21, Gale, 1987, pp. 438-442.

FOR MORE INFORMATION SEE:

BOOKS

Blount, Margery, *Animal Land: The Creatures of Children's Fiction,* Morrow, 1975, pp. 131-151.
Children's Literature Review, Volume 8, Gale, 1985, pp. 195-203.

PERIODICALS

Bulletin of the Center for Children's Books, February, 1984; February, 1987; January, 1988.
Children's Book Review, June, 1971, p. 92.
Christian Science Monitor, October 3, 1973.
Growing Point, March, 1984, p. 4213.
Horn Book, August, 1969; August, 1973, pp. 382-383; October, 1974.
Junior Bookshelf, June, 1971, p. 187; August, 1978, p. 195; February, 1984, p. 29.
Kirkus Reviews, December 15, 1974, p. 1305; September 15, 1981, p. 1161.
National Observer, June 9, 1969, p. 23.
New York Times Book Review, September 20, 1964, p. 26; June 24, 1973, p. 8; March 13, 1983, p. 29; January 22, 1984, p. 24.
School Library Journal, September, 1969, p. 161; November, 1982, p. 104.
Times Literary Supplement, April 7, 1978; July 23, 1982.
Washington Post Book World, August 9, 1981, p. 9.
Young Readers Review, December, 1965.

Harry Cat gets a new "pet" in this sequel to *The Cricket in Times Square.* (Cover illustration by Williams.)

OBITUARIES:

PERIODICALS

Los Angeles Times, December 10, 1989.
New York Times, December 6, 1989.
School Library Journal, January, 1990, p. 18.*

TOLLAND, W. R.
  See HEITZMANN, William Ray

*   *   *

VINCENT, W. R.
  See HEITZMANN, William Ray

W

WAHL, Jan (Boyer) 1933-

PERSONAL: Born April 1, 1933, in Columbus, OH; son of Russell Rothenburger (a physician) and Nina Marie (Boyer) Wahl. *Education:* Cornell University, B.A., 1953; graduate study at University of Copenhagen, 1954-55; University of Michigan, M.A., 1958. *Religion:* Presbyterian. *Hobbies and other interests:* Collecting old films, particularly animated films; collecting old toys and comic strip and animation art; traveling from the Sahara Desert to Lapland to the Yucatan.

ADDRESSES: Home—6766 Carrietowne Ln., Toledo, OH 43617; and Apartado Postal 33, San Miguel Allende, Guanajuato, Mexico. *Agent*—Mary Jack Wald, 111 East 14th St., New York, NY 10003; Rogers, Coleridge and White, 20 Powis Mews, London W11 1JN, England.

CAREER: Worked with Danish film director Carl Theodor Dreyer during the making of Dreyer's prize-winning *Ordet,* 1954-55; returned to Denmark as secretary to writer Isak Dinesen, 1957-58; later worked with illustrator Garth Williams in Mexico, and with Erik Blegvad in England, 1966-67; writer for young people. Served as correspondent from Copenhagen for *Dance* during the 1950s and worked as a translator of French communiques for two Danish newspapers.

AWARDS, HONORS: Fulbright scholar in Copenhagen, 1953-54; Avery Hopwood Award in fiction, University of Michigan, 1955, for a group of short stories collectively titled *Seven Old Maids* (the stories appeared in various periodicals); Young Critics' award at International Children's Book Fair, Bologna, Italy, 1969, for *Pocahontas in London;* Ohioana Book Award winner, 1970, for *The Norman Rockwell Storybook;* American Library Association (ALA) Notable Book citation, 1974, for *The Woman with the Eggs;* Bowling Green State University, Ohio, declared May 1, 1980, as "Jan Wahl Day"; Parents' Choice literary award, 1982, for *Tiger Watch; Redbook* award, 1987, for *Humphrey's Bear.*

WRITINGS:

CHILDREN'S FICTION

Pleasant Fieldmouse, illustrated by Maurice Sendak, Harper, 1964.
The Howards Go Sledding, illustrated by John E. Johnson, Holt, 1964.
Hello, Elephant, illustrated by Edward Ardizzone, Holt, 1964.
Cabbage Moon, illustrated by Adrienne Adams, Holt, 1965.

JAN WAHL

222

The Muffletumps: A Story of Four Dolls, illustrated by E. Ardizzone, Holt, 1966.

Christmas in the Forest, illustrated by Eleanor Schick, Macmillan, 1967.

Pocahontas in London, illustrated by John Alcorn, Delacorte, 1967.

Cobweb Castle, illustrated by Edward Gorey, Holt, 1968.

The Furious Flycycle, illustrated by Fernando Krahn, Delacorte, 1968.

Push Kitty, illustrated by Garth Williams, Harper, 1968.

Rickety Rackety Rooster, illustrated by J. E. Johnson, Simon & Schuster, 1968.

Runaway Jonah, and Other Tales (adapted from biblical stories), illustrated by Uri Shulevitz, Macmillan, 1968, illustrated by Jane Conteh-Morgan, Caedmon, 1985.

The Fishermen, illustrated by Emily Arnold McCully, Norton, 1969.

How the Children Stopped the Wars (fable), illustrated by Mitchell Miller, Farrar, Straus, 1969, illustrated by Gerald Rose, Abelard Schuman, 1975, illustrated by Maureen O'Keefe, Ten Speed Press, 1993.

May Horses, illustrated by Blair Lent, Delacorte, 1969.

The Norman Rockwell Storybook, illustrated by Norman Rockwell, Windmill/Simon & Schuster, 1969.

A Wolf of My Own, illustrated by Lillian Hoban, Macmillan, 1969.

The Animals' Peace Day, illustrated by Victoria Chess, Crown, 1970.

Doctor Rabbit, illustrated by Peter Parnall, Delacorte, 1970.

The Mulberry Tree, illustrated by Feodor Rojankovsky, Grosset, 1970.

The Prince Who Was a Fish, illustrated by Robin Jacques, Simon & Schuster, 1970.

Abe Lincoln's Beard, illustrated by F. Krahn, Delacorte, 1971.

Anna Help Ginger, illustrated by Lawrence Di Fiori, Putnam, 1971.

Crabapple Night, illustrated by Steven Kellogg, Holt, 1971.

Lorenzo Bear and Company, illustrated by F. Krahn, Putnam, 1971.

Margaret's Birthday, illustrated by Mercer Mayer, Four Winds Press, 1971.

The Six Voyages of Pleasant Fieldmouse, illustrated by P. Parnall, Delacorte, 1971.

The Wonderful Kite, illustrated by U. Shulevitz, Delacorte, 1971.

Cristobal and the Witch, illustrated by Janet McCaffery, Putnam, 1972.

Grandmother Told Me, illustrated by M. Mayer, Little, Brown, 1972.

Magic Heart, illustrated by Trina Schart Hyman, Seabury, 1972.

The Very Peculiar Tunnel, illustrated by S. Kellogg, Putnam, 1972.

Crazy Brobobalou (adapted from *Le Prince spirituel,* by Countess Prince de Beaumont), illustrated by Paula Winter, Putnam, 1973.

Wahl's sense of whimsy is evident in this book of action-packed verse. (Cover illustration by David Allender.)

S.O.S. Bobomobile! or, The Future Adventures of Melvin Spitznagle and Professor Mickimecki, illustrated by F. Krahn, Delacorte, 1973.

Jeremiah Knucklebones, illustrated by Jane Breskin Zalben, Holt, 1974.

(With Spanish translation by Dolores Janes Garcia) *Juan Diego and the Lady/La dama y Juan Diego* (bilingual edition), illustrated by Leonard Everett Fisher, Putnam, 1974.

Mooga Mega Mekki, illustrated by F. Krahn, O'Hara, 1974.

Pleasant Fieldmouse's Halloween Party, illustrated by Wallace Tripp, Putnam, 1974.

The Five in the Forest, illustrated by Erik Blegvad, Follett, 1974.

The Woman with the Eggs (adapted from the fable by Hans Christian Andersen), illustrated by Ray Cruz, Crown, 1974.

Bear, Wolf, and Mouse, illustrated by Kinuko Craft, Follett, 1975.

The Clumpets Go Sailing, illustrated by Cyndy Szekeres, Parents' Magazine Press, 1975.

The Muffletumps' Christmas Party, illustrated by C. Szekeres, Follett, 1975.

The Muffletump Storybook, illustrated by C. Szekeres, Follett, 1975.

The Screeching Door; or, What Happened at the Elephant Hotel, illustrated by J. Winslow Higginbottom, Four Winds Press, 1975.

Follow Me Cried Bee, illustrated by John Wallner, Crown, 1976.

A group of animal friends find excitement when they go on a nature walk in Wahl's 1979 work. (Cover illustration by Cyndy Szekeres.)

Grandpa's Indian Summer, illustrated by Joanne Scribner, Prentice-Hall, 1976.

Great-Grandmother Cat Tales, illustrated by C. Szekeres, Pantheon, 1976.

Doctor Rabbit's Foundling, illustrated by C. Szekeres, Pantheon, 1977.

Frankenstein's Dog (also see below), illustrated by Kay Chorao, Prentice-Hall, 1977.

The Muffletumps' Halloween Scare, illustrated by C. Szekeres, Follett, 1977.

The Pleasant Fieldmouse Storybook, illustrated by E. Blegvad, Prentice-Hall, 1977.

Pleasant Fieldmouse's Valentine Trick, illustrated by E. Blegvad, Windmill/Dutton, 1977.

Carrot Nose, illustrated by James Marshall, Farrar, Straus, 1977.

Dracula's Cat (also see below), illustrated by K. Chorao, Prentice-Hall, 1977.

Drakestail (adapted from the French folktale), illustrated by Byron Barton, Greenwillow, 1978.

Jamie's Tiger, illustrated by Tomie dePaola, Harcourt, 1978.

Who Will Believe Tim Kitten?, illustrated by C. Szekeres, Pantheon, 1978.

Doctor Rabbit's Lost Scout, illustrated by C. Szekeres, Pantheon, 1979.

Needle Noodle, and Other Silly Stories (English folktales), illustrated by Stan Mack, Pantheon, 1979.

Sylvester Bear Overslept, illustrated by Lee Lorenz, Parents' Magazine Press, 1979.

The Teeny Tiny Witches, illustrated by Margot Tomes, Putnam, 1979.

Button Eye's Orange, illustrated by Wendy Watson, Warne, 1980.

Old Hippo's Easter Egg, illustrated by Lorinda Bryan-Cauley, Harcourt, 1980.

The Cucumber Princess, illustrated by Caren Caraway, Stemmer House, 1981.

Grandpa Gus's Birthday Cake, illustrated by J. Wallner, Prentice-Hall, 1981.

The Little Blind Goat, illustrated by Antonio Frasconi, Stemmer House, 1981.

The Pipkins Go Camping, illustrated by J. Wallner, Prentice-Hall, 1982.

Tiger Watch, illustrated by Charles Mikolaycak, Harcourt, 1982.

More Room for the Pipkins, illustrated by J. Wallner, Prentice-Hall, 1983.

Peter and the Troll Baby, illustrated by E. Blegvad, Golden Press, 1984.

Cheltenham's Party, illustrated by Lucinda McQueen, Golden Press, 1985.

So Many Raccoons, illustrated by Beth Lee Weiner, Caedmon, 1985.

Rabbits on Roller Skates!, illustrated by David Allender, Crown, 1986.

The Toy Circus, illustrated by Tim Bowers, Gulliver Books-Harcourt, 1986.

Let's Go Fishing, illustrated by Bruce Lemorise, Golden Press, 1987.

Humphrey's Bear, illustrated by William Joyce, Holt, 1987.

Timothy Tiger's Terrible Toothache, illustrated by Lisa McCue, Golden Press, 1988.

Little Dragon's Grandmother, illustrated by L. McQueen, Golden Press, 1988.

Tim Kitten and the Red Cupboard, illustrated by Bruce Degen, Simon & Schuster, 1988.

The Golden Christmas Tree, illustrated by Leonard Weisgard, Golden Press, 1988.

Tales of Fuzzy Mouse: Six Cozy Stories for Bedtime, illustrated by L. Hoban, Golden Press, 1988.

The Adventures of Underwater Dog, illustrated by Tim Bowers, Grosset, 1989.

The Wizard of Oz Movie Storybook, Golden Press, 1989.

Dracula's Cat [and] *Frankenstein's Dog,* illustrated by K. Chorao, Simon & Schuster, 1990.

A Gift for Miss Milo, illustrated by Jeff Grove, Ten Speed Press, 1990.

The Rabbit Club, illustrated by Tim Bowers, Harcourt, 1990.

Mrs. Owl and Mr. Pig, illustrated by Eileen Christelow, Lodestar/Dutton, 1991.

(Reteller) *Tailypo!,* illustrated by Wil Clay, Holt, 1991.

The Sleepytime Book, illustrated by Arden Johnson, Tambourine Books, 1992.

(Reteller) *Little Eight John,* illustrated by W. Clay, Lodestar/Dutton, 1992.

My Cat Ginger, illustrated by Naava, Tambourine Books, 1992.

Suzy and the Mouse King, illustrated by Catherine A. Macaro, Monroe County Library, 1992.

Little Gray One, illustrated by Frane Lessac, Tambourine Books, 1993.

OTHER

Paradiso! Paradiso! (play), first produced at Cornell University, 1954.

The Beast Book (children's verse), illustrated by E. W. Eichel, Harper, 1964.

Youth's Magic Horn: Seven Stories (young adult fiction), Thomas Nelson, 1978.

Contributor to periodicals, including *Transatlantic Review, Prairie Schooner, Films in Review,* and *Epoch.* Wahl's manuscripts are housed in a Jan Wahl Collection at the University of Wyoming, Laramie, at Bowling Green State University, Bowling Green, Ohio, and at the Kerlan Collection at the University of Minnesota, Minneapolis.

ADAPTATIONS: An animated film entitled *Why We Need Each Other: The Animals' Picnic Day,* adapted from *The Animals' Peace Day,* was produced by Bosustow/Learning Corporation, 1973; a filmstrip with cassette of *The Clumpets Go Sailing* was produced by Listening Library, 1979; an animated film based on *The Furious Flycycle* was produced by Bosustow/Churchill and was later presented on CBS-TV, 1980; an opera based on *How the Children Stopped the Wars* was produced by Northwestern University in 1986, and at Fairfield University in 1991; an album and audiocassette of *Runaway Jonah, and Other Tales* with orchestra and songs, read by E. G. Marshall, was produced by Caedmon, c. 1986; a filmstrip of *The Toy Circus* was produced by Random House, 1988.

SIDELIGHTS: Jan Wahl is an imaginative and prolific writer of children's books, many of which are graced by the work of the most notable of illustrators. When he was born in Columbus, Ohio, in 1933, his father was a pre-medical student at Ohio State University and his mother was an art student; therefore, Wahl spent a good portion of the Great Depression years with both sets of

Pleasant Fieldmouse's sense of adventure and fun make him a favorite with all of his animal neighbors. (Cover illustration by Maurice Sendak.)

grandparents in northwest Ohio improvising stories for his own amusement and later for the amusement of his five other brothers. One of his first literary efforts involved trying to improve upon the story of "Jack and the Beanstalk." At the age of three, though, he remembers being enthralled as his great-grandmother sketched a chicken on what had previously been a blank sheet of paper. "And I believe at that moment I became 'hooked' on art in general," says Wahl in an autobiographical essay in *Something about the Author Autobiography Series (SAAS).* "Virtually the whole of my adult life has been spent in writing and scribbling so that some artist might make interesting pictures. Much of my life, too, has been spent recalling the freshness of that morning on an Ohio farm where I spent much of my childhood."

As the Great Depression was ending, Wahl's family settled in Toledo, Ohio, where his father had established his medical practice. Since one of his mother's cousins happened to be the music director for a local broadcasting company, Wahl was invited to play on a Saturday morning radio program. He describes his life at the time: "I did puppet shows, magic shows; I pretended to be Danny Kaye and lip-synched his records. I performed before church groups, traveled to other schools, made a buffoon of myself in front of parent-teacher groups. And on Saturday mornings did 'The Kiddies' Karnival.'" Wahl also fell in love with the movies, a passion retained in his collection of old films, particularly animated films by Lotte Reiniger, Ladislas Starevitch, Max Fleisher, Walt Disney, Hugh Harman, and Rudolf Ising. Although Wahl, with an early training in piano, wanted to write music for film, he believes that movies have helped him in his career as a writer, enabling him to think visually.

After high school graduation, Wahl entered Cornell University where he began to study creative writing and published stories in a few small magazines. After finishing his bachelor's degree, he won a Fulbright scholarship to the University of Copenhagen. While studying there, he met several influential people, including writer Isak Dinesen. Also, a fortuitous invitation allowed him to work on director Carl Theodor Dreyer's classic film, *Ordet.* Upon his return to the United States, Wahl accepted a scholarship to earn a master's degree at the University of Michigan and continued his efforts to become a writer, winning the Avery Hopwood Award in fiction for a group of short stories collectively titled *Seven Old Maids.* Then came an unexpected cable from an ailing Isak Dinesen in Denmark requesting Wahl to join her there so that she could dictate her last tales. Although he was neither a stenographer nor a professional typist, he was eager to assist the writer; however, the arrangement proved unsatisfactory to her and he was soon dismissed. While in Denmark, Wahl also did research for the Danish Film Museum and became a correspondent from Copenhagen for *Dance* magazine and worked briefly for Danish newspapers.

Upon his return to the United States, Wahl began work on a novel as well as a few little animal stories for children. "This was a lot more fun. I had found what I could do. I MUST write for children. In a way, I was writing the films I wished I could see. A picture book is related to an animated cartoon." Although his first efforts to publish children's books were unsuccessful, Wahl once commented: "When my first children's book, *Pleasant Fieldmouse,* won reviews such as 'belongs on the same high shelf as Beatrix Potter' and 'not since *Wind in the Willows*' and 'if you buy only one book this year, make it this one,' all my own childhood dreams seemed to come true." *Pleasant Fieldmouse,* published in 1964 and still in print, is a story about an optimistic fieldmouse who philosophizes that "things cannot remain unpleasant." He resides in a forest with diverse animals, such as Worry-Wind Hedgehog, Haunted Beaver, Tired Fox, and Terrible Owl. In his community Pleasant Fieldmouse presumes the responsibility of protector. When a fire rages through the forest, Pleasant Fieldmouse wishes for rain, and soon after, the fire is doused; and in an attempt to unite the forest animals, he invites every good creature to a picnic. After he lays out food for the picnic, Pleasant Fieldmouse falls asleep. He rises from his slumber to find the food gone, and he happily assumes everyone came to the picnic. However, the only animals who actually attended the feast were the beetles and caterpillars who could not read, because the animals did not feel that they were good enough to attend.

Some years after publishing *Pleasant Fieldmouse,* Wahl stated in *SAAS,* he was recommended to illustrator

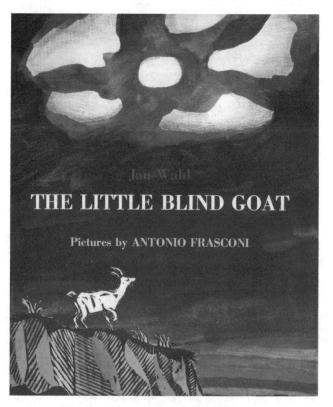

On the advice of El Puerco Espin the hedgehog, Casimiro the blind goat decides to work on enhancing his other senses. (Cover illustration by Antonio Frasconi.)

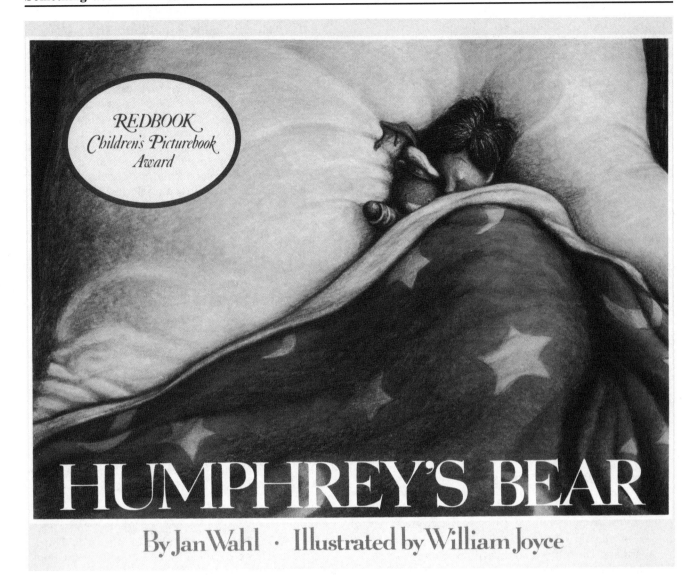

Humphrey's father is reminded of his own happy childhood dreams when he sees his son sleeping with his old teddy bear.
(Cover illustration by William Joyce.)

Norman Rockwell as the "the man for the job" of writing a storybook for Rockwell's illustrations. According to Wahl, Rockwell contacted him personally to request his assistance, and Wahl agreed to write the stories for the book. *The Norman Rockwell Storybook,* released in 1969, features Rockwell's illustrations accompanied by Wahl's detailed characterizations of each picture. *Horn Book* called it "an unusual and successful collaboration."

Another of Wahl's publications, *The Little Blind Goat* follows a blind goat, Casimiro, through a day of exploring the pastures in which he lives. In a conversation between Casimiro and hedgehog El Puerco Espin, the goat explains that he ran into a thorny bush because he could not see it. El Puerco Espin responds by telling the goat to "learn to FEEL. Feel what is on the ground. Feel what is in the air. Feel what is *near.*" With help from other animals in the pasture, Casimiro learns to rely on his senses of touch, smell, taste, and hearing. At the end of the day Casimiro sets out to find his sister,

Todomira, whom he had been separated from earlier in the day, and it is with his keen senses of hearing and smell that he is able to find and save her from captors.

Winner of the 1982 Parents' Choice literary award, *Tiger Watch* continues the lineage of Wahl's animal books. In this book an Indian tiger kills a woman, and the husband and son avenge her death by hunting for and killing the tiger. According to Patricia Dooley's review in *School Library Journal,* the illustrations by Charles Mikolaycak "bring a foreign world very near" and together with Wahl's story "make India at once exotic and familiar." In 1987 Wahl produced another award-winning children's book called *Humphrey's Bear.* Humphrey, a young boy, sleeps with his father's childhood bear, but now his father feels that Humphrey is too old for the bear. When Humphrey wakes from a dream in which he and the bear went on a sailing journey, his father, leaning over his bed, remembers the adventures he had with the bear in his dreams as a young boy, and consequently, allows Humphrey to keep the bear. *School*

Library Journal contributor Anna Biagioni Hart commented in her review of *Humphrey's Bear* that "this team [author and illustrator] is too good and the book too carefully made to disregard." In his autobiographical essay, Wahl reflects on his aspirations for his children's books: "My promise to myself was to write in a positive way. To connect with children and their parents through fables and animal stories. To know that truth can be reached via fantasy."

WORKS CITED:

BOOKS

Something about the Author Autobiography Series, Volume 3, Gale, 1986, pp. 293-311.
Wahl, Jan, *The Little Blind Goat,* Stemmer House, 1981.

PERIODICALS

Dooley, Patricia, review of *Tiger Watch, School Library Journal,* October, 1982, p. 146.
Hart, Anna Biagioni, review of *Humphrey's Bear, School Library Journal,* August, 1987, p. 76.
Review of *The Norman Rockwell Storybook, Horn Book,* February, 1970, p. 34.
Review of *Pleasant Fieldmouse, Times Literary Supplement,* December 4, 1969, p. 1386.

FOR MORE INFORMATION SEE:

BOOKS

Authors of Books for Young People, edited by Martha E. Ward and Dorothy A. Marquardt, Scarecrow, 1971.
Twentieth-Century Children's Writers, 3rd edition, St. James Press, 1989.

PERIODICALS

Book World, December 10, 1967.
Kirkus Reviews, October 15, 1971, p. 1117; March 15, 1986, p. 474; April 15, 1991, p. 540.
National Observer, December 11, 1967.
Newsweek, December 6, 1982.
New York Times Book Review, December 3, 1967; November 7, 1971, p. 46; November 11, 1984, p. 48; August 9, 1987, p. 29.
Ohioana Quarterly, Autumn, 1980.
Publishers Weekly, December 14, 1970, p. 39; February 8, 1971, p. 81; November 11, 1974, p. 48; December 5, 1980, p. 53; January 17, 1986, p. 69; April 25, 1986, p. 72; October 31, 1986, p. 66; April 24, 1987, p. 69; October 13, 1989, p. 56; June 8, 1990, p. 54; May 10, 1991, p. 283.
School Library Journal, January, 1985, p. 48; May, 1986, p. 114; February, 1987, p. 75; January, 1990, p. 92; August, 1990, p. 135; September, 1990, p. 232.
School Library Media Activities Monthly, February, 1990, pp. 33-35.

WARNER, Gertrude Chandler 1890-1979

OBITUARY NOTICE —See index for *SATA* sketch: Born April 16, 1890, in Putnam, CT; died August 30, 1979. Teacher and author. Warner was best known for *The Boxcar Children,* her 1924 tale of a young family living on the railways; a second edition, rewritten in 1942 with a prescribed vocabulary, became a common reader in schools. The author spent over thirty years as an elementary school teacher in Connecticut; during her time off she wrote several children's books, and after retirement penned over fifteen mysteries, including *The Schoolhouse Mystery* and *The Caboose Mystery.* Her works also included *Life's Minor Collisions* and *Pleasures and Palaces,* written with her essayist sister Frances Warner.

OBITUARIES AND OTHER SOURCES:

Date of death provided by publisher, Albert Whitman & Co.

*   *   *

WAX, Wendy A. 1963-

PERSONAL: Born October 9, 1963, in Detroit, MI. *Education:* Received B.F.A. from University of Michigan; attended New York University School of Continuing Education, 1985-91.

ADDRESSES: Home—322 East 55th St., # 2A, New York, NY 10022.

CAREER: Writer.

AWARDS, HONORS: Two books from the "Ten Things I Know" series were named to the Children's Best Book List in *Parents* magazine, 1990.

WRITINGS:

"TEN THINGS I KNOW" SERIES; ILLUSTRATED BY THOMAS PAYNE

Ten Things I Know about Kangaroos, Contemporary Books, 1989.
Ten Things I Know about Penguins, Contemporary Books, 1989.
Ten Things I Know about Elephants, Contemporary Books, 1990.
Ten Things I Know about Whales, Contemporary Books, 1990.

OTHER

Where Does Bubble Gum Come From?, illustrated by Tom Payne, Contemporary Books, 1989.
Inside the Aquarium, illustrated by Joe Murray, Contemporary Books, 1989.
The Autograph Book, Parachute Press, 1990.
My Sticker Book, Parachute Press, 1990.
Me and My Friends, Parachute Press, 1991.
My Book about Me, Parachute Press, 1991.
Say No and Know Why, photographs by Toby McAfee, Walker Publishing, 1992.

Work included in *Time-Life* "Little People Big Book" series.

WORK IN PROGRESS: Novelizations of the television series *Full House*, the animated television series *The Addams Family*, and the "movie *Tom and Jerry*."

SIDELIGHTS: Wendy A. Wax is the author of a number of books that inform young people on subjects ranging from aquariums to bubble gum. Her "Ten Things I Know" series, illustrated by Thomas Payne, was acclaimed for its presentation of facts about various land and sea animals. In 1991 she released *Say No and Know Why*, a book that teaches children about the value of achievement and argues against the use of drugs. She has also illustrated a young adult book cover for Dell. Wax has worked in an editorial capacity for several presses and is involved in merging her interests in writing and illustration.

* * *

WEBER, Bruce 1942-

PERSONAL: Born November 20, 1942, in Brooklyn, NY; son of Paul Karl (an educator) and Miriam Lillian (a homemaker; maiden name, Goldstein) Weber; married Annette Katz (in sales), May 30, 1968; children: Allison Emma, Jonathan Russell. *Education:* University of Maryland, B.S., 1964; Pace University, M.B.A., 1968. *Politics:* Democrat. *Religion:* Jewish. *Hobbies and other interests:* Sports, music.

ADDRESSES: Home—511 Marion Ln., Paramus, NJ 07652. *Office*—Scholastic Inc., 730 Broadway, New York, NY 10003.

CAREER: Scholastic Coach magazine, New York City, assistant editor, 1965-70, associate editor, 1970-81, publisher, 1981—; New York City Board of Education, Brooklyn, NY, music teacher, 1968-72; writer. *Scholastic Sports Academy* (television series), writer, 1981-84. Paramus, New Jersey Board of Education, member, 1978-87, president, 1981-83; Devonshire School Board of Governors, president, 1988-90. Director of Paramus Run, 1979—; director of Athletic Institute, 1991—.

MEMBER: National Soccer Coaches Association of America, Football Writers Association of America, American Football Coaches Association.

AWARDS, HONORS: Action for Children's Television (ACT) Award, 1982, for *Scholastic Sports Academy*; award from Sports in America, 1987, for his work for the Athletic Institute.

WRITINGS:

(With William Hongash) *Questions and Answers about Baseball*, Scholastic Book Services, 1974.
The Funniest Moments in School, illustrated by Kevin Callahan, Lippincott, 1974, reprinted as *School Is a Funny Place*, Scholastic Book Services, 1977.

Weird Moments in Sports, Scholastic Book Services, 1975.
The Pro Football Quiz Book, Scholastic Book Services, 1976.
The Pro Basketball Reading Kit, Bowmar, 1976.
All-Pro Baseball Stars, annual editions, Scholastic Book Services, 1976-81, Scholastic Inc., 1982-83.
All-Pro Basketball Stars, annual editions, Scholastic Book Services, 1976-81, Scholastic Inc., 1982-83.
The Dynamite Animal Hall of Fame, Scholastic Book Services, 1979.
The T.V. Olympic Program Guide, Scholastic Book Services, 1980.
More Weird Moments in Sports, Scholastic Inc., 1983.
Bruce Weber's Inside Pro Football, annual editions, Scholastic Inc., 1983-85.
Bruce Weber's Inside Baseball, annual editions, Scholastic Inc., 1984-85.
Athletes: Photographs by Bruce Weber, Twelvetrees, 1985.
Sparky Anderson, edited by Michael E. Goodman, Crestwood, 1988.
The Indianapolis 500, Creative Education, 1990.

Also author of *All-Pro Football Stars*; author of sixty-five half-hour instructional programs for the USA Network television series *Scholastic Sports Academy*, 1981-84; contributor to *Modern Encyclopedia of Basketball*, edited by Zander Hollander, Doubleday, 1979, and *Eevetec*, Houghton; columnist for *Junior Scholastic, Science World, Voice, Scope, Dynamite, Scholastic Math, Sprint*, and *Action*; contributor to periodicals, including *Teen Age* magazine.

SIDELIGHTS: Bruce Weber told *SATA:* "When I found myself sitting farther and farther away from the coach on the bench, it didn't take a genius to figure out that if I wanted to stay in sports, I'd have to find some other route than the locker-room door. I found my entrance at the press gate and I've been working my way in there ever since.

"It has been wonderful. I know a great many adults who are fed up with their professional lives, doing something every day that they hate. Not me. As Garrett Morris used to say on *Saturday Night Live*, 'Baseball been very, very good to me.' The same goes for football and basketball and soccer and track and field, among other things. There is a genuine fraternity of sports, and most of my professional relationships, many of which are a quarter-century or more old, begin with sports.

"But my greatest pleasure comes from the young people for whom I write. I've been fortunate to work at Scholastic, Inc. for twenty-seven years, and although my basic job involves coaches at all levels, my writing for children produces the most—and most interesting—mail. I try to ignore the sometimes lavish praise these young readers send along, but I'm pleased with the depth of feeling (and often, the quality of writing) I get from the children of America. Once when we ran a contest to determine what changes the readers would make if they were running baseball, we were inundated with suggestions (which we shared with the Commissioner). That's what makes sports great. Everyone can be involved; everyone can be an expert. Can you think of any other subject in which young people can be as totally involved as they are in sports?

"I make every effort to answer every letter or request from a fan (of sports, if not of me), and I try to make every response personal (though that's not always possible). My wife explains this idiosyncrasy of mine by telling friends that that's how I'd have wanted to be treated by an author when I was a kid. She's right, of course.

"When did my involvement with writing begin? As a child—I was eleven, I think—I loved newspapers. But for some reason (possibly cost), we did not get a Sunday paper at home. So my brother (four years younger and now a top antitrust attorney in New York) and I started our own. We began by rising very early on Sunday and listening to the news on the radio. We then wrote short stories (the forerunner of *USA Today?*), and then printed them up in newspaper format on an old-fashioned toy typewriter, which required the spinning of a wheel for each letter. It was hard and tedious, but by the time our folks woke up, the *Weber Times* was ready for them. We added sections and then began pre-printing special sections earlier in the week for inclusion in the Sunday edition. If I remember (this was around 1953), the Sunday *New York Times* cost around a quarter. We probably could have afforded a copy. But this was infinitely more fun, and I think our parents enjoyed our news more than anything the 'old gray lady of Times Square' ever could have done. If that was the start of a career, so be it. It's fun. And so, in the words of Dean Martin, 'Keep those cards and letters coming in!'"

* * *

WEINSTEIN, Nina 1951-

PERSONAL: Born November 30, 1951, in Inglewood, CA; daughter of Herman (a retired flight engineer) and Bernice (a homemaker) Weinstein; married David Van Zak (a psychologist), February 15, 1981; children: Joshua Jordan. *Education:* University of California, Los Angeles, B.A. (world literature), 1975, teaching certificate in English as a second language, 1976, M.A., 1984.

ADDRESSES: Office—c/o The Seal Press, 3131 Western Ave., Suite 410, Seattle, WA 98121.

CAREER: Long Beach City College, Long Beach, CA, instructor, 1977-81. Instructor, Centinela Valley Adult School, 1975-77, Hamilton Adult School, 1977-78, Mazda Motors of America, 1979-89. Also taught summer courses in English as a second language at the University of California, Los Angeles, 1976 and 1978, and Harvard University, 1981.

AWARDS, HONORS: No More Secrets was selected as one of the Best Books for Teenagers, New York Public Libraries, and nominated for Best Book for Young

NINA WEINSTEIN

Adults and Best Book for Reluctant Readers, American Library Association, all 1991.

WRITINGS:

TEXTBOOKS

New English Course, Prentice-Hall, 1979.
Whaddaya Say? A Guide to Relaxed Spoken English, Prentice-Hall, 1982.
Communication Skits, Prentice-Hall, 1983.
Whaddaya Mean? When to Use Formal and Everyday English, Language Services (Japan), 1983, revised, 1985.
Voices of America, Addison-Wesley, 1984
Listen and Say It Right in English, National Textbook, 1985.
Whattaya Do? Business English, Language Services, 1986.
Whattaya Hear? Listening Strategies and Culture through American Jokes, Language Services, 1987.
Say What You Feel, Macmillan, 1990.
Crazy Idioms, Macmillan, 1990.
Reading Snacks, Macmillan, 1991.
(Editor) *Sunshine Series,* Kariyudo (Japan), 1991.

FICTION

No More Secrets, Seal Press, 1991.

WORK IN PROGRESS: The Cheerleader, the Football Star and the Homeless Guy.

SIDELIGHTS: "I love to write," Nina Weinstein told *SATA.* "I wrote *No More Secrets* hoping to open myself emotionally because my life goal is to face all of my fears. *No More Secrets* is semi-autobiographical. I was molested, but not raped as the girl in the story was. Most of the book really happened, although not in the order presented necessarily. Like Mandy in the story, these things were never acknowledged in our house.

"I think the most important message in the book is that every human being's emotions are real and important, no matter what those emotions are, and no matter who opposes them. If something bad happens to you, talk about it to the right person. If you try someone and they don't listen, try someone else until you find someone who takes you as seriously as you deserve to be taken.

"I will continue to write about serious subjects because I think people learn how to better their lives through books."

* * *

WILLIAMS, Ursula Moray
See MORAY WILLIAMS, Ursula

* * *

WILSON, Hazel (Hutchins) 1898-1992

OBITUARY NOTICE —See index for *SATA* sketch: Born April 8, 1898, in Portland, ME; died of congestive heart failure, August 20, 1992, in Bethesda, MD. Librarian, educator, book reviewer, and author. Wilson is remembered for her "Herbert" series of children's books, including *Herbert's Homework, Herbert's Space Trip,* and *Herbert's Stilts.* The ten-year-old character of Herbert was based on Wilson's own son. The subjects of Wilson's writings ranged from geographic features, as in *The Seine: River of Paris,* to historical figures, such as *The Years Between: Washington at Home at Mt. Vernon* and *The Story of Lafayette.* After a career as a librarian in Maine, Missouri, Paris, and Massachusetts, Wilson taught at George Washington and Georgetown universities and wrote book reviews for periodicals.

OBITUARIES AND OTHER SOURCES:

BOOKS

Authors of Books for Young People, 3rd edition, Scarecrow, 1990.

PERIODICALS

Washington Post, August 21, 1992, p. D5.

* * *

WRIGHT, David K. 1943-

PERSONAL: Born January 10, 1943, in Richmond, IN; son of Richard M. (a teacher) and Wilma S. (a teacher) Wright; married Grace Snyder (a teacher), June 27, 1970; children: Austin D., Monica G. *Education:* Wittenberg University, B.A., 1966. *Politics:* Independent. *Religion:* None.

ADDRESSES: Home—452 S. 7th Ave., West Bend, WI 53095. *Office*—P.O. Box 353, West Bend, WI 53095.

CAREER: Chicago Tribune, Chicago, IL, copy editor, 1970-75; *Truth,* Elkhart, IN, city editor, 1975-77; *Monroe Evening Times,* Monroe, WI, editor, 1976-77; freelance writer, 1977—. Member of advisory committee for public television station; publicity chair of Citizens

Advocacy. *Military service:* U.S. Army, 1966-68, served in Vietnam; became sergeant.

WRITINGS:

"ENCHANTMENT OF THE WORLD" SERIES; FOR CHILDREN

Vietnam, Childrens Press, 1988.
Malaysia, Childrens Press, 1988.
Brunei, Childrens Press, 1991.
Burma, Childrens Press, 1991.
Albania, Childrens Press, 1992.

"CHILDREN OF THE WORLD" SERIES; FOR CHILDREN

Hong Kong, Gareth Stevens, 1990.
Singapore, Gareth Stevens, 1990.
Canada, Gareth Stevens, 1991.

OTHER

The Harley-Davidson Motor Company: An Official Eighty-Year History, Classic Motorbooks, 1983.
(Contributor) *Great National Park Vacations,* Rand-McNally, 1987.
War in Vietnam, Volume 1: *Eve of Battle,* Volume 2: *A Wider War,* Volume 3: *Vietnamization,* Volume 4: *Fall of Vietnam,* Childrens Press, 1989.
The Story of the Vietnam Memorial, Childrens Press, 1989.
Censorship, Lerner, 1992.
(With Clarence Jungwirth) *Oshkosh Truck Corporation,* Classic Motorbooks, 1992.

David K. Wright explores the Vietnam war in a four-part series that emphasized the complex nature of the engagement. (Cover photograph by Wang Tzi.)

Contributing editor of bimonthly business magazine. Editor of other works in the "Children of the World" series, Gareth Stevens, 1989-91. Writer, editor, and publisher for *Working Writers* (monthly newsletter), 1991-92.

WORK IN PROGRESS: Self-publishing a book on corporate management.

SIDELIGHTS: David K. Wright, author of some ten books for children, has sought to educate the young about the histories and cultures of various countries with his works. In particular, Wright, a former U.S. soldier who served in the Vietnam War, has written several books about Vietnam. *Vietnam,* his first volume in the "Enchantment of the World" series for Childrens Press, examines Vietnam's history, culture, geography, religion, and politics. Wright explores the country's history beginning with the French occupation in 1874. He details the civil war in Vietnam, which involved the U.S. military troops aiding the South Vietnamese against the invasion and subsequent takeover in 1975 by Communist North Vietnam. The author emphasizes postwar effects on Vietnam, especially environmental, and the problems associated with the flux of refugees fleeing the country. Wright includes color photographs and maps to explain various aspects of the region.

In 1989, a year after publishing *Vietnam,* Wright produced *War in Vietnam,* a four-volume set providing a more detailed account of the Vietnam conflict. In this book Wright recounts the situations leading up to the war and how the U.S. became entangled in the fighting. He discusses the effects of the war, both during and after, on the Vietnamese and U.S. soldiers and civilians. He includes discussion of American anti-war protests and the formation and actions of the Vietnam Veterans Against the War (VVAW) association. Leaders of the war are featured in separate biographies, which *School Library Journal* contributor Mary Mueller lauded as "a strong point in the books." In *War in Vietnam* Wright also reports on the country in the late 1980s. In a review for *Booklist,* Denise Wilms praised the book to be "a staple item for the history or reference shelves."

Wright told *SATA:* "I'm successful, I think, because I'm willing to attempt any assignment. Consequently, the quality of the finished product may fluctuate. But I need to feed my family and spend lots of time at the keyboard."

WORKS CITED:

PERIODICALS

Mueller, Mary, review of *War in Vietam, School Library Journal,* June, 1989, p. 131.
Wilms, Denise, review of *War in Vietnam, Booklist,* June 1, 1989, p. 1727.

FOR MORE INFORMATION SEE:

PERIODICALS

Booklist, August, 1989, p. 1972-1973.
School Library Journal, January, 1990, p. 118; September, 1991, p. 274.

Cumulative Indexes

Illustrations Index

(In the following index, the number of the volume in which an illustrator's work appears is given *before* the colon, and the page number on which it appears is given *after* the colon. For example, a drawing by Adams, Adrienne appears in Volume 2 on page 6, another drawing by her appears in Volume 3 on page 80, another drawing in Volume 8 on page 1, another drawing in Volume 15 on page 107, and so on and so on....)

YABC

Index citations including this abbreviation refer to listings appearing in *Yesterday's Authors of Books for Children,* also published by Gale Research Inc., which covers authors who died prior to 1960.

Author Index

The following index gives the number of the volume in which an author's biographical sketch, Brief Entry, or Obituary appears.

This index includes references to all entries in the following series, which are also published by Gale Research Inc.

YABC—*Yesterday's Authors of Books for Children: Facts and Pictures about Authors and Illustrators of Books for Young People from Early Times to 1960*
CLR—*Children's Literature Review: Excerpts from Reviews, Criticism, and Commentary on Books for Children*
SAAS—*Something about the Author Autobiography Series*

Clark, Leonard 1905-1981 ....*30*
  Obituary *29*
Clark, Margaret Goff 1913- *8*
Clark, Mary Higgins....................*46*
Clark, Mavis Thorpe....................*8*
  See also CLR *30*
  See also SAAS *5*
Clark, Merle
  See Gessner, Lynne
Clark, Patricia (Finrow) 1929- *11*
Clark, Ronald William 1916-1987 ....*2*
  Obituary *52*
Clark, Van D(eusen) 1909- *2*
Clark, Virginia
  See Gray, Patricia
Clark, Walter Van Tilburg 1909-1971 ....*8*
Clarke, Arthur C(harles) 1917- *70*
  Earlier sketch in SATA *13*
Clarke, Clorinda 1917- *7*
Clarke, Joan 1921- *42*
  Brief Entry *27*
Clarke, John
  See Laklan, Carli
Clarke, Mary Stetson 1911- *5*
Clarke, Michael
  See Newlon, Clarke
Clarke, Pauline
  See Hunter Blair, Pauline
Clarkson, E(dith) Margaret 1915- *37*
Clarkson, Ewan 1929- *9*
Claverie, Jean 1946- *38*
Clay, Patrice 1947- *47*
Claypool, Jane
  See Miner, Jane Claypool
Cleary, Beverly (Bunn) 1916- *43*
  Earlier sketch in SATA *2*
  See also CLR *2, 8*
Cleaver, Bill 1920-1981 ....*22*
  Obituary *27*
  See also CLR *6*
Cleaver, Carole 1934- *6*
Cleaver, Elizabeth (Mrazik)
  1939-1985 ....*23*
  Obituary *43*
  See also CLR *13*
Cleaver, Hylton (Reginald) 1891-1961 ...*49*
Cleaver, Vera............................*22*
  See also CLR *6*
Cleishbotham, Jebediah
  See Scott, Sir Walter
Cleland, Mabel
  See Widdemer, Mabel Cleland
Clemens, Samuel Langhorne 1835-1910
  See YABC *2*
Clemens, Virginia Phelps 1941- *35*
Clements, Bruce 1931- *27*
Clemons, Elizabeth
  See Nowell, Elizabeth Cameron
Clerk, N. W.
  See Lewis, C. S.
Cleveland, Bob
  See Cleveland, George
Cleveland, George 1903(?)-1985
  Obituary *43*
Cleven, Cathrine
  See Cleven, Kathryn Seward
Cleven, Kathryn Seward..................*2*
Clevin, Jörgen 1920- *7*
Clewes, Dorothy (Mary) 1907- *1*
Clifford, Eth
  See Rosenberg, Ethel
Clifford, Harold B. 1893- *10*
Clifford, Margaret Cort 1929- *1*
Clifford, Martin
  See Hamilton, Charles H. St. John
Clifford, Mary Louise (Beneway)
  1926- *23*
Clifford, Peggy
  See Clifford, Margaret Cort
Clifford, Rachel Mark
  See Lewis, Brenda Ralph
Clifton, Harry
  See Hamilton, Charles H. St. John
Clifton, Lucille 1936- *69*
  Earlier sketch in SATA *20*
  See also CLR *5*

Clifton, Martin
  See Hamilton, Charles H. St. John
Climo, Shirley 1928- *39*
  Brief Entry *35*
Clinton, Jon
  See Prince, J(ack) H(arvey)
Clish, (Lee) Marian 1946- *43*
Clive, Clifford
  See Hamilton, Charles H. St. John
Clokey, Art 1921- *59*
Cloudsley-Thompson, J(ohn) L(eonard)
  1921- *19*
Clymer, Eleanor 1906- *9*
Clyne, Patricia Edwards..................*31*
Coalson, Glo 1946- *26*
Coates, Anna 1958- *73*
Coates, Belle 1896- *2*
Coates, Ruth Allison 1915- *11*
Coats, Alice M(argaret) 1905- *11*
Coatsworth, Elizabeth (Jane)
  1893-1986 ....*56*
  Obituary *49*
  Earlier sketch in SATA *2*
  See also CLR *2*
Cobalt, Martin
  See Mayne, William (James Carter)
Cobb, Jane
  See Berry, Jane Cobb
Cobb, Vicki 1938- *69*
  Earlier sketch in SATA *8*
  See also CLR *2*
  See also SAAS *6*
Cobbett, Richard
  See Pluckrose, Henry (Arthur)
Cober, Alan E. 1935- *7*
Cobham, Sir Alan
  See Hamilton, Charles H. St. John
Cocagnac, A(ugustin) M(aurice-Jean)
  1924- *7*
Cochran, Bobbye A. 1949- *11*
Cockett, Mary............................*3*
Coe, Douglas [Joint pseudonym]
  See Epstein, Beryl and Epstein, Samuel
Coe, Lloyd 1899-1976
  Obituary *30*
Coen, Rena Neumann 1925- *20*
Coerr, Eleanor (Beatrice) 1922- *67*
  Earlier sketch in SATA *1*
Coffin, Geoffrey
  See Mason, F. van Wyck
Coffman, Ramon Peyton 1896- *4*
Coggins, Jack (Banham) 1911- *2*
Cohen, Barbara 1932- *10*
  See also SAAS *7*
Cohen, Daniel (E.) 1936- *70*
  Earlier sketch in SATA *8*
  See also CLR *3*
  See also SAAS *4*
Cohen, Jene Barr
  See Barr, Jene
Cohen, Joan Lebold 1932- *4*
Cohen, Miriam 1926- *29*
  See also SAAS *11*
Cohen, Paul S. 1945- *58*
Cohen, Peter Zachary 1931- *4*
Cohen, Robert Carl 1930- *8*
Cohn, Angelo 1914- *19*
Coit, Margaret L(ouise)..................*2*
Colbert, Anthony 1934- *15*
Colby, C(arroll) B(urleigh) 1904-1977 ...*35*
  Earlier sketch in SATA *3*
Colby, Jean Poindexter 1909- *23*
Cole, Annette
  See Steiner, Barbara A(nnette)
Cole, Babette 1949- *61*
Cole, Brock 1938- *72*
  See also CLR *18*
Cole, Davis
  See Elting, Mary
Cole, Jack
  See Stewart, John (William)
Cole, Jackson
  See Schisgall, Oscar
Cole, Jennifer
  See Stevens, Serita (Deborah)
Cole, Jennifer
  See Zach, Cheryl (Byrd)

Cole, Joanna 1944- *49*
  Brief Entry *37*
  See also CLR *5*
Cole, Lois Dwight 1903(?)-1979 ....*10*
  Obituary *26*
Cole, Michael 1947- *59*
Cole, Sheila R(otenberg) 1939- *24*
Cole, William (Rossa) 1919- *71*
  Earlier sketch in SATA *9*
  See also SAAS *9*
Coleman, William L(eRoy) 1938- *49*
  Brief Entry *34*
Coles, Robert (Martin) 1929- *23*
Colin, Ann
  See Ure, Jean
Collier, Christopher 1930- *70*
  Earlier sketch in SATA *16*
Collier, Ethel 1903- *22*
Collier, James Lincoln 1928- *70*
  Earlier sketch in SATA *8*
  See also CLR *3*
Collier, Jane
  See Collier, Zena
Collier, Steven 1942- *61*
Collier, Zena 1926- *23*
Collington, Peter 1948- *59*
Collins, David 1940- *7*
Collins, Hunt
  See Hunter, Evan
Collins, Michael
  See Lynds, Dennis
Collins, Michael 1930- *58*
Collins, Pat Lowery 1932- *31*
Collins, Ruth Philpott 1890-1975
  Obituary *30*
Collodi, Carlo
  See Lorenzini, Carlo
  See also CLR *5*
Colloms, Brenda 1919- *40*
Colman, Hila.............................*53*
  Earlier sketch in SATA *1*
  See also SAAS *14*
Colman, Morris 1899(?)-1981
  Obituary *25*
Colman, Warren (David) 1944- *67*
Colombo, John Robert 1936- *50*
Colonius, Lillian 1911- *3*
Colorado (Capella), Antonio J(ulio)
  1903- *23*
Colt, Martin [Joint pseudonym]
  See Epstein, Beryl and Epstein, Samuel
Colum, Padraic 1881-1972 ....*15*
Columella
  See Moore, Clement Clarke
Colver, Anne 1908- *7*
Colwell, Eileen (Hilda) 1904- *2*
Colwyn, Stewart
  See Pepper, Frank S.
Combs, Robert
  See Murray, John
Comfort, Jane Levington
  See Sturtzel, Jane Levington
Comfort, Mildred Houghton 1886- *3*
Comins, Ethel M(ae).....................*11*
Comins, Jeremy 1933- *28*
Commager, Henry Steele 1902- *23*
Comus
  See Ballantyne, R(obert) M(ichael)
Conan Doyle, Arthur
  See Doyle, Arthur Conan
Condit, Martha Olson 1913- *28*
Cone, Ferne Geller 1921- *39*
Cone, Molly Lamken 1918- *28*
  Earlier sketch in SATA *1*
  See also SAAS *11*
Coney, Michael (Greatrex) 1932- *61*
Conford, Ellen 1942- *68*
  Earlier sketch in SATA *6*
  See also CLR *10*
Conger, Lesley
  See Suttles, Shirley (Smith)
Conklin, Gladys (Plemon) 1903- *2*
Conklin, Paul S..........................*43*
  Brief Entry *33*
Conkling, Hilda 1910- *23*
Conlon-McKenna, Marita 1956- *71*
Conly, Robert Leslie 1918(?)-1973 ......*23*

Duchacek, Ivo D(uka) 1913-1988
  Obituary *55*
Du Chaillu, Paul (Belloni)
  1831(?)-1903 ....*26*
Duchesne, Janet 1930-
  Brief Entry *32*
Ducornet, Erica 1943- *7*
Dudley, Martha Ward 1909(?)-1985
  Obituary *45*
Dudley, Nancy
  See Cole, Lois Dwight
Dudley, Robert
  See Baldwin, James
Dudley, Ruth H(ubbell) 1905- *11*
Due, Linnea A. 1948- *64*
Dueland, Joy V(ivian)....................*27*
Duff, Annis (James) 1904(?)-1986
  Obituary *49*
Duff, Maggie
  See Duff, Margaret K.
Duff, Margaret K........................*37*
Dugan, Michael (Gray) 1947- *15*
Duggan, Alfred Leo 1903-1964 ....*25*
Duggan, Maurice (Noel) 1922-1974 ......*40*
  Obituary *30*
du Jardin, Rosamond (Neal)
  1902-1963 ....*2*
Duka, Ivo
  See Duchacek, Ivo D(uka)
Dulac, Edmund 1882-1953 ....*19*
Dumas, Alexandre (the elder)
  1802-1870 ....*18*
Dumas, Jacqueline (Claudia) 1946- *55*
Dumas, Philippe 1940- *52*
du Maurier, Daphne 1907-1989 ....*27*
  Obituary *60*
Dumbleton, Mike 1948- *73*
Dunbar, Paul Laurence 1872-1906 ......*34*
Dunbar, Robert E(verett) 1926- *32*
Duncan, Frances (Mary) 1942-
  Brief Entry *48*
Duncan, Gregory
  See McClintock, Marshall
Duncan, Jane
  See Cameron, Elizabeth Jane
Duncan, Julia K. [Collective
  pseudonym].................................*1*
  See also Benson, Mildred (Augustine
  Wirt)
Duncan, Lois S(teinmetz) 1934- *36*
  Earlier sketch in SATA *1*
  See also SAAS *2*
Duncan, Norman 1871-1916
  See YABC *1*
Duncombe, Frances (Riker) 1900- *25*
Dunlop, Agnes M.R......................*3*
Dunlop, Eileen (Rhona) 1938- *24*
  See also SAAS *12*
Dunn, Harvey T(homas) 1884-1952 .....*34*
Dunn, Judy
  See Spangenberg, Judith Dunn
Dunn, Mary Lois 1930- *6*
Dunnahoo, Terry 1927- *7*
Dunne, Jeanette 1952- *72*
Dunne, Mary Collins 1914- *11*
Dunnett, Margaret (Rosalind)
  1909-1977 ....*42*
Dunrea, Olivier 1953- *59*
  Brief Entry *46*
Dupuy, T(revor) N(evitt) 1916- *4*
Durant, John 1902- *27*
Durell, Ann 1930- *66*
Durrell, Gerald (Malcolm) 1925- *8*
Du Soe, Robert C. 1892-1958
  See YABC *2*
Dutz
  See Davis, Mary Octavia
Duval, Katherine
  See James, Elizabeth
Duvall, Evelyn Millis 1906- *9*
Duvoisin, Roger (Antoine) 1904-1980 ...*30*
  Obituary *23*
  Earlier sketch in SATA *2*
  See also CLR *23*
Dwiggins, Don 1913-1988 ....*4*
  Obituary *60*

Dwight, Allan
  See Cole, Lois Dwight
Dyer, James (Frederick) 1934- *37*
Dygard, Thomas J. 1931- *24*
  See also SAAS *15*
Dyke, John 1935- *35*

E

Eagar, Frances (Elisabeth Stuart)
  1940-1978 ....*11*
  Obituary *55*
Eager, Edward (McMaken) 1911-1964 ...*17*
Eager, George B. 1921- *56*
Eagle, Ellen 1953- *61*
Eagle, Mike 1942- *11*
Earle, Olive L.............................*7*
Earle, William
  See Johns, W(illiam) E(arl)
Early, Jon
  See Johns, W(illiam) E(arl)
Early, Margaret 1951- *72*
Earnshaw, Brian 1929- *17*
Eastman, Charles A(lexander) 1858-1939
  See YABC *1*
Eastman, P(hilip) D(ey) 1909-1986 ......*33*
  Obituary *46*
Eastwick, Ivy O...........................*3*
Eaton, Anne T(haxter) 1881-1971 ....*32*
Eaton, George L.
  See Verral, Charles Spain
Eaton, Janet
  See Givens, Janet E(aton)
Eaton, Jeanette 1886-1968 ....*24*
Eaton, Tom 1940- *22*
Ebel, Alex 1927- *11*
Eber, Dorothy (Margaret) Harley
  1930- *27*
Eberle, Irmengarde 1898-1979 ....*2*
  Obituary *23*
Eccles
  See Williams, Ferelith Eccles
Eckblad, Edith Berven 1923- *23*
Ecke, Wolfgang 1927-1983
  Obituary *37*
Eckert, Allan W. 1931- *29*
  Brief Entry *27*
Eckert, Horst 1931- *72*
  Earlier sketch in SATA *8*
Ede, Janina 1937- *33*
Edell, Celeste.............................*12*
Edelman, Elaine
  Brief Entry *50*
Edelman, Lily (Judith) 1915- *22*
Edelson, Edward 1932- *51*
Edens, Cooper 1945- *49*
Edens, (Bishop) David 1926- *39*
Edey, Maitland A(rmstrong)
  1910-1992 ....*25*
  Obituary *71*
Edgeworth, Maria 1767-1849 ....*21*
Edler, Tim(othy) 1948- *56*
Edmonds, I(vy) G(ordon) 1917- *8*
Edmonds, Walter D(umaux) 1903- *27*
  Earlier sketch in SATA *1*
  See also SAAS *4*
Edmund, Sean
  See Pringle, Laurence P(atrick)
Edsall, Marian S(tickney) 1920- *8*
Edwards, Al
  See Nourse, Alan E(dward)
Edwards, Alexander
  See Fleischer, Leonore
Edwards, Anne 1927- *35*
Edwards, Audrey 1947- *52*
  Brief Entry *31*
Edwards, Bertram
  See Edwards, Herbert Charles
Edwards, Bronwen Elizabeth
  See Rose, Wendy
Edwards, Cecile (Pepin) 1916- *25*
Edwards, Dorothy 1914-1982 ....*4*
  Obituary *31*
Edwards, Gunvor..........................*32*
Edwards, Harvey 1929- *5*
Edwards, Herbert Charles 1912- *12*

Edwards, Jane Campbell 1932- *10*
Edwards, Julia
  See Stratemeyer, Edward L.
Edwards, Julie
  See Andrews, Julie
Edwards, June
  See Forrester, Helen
Edwards, Linda Strauss 1948- *49*
  Brief Entry *42*
Edwards, Margaret (ALexander) 1902-1988
  Obituary *56*
Edwards, Michelle 1955- *70*
Edwards, Monica le Doux Newton
  1912- *12*
Edwards, Olwen
  See Gater, Dilys
Edwards, Page L., Jr. 1941- *59*
Edwards, Sally 1929- *7*
Edwards, Samuel
  See Gerson, Noel B(ertram)
Egan, E(dward) W(elstead) 1922- *35*
Egermeier, Elsie E(milie) 1890-1986 .....*65*
Eggenberger, David 1918- *6*
Eggleston, Edward 1837-1902 ....*27*
Egielski, Richard 1952- *49*
  Earlier sketch in SATA *11*
Egypt, Ophelia Settle 1903-1984 ....*16*
  Obituary *38*
Ehlert, Lois 1934- *69*
  Earlier sketch in SATA *35*
  See also CLR *28*
Ehrlich, Amy 1942- *65*
  Earlier sketch in SATA *25*
Ehrlich, Bettina (Bauer) 1903- *1*
Eichberg, James Bandman
  See Garfield, James B.
Eichenberg, Fritz 1901- *50*
  Earlier sketch in SATA *9*
Eichler, Margrit 1942- *35*
Eichner, James A. 1927- *4*
Eifert, Virginia S(nider) 1911-1966 ....*2*
Eige, (Elizabeth) Lillian 1915- *65*
Einsel, Naiad..............................*10*
Einsel, Walter 1926- *10*
Einzig, Susan 1922- *43*
Eiseman, Alberta 1925- *15*
Eisenberg, Azriel 1903- *12*
Eisenberg, Lisa 1949- *57*
  Brief Entry *50*
Eisenberg, Phyllis Rose 1924- *41*
Eisner, Vivienne
  See Margolis, Vivienne
Eisner, Will(iam Erwin) 1917- *31*
Eitzen, Allan 1928- *9*
Eitzen, Ruth (Carper) 1924- *9*
Ekwensi, C. O. D.
  See Ekwensi, Cyprian (Odiatu Duaka)
Ekwensi, Cyprian (Odiatu Duaka)
  1921- *66*
Elam, Richard M(ace, Jr.) 1920- *9*
Elfman, Blossom 1925- *8*
Elgin, Kathleen 1923- *39*
Elia
  See Lamb, Charles
Eliot, Anne
  See Cole, Lois Dwight
Elish, Dan 1960- *68*
Elisofon, Eliot 1911-1973
  Obituary *21*
Elkin, Benjamin 1911- *3*
Elkins, Dov Peretz 1937- *5*
Ellacott, S(amuel) E(rnest) 1911- *19*
Elliott, Sarah M(cCarn) 1930- *14*
Ellis, Anyon
  See Rowland-Entwistle, (Arthur)
  Theodore (Henry)
Ellis, Edward S(ylvester) 1840-1916
  See YABC *1*
Ellis, Ella Thorp 1928- *7*
  See also SAAS *9*
Ellis, Harry Bearse 1921- *9*
Ellis, Herbert
  See Wilson, Lionel
Ellis, Mel 1912-1984 ....*7*
  Obituary *39*
Ellis, Sarah 1952- *68*

Leonard, Constance (Brink) 1923- *42*
  Brief Entry *40*
Leonard, Jonathan N(orton)
  1903-1975 ....*36*
Leong Gor Yun
  See Ellison, Virginia Howell
Lerangis, Peter 1955- *72*
Lerner, Aaron B(unsen) 1920- *35*
Lerner, Carol 1927- *33*
  See also SAAS 12
Lerner, Gerda 1920- *65*
Lerner, Marguerite Rush 1924-1987 .....*11*
  Obituary *51*
Lerner, Sharon (Ruth) 1938-1982 ....*11*
  Obituary *29*
Leroe, Ellen W(hitney) 1949- *61*
  Brief Entry *51*
Leroux, Gaston 1868-1927 ....*65*
LeRoy, Gen............................*52*
  Brief Entry *36*
Lerrigo, Marion Olive 1898-1968
  Obituary *29*
LeShan, Eda J(oan) 1922- *21*
  See also CLR 6
LeSieg, Theo.
  See Geisel, Theodor Seuss
Leslie, Robert Franklin 1911- *7*
Leslie, Sarah
  See McGuire, Leslie (Sarah)
Lessac, Frane 1954- *61*
Lesser, Margaret 1899(?)-1979
  Obituary *22*
Lesser, Rika 1953- *53*
Lester, Alison 1952- *50*
Lester, Helen 1936- *46*
Lester, Julius B. 1939- *12*
  See also CLR 2
Le Sueur, Meridel 1900- *6*
Le Tord, Bijou 1945- *49*
Leutscher, Alfred (George) 1913- *23*
Levai, Blaise 1919- *39*
LeVert (William) John 1946- *55*
Levin, Betty 1927- *19*
  See also SAAS 11
Levin, Ira 1929- *66*
Levin, Marcia Obrasky 1918- *13*
Levin, Meyer 1905-1981 ....*21*
  Obituary *27*
Levine, Abby 1943- *54*
  Brief Entry *52*
Levine, Betty K(rasne) 1933- *66*
Levine, David 1926- *43*
  Brief Entry *35*
Levine, Edna S(imon)........................*35*
Levine, I(srael) E. 1923- *12*
Levine, Joan Goldman........................*11*
Levine, Joseph 1910- *33*
Levine, Rhoda............................*14*
Levine, Sarah 1970- *57*
Levine-Freidus, Gail
  See Provost, Gail Levine
Levinson, Nancy Smiler 1938- *33*
Levinson, Riki............................*52*
  Brief Entry *49*
Levitin, Sonia (Wolff) 1934- *68*
  Earlier sketch in SATA 4
  See also SAAS 2
Levitt, Sidney (Mark) 1947- *68*
Levoy, Myron..............................*49*
  Brief Entry *37*
Levy, Constance 1931- *73*
Levy, Elizabeth 1942- *69*
  Earlier sketch in SATA 31
Levy, Marilyn 1937- *67*
Levy, Nathan 1945- *63*
Lewees, John
  See Stockton, Francis Richard
Lewin, Betsy 1937- *32*
Lewin, Hugh 1939- *72*
  Brief Entry *40*
  See also CLR 9
Lewin, Ted 1935- *21*
Lewis, Alfred E. 1912-1968
  Brief Entry *32*
Lewis, Alice C. 1936- *46*
Lewis, Alice Hudson 1895(?)-1971
  Obituary *29*

Lewis, (Joseph) Anthony 1927- *27*
Lewis, Barbara A. 1943- *73*
Lewis, Brenda Ralph 1932- *72*
Lewis, Claudia (Louise) 1907- *5*
Lewis, C(live) S(taples) 1898-1963 ....*13*
  See also CLR 3, 27
Lewis, Elizabeth Foreman 1892-1958
  See YABC 2
Lewis, E. M............................*20*
Lewis, Francine
  See Wells, Helen
Lewis, Hilda (Winifred) 1896-1974
  Obituary *20*
Lewis, Jack P(earl) 1919- *65*
Lewis, Jean 1924- *61*
Lewis, J. Patrick 1942- *69*
Lewis, Linda (Joy) 1946- *67*
Lewis, Lucia Z.
  See Anderson, Lucia (Lewis)
Lewis, Marjorie 1929- *40*
  Brief Entry *35*
Lewis, Mary (Christianna)
  1907(?)-1988 ....*64*
  Obituary *56*
Lewis, Paul
  See Gerson, Noel B(ertram)
Lewis, Richard 1935- *3*
Lewis, Rob 1962- *72*
Lewis, Roger
  See Zarchy, Harry
Lewis, Shari 1934- *35*
  Brief Entry *30*
Lewis, Thomas P(arker) 1936- *27*
Lewiton, Mina 1904-1970 ....*2*
Lexau, Joan M............................*36*
  Earlier sketch in SATA 1
Ley, Willy 1906-1969 ....*2*
Leydon, Rita (Flodén) 1949- *21*
Leyland, Eric (Arthur) 1911- *37*
L'Hommedieu, Dorothy K(easley) 1885-
  1961
  Obituary *29*
Libby, Bill
  See Libby, William M.
Libby, William M. 1927-1984 ....*5*
  Obituary *39*
Liberty, Gene 1924- *3*
Liddell, Kenneth 1912-1975 ....*63*
Lieberman, E(dwin) James 1934- *62*
Liebers, Arthur 1913- *12*
Lieblich, Irene 1923- *22*
Liers, Emil E(rnest) 1890-1975 ....*37*
Liestman, Vicki 1961- *72*
Lietz, Gerald S. 1918- *11*
Lifton, Betty Jean.........................*6*
Lifton, Robert Jay 1926- *66*
Lightner, Alice
  See Hopf, Alice (Martha) L(ightner)
Lightner, A. M.
  See Hopf, Alice (Martha) L(ightner)
Lignell, Lois 1911- *37*
Lillington, Kenneth (James) 1916- *39*
Lilly, Charles
  Brief Entry *33*
Lilly, Ray
  See Curtis, Richard (Alan)
Lim, John 1932- *43*
Liman, Ellen (Fogelson) 1936- *22*
Limburg, Peter R(ichard) 1929- *13*
Lincoln, C(harles) Eric 1924- *5*
Lindbergh, Anne
  See Sapieyevski, Anne Lindbergh
Lindbergh, Anne Morrow (Spencer)
  1906- *33*
Lindbergh, Charles A(ugustus, Jr.)
  1902-1974 ....*33*
Lindblom, Steven (Winther) 1946- *42*
  Brief Entry *39*
Linde, Gunnel 1924- *5*
Lindgren, Astrid 1907- *38*
  Earlier sketch in SATA 2
  See also CLR 1
Lindgren, Barbro 1937- *63*
  Brief Entry *46*
  See also CLR 20
Lindman, Maj (Jan) 1886-1972 ....*43*
Lindop, Edmund 1925- *5*

Lindquist, Jennie Dorothea
  1899-1977 ....*13*
Lindquist, Willis 1908- *20*
Lindsay, Norman (Alfred William)
  1879-1969 ....*67*
  See also CLR 8
Lindsay, (Nicholas) Vachel 1879-1931 ...*40*
Line, Les 1935- *27*
Lines, Kathleen Mary 1902-1988
  Obituary *61*
Linfield, Esther............................*40*
Lingard, Joan............................*8*
  See also SAAS 5
Link, Martin 1934- *28*
Lionni, Leo(nard) 1910- *72*
  Earlier sketch in SATA 8
  See also CLR 7
Lipinsky de Orlov, Lino S. 1908- *22*
Lipkind, William 1904-1974 ....*15*
Lipman, David 1931- *21*
Lipman, Matthew 1923- *14*
Lippincott, Bertram 1898(?)-1985
  Obituary *42*
Lippincott, Gary A. 1953- *73*
Lippincott, Joseph Wharton
  1887-1976 ....*17*
Lippincott, Sarah Lee 1920- *22*
Lippman, Peter J. 1936- *31*
Lipsyte, Robert (Michael) 1938- *68*
  Earlier sketch in SATA 5
  See also CLR 23
Lisker, Sonia O. 1933- *44*
Lisle, Janet Taylor 1947- *59*
  Brief Entry *47*
  See also SAAS 14
Lisle, Seward D.
  See Ellis, Edward S(ylvester)
Lisowski, Gabriel 1946- *47*
  Brief Entry *31*
Liss, Howard 1922- *4*
Lissim, Simon 1900-1981
  Brief Entry *28*
Lisson, Deborah 1941- *71*
List, Ilka Katherine 1935- *6*
Liston, Robert A. 1927- *5*
Litchfield, Ada B(assett) 1916- *5*
Litowinsky, Olga (Jean) 1936- *26*
Littke, Lael J. 1929- *51*
Little, A. Edward
  See Klein, Aaron E.
Little, (Flora) Jean 1932- *68*
  Earlier sketch in SATA 2
  See also CLR 4
Little, Lessie Jones 1906-1986 ....*60*
  Obituary *50*
Little, Mary E. 1912- *28*
Littledale, Freya (Lota)....................*2*
Lively, Penelope 1933- *60*
  Earlier sketch in SATA 7
  See also CLR 7
Liversidge, (Henry) Douglas 1913- *8*
Livingston, Carole 1941- *42*
Livingston, Myra Cohn 1926- *68*
  Earlier sketch in SATA 5
  See also CLR 7
  See also SAAS 1
Livingston, Richard R(oland) 1922- *8*
Llerena-Aguirre, Carlos Antonio
  1952- *19*
Llewellyn, Richard
  See Llewellyn Lloyd, Richard Dafydd
  Vyvyan
Llewellyn, T. Harcourt
  See Hamilton, Charles H. St. John
Llewellyn Lloyd, Richard Dafydd Vyvyan
  1906-1983 ....*11*
  Obituary *37*
Lloyd, E. James
  See James, Elizabeth
Lloyd, Errol 1943- *22*
Lloyd, Hugh
  See Fitzhugh, Percy Keese
Lloyd, James
  See James, Elizabeth
Lloyd, Norman 1909-1980
  Obituary *23*
Lloyd, (Mary) Norris 1908- *10*

Author Index